'A long and

SY

'A manual on how to look at things, how to pay attention. It is a hymn to receptivity as much as it is to creativity, a portrait of the artist in full creative health, consuming and producing in equal measure.'
AUSTRALIAN BOOK REVIEW

'Paul Kelly's reminiscences about 30 years of creative endeavour have it all. Call it a gift.'
THE AGE

'Totally original. The writing is to die for.'
THE AUSTRALIAN

'This book delivers.'
SUN-HERALD

'Every line is an enlightening treat.'
CANBERRA TIMES

'The Bard of the People has turned his career-spanning A–Z shows into a fascinating autobiography . . . Often hilarious.'
TIME OUT, SYDNEY

'Stands apart from the run-of-the-mill rock biography template . . . A rare peek into his very private world.'
X-PRESS MAGAZINE

'Funny, moving, entertaining and perilously easy to read.'
SUNDAY TELEGRAPH

'Kelly is a consummate storyteller.'
AUSTRALIAN BOOKSELLER & PUBLISHER

'Not just for fans.'
HERALD SUN

'Fascinating . . . It has a vigour, intelligence and humanity . . . a wealth of insider detail about life at the coalface of the music industry.'
WEST AUSTRALIAN

'A hundred tales that traverse the emotional, the personal, the historical, the factual and the political.'
YEN

PENGUIN BOOKS

How to Make Gravy

Paul Kelly has recorded twenty-three studio albums as well as several film soundtracks and live albums, in an influential career spanning more than thirty years. His prose has appeared in *Meanjin*, *The Monthly*, *Rolling Stone* and *The Age*.

paulkelly.com.au

PAUL KELLY

How to Make Gravy

PENGUIN BOOKS

PENGUIN BOOKS

UK | USA | Canada | Ireland | Australia
India | New Zealand | South Africa | China

Penguin Books is part of the Penguin Random House group of companies
whose addresses can be found at global.penguinrandomhouse.com.

Penguin
Random House
Australia

First published by Penguin Random House Australia Pty Ltd, 2010
This revised edition published by Penguin Random House Australia Pty Ltd, 2018

Cover design © Penguin Random House Australia Pty Ltd
Cover photograph by Wendy McDougall (www.wendymcdougall.com.au)
Typeset in Adobe Garamond by Post Pre-press Group, Brisbane, Queensland
Printed and bound in Australia by Griffin Press, an accredited ISO AS/NZS 14001
Environmental Management Systems printer.

A catalogue record for this
book is available from the
National Library of Australia

ISBN: 978 0 14379 599 5

penguin.com.au

Contents

A story should have a beginning, a middle, and an end . . . but not necessarily in that order.

JEAN-LUC GODARD

*I have read many books but I don't believe them.
When it hurts we return to the banks of certain rivers.*

CZESŁAW MIŁOSZ

Introduction

In the middle of the journey of my life I found myself inside a tent of mirrors. Ahead lay a labour of trouble. All around, a thronging darkness. A deep slumber had caused me to stray, and to go forward was the only way back.

Six weeks previously, in October 2004, my manager Rob had rung to say the Spiegeltent was coming to Melbourne for the summer. Would I do some shows? I'd played in the tent before, at the Edinburgh Festival. Built by Belgians in 1920 of wood and canvas, and decorated with mirrors, velvet, brocade and leaded glass, it travels around the world hosting cabaret shows. *Spiegel* is Flemish for mirror, and the mirrors in the booths and on poles all around are the main feature, multiplying the audience in the intimate circular space. The staff like to tell you that Marlene Dietrich performed there back in the day. It's a fun place to play, fits around three hundred people. They walk in with a different kind of buzz, like children at the circus.

'They've suggested you put together a show you wouldn't do elsewhere,' said Rob. 'You know, an exclusive. They'll give you a few nights.'

I said I'd think about it, and not long afterwards found myself awake in the middle of the night with an idea fully formed in my brain: I know! I'll sing a hundred of my songs in alphabetical order over four nights. Twenty-five songs a night, each night a different song list. I called Rob the next morning before I had time to talk myself out of it, wrote a blurb for the Spiegeltent's program and started a list.

Preparing for and performing that first A–Z season was like running a marathon. I'd written close to three hundred songs in the decades since I started out, but had lost touch with many of them. I had to relearn words and chords as well as work on pared-back arrangements that would sound good without the colour and rhythm of a band. Some songs I had lost touch with due to natural attrition. I no longer had a connection to them, and couldn't sing them in a true way any more. Their faults outweighed their virtues. Clunky rhymes, false conceits, banal verses. They'd worked for me once, but, badly made, had long since worn out. Those songs wouldn't come back.

Others, however, had been neglected due to the performer's eternal problem – balancing the old and the new. Your audience have paid their money and want to hear their favourites. So inside you, two people are at war: the stern artist who wants to keep his art fresh, testing out new and obscure material, and the needy show-off who wants to get over right here, right now to the audience in front of him. To harness that hunger in the room and give it satisfaction. And so release yourself and them.

My strategy with the band had been to rotate the songs, the familiar and the unfamiliar. So we had a set each night that gave us a kick to play and also included enough songs to keep the audience happy. But over the course of a tour, a set would evolve that worked really well and we'd tend to stick to it, with only minor tinkering. This meant that perfectly good songs weren't getting a run often enough. I was like the coach of a sporting team with a huge squad, relying too much on his stars, proven match-day winners. Meanwhile talented players languished on the bench, some for so long that they didn't turn up to training any more.

The decision to field four separate teams over four nights changed all that. By the end of the first season I realised I was onto something. The audiences had enjoyed these shows in a different way. They felt they were part of a game. Some came one night, some two or three, some all four. Those who'd come every night exchanged addresses with some of their fellow 'completists', previously strangers but now bonded as if they'd walked the Kokoda Trail together. Others said to me, 'Will you do it again? We came on night three but we'll pick another night next time.'

Next time? The last thing I wanted to think about was a next time as I headed home to lie down for a couple of days. But there was a next time. Then another and another. The memory feat became easier and my fingers began to know where to go without stumbling; I was no longer searching for old friends who'd dropped off the radar. I'd held a reunion and they'd all come, and now we were keeping in touch regularly. I'd found the gift that keeps on giving.

Right from the start, I realised the shows needed theatricalising, something to spruce up the doggedness of one man singing a list. So I decided to add some storytelling around the songs for variety, and not being a natural raconteur, wrote and memorised a script. Guests joined me onstage now and then, including my nephew Dan Kelly playing guitar. His role grew larger over time as I took the shows to other cities and countries. The performances were recorded with a view to releasing them eventually as a CD collection, and I began to imagine a book to go with it.

I went back to my show notes, put them next to the song lyrics and let my mind brew. I wanted to find a key I could turn, to feel a little click that would set me writing in a new way. Over time I found a series of keys, some to big rooms, some to little rooms, some to dark cupboards. Many days I was locked out of the house altogether.

Before too long a mongrel beast emerged. Was I writing an idiosyncratic history of music, a work diary or a hymn to dead friends? There were lists, letters, quotes, confessions, essays and road stories. Could I get them all to fit? Could I make the architecture sing? And what kind of megalomaniac would assume that setting his lyrics down and writing commentary around them – a kind of Midrash – would be interesting to others?

Just your everyday writer kind of megalomaniac, I suppose. The kind that says, Homer sang of heroes and so shall I. Of all the good people who travelled with me, who shared the dark hours and sweet moments, my twentieth- and 21st-century chums whom the gods neither helped nor hindered, I'll sing. Of those who helped me make the sounds I couldn't make on my own, the sounds that make me swoon, I'll sing. Of those I never met who sang to me across space and time, I'll sing. And hope my song becomes a charnel house, a place for those not yet born to visit, where my companions and I will remain strewn among each other, long after our days are done.

The kind of dreamer who hopes to make a new kind of book for new machines. A book for the ears as well as the eyes. A book that sings and talks and plays.

The kind of man who, appalled at his poor memory, throughout his life and in the middle of his life – though who's to say it's the middle? – kept putting out a net to catch scraps from the rushing river on its way to the wine dark sea.

How to hear this book

The companion CD box set, *The A to Z Recordings*, contains previously unreleased versions of the songs that form this book's chapters, mainly live solo or duo performances from 2004–10. They can also be purchased as downloads or streamed on various platforms. (Two songs, 'This Land Is Mine' and 'Treaty', are not included in the box set as they defy stripped-back reworking.) For details of other recordings described in the text, see the discography.

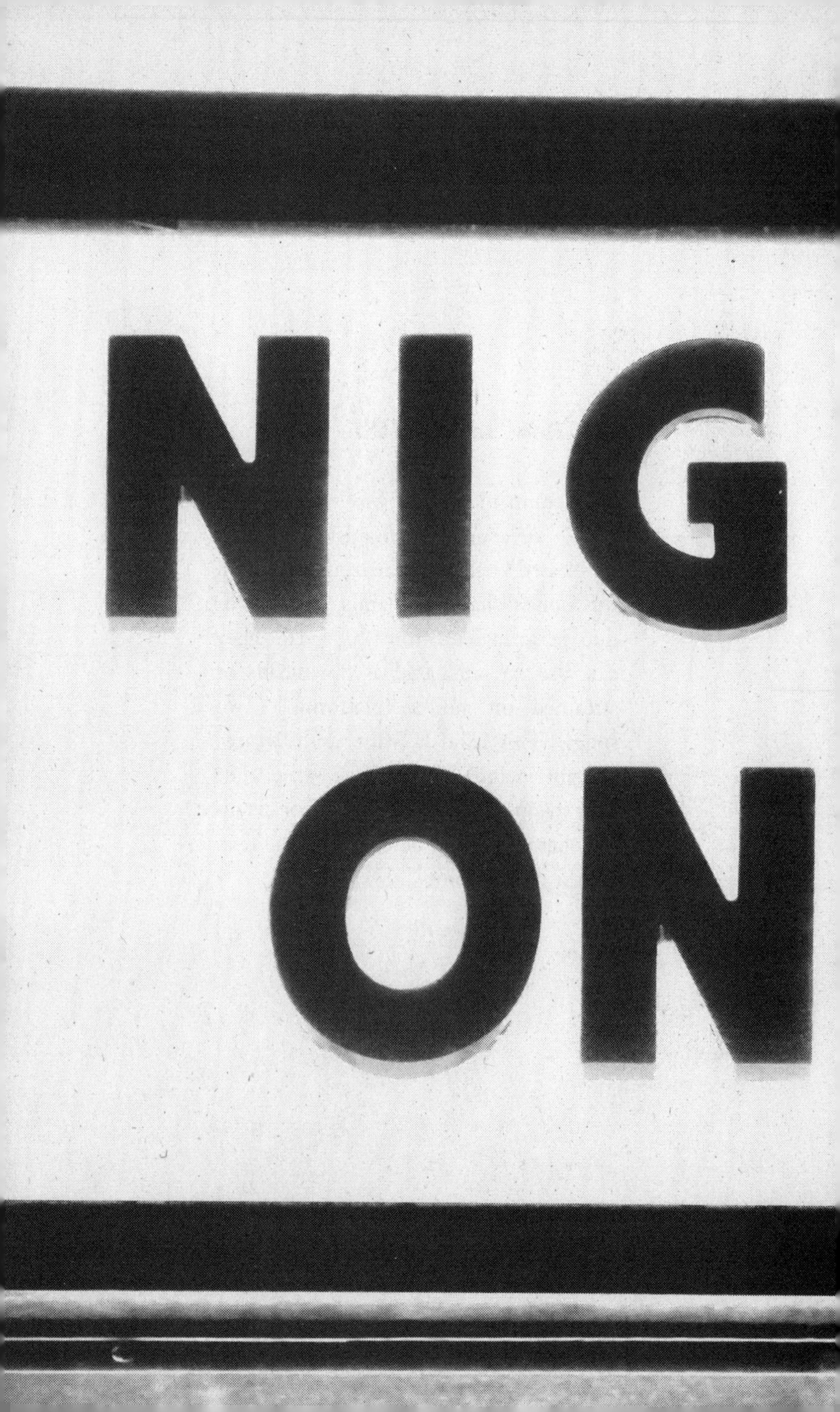
NIG
ON

ADELAIDE
AFTER THE SHOW
ANASTASIA
BE CAREFUL
BEAUTIFUL
BEFORE
BEGGAR
BEHIND THE BOWLER
BIG FINE GIRL
BLUES
BRADMAN
CAKE
CARELESS
CHANGE YR MIND
CHARLIE
CITIES O' TEXAS

COMA
CRADLE
DEEPER
DESDEMONA
DIFFICULT WOMAN
DON'T EXPLAIN
MESSENGER
WINDOW
DON'T START
DOWN TO MY SOUL
DUMB THINGS
EMOTIONAL
E F C
EVERYBODY
WHITE

ADELAIDE

The wisteria on the back verandah is still blooming
And all the great-aunts are either insane or dead
Kensington Road runs straight for a while before turning
We lived on the bend – it was there I was raised and fed
Counting and running as I go
Down past the hedges all in a row
In Adelaide, Adelaide

Dad's hands used to shake but I never knew he was dying
I was thirteen, I never dreamed he could fall
And all the great-aunts were red in the eyes from crying
I rang the bells, I never felt nothing at all
All the king's horses, all the king's men
Cannot bring him back again

Find me a bar or a girl or guitar, now where do you go
    on a Saturday night?
I own this town, I spilled my wine at the bottom of the statue
    of Colonel Light
And the streets are so wide, everybody's inside
Sitting in the same chairs they were sitting in last year
Talking about the crows, the crows

All the king's horses, all the king's men
Wouldn't drag me back again
To Adelaide, Adelaide,
Adelaide, Adelaide

City Of The Plain

All heroes have to leave home at some stage. Odysseus did. Frodo too. I left a city that sits on a plain between round hills and flat sea. The oldest hills in the world, we were told as children. Once they had been mountains, higher than the Himalayas, but erosion wore them down over aeons, down to unprepossessing nubs topped by the gently mounded and hopefully named Mount Lofty. 'You can have your Rockies, your Swiss Alps,' said our elders. 'Mere babes they are compared to our venerables.'

The hills were high enough, however, to trap the smog. Smog that could get as bad as Los Angeles, though we were less than a million. On those days, from the lookout at Eagle-on-the-Hill, the gridded city below looked to be stewing in brown soup. Not far north of those ancient hills the desert began, thousands of miles of it stretching towards the Gulf of Carpentaria. The hot breath of summer never let us forget it, drying dripping towels and trousers on clotheslines within minutes. We were the capital of the driest state in the driest continent. Our water was pumped in via pipeline from the turbid, slow-moving lower reaches of the Murray River.

'Did you know,' we heard, 'that Adelaide and Aden are the only two places in the world where ships don't take on water? They say it's too hard, full of minerals, but it's very good for you; prevents heart attacks.' It didn't help Dad, though – father of nine, dead from a heart attack two days after his fifty-second birthday.

Over several years huge, slow-rolling dust storms blanketed the city and darkened the sky. Oblivion stalked us. But when The Beatles came to town in 1964 and waved to nearly a third of the population from the town-hall balcony (my two older sisters were there) it was the highest per-capita turnout for the Fab Four in any city in the world.

The big smokes to the east couldn't give a toss about us. Melbourne stole our best young footballers, chewed them up and spat them out, arthritic in young old age. Sydney was spoilt and beautiful, too preoccupied with preening itself in its harbour mirror to lift its gaze elsewhere. But hadn't Don Bradman, the greatest cricketer the world has ever seen, chosen to live in Adelaide at the height of his fame? And hadn't we invented the wine cask, that ingenious plastic bladder inside a cardboard box with a tap attached to keep your value-for-money wine fresh?

The wine came from the Barossa Valley and McLaren Vale, not far from the city, much of it better than the French only the French didn't know it yet. This was due to our climate's similarity to that of the Mediterranean – cool but not too cold winters to nurse the grapes along, and hot dry summers to intensify the flavour – coupled, of course, with good old South Australian know-how.

Adelaide hadn't begun in rum and riot like Sydney – a poor huddle of huts built by convicts under the lash and on the chain. Clear-eyed citizens chose to live here. Men of vision and stamina, men such as Colonel Light, surveyor-general, who laid out the town in an elegant and spacious manner – the city centre a perfect one-mile square, surrounded on all sides by parkland, the 'lungs of the city', which our forefathers had the good sense to preserve against the designs of developers.

South Australia, state of enlightenment, was the first state in Australia and one of the first places in the world to give women the vote; it was also home to the country's first woman judge. The Athens of the South, we called ourselves. After the reign of Premier Don Dunstan – who wore pink hotpants to parliament in 1972, who introduced laws against discrimination on the basis of race, sexuality and religion, and who liberated the licensing laws – you could drink wine at tables on the pavement, just like they did in Europe. He poured money into the arts and established the South Australian Film Corporation. The biennial Adelaide Festival of Arts blossomed under his patronage to become 'world-class'.

'Why, many of the overseas acts come only for our festival and don't bother with the other cities, don't you know.'

Methinks we proclaim too much, murmured my seventeen-year-old self. I was reading Hermann Hesse, Arthur Rimbaud, Jack Kerouac, Henry Miller. They or their heroes had all fled home. Henry was dancing with taxi girls, raving about art, walking past packed Paris restaurants cold and hungry without a sou in his pocket, fucking himself silly, writing whole pages in praise of the variety of cunts. Hesse's Goldmund was roaming the world, sucking it and squeezing it, princesses and peasant girls too. Arthur was reinventing poetry and pouring forth manifestos; and Jack, sweet Jack, drunk Jack, was trailing after 'the mad ones', sleeping in boxcars, musing on mountains and staying up for days on Benzedrine to put it all down, every last drop. Real life was elsewhere. I couldn't get out of town fast enough.

Of course, everything was happening in Adelaide all along, and still is – dark secrets, 'dithyrambic cunts', heroism, heroinism, ecstasy, stoicism, every low and high drama, men with large young families cut down in their prime, too soon, too soon – enough for a thousand novels, movies, songs. I never had to leave home at all.

But you don't know you don't until you do.

About fifteen years after I left, I was back in town with the band. Our record *Gossip*, which included the song 'Adelaide', had been out for a year or two. We played a show on a Friday night, and the next afternoon I went to the Norwood Oval – scene of early sorrows – to see my old football team the Redlegs play. I'd just sat down when the man in front turned around: 'I thought you said you were never coming back here?'

All the great-aunts *were* dead by then. None of them had been crazy, though, so a couple of the living aunts weren't too happy with the second line of the song – a line that had slipped out quick and was loosely connected to distant memories of visiting fond, bosomy, spinster great-aunts as a child. I remembered that during the writing of the song, as the other details accrued, all of them true – the wisteria, the hedges, the counting, Dad's Parkinson's, the altar bells at his funeral – I'd thought to myself, I'm going to get in trouble for this.

You can't have everything true and one thing not. Everyone will think that it's true too. I'll have to change that line.

But I never did. It sang well. The drawn out 'insane', the short sharp 'dead'. Should I call them 'eccentric' rather than 'insane'? But that had too many syllables to fit right. And I liked the punch the line gave the opening of the song. When you get a good first line you don't want to give it up.

'It's just a song,' I said to the living aunts. 'It's a mix of made-up stuff and true stuff, like most songs. I'm writing fiction, not autobiography, even though a lot of the things I say sound familiar.'

'It's just a song,' I said to my friends and journalists. 'I'm not having a go at Adelaide. I would have written this kind of song no matter where I was born. The character's an archetype – the young man who leaves home to see the world.'

They didn't look convinced. I probably didn't sound convincing. They were right to be wary, to sniff the answer with suspicion. You shouldn't trust a songwriter. They distort, they exaggerate, they juggle things around to get what they want. They grab whatever's at hand to assemble their montages. Know that if you get close to them they'll grab bits of you, too. Out of their mouths true things become lies and lies become true. They'll rhyme, and murder while they rhyme. They'll take your precious wine and spill it all over town.

AFTER THE SHOW

After the show
Where shall we go?
I want to go downtown
I don't want to go uptown no more
Just want to go downtown

Wasn't it grand?
The music, the band
I know it ain't cheap
But I just can't sleep
Know what I mean?

I get this feeling inside
It's a feeling I can't hide
Oh we're gonna have some fun tonight
We're gonna ball and shout
We're gonna have a real good time
After the show

My First Love And Other Longs

Hobart in the winter of 1974 was cold, the coldest I'd ever been. Mount Wellington, snow-dusted, brooded over the town. Some days it was just an idea wreathed in clouds. First there is a mountain, then there is no mountain, then there is. I was nineteen years old and renting a room from a man who liked to go shooting. We ate a lot of wallaby stew. Cats pissed inside the house. I tried to keep warm in the bare living room, huddled close to a single-bar electric heater, playing *Astral Weeks* on the old record player over and over again.

I got a job in a foundry. I don't recall much about it but I remember walking down to the harbour on weekends and staring at the big ships from other countries, with Russian, Norwegian, Chinese writing on the sides. I imagined sneaking on board, or getting taken on as a sailor, and going all over the world, stopping off at tropical ports, singing and playing guitar to dusky señoritas who'd lead me down dark hallways into cool chambers.

Back at Cat Wallaby Manor, I'd finger the chords to 'Madame George' and sing along with Van. I hadn't written a song myself yet but I was writing words in a journal. They mostly disappointed me, and though I put some scraps to music, they were nothing I wanted to play to anyone. *Astral Weeks* was so beautiful and so beyond me it made me depressed. So did the cats' piss and the single-bar heater. I had to get out.

I moved into a share house down the road in Sandy Bay. Threw my rucksack into the corner of a small room with a mattress on the floor, kept my tattered copy of *Leaves of Grass* by the pillow. I hadn't been there long when a couple from Adelaide came to visit: John and Rosie. They were tall and slim, pale and intellectual. John had long blond hair and a beard, Rosie big deep eyes in a rag-doll face. They talked about Jean Paul Sartre and Simone de Beauvoir. They *were* Jean Paul Sartre and Simone de Beauvoir, and had come to Tasmania to write.

Rosie was working at Cadbury's chocolate factory and writing poetry. John was a couple of years older than me, had read my men Kerouac, Hesse, Miller, but had already moved on. According to him they were woolly, soft, sentimental – unlike the French existentialists, who saw things true. He gave me *Nausea* and *The Stranger* to read, tried to explain to me the idea that existence precedes essence; that a person is not like a table, not something conceived of by a creator and then built; that people make themselves by their actions; that they are not innately good or cruel, but choose to be either; that there is no such thing as human nature. This was news to me.

One cold night, walking home with a group from the St Ives pub after listening to jazz, we got ahead of the gang. Standing on a street corner, our mouths blowing steam as we waited for the others to catch up, we pledged to show each other our writing by exchanging our journals. It was a declaration of love. One of the first things I read in John's black book was 'Intimacy involves shame and is therefore precious', a quote from Friedrich Nietzsche, anti-godfather of the existentialists. There were other quotes too, by Sartre and Kafka, along with John's own diamond-hard sentences which suggested a mind of depth and complexity far beyond my fathoming. Totally unsentimental.

As I read I remembered being anxious as a child in a room full of adults, unable to understand the conversation, and my mortification increased at the thought of John reading my thin scribbles, my Zen mysticism, my hero-on-a-quest dreams, my banal longing for transcendence and glory. Mostly I wrote about following my cock around, wanting to fuck the whole world, wanting to swallow it whole and spit it out different. I had huge, vague plans.

I came across another Nietzsche quote: 'In man, creature and creator are united. In man there is material, fragment, excess, clay, dirt, nonsense, chaos; but in man there is also creator, form-giver, hammer hardness, spectator divinity and seventh day.'

In my mind I was all chaos and clay. I could be all things. John was kind to me, patient and sceptical, like a good teacher. At the grand old age of twenty he said I reminded him of his lost youth. 'We all tend to see other people as fixed solid entities but ourselves as fluid,' he said. 'You think you're all possibility, that you can't be pinned down. But what you are is as much how others see you as how you see yourself. You can't step back from the human race and say, I'm nothing and everything. You already are the things you've done. And you will be all the things you do next.'

I'd heard of a folk club down by the port in Salamanca Place where they had an open mic on Sunday nights. I could play and sing a few songs by now but I'd never done so in public. I told John I might go down there and give it a try, and asked if he wanted to come with me.

Salamanca Place was a row of warehouses gradually being converted into galleries, shops and cafés. The club was upstairs above a jewellery and craft store. Tables and chairs on a wooden floor with a small stage. I put my name down on a list and John and I secured a table. Waiting my turn I drank a few beers to settle my nerves but they didn't do a thing. I remember nothing of the other performers except that they all seemed confident. By the time I got onstage I was shaking. I sang Bob Dylan's 'Girl From The North Country', the *Nashville Skyline* version, and 'The Streets Of Forbes', a folk song about the bushranger Ben Hall. Somehow I got through my two-song gig, headed straight to the bar for more beer and some whisky, and an hour later went up to a 35-year-old woman and asked if she'd like to take me home. She looked at me as if I were twelve and laughed.

Not that I recall any of this. John had to fill me in the next day. How I'd been about to leave without my guitar until he reminded me to get it, how he helped me walk home, helped put my key in the door and helped me find my room. Thirty years later, he made a speech at my fiftieth birthday and mercifully didn't tell that story, though he spoke about the swapping of the black books.

Not long after my glorious debut, I hitchhiked north-west out of Hobart on a crisp sunny day and ended up in Savage River, where I got a job for a couple of months working at the iron-ore mine. I spent most of my days skulking around the plant trying to look busy with a broom, most of my nights in my single man's donga reading, drinking beer and dreaming of women. John and I started writing letters to each other that haven't stopped. It wasn't 'til nearly two years later that I set foot on a stage again. By then I had a couple of songs of my own, more on the way.

That Beautiful Oceanic Feeling

There's a story about a famous Irish entertainer who liked to have a beautiful woman standing by backstage to service him immediately he finished one of his dance extravaganzas. He would be so pumped, so high, so flooded with adrenalin after fifteen thousand fans had screamed, hollered, clapped and stamped their love for him that he would have to have sex as soon as he stepped off stage. It sounds like scurrilous gossip but it's fun to wonder, if it *is* true, who waited for him. The same woman each night? Or were the young female dancers on a roster system?

'It's your turn tonight, Bernadette. Skip the last big chorus number and get yourself ready.'

'I thought Rhiannon was on tonight. I'm down for the Saturday matinée.'

'Rhiannon swapped with Sinead. Now Sinead's got her family coming after the show.'

'Oh, Jesus, Mary and Joseph, all right. But can I have a towel to wipe him down this time? He's always dripping wet when he comes off.'

'No. No towels. You know the rules. He likes to stay sweaty.'

Some nights onstage you do feel like a lord-god. My friend James, piano player and guitarist, describes those nights as having 'a beautiful oceanic feeling'. Nights when you can't put a foot wrong, when everything's coming out just right and the band seems to have one mind. The sound onstage is a glorious river and your voice is gliding like an eel in the torrent – strong, flexible, electric. The music and your singing are full of fresh detail and everything you do seems brand new. You're totally in control but loose, as all the right choices in notes, tempo, intonation, rhythm, sound and intensity unfold. It's not a matter of choice, though. You're way beyond choice because your left-brain chatter has shut down and you're riding a long wave to the shore. You trust your band mates completely, not knowing any more where you end and they begin. Or where you stop and the world starts.

The audience knows something special's going on too. You can see it in their faces, or sense it coming towards you from the dark, hear it in the pin-drop silence during a quiet song, in the noise they make after it finishes and in their laughter at the slyest joke. Their feeling feeds your feeling and lifts you higher. By the end of the show you're ten foot tall.

You walk off stage after a gig like that and the night feels like it could go on forever. You're ready to step out into the city with your boon companions, put your arms around the whole wide world and drink it dry.

Then there are the other nights. Nights like Mittagong RSL, 1985. It's the first show of a tour. We've hired a mate of a mate's PA and, alas, it's junk. When we walk into the vast auditorium for the sound check my stomach clenches at the sight before us. The stage is covered in a spaghetti of cables, multi-cores and leads. No mics or mic stands are up yet. Our sound guy battles for around five hours to get it working while we hang around and wait. We're over an hour late going on and the DJ's making snide remarks about the band maybe getting onstage sometime before Christmas. He cranks up The Doors' 'Roadhouse Blues': 'Keep your eyes on the road, your hands upon the wheel . . .' His sound system is pumping! Around fifty people are there, in a room that fits six hundred. They're all on the dance floor but as soon as we walk onstage they retreat to the bar way at the back of the room.

Finally we start to play. The monitors sound like shit – muddy and harsh at the same time. How is that possible? They keep cutting in and out and we can never settle down with the music. There's a hovering high-feedback frequency which every now and then intensifies into a fierce spike. We battle gamely on and get through a few songs, wondering if we'll ever be able to hear properly again, and after each song there's deafening silence, except for the feedback. At the back bar they're all talking amongst themselves. Mentally the whole band is disintegrating. I want to kill myself.

Eventually a girl detaches herself from the small knot of drinkers and walks all the way across the empty dance floor to the front of the stage. She takes up a position, hands on hips, in front of Steve on guitar and beckons to him. She has something urgent she wants to say. We're in the middle of a song so he can't respond immediately, but she's quite insistent. Well, at least one person likes it, I think to myself. Maybe she has a request.

The song over, Steve bends down to her in the yawning silence to hear what she wants.

'Hi, my friends and I are leaving now but I just wanted to tell you before I go – you're the worst band I've ever heard in my life.'

Most gigs are somewhere in between the Mittagong RSL and that beautiful oceanic feeling. The ratio of good to bad ones has improved over the years, and usually when I come off stage now it feels like a job well done. We kick back in the band room with a couple of drinks, maybe have a laugh about a little stuff-up somewhere, talk about the songs that sounded extra good, say hello to a few well-wishers, and after the unwind head back to our hotel. In a strange way, the truly great and the truly awful gigs are more alike than all the ones in between. After both, all you want to do is stay lost.

ANASTASIA CHANGES HER MIND

Anastasia left a kiss on the mirror
And a couple of condoms by the bed
I tried to find her on her old number
But I just got her boyfriend instead
Oh it's hard, so hard
When Anastasia changes her mind

So I went back to working the quadrellas
I collected three times in a row
I swear it must have been that kiss on the mirror
That I'd touch with my lips just for luck each time I'd go
Oh it's hard, so hard
When Anastasia changes her mind

Now the numbers were my daily devotion
I was stashing big bills in the floor
Then one night at my door a commotion
Anastasia – at some ungodly hour!
I said 'Baby can I fix you a coffee?
Tomorrow let me buy you a dress
Since you've been gone I got lucky'
She just nodded her head and said 'I guess'
Oh it's hard, yeah it's hard
When Anastasia changes her mind

Now 'Stacey' takes the crumbs from the table
And feeds them out back to the birds
Me I can't even pick the daily double
Since that kiss on the mirror disappeared
Yeah it's hard, ain't it hard
When Anastasia changes her mind

Connect And Cut

John Updike once said about his stories that sometimes he would write two or more unrelated sentences on a page and stare at them until they connected. Songwriting's similar. You carry around your scrips and scraps in your pocket for long enough and eventually some of them stick to each other.

My second wife Kaarin once had to leave early in the morning on a work trip. She left a lipstick kiss on the mirror in our daughters' bedroom, which stayed there for months until it gradually faded away. It didn't fade from my mind, though. A year later I was talking to my friend Stella about her daughter's upcoming trip to Greece. The girl she'd planned to travel with had fallen in love with a sailor and cancelled at the last moment. 'Anastasia always changes her mind,' sighed Stella. I put down the phone and picked up a pen.

I never met the mind-changing sailor lover, but I've met several other Anastasias over the years. One of them used to book a club called Schubas in Chicago, where we played a few times in the nineties. She told me she'd hated her name as a child – it was too weird among the Janes and the Lisas and the Sally-Annes – so she decided to call herself Stacey. It was only as an adult she'd switched back, proud that her name came from the Greek word for resurrection.

Schubas was a good place to play, what they call in America a 'listening room'. People buy their drinks at the adjacent bar or get served at the tables and booths. Talking during a song is frowned upon. John and Rosie came to see me play a solo show there once; they were long separated at the time, travelling on holiday as friends. Schubas was a long way from Salamanca Place but about the same size. Wooden floors too. This time I held the room for an hour and a half, singing my own folk songs. Afterwards I didn't proposition any women of any age, and walked back to the hotel unassisted.

These days, John writes a sports column for *The Adelaide Review*. He likes to visit Melbourne for the Spring Racing Carnival, having once owned one-twentieth of a racehorse that came second-last in the

Melbourne Cup. He shepherds me around Flemington or Caulfield, advising me on the odds; puts horses into (metaphorical) boxes – trifectas, quadrellas, quinellas, daily doubles. I might chip in for a share of his bets, or place my own simpler ones – on the nose, each way, place. We wander around the mounting yard as he scans the horses, their heads and eyes, flanks and fetlocks, shudders and twitches, for signs. Such magnificent creatures. Friend to man for thousands of years, so exquisitely evolved with their tapered legs, big liquid eyes and handsome hairdos. All that massive power idling within a fine, intricate mechanism. How does 'horseness' hold together as a whole and not fly apart in a thousand directions? I could stare at them all day.

After seeing me in Chicago, John and Rosie headed to New York to meet John's old friend Richard, now working as an architect in Connecticut. He drove them back to his place, an hour and a half away, where they stayed two nights. Richard and Rosie, strangers to each other, fell in love in a heartbeat. She and John returned to Manhattan as planned, but after a couple of days she changed her mind and went back to Connecticut. A year later Richard and Rosie were married and living in Yale, where she teaches and still writes.

Triangles. Rosie is my ex-girlfriend too. We got together not long after she and John split up. Pieces of her appeared in my early songs and pieces of me in her poetry. She gave me *To the Lighthouse* to read. She was more Virginia Woolf than Simone de Beauvoir. Some days I imagined us being married and living in the country, writing in rooms of our own. Other days she spoke in voices and didn't know who I was, as if her mind had completely changed. My mind kept changing too. I was in awe of her one minute, irritated the next. Then amazed at the difference in my feelings. Isn't that the story of love? We were together through most of 1976 and some of '77. I still see her, my initiator into the mysteries, at one end of the long bath in my North Adelaide flat, shoulders peeping out of the water, face floating in the steam. She taught me to pay attention.

One day maybe I'll rhyme 'architect' and 'Connecticut' in a song. It's a rough rhyme but it's allowed. The rest I'll make up.

BE CAREFUL WHAT YOU PRAY FOR

Be careful what you pray for
You just might get it
Be careful what you pray for
You might regret it
You get your hands on that glittering prize
Now everybody's coming at you from every side
Be careful what you pray for
You just might get it

Be careful what you want now
You might be sorry
Be careful what you want now
You might be sorry
You finally make it to your place in the sun
You stop and look around you – you're friends with no one
Be careful what you want now
You might be sorry

Go ahead like a moth to the flame
Go ahead

Be careful what you dream on
Dreams come true
Be careful what you dream on
They can turn on you
Revenge is a dish they say best tasted cold
But revenge digs two graves, makes a young person old
Be careful what you dream on
It might come true

Harry Was A Bad Bugger

'Lucky in cards, unlucky in love,' my mother, a keen bridge player, used to say. She was good at most card games and a demon at Scrabble. Dad loved Coopers Ale, the Brandenburg Concertos, puns and thinking about where words came from ('ale' from the Old English *ealu* and Old Norse *öl*, possibly from the proto-Indo-European *al*, which may mean 'bitter'). He never travelled outside Australia, though he knew several languages – French, Italian, Latin and Ancient Greek – and could trace the journey of words from those languages into modern English. His linguistic ability helped him as a lawyer working with immigrants from southern Europe, or New Australians as they were called then.

Norwood, our suburb in Adelaide, had a big Italian population. Some of Dad's work was *pro bono*, which, he explained to me, was Latin for 'for the good' – in other words, for the public good, for free. The *pro bono* worked both ways. Dad's clients often paid him in homemade wine, olives and rabbits, or let us come and pick cherries and apples *gratis* from their orchards in the hills.

Dad also represented some Greek fishermen, who brought fresh seafood around, including octopus and squid, food not many Australians ate in the fifties and sixties. Mum would tell the story of cooking calamari at a dinner party one night. She made a nice sauce and everyone loved it, but when she told them after the meal what they'd been eating, one of them rushed to the toilet and threw up.

I did Latin in high school for five years, all the way through to my last year, when there were only two of us in the class. Having inherited along with most of my siblings a love of words, wordplay and the history of language, I'm often given 'wordie' presents. Steven Pinker's *Words and Rules* came several Christmases ago. Other years have brought *Shakespeare's Insults*, *Ad Nauseam* (a study of the Roman world behind Latin phrases used in English), David Sacks' *The Alphabet* (ding!), Bill Bryson's *Mother Tongue* and *Troublesome Words*, as well as *The Penguin Dictionary of Proverbs*, various other dictionaries, rhyming and otherwise, and *Roget's Thesaurus*.

I've been to the rhyming dictionary a few times, so far fruitlessly. It's nice to know it's there, though I know I'll never find a good rhyme for 'orange'. It appears squeezed between 'syringe' and 'infringe' but I'm not convinced – the emPHAsis is on the wrong syllAHble. The dictionary of proverbs gets a glance once in a while. What's noticeable about proverbs is how often they contradict each other:

He who hesitates is lost / Look before you leap

Birds of a feather flock together / Opposites attract

Silence is golden / The squeaky wheel gets the grease

Many hands make light work / Too many cooks spoil the broth

Don't judge a book by its cover / The apparel oft proclaims the man

Familiarity breeds contempt / Better the devil you know

Never look a gift horse in the mouth / Beware of Greeks bearing gifts . . .

And so on. My favourite arguing pair, though, are two Italian proverbs about revenge: 'Revenge is a dish best served cold' and 'Revenge digs two graves'. The argument is clear-cut if you read the first as saying revenge is worth it, the second as saying it's not. On the other hand, the second may be used in support of the first: Don't be a hothead and fly off the handle; think your way through it.

Revenge is clearly on the mind of the narrator in Don Walker's song 'Harry Was A Bad Bugger'. Don, the Clint Eastwood of Australian rock, piano player and songwriter for the hugely successful Cold Chisel, has been making peerless solo records since the band's break-up in the eighties. He toured with us in 1998, playing songs from his cheerfully entitled *We're All Gunna Die*. Some people might call Don's voice lugubrious, perhaps comparing it to Leo Kottke's description of his own singing – 'geese farts on a muggy day' – but I like it. Sort of a tuneful, deeper Bryan Brown.

Charlie Owen, another heavy hombre, was playing lap steel with Don at the time he toured with us. Every night they broke down the band and performed 'Harry' as a duo. Don would get up from the piano, pour himself a big glass of Johnnie Walker Black, stand at the mic and talk-sing its many verses.

Harry did a lot of bad things, criminal things; he ruined lives then mysteriously disappeared. Nobody's really sure what happened to him, or if they are, nobody's talking. There's a rumour his body's inside one of the pylons of Sydney's Glebe Island Bridge, but it's barely a skerrick of a scrap of a whisper, heard once on a screeching wind. Don, as the narrator with a score to settle, intones towards the end, 'Revenge is a dish best tasted cold,' just before he tells us one more time, 'Harry was a bad bugger.'

It's a ripper song. By the end of the tour we had an extra bottle of Johnnie Walker each night on the rider, now called a bottle of Harry. We would crowd around the monitor desk on the side of the stage, glasses in hand, saluting the Don, who sipped from his own glass of Harry as he conjured once again the eternal, infernal Bad Bugger.

'Be Careful What You Pray For' was written for Vika and Linda Bull, two Melbourne sister-singers with Australian-Tongan ancestry. They grew up listening to big, hymn-singing Tongan choirs and were looking for gospel songs for their album *Two Wings*. The chords of 'Be Careful' are pure gospel and so is the tune, which sounds like a thousand other tunes. The song groans with clichés; it's packed to the gills, you might say – the title itself, of course, followed by 'glittering prize', 'place in the sun', 'moth to a flame' and 'dreams come true'.

Clichés are the songwriter's friend, and gospel music in particular derives its comfort and power from familiar phrases, but this, I realised, was pushing it too far. I was in danger of ending up with a bowl of plain pasta. Those two salty Italian proverbs gave me the pungent dash of flavour – the anchovies and olives – I needed.

It's not every day you get to double the Don. Wine is wine and ale is ale, and all praise to the humans who make them, but a glass of whisky is, to me, forever now a glass of Harry.

BEAUTIFUL PROMISE

You made me a beautiful promise
You told me a wonderful lie
Can you keep that beautiful promise?
I've seen tall fountains dwindle and die

We're chasing a beautiful rainbow
Our story hasn't been told
It takes rain to make a rainbow
Takes a sun dying to turn the world gold

The days run outside the window
Like horses across the plains
Fireflies dance in the shadows
Love don't shine steady – it waxes and wanes

It's All Too Beautiful

'Itchycoo Park' – The Small Faces
'Beautiful Brother Of Mine' – Curtis Mayfield
'The Most Beautiful Girl In The World' – Prince
'But Beautiful' – Mel Tormé
'Beautiful Day' – U2
'You Must Have Been A Beautiful Baby' –
    Bing Crosby, Bobby Darin
'A Beautiful Morning' – The Rascals
'Beautiful Child' – Archie Roach
'Up, Up And Away' – The 5th Dimension
'Bathe In That Beautiful Pool' – Dock Walsh
'Beautiful Waste' – The Triffids
'Beautiful' – Snoop Dogg

'Beautiful Brown Eyes' – Rosemary Clooney
'Beautiful Way'– Beck
'Beautiful Dreamer'– Roy Orbison

Dear Friends And Gentle Hearts

One morning on tour during the American spring of 2002, I took a stroll around Pittsburg. It was a beautiful day, a day off, which made it even more beautiful, and I wandered happily with no particular place to go. I found myself in the handsome grounds of the university and came upon a small building called the Stephen Foster Memorial. I remembered singing his songs around the house as a child, from Pete Seeger's book of American folk songs. Foster wrote 'Beautiful Dreamer' but never recorded it. He also wrote 'Oh! Susannah', 'Camptown Races' and 'Old Folks At Home' (first line: 'Way down upon the Swanee River') but never recorded them either. He died before Edison developed the wax cylinder.

I knew that a lot of his songs had come out of the blackface minstrel shows that were the most popular form of American entertainment from the mid-nineteenth century on. I was curious to learn more but the door to the museum was locked and a sign on it read, 'Sorry, we're closed today – any enquiries, call this number.'

I went down the street and called from a payphone. The fellow who answered said his assistant hadn't been able to come in today and he had a class to teach in an hour's time, but as I was a songwriter *all* the way from Australia and in town *only* for *one* day (you have to work these things), he would be happy to show me around the museum for forty-five minutes.

Touring is often a grind, touring America in particular – the absence of family, the endless interstates, the queues at airports, the incomprehensibility of the sports pages in the newspapers, the indifference of promoters, the struggle of sound checks. But every once in a while, unbidden and unforeseen, a golden day or hour bowls up to you. The professor arrived ten minutes later, unlocked the modest museum and took me through its several small rooms, chatting all the while. Among other things, we discussed the influence on Foster of African-American music – 'Camptown Races' has an obvious call-and-response element ('Doodah! Doodah!') – and whether he borrowed much from existing folk songs. Evidently not, according to the prof, though popular expressions of the day made their way into his songs. (What else is new?)

We also pondered the perennial question, Did he write the words or the music first?, as we looked into a glass cabinet at a notebook containing two separate lyrics for 'Old Folks At Home', displayed side by side. They were different metrically, which suggested to the prof that the lyrics came first. But Foster could have had two different melodies he was kicking around, I suggested. It happens sometimes.

The first line of one of the manuscripts read, 'Way down upon the Pedee river', with 'Pedee' crossed out and 'Swanee' substituted.

'Just as well he changed that,' I said, and told the story of Paul McCartney changing 'Scrambled eggs' to 'Yesterday' while keeping the tune. (Try it, 'Yesterday' will never sound the same.) This seemed to tickle the prof as much as it's tickled me for many years.

The charge has been made in recent decades that Stephen Foster perpetuated racial stereotypes in his songs. The prof argued that, true, the blackface minstrel shows depicted African Americans in crude, almost subhuman caricature, but this had been going on for some time before Foster started writing. His aim, which has to be seen in the context of his time, was to raise the art form by humanising the characters in his songs, so that audiences could empathise with them.

His song 'Nelly Was A Lady', a slave's lament upon the death of his wife, is a good example of this. The dignity and poignancy of the words and tune shine through the idiomatic dialect of his day.

When I saw my Nelly in de morning,
Smile 'til she opened up her eyes,

Seemed like de light ob day a-dawning,
Jist 'fore de sun begin to rise.

Nelly was a lady
Last night she died,
Toll de bell for lubly Nell,
My dark Virginny bride.

Blackface minstrelsy is the hidden heart of American popular music. All the country-music pioneers – Jimmie Rodgers, Roy Acuff, Bill Monroe – put on the burnt cork when they worked with the medicine shows, but nobody likes to talk about it all that much these days. Minstrelsy still lives, more disguised now, in the ongoing imitation and exaggeration of Afro-American culture – a constant leaven in the dough of Western popular art. It worked for Elvis Presley, The Rolling Stones, and Moby, and still works for Tom Waits, C. W. Stoneking, Eminem and many others. Young white folks have been sneaking down to the slave shacks on the plantation and borrowing the dances and tunes ever since the first boats from Africa dropped their human cargo on the auction blocks of New Orleans' Congo Square.

And not just white folks. It's paid blacks well to put on the mask of minstrelsy, too, from early times to the present. Louis Armstrong's eye-rolling, face-pulling, hanky-dabbing was straight from the vaudeville stage. And Michael Jackson's flash dancing in sharp suits, a little short in the arm and leg, with one gloved hand, draws directly from two staple characters of blackface – Zip Coon, the uptown dandy, and Jim Crow, the hayseed whose clothes don't fit quite right. As a child, Jackson also had the Cute Piccaninny role, another staple, well stitched up. Under their disguises, with their subliminal signals that said, 'Fear us not, we know our place,' Michael and Louis gained safe passage to the big house of pop stardom.

In the museum in Pittsburgh I saw the piano where Stephen Foster wrote his famous songs, and heard from the prof how Foster's business arrangements – he didn't perform, he relied for income solely on publishing his song sheets – pioneered the standard music practices regarding royalties, copyright, and so on, in place today. In this he could be considered the first professional songwriter of modern times. (I say 'modern times' because I bet Homer and the old Irish bards got paid one way or another.)

Unfortunately things didn't work out so well for poor Stephen. His songs went out of fashion and the Civil War ruined him financially. In 1864 he died of a fever in a New York room. He was thirty-eight years old with thirty-eight cents to his name. There was a note in his pocket that read 'Dear friends and gentle hearts.' I wonder if the copyright's expired on that yet.

'Beautiful Dreamer', the last song Foster completed, was published the year of his death. It's still going strong. Lots of people have sung it, including Bing Crosby and Roy Orbison. It was the Joker's love song in the first Batman movie. But it's a shame Steve never heard the Big O sing his words.

> Beautiful dreamer, wake unto me,
> Starlight and dewdrops are waiting for thee;
> Sounds of the rude world, heard in the day,
> Lull'd by the moonlight have all pass'd away!

BEFORE TOO LONG

Before too long
The one that you're loving will wish that he'd never met you
Before too long
He who is nothing will suddenly come into view
So let the time keep rolling on
It's on my side
Lonely nights will soon be gone
High is the tide

Before too long
We'll be together and no-one will tear us apart
Before too long
The words will be spoken, I know all the action by heart
As the night time follows day
I'm closing in
Every dog will have his day
Any dog can win

Shut the shade do not fear anymore
Here I come creeping round your back door

Before too long
I'll be repeating what's happened before in my mind
Before too long
Over and over just like a hammer inside
As the night time follows day
I'm closing in
Every dog will have his day
Any dog can win
Before too long, before too long

Strawberry Hills Forever

Steve Connolly, who played guitar with me for seven years, came from a line of vaudevillians, writers and communists. He had a prodigious memory, a capacity for alcohol and drugs, and loved the Essendon football club, American Civil War history, Howlin' Wolf, Abba, and The Beach Boys. He died too young, at the age of thirty-six, from a heart infection.

In 1984 I was living in Melbourne and coming out of a rough patch. I'd made a couple of records that had stiffed, was without a band and had hardly written a song in two years. My friend Ronnie took me to see The Cuban Heels, who were playing at a hotel in Richmond. His friend Steve was the front man, singing bittersweet punk-pop songs and playing guitar like a cross between Hubert Sumlin, Steve Cropper and James Burton. He was wearing tight black jeans above R. M. Williams boots with, yes, Cuban heels.

They did two covers – Neil Young's 'The Losing End' and 'Fa-Fa-Fa-Fa-Fa' by Otis Redding. I thought to myself, I should get to know this guy, and hung around afterwards to have a drink with the band. A couple of weeks later we were sitting in his kitchen with guitars and he was playing little melody lines and in-the-pocket parts to some new songs of mine that were finally starting to come.

My first wife Hilary and I broke up around that time and she moved to Sydney. I stayed in Melbourne looking after our 3½-year-old son Declan, and jamming with Steve. A young surfie friend of his who played drums and sang high harmonies joined us, banging a tambourine and shaking maracas. His name was Michael Barclay.

Three months later, Declan and I moved to Sydney where Hilary and I took turns looking after him. After a while Steve and Michael headed north as well, and the three of us moved into an apartment in Randwick, just around the corner from a church. On Saturday and Sunday mornings the bells ringing out of tune would wake us up. On Sunday nights we played as a trio at an inner-city hotel called the Strawberry Hills, where we'd been offered a residency. It was a dingy little room, but they guaranteed us a hundred and fifty dollars a night even though we were only averaging around thirty people. The publicans liked us – one acoustic guitar, one chiming-stinging Stratocaster, and sweet high harmonies. Maybe it was a nice break from the Friday- and Saturday-night bands with names like The Slugfuckers, Thug, and Severed Heads.

Every Sunday evening we'd pile ourselves, the amp and the guitars into the Kingswood, Hilary's father's old car, and drive into the city. We'd slow down as we went past the Hopetoun Hotel in Surry Hills, a popular rock'n'roll pub that was always packed. It sat on a corner, lights blazing, music pumping, like a nonstop-party cruise ship. People spilled out onto both streets, shining schooners of beer in their hands, talking, smiling and laughing without a care in the world.

'We're gonna play there one day,' I said to the others as we drove down the hill to our sparse assignment.

A year later we'd made a record called *Post* and become a five-piece band called Paul Kelly and The Coloured Girls (after Lou Reed's reference to his sweet harmony singers in 'Walk On The Wild Side'). A few more people were starting to come along to see us play, and the Hopetoun eventually offered us a gig.

In 1986 we recorded and released our double album *Gossip*. Not long after it came out, we were driving the 880 kilometres from Sydney to Melbourne, a regular occurrence back then, and 'Before Too Long', the first single from the record, came on the radio somewhere between Yass and Gundagai. It was the first time we'd heard it in public coming at us, rather than from us.

Electrified, we jumped up as one in our seats, turned the radio up to the max and sang along at the tops of our voices. If memory serves me well, we ripped the scabs off a few more cold little vicious ones from the perennial slab of Victoria Bitter, to help wash down another round of Sudafed. In the days before drug manufacturers got wise, a packet of Sudafed – white cold-and-flu pills containing a little yellow, easily extractable nucleus of pseudoephedrine – combined with the aforementioned 24-can slab was the human petrol of choice for long-distance trips. The speed kept you sober and the beer took the edge off the speed. A great buzzy way to make the miles fly by.

The guitar break on the recording of 'Before Too Long' is typical of Steve's style. He didn't like to play a lot of notes. He simply took the melody of the song as a starting point then bent it a little.

Some songs are more elastic than others. They can be played in many different ways, Gershwin's 'Summertime' being a good example. There's space between the change of chords for a variety of arrangements to breathe. The chords of 'Before Too Long' move very quickly from one to another, locking it, like tight links in a chain, into a set structure. For some years I tried to take this song away from the original recording, tried it as a waltz even, but I kept coming back to that old arrangement. Now I'm content to stay there, let the parts of the song move me along and ring the changes in honour of my dead friend.

Steve Connolly was a proud, stubborn man with deep hates and loves. He didn't like jazz (couldn't stand the noodling) or reggae (too sleepy). But he loved all kinds of pop music. He was always pushing the band to be concise – to define parts, to find hooks, to tighten arrangements. The infuriating, charming, strutting little bugger shouldn't have died when he did. He thought he was indestructible but he got careless.

Oh, we all could have died on that Hume Highway singing our happy guts out.

BEGGAR ON THE STREET OF LOVE

In my time I have been a rich man giving favours
All the world at my feet and its many different flavours
I sucked it all dry, now I realise
I'm a beggar on the street of love

All the rest have no charm
There's nothing they can give me
What I want makes me poor
In this great big world of plenty
I'm holding out my cup, only you can fill it up
I'm a beggar on the street of love

On my own I'm standing, so patiently
And my heart keeps calling, calling out for you to see
You look right through me and you pass me by

Take my hand, lead me to your loving milk and honey
Cover me, keep me from the night so cold and rainy
Please, I'm down on my knees
I'm a beggar on the street of love

Big Blue Frog

The first song I ever learnt on guitar was 'I'm In Love With A Big Blue Frog', recorded by Peter, Paul and Mary. My second-eldest sister Sheila taught it to me when I was thirteen. The chords are G, C, D and A, and they've come in handy since. Around ninety percent of my songs contain one or more of them.

I liked the words to 'Big Blue Frog' too.

I'm in love with a big blue frog
A big blue frog loves me
It's not as bad as it appears
He's got rhythm and a PhD

On the cover of Sheila's record there was a name in brackets, (Braunstein), next to the title of the song. Braunstein, the songwriter. I wonder now who he or she was. A sit-down-every-day-at-the-piano type? A writer of children's songs only? And that question again – I'd love a dollar for each time I've been asked it – What came first, the words or the music?

I could spiral down the Google whirlpool, disappear for days and come up with a net full of wondrous knowledge and falsehoods, but part of me prefers to leave (Braunstein) in his or her mysterious brackets. I'd rather meditate on the titles of other songs sung by Peter, Paul and Mary – 'Lemon Tree', '500 Miles', 'Go Tell It On The Mountain', 'Blowin' In The Wind' – as they bring, swimming up to me from the depths, the image of Sheila strumming and singing and forever trying to straighten her curly hair to look like Mary Travers.

At home there were long-playing albums belonging to our parents – comedy records by Barry Humphries and Victor Borge, classical, opera, and Harry Belafonte's *Greatest Hits* – but Sheila and the eldest of the family, Anne, were the first to buy singles – 'The Battle Of New Orleans' by Johnny Horton, 'Sheila' (of course) by Tommy Roe, Chubby Checker's 'Let's Twist Again' and 'Limbo Rock'; 'Love Me Do' and 'All My Loving' by The Beatles. Later on came the albums of our generation – *High Tide and Green Grass, Highway 61 Revisited, The Best of Françoise Hardy, Sweet Soul Music* . . .

Anne was a year and a day older than Sheila and they both had December birthdays. There were big, teenage boy-girl parties coinciding with the end of the school year, the start of the long hot summer vacation and the delicious, stretched-out feeling of no-school-for-two-months. 'Limbo Rock' was played on high rotation and we wide-eyed younger ones, staying up late in our shortie pyjamas, were allowed to take our turn under the limbo stick before being bundled off to bed.

Lying in our bunks in the dark, we heard songs from another planet drifting through the chat and laughter down the hall – Wilson Pickett's 'Land Of A Thousand Dances', 'Sweet Soul Music' by Arthur Conley, 'What'd I Say' (a song that sounded like it was recorded at a party to be played at a party), 'Spanish Harlem' and 'Stand By Me' – as the dancers in my mind's eye moved closer to each other.

Many years on, in the late seventies, wearing long pants and living in Melbourne, I would go and see Jo Jo Zep and The Falcons playing in crowded pubs – the Kingston, Martinis, Bananas and other places. Joe Camilleri, their lead singer, had a Wilson Pickett thing going on. The Falcons were sharp dressers – waistcoats, natty shirts, shiny shoes – but Joe dressed the sharpest of them all. Most other bands of the time were wearing black jeans and ripped T-shirts and snarling at the audience. But The Falcons wore suits of arresting colours and believed it was their duty to entertain. They did house-rocking, roof-raising versions of classic and obscure soul, R'n'B and reggae songs: 'Security', 'The Honeydripper', 'Dancing Mood'. A lot of their songs were about dancing. The band had horns and strut, stage moves and smiles on their faces. They waved their guitars and saxophones in the air, did everything they could to get over to a crowd. And get over they did. The sweat poured off them and their audience in heaving rooms.

The Falcons were yet to develop their full-blown style. The great nutty soulfulness of 'Hit And Run', 'Sweet' and 'Taxi Mary' was still to come. Joe was just starting to write his own songs. And so was I. Meanwhile he was looking for people to collaborate with. He took a song of mine called 'Only The Lonely Heart', containing the chords G, C and D, into the studio and recorded it. For some reason it was released as 'Only The Lonely Hearted' – maybe it was a typo, maybe he just liked the sound of that title better – and the words weren't exactly the same as I remembered giving him, but I wasn't complaining. It was my first cover. My name was in brackets on someone else's record. Now I was a real songwriter.

Joe was like a big brother to me and helped me get up and running. He recorded another song of mine, 'Hand Me Down', mysteriously adapting the words again, and invited me to write with him for The Falcons. Through his influence Mushroom Records offered me a recording deal, putting up the money for my first album, which he produced.

Sadly, I don't have great memories of our time in the studio. I'd done my back badly and couldn't stand or sit for any length of time, so I had to do most of my vocals lying on the floor. I hated listening back to my singing. It worried me that the studio cost a thousand dollars a day and everything seemed to take so long. I had no idea what I was doing and felt like a fake. If I could gather up every copy of that first record and bury them all in a big hole, I would. But that's no fault of Joe's. He put his heart and soul into it. The songs were the problem. And the flailing singer.

In 1986 the New Zealand singer Jenny Morris asked me for a soul-pop song. I'd written and made three records by then and was beginning to get the hang of it; had a few songs that were starting to stick, that I didn't feel like tossing out after a year. Listening to The Temptations and thinking about Ben E. King, I wrote 'Beggar On The Street Of Love' pretty quickly for her. She called it 'Street Of Love', changed the first three notes so the rip from 'Stand By Me' wasn't so obvious, and did quite well with it.

Not long after that, Melbourne folk-rock band Weddings, Parties, Anything recorded a song of mine called 'Laughing Boy', based on the life of Irish playwright and poet Brendan Behan. They added a sweet tin-whistle intro and instrumental break to it, but otherwise stuck with the template I'd given them. Same chords – G, D, A and Bm – same melody, same words, same title.

We did a lot of shows with The Weddos in the late eighties and early nineties and had all-night singalongs with them after gigs in hotel rooms – sorry, long-ago neighbours – and at afternoon barbecues in lead singer Mick's big backyard down by the river. Onions, sausages and chops frying under the gum trees, guitars strewn in the long grass. They were influenced by bands like The Pogues and Fairport Convention, and by early Australian bush-ballad poets Henry Lawson and Banjo Paterson.

Between us all we knew a lot of songs. Steve Connolly, who had the great party ability to remember whole songs, not just bits, with the right chords, could pull out 'Video Killed The Radio Star' or 'Money, Money, Money' right alongside Mick singing 'Moreton Bay' or our bass player Jon Schofield tearing into 'Hawaii'. We liked a drink and weren't shy about it, but The Weddos made us look like ladies at a vicar's tea party.

Both bands performed together on a radio show one time, squeezed into a little studio. We sang raggedy versions of 'Beggar On The Street Of Love' and Woody Guthrie's 'Deportees', the former turning up as a B-side (nowadays known as a bonus track) and the latter floating around out there somewhere in bootleg land.

One of these days I may record 'Beggar' in a more considered fashion, with a tight soul combo approach – bass, drums, spooky Hammond organ, dry guitar, and add strings, perhaps. I might play around with the melody some. The chords – my sturdy friends G, C, D, plus a couple of extras – I'll stick with.

Thanks, Sheila, and thank you, (Braunstein), for all that lovely frog spawn.

BEHIND THE BOWLER'S ARM

Oh it's been a hard, hard year
Pushing shit uphill
But shit happens all the time
And I guess it always will
Now the days are getting long
Summer's on its way
And I can't wait for Christmas
'Cause the day after Christmas is Boxing Day
And you'll know where to find me
Ten rows back at the MCG
Right behind the bowler's arm

So leave your worries at the farm
Don't fret about the rain
Hold your credit over at the store
Bring the kids down on the train
Meet me on the Richmond side
Just outside the gate
I want to see that very first ball
But don't sweat if you're running late
'Cause you'll know where to find me
There's no other place I'd rather be
But right behind the bowler's arm

And if we're lucky we might see
Someone make a ton or a slashing fifty
Yeah, if we're lucky there might be
A bowling spell of sheer wizardry
But most probably
Nothing much will happen at all

And when the angels add my days
And say my time is up

I'll say to them 'Now hold on please
There's just one thing that you forgot

I know each man must leave this world
Behind when he gets called

But we had a deal that you won't count
The days I watched the bat and the ball
And the angels . . .

They'll know where to find me
There's no other place I'd rather be
But right behind the bowler's arm
Yeah, they'll know where to find me
Ten rows back with sunburnt knees
Right behind the bowler's arm

Demos And Me

Test cricket is a slow game, which is why I like it – a game you can
drop in and out of. You might be at work all day but you switch the
radio on at lunch to check the score and glean from the commentary
what's transpired over the past two hours. You turn it on again mid-
afternoon during a break, or if your kind of work allows it you have
it on the whole seven or eight hours, easing the passage of time with
its lulling drone. Every now and then something exciting happens and
you cock your head and tune your ear in to the suddenly urgent tone
of the announcers. You may finish work a little early to catch the last
hour on TV at home. Or maybe the match is on in Perth, three hours
behind, in which case you watch it with dinner and a bottle of wine.

Tests played in England start at eight or nine o'clock at night,
Australian time. As children, my brothers and I would lie in bed

listening to the voices of the announcers – kindly, measured McGil-vray; plummy, rambling Arlott – coming to us from impossibly faraway places, sports grounds with heraldic names: Old Trafford, Lords, the Oval. We willed on Hassett, Benaud, Simpson, Lawry, McKenzie, eventually falling asleep only to be woken with a start in the middle of the night if a wicket fell – English: joy! Australian: disaster! – or a catch was dropped or a six hit, the crackling, distorted applause crossing vast oceans to bleed out of our tiny transistor radio.

Deep sleep would often blanket all happenings, or Mum or Dad would quietly come in and turn the sound off during the first period of REM. I'd wake up in the morning and switch it on again, anxious to hear the latest news of the distant battle from the war correspondents on the scene.

I get less anxious now. Instead, watching cricket is a way of switching off from the cares of life – debt, death, marriage, children, work, reputation – to concentrate intently on little things: why the bowler has changed from over the wicket to around; why silly short leg has dropped back to square; whether the out-of-form opener, scratching away for runs, will be able to get his flow going; the danger developing for the left-handed batsmen in the ever-deepening rough made by the bowler's footmarks at the other end, and other pressing issues.

There are always numbers to ponder too – runs per over, runs by each batsman per ball, wickets in hand, the bowlers' averages, the number of overs until the new ball can be taken, previous records, the time left in the match and the timing of a declaration. I've heard of a Chinese folk belief that we have a certain number of days allotted to us in our lives but any time spent fishing doesn't count. It's an appealing notion, the idea that some activities are outside time. Watching or playing cricket's like that for me.

The term 'Boxing Day' holds hidden folk memories, traditions that have to do with the distribution of gifts, money or food to the poor. The box of money from the church Christmas service collection was divided up the next day among the deserving of the parish. Or the servants, having served their masters on Christmas Day, were given the leftovers, boxed up to take home to their families. Or wealthy families would box presents to give to the less fortunate, and so on.

You don't see a lot of that these days. Boxing Day now mainly means shop 'til you drop at the post-Christmas sales. In Melbourne it's also the first day of the test match at the Melbourne Cricket Ground – a five-day match that has been 'traditional' since 1980.

My friend Demos and I and various family members always used to go on the first day. It was a point of honour to be there for the very first ball of the first session. The Boxing Day crowds can be huge, up to ninety thousand people. Somehow, over the years, a popular folk event has become a Traditional Corporate Blockbuster, with the scoreboard shouting at you, ads and music blaring, ground announcers stating the bleeding obvious, Mexican waves and huge bouncing beach balls. This is the way of modern times – to pump up the authentic 'til it becomes hyper-authentic, keep pumping 'til the bladder bursts, the hyper turns hypo, and everybody feels like an actor in a world turned inside out.

Demos and his daughters still go on day one, but I'm more inclined in recent times to join them on the second and third days, when things have settled down. Maybe it's a sign of old age, though Demos is older than me. We usually get a spot not too far back from the fence and behind the bowler's arm so we can see the deviation of the ball off the pitch. It means that the sightscreen blocks our view of part of the ground and we have to shift seats every time it moves. We don't mind, though. It keeps us from seizing up.

Demos brings a thermos of coffee and Greek sweets – blissful little horseshoe kourabiedes – made by his mother-in-law. I bring mince pies and ham sandwiches with hot mustard. We drink cold beer in the sun and wouldn't be anywhere else.

BIG FINE GIRL

She's a big fine girl from the country
A big fine girl from the country
She's a rolling queen and she wants me
A rolling queen and she wants me
Well, I'm gonna ride with my big fine girl all night long

We met beneath the tall pines
Met beneath the tall pines
We lay down on the green grass
Lay down on the green grass
Yeah, I'm gonna ride with my rolling queen all night long

I woke up to a knocking
Woke up to a knocking
She stood and darkened my door
Stood and darkened my door
Oh, I'm gonna ride with my big fine girl all night long

Caltowie Bells

In the couple of photographs I've seen of her, my great-grandmother
Catherine is tall, and angular of face – an imposing figure with her
hair pulled back into a tight bun. She looks formidable. From the
snippets I've gleaned, though, it seems her grandchildren were very
fond of her, so the severity of her expression probably has more to
do with unease in front of a camera, or the necessity of keeping still
for an unblurred picture. No-one on a mobile phone ever snapped
her with her head thrown back and laughing. No photo exists of her
playing with her children or hugging them close to her bosom and
smothering them with kisses.

She would have been a good rider, living on a farm north of Adelaide. Her straight back suggests she cut a fine figure on horseback, on her way to meet her beau James Kelly, an ambitious young farmer from the neighbouring area. He certainly appears to have been quite taken with her, as evidenced in a letter he wrote to one of his cousins saying he had his eye on a 'big fine girl'.

James later told his grandchildren that he courted her, when he was twenty-one and she sixteen, 'around the pine trees of Sevenhill', the winery run by the Jesuits and still in operation today. But it would be six years before wedding bells rang for them at the Catholic church in Caltowie. Their first child was born a year later and died from pneumonia the year after that. That would hollow a face.

BLUES FOR SKIP

Babe, there's no water in the well
Babe, there's no water in the well
I got a funny feeling we're in for quite a spell

Babe, I can't find a vein
Babe, I can't find a vein
I'm digging and I'm digging, I got the shaft again

Little cloud, little cloud way up in the air
Little cloud, little cloud way up in the air
Well I just ain't receiving, little cloud's moved on somewhere

Babe, there's no water in the well
Babe, there's no water in the well
I'm digging and I'm digging . . .

Borrowed Tune

On Neil Young's dark and desolate record *Tonight's the Night*, recorded not long after two friends died from drug overdoses, he sings a song called 'Borrowed Tune', saying in the fourth verse that he's too wasted to write his own.

'Lady Jane' was the song he borrowed. I know the feeling. The only song I wrote in 1982 was a song about not being able to write a song. The minor key and the falsetto were borrowed from the late great bluesman Skip James, who wrote 'Devil Got My Woman', 'Hard Time Killing Floor' and 'Cypress Grove Blues'. These three tunes alone are reason enough to live.

**Other Reasons To Live
(Besides The Ones You Love)**

Act Three of *Der Rosenkavalier*
Bondi Beach
Cézanne's watercolours
Elvis, twenty years old, singing 'Blue Moon'
Kicking the football in dying autumn light
'Ode to a Nightingale'
Rain on the roof
Roast lamb with rosemary and garlic
The first beer after hard work

BRADMAN

Sydney, 1926, this is the story of a man
Just a kid in from the sticks, just a kid with a plan
St George took a gamble, played him in first grade
Pretty soon that young man showed them how to flash the blade
And at the age of nineteen he was playing for the State
From Adelaide to Brisbane the runs did not abate
He hit 'em hard, he hit 'em straight

He was more than just a batsman
He was something like a tide
He was more than just one man
He could take on any side
They always came for Bradman 'cause fortune used to hide in the
    palm of his hand

A team came out from England
Wally Hammond plundered like a chief
All through the summer of '28, '29 they gave the greencaps no relief
Some reputations came to grief
They say the darkest hour is right before the dawn
And in the hour of greatest slaughter the great avenger is being born
But who then could have seen the shape of things to come?
In Bradman's first test he went for eighteen and for one
They dropped him like a gun
Now big Maurice Tate was the trickiest of them all
And a man with a wisecracking habit
But there's one crack that won't stop ringing in his ears
'Hey Whitey, that's my rabbit'
Bradman never forgot it

He was more than just a batsman
He was something like a tide

He was more than just one man
He could take on any side
They always came for Bradman 'cause fortune used to hide in the
    palm of his hand

England 1930 and the seed burst into flower
All of Jackson's grace failed him, it was Bradman was the power
He murdered them in Yorkshire, he danced for them in Kent
He laughed at them in Leicestershire, Leeds was an event
Three hundred runs he took and rewrote all the books
That really knocked those gents
The critics could not comprehend this nonchalant phenomenon
'Why, this man is a machine,' they said. 'Even his friends say
    he isn't human'
Even friends have to cut something

He was more than just a batsman
He was something like a tide
He was more than just one man
He could take on any side
They always came for Bradman 'cause fortune used to hide in the
    palm of his hand

Summer 1932 and Captain Douglas had a plan
When Larwood bowled to Bradman it was more than man to man
And staid Adelaide nearly boiled over as rage ruled over sense
When Oldfield hit the ground they nearly jumped the fence
Now Bill Woodfull was as fine a man as ever went to wicket
And the bruises on his body that day showed that he could
    stick it
But to this day he's still quoted and only he could wear it
'There's two sides out there today and only one of them's
    playing cricket'

He was longer than a memory, bigger than a town
His feet they used to sparkle and he kept the ball along the ground
Fathers took their sons who never lost the sound of the roar of
    the grandstand

Now shadows they grow longer and there's so much more yet
    to be told
But we're not getting any younger, so let the part tell the whole
Now the players all wear colours, the circus is in town
I can no longer go down there, down to that sacred ground

He was more than just a batsman
He was something like a tide
He was more than just one man
He was a match for any side
They always came for Bradman 'cause fortune used to hide in the
    palm of his hand

Leg Theory

A miracle has been removed from among us. So must ancient
Italy have felt when she heard of the death of Hannibal.

> English cricket writer, R. C. Robertson
> Glasgow, on Bradman's retirement

I rode with Sir Donald Bradman in a taxi once but I was only five
years old and don't remember a thing. Dad knew him through the
professional circles of Adelaide in the 1950s and '60s. Don, the greatest cricketer of all time by most reckonings, had moved there in the
mid-1930s to work for a stockbroking firm. He lived in our neighbourhood and played for my local cricket club, Kensington, after his
international retirement. He gave Dad replicas of the baggy green

caps worn by the Australian cricket team, to pass on to me and my brothers. (Oh, Time, where are they now?)

Bradman's status in the game is forever fixed by his famous, freaky batting average of 99.94. If he'd scored a mere four more runs in his last innings his average would have been a perfect 100, but he was bowled second ball by leg spinner Eric Hollies. The story goes, denied by the Don, that there were tears in his eyes from the ovation given him by the crowd beyond the fence and by the opposing England team within it.

Don Bradman came along at a time when Australia was hungry for heroes, clawing its way out of the Depression and defining itself against the Mother Country. The Don stood for Australian prowess, independence and freedom of spirit. He was the Boy From The Bush, a self-taught loner-genius, the diminutive David who strode out of the wilderness slinging his stick against the imperial Goliath.

The whole country loved him but not all of his teammates did. His huge fame sat as uneasily with them as it did with him. He wasn't considered one of the boys – very un-Australian then, as now – and didn't drink. Not only that, he played piano and liked to spend his free time writing in his room. This was even more un-Australian.

I played a lot of cricket as a child and teenager – opened the batting generally for school teams, bowled leg spin, and was in the First Eleven in my last year. I also played for Kensington Schoolboys and took guard at the crease on the same wicket Don would have many years before, or so I imagined.

Cricket books often turned up in my Christmas stocking. (The wordie books came later.) A biography of Bradman written by Irving Rosenwater gripped me all through the summer of its arrival, in particular the account of the Bodyline series in 1932–33. A cavalcade of villains, heroes and those who were a bit of both stalked its pages as the England captain, Douglas Jardine, employed his infamous leg theory – bowling dangerously fast at the batsman's body and stacking the field on the leg side – designed specifically to curb Bradman and considered unsporting not just by the Australians but by several members of the England team.

Years later I was fooling around with a circular series of three chords – the usual suspects D, G, A – over which I was singing a melancholy, falling tune. Each chord was the same length, so the cycle was three bars long – not a normal song structure. On a hunch I went back to Bradman's biography and dipped into it again. The music worked well for a long narrative, for moving between talking and singing. Verses could start anywhere and go as long as they wanted. Rosenwater's heroes and villains and in-between men began rolling out of my mouth. The random structure and odd length of the bar progression seemed to make the song float free of time, suiting the subject matter and suggesting a narrator's point of view – that of an old man nearing the end of his days, looking back.

The song was recorded in 1986 with The Coloured Girls. To accompany it we released a video made up of photos and archival film footage, put together by author and documentary maker Jack Egan. I've made a lot of videos but this is one of my favourites. Jack pulled a few favours to get the footage at an affordable rate and agreed we didn't need to have me and the band miming the song. My kind of film clip.

Songwriters never quite know what they're doing. The action of 'Bradman' ended in 1933, only five years into the Don's test career. He played on, with a substantial break during World War II, for another fifteen years, but the song already went for seven and a half minutes, which seemed long enough to me. At the time, though I'd called a halt to the story prematurely and written a last verse to justify my action, I had a nagging feeling that I'd abandoned the song, or it had abandoned me, that somehow I'd run out of puff.

It was not 'til much later that I came to feel I'd got out at the right time. Bradman's final tour, his last-innings duck notwithstanding, was an unprecedented triumph. His team, known from then on as The Invincibles, was the only cricket side ever to tour England undefeated in every match they played – test and county. The music of the song would not have suited such a grand finale. Much better to leave him in the middle of uncertainty, crowded by the old enemy, at the point of his greatest vulnerability.

I sent Sir Donald the video and a single and wrote him a letter mentioning my father, who'd died many years before. It's said that Bradman answered every fan letter written to him – sat down every morning and knocked them off – and sure enough, I received a reply in fairly short time.

He remembered my father warmly, then said he didn't have a video player but would watch the clip soon at his daughter's place. The letter ended: 'Thank you. I am flattered by your attempt.'

Who is it that all Australia raves about?
Who has won our very highest praise?
Now is it Amy Johnson, or little Mickey Mouse?
No! It's just a country lad who's bringing down the house
And he's Our Don Bradman – I ask you is he any good?
Our Don Bradman – As a batsman he can sure lay on the wood
For when he goes in to bat
He knocks ev'ry record flat
For there isn't any thing he cannot do

Jack O'Hagan, from 'Our Don Bradman'

(THE) CAKE AND THE CANDLE

I don't ask much
Only what's mine
I know just what I'm worth
I'll get what I deserve
Look at me now
I'm in my prime
My eyes are on the prize
There'll be no compromise this time
You can still change your mind
If this is more than you can handle
'Cause I want it all, that's what I'm here for
I want the cake
I want the candle

You've had your share
Of pleasure and pain
All that was just a taste
Before the feast
So bring me your body
Bring me your flame
I'll make you burn so bright
I'll make you shout my name
You can still change your mind
If you can't afford the scandal
Yeah, I want it all
Body and soul
I want the cake
And I want the candle
I want the whole damn cake and candle

Cakewalk

Put the following phrases into a story (example at back of book):
   Life is not all cakes and ale
   It's a piece of cake
   My cake is dough
   They sold like hot cakes
   Hey, sweet baby-cakes
   Someone left the cake out in the rain
   He's not fit to hold a candle to her
   The game is not worth the candle
   You've been burning the candle at both ends
   You're holding a candle to the devil
   It seems to me you've lived your life like a candle in the wind
   (Optional extra: The proof of the pudding is in the eating)

I puzzled for years over the expression 'You can't have your cake and eat it too.' What's the point of having a cake, I thought, if you can't eat it? Eventually it was pointed out to me that the correct form of the expression is 'You can't eat your cake and have it.' This made more sense. You use something up, it's gone. You eat your cake, you don't have it any more. Unless it's a magic pudding.

In 1993 Melbourne singer Kate Ceberano approached me for a song. Kate has an expressive, supple voice, equally at home singing pop or jazz. I jumped at the chance. She was after a big song, she said, about reaching out for what you want – a statement of intent. She and her family are Scientologists and it seemed to me they were big believers in the power of positive thinking.

I was reading Tim Winton's *Cloudstreet* at the time. One of the many short chapters was entitled 'The Whole Damn Cake and Candles', a phrase I hadn't come across before. It jumped off the page and into the folds of my brain like a flea burrowing into the coat of a dog.

Most of my songs are written on guitar but I went to the piano for this one, looking to pump it up, in search of grandeur. Since I'm limited on the piano and unable to change chords that quickly, the songs I write on it seem to have more space and air. I can get hold of a more stately feeling.

It's a fine line between stately and bombastic, though, and I wasn't sure which side of the line I was on when I finished the song. I could hear Helen Reddy's 'I Am Woman' roaring in the background – 'I've paid the price but look how much I've gained . . . I am strong, I am invincible.' Was that a good thing or a bad thing? One person's inspiring self-affirmation is another person's turn-off. But Kate liked the song and said she'd have a go at it.

Soon afterwards she landed a job as the host of a TV show called *Kate Ceberano and Friends* and invited me on for an episode. The idea was for the guests to sing something they didn't normally, before joining Kate. I chose Frank Sinatra's 'All The Way', which was a big challenge for me. What Frank makes sound easy isn't. I put on a suit and gave it my best shot but to my mind didn't quite pull it off. Kate pulled off 'The Cake And The Candle', though, as I sat in with her band playing rhythm. She walked that fine line, found the balance, holding the reins lightly with a playfulness that lifted the ponderousness of the lyric.

When she put together a record featuring the highlights from her TV show, 'Cake' made the cut. 'All The Way', to my relief, didn't. It was a good call. Both songs pretty much say the same thing anyway.

Kate's kept her light touch, maintaining a diverse career in show business for over twenty-five years. She was a teenage sensation in I'm Talking, a seminal pop-dance band of the eighties. She's made jazz albums, sung with symphony orchestras and collaborated with a range of singers. She went to New York and made a soul record. She's been a judge on a talent program and a successful contestant on a popular dancing show, played Mary in *Jesus Christ Superstar* and liquefied the house singing 'I Don't Know How To Love Him'. She's writing songs, interpreting other songwriters and raising a family. At last count she'd made eighteen albums.

She's doing it all, eating her cake and having it too.

CARELESS

How many cabs in New York City, how many angels on a pin?
How many notes in a saxophone, how many tears in a bottle of gin?
How many times did you call my name, knock at the door but you
    couldn't get in?
I know I've been careless

I've been wrapped up in a shell, nothing could get through to me
Acted like I didn't know I had friends or family
I saw worry in their eyes, it didn't look like fear to me
I know I've been careless (I took bad care of this)

Like a mixture in a bottle, like a frozen-over lake
Like a longtime painted smile I got so hard I had to crack
You were there, you held the line, you're the one that brought me back
I know I've been careless (I lost my tenderness)
I've been careless (I took bad care of this)

How many cabs in New York City, how many angels on a pin?
How many notes in a saxophone, how many tears in a bottle of gin?
How many times did you call my name, knock at the door but you
    couldn't get in?
How many stars in the Milky Way, how many ways can you lose
    a friend?

Circle Songs

You don't learn how to write a song at school. You can't buy a manual
and follow steps A, B and C, like you do to build a model aeroplane.
Or a table. But there are many teachers for the attentive student,
teachers who teach unknowingly. Some of mine were The Saints, The

Hoodoo Gurus, The Go-Betweens, The Triffids, and Died Pretty, all Australian bands from the late seventies and eighties. Three of them fled the country to live elsewhere. None of them lived in Melbourne. They were my school of the air.

I saw Died Pretty a number of times after I moved to Sydney. They used to pack out The Trade Union Club down the road from my house in Surry Hills. Brooding Frank Brunetti on the keyboards. Tall handsome Brett Myers on guitar, pealing his majestic tones. Their diminutive singer Ron Peno jerked around the stage like a puppet pulled by invisible strings, and howled and crooned into the mic. They were a dangerous band. Some nights they fell in a heap. Other nights they were incandescent.

The Triffids had an album called *Born Sandy Devotional*, a great cathedral of a record inside which singer David McComb preached on love, lust and loneliness, surrounded and uplifted by the soaring architecture of 'Evil' Graham Lee's pedal steel. Nashville never sounded like this. For months I worshipped there daily.

The Saints' first two records, despite the raves, underwhelmed me. They sound great to me now but at the time all I heard was the sneer. With the release of their third album, *Prehistoric Sounds*, I got it. The Bo Diddley beat and the rambunctious horns of 'Swing For The Crime' made a swaggering carriage for singer Chris Bailey, who managed to sound jaded and passionate at the same time. Later on came the EP *Paralytic Tonight, Dublin Tomorrow*. In a cold flat on Punt Road I played those four songs over and over.

I was driving somewhere in Melbourne when I first heard The Go-Betweens' 'Cattle And Cane'. My skin started tingling and I had to pull over to the side of the road. The song had an odd, jerky time signature which acted as a little trip-switch into another world – weird and heavenly and deeply familiar all at once.

> A schoolboy coming home through fields of cane
> To a house of tin and timber
> And in the sky a rain of falling cinders . . .

I could *smell* that song. And then came the droll talking bit – 'So I knew where I was, alone and so at home' – followed by the dreamy 'da da da das'. What planet was this from? When did The Stranglers go to northern Queensland and get all arty? How the fuck did they *do* that? I wondered, slumped and goose-bumped on the steering wheel.

A few years later I was playing around with the chords to another Go-Betweens song, 'Apology Accepted', and came up with the tune for 'Careless'. Like its progenitor, 'Careless' is a circle song, with a progression of chords cycling in the same order all the way through. I have a lot of these – 'Deeper Water', 'From Little Things Big Things Grow' being two. The melody may change for the chorus but the chords don't. There is no 'new bit', no change-up via a bridge or middle eight, no modulation.

A lot of folk music is like this, verses and choruses sung over the same chords. Lots of African music too – the complexity is in the rhythms and the phrasing of the singers – and coming out of that, much funk, hip-hop, modern dance music and electronica. Sometimes there are only two chords, or no chord change at all. In pop music, which borrows from all these forms, it follows that this kind of song turns up regularly, from 'La Bamba' to 'Wanna Be Starting Something' to 'Sweet About Me'. Circle songs are useful when you're jamming with strangers or people who don't have the same repertoire. Everybody can jump on board and stay on the tracks, confident there won't be a sudden shunt to another line and a massive train wreck.

In 1996 the WOMADelaide festival gathered a group of artists from around the world to journey across the great Nullarbor Plain by non-metaphorical train from west to east. ('Nullarbor': Latin for 'no tree'.) Lucky Oceans, one of the world's great pedal steel players, and I were invited to join The Bauls of Bengal, Shu-De, Remy Ongala, Archie Roach and Ruby Hunter and others on the trip. Lucky hails from Pennsylvania, started out life as Reuben Gosfield, and played for many years with Grammy Award-winning western swing band, Asleep at the Wheel. He now lives in Perth, by the mighty Indian Ocean, plays sweet, raw R&B with his friends in a pub on a Sunday afternoon, and hosts a world-music radio program that's broadcast all around the country, playing whatever the hell he wants to. Lucky indeed.

We assembled at Perth railway station and set out on a warm, late-summer evening. Three days later we arrived in the small desert town of Pimba, in the mid-north of South Australia, and performed to three thousand people. Along the way we made music on the train.

Lucky and I were the only musicians who didn't belong to a group, so we floated between them. Lucky, who was travelling with a few instruments – lap steel, acoustic guitar and accordion – can play with anyone, anytime. He's a maestro with an encyclopaedic knowledge of music. I had very limited musical chops, and still do, but I had my circle songs.

Sometime on day two, Remy Ongala and his band jumped on 'Careless' and rode it for twenty joyful minutes. Later that afternoon Shu-De, throat singers from Tuva, built up a drone over the two chords of 'Maralinga', a lament set in the very country we were bisecting. Through the window the sun was going down over red earth and stunted trees.

Throat singers can sing two or more notes at the same time by creating harmonics in their heads. The Tuvans began softly in a low guttural tone. As their sound built up, the whistling harmonics began to fly around the carriage. To be right next to someone who's singing three notes at once feels like you've stepped into a supernatural world and are in the presence of shamans. Lucky's rising and falling steel guitar, not to be outdone in sorcery, wept for the fiery land outside.

Goose bumps again. Weird and heavenly and familiar. Sometimes you wouldn't be dead for quids.

I'd noticed years before, when the paint was still wet on 'Careless', that not only had I lifted the chords from 'Apology Accepted' – nothing unusual about them, variations on the repeat offenders, G, C and D – but my chorus used the same two notes as 'Further, longer, higher, older', the closing refrain of 'Cattle And Cane'.

Apology offered. Forgiveness not required. We just pick it up and pass it on. Further, longer, higher, older.

CHANGE YOUR MIND

Staring at the river
Watching the water flow
I can't stop the river
Never, no

If I could make the mountains
Fall into the sea
Maybe I could make you
Fall for me

(Would you) change your mind
Change your mind, change your mind

All the stars keep turning
Wheeling all night long
I wish you'd turn
And hear my song

If I could make wild horses
Come and get their hay
Maybe I could make you
Sway my way

(Would you) change your mind
Change your mind, change your mind

Maybe when you're sleeping
I can make a spell
And when you wake up
I won't tell

(Would you) change your mind
Change your mind, change your mind

The Motley Cape

Bob Dylan made a record in 1997 called *Time Out of Mind*. Some critics got themselves in a lather writing about his use of 'borrowed language', as if he'd just stepped down from the mountain with the holy tablets. The Bobmeister has that effect on people.

I thought it was a great record about growing old: 'It's not dark yet but it's getting there.' And: 'All the young men with the young women lookin' so good/Well I'd trade places with any of 'em, in a minute if I could.'

As for the borrowed language, ever since Homer's repeated use of 'rosy-fingered dawn', 'wine dark sea' and other formulas in *The Odyssey*, songwriters have been drawing on the communal pool of phrases and images available to anyone with ears. In blues, folk, country and soul music – the building blocks of pop – words, lines and whole verses have been swimming around forever from song to song. Melodies too. Nearly all of Woody Guthrie's tunes are borrowed.

That old tune borrower Neil Young came up in conversation with a friend not long after 'Change Your Mind' was released. 'Did you know he has a song with the same title as yours? It's on *Sleeps With Angels*.'

I went back to my old copy of *Sleeps With Angels* and played the song in question. Beautiful. No problem, though. Titles aren't copyrightable and they've been swimming around for years too. It wasn't the first time I'd recycled one.

Still, I feel like a burglar sneaking across the lawn with a swag of loot over my shoulder every time I pull 'Change Your Mind' out of the drawer. The title's not the only line I've borrowed. Nearly every line in the song comes from somewhere else. From 'Watching The River Flow', 'Stand By Me', 'I Put A Spell On You', 'The Wagoner's Lad', 'Wild Horses', to mention a few. Some people continue to be surprised by this – those who have notions of the artist as some kind of self-dredger, dragging precious originality up from the depths of their soul. Self-expression is overrated, though. There's so much of it around these days. And a good line is worth using again. And again.

I remember when sampling first became popular with the rise of hip-hop. A lot of musicians I knew, who prided themselves on being able to play their instruments properly, were dismissive. 'That's not music,' they sniffed. 'Anyone could do that.' But sampling made perfect sense to me; I'd been doing it since I first started making songs.

'Change Your Mind' is my patchwork quilt. My motley cape. The stitching is visible but it works well – a good item to have in the kit as I go about my night-work. I spread my arms and glide.

CHARLIE OWEN'S SLIDE GUITAR

I was crawling, in need of inspiration
So disgusted, aching for a cure
Right there in my neighbourhood
A spell from the old, dark wood
Charlie Owen's slide guitar

The usual murmurs, the clinking of the glasses
The usual rumours drifting round the bar
He made the same mistake twice
My tears took me by surprise
Charlie Owen's slide guitar

Charlie, I can't see your face
Your good friends are in disgrace
And at the crossroads I am told
The devil's waiting for your soul

If I ever find my way to heaven
I promise I'll throw a party there
The band will be from Brazil
I know he'll be sitting in as well
Charlie Owen with his slide guitar

Songs Praising Musicians (Well, Mostly)

'Angel Of Harlem' – U2 (for Billie Holiday)
'Nightshift' – The Commodores (for Marvin Gaye
   and Jackie Wilson)
'Blind Willie McTell' – Bob Dylan
'Blind Lemon Jefferson' – Nick Cave

'Song For Bob Dylan' – David Bowie

'Master Blaster (Jammin')' – Stevie Wonder (for
  Bob Marley)

'Jackie Wilson Said (I'm In Heaven When You
  Smile)' – Van Morrison

'When Smokey Sings' – ABC (for Smokey Robinson.
  Classic '80s New Romantic schlock. Brilliant video:
  poncy young men hug themselves and sniff roses)

'Elvis Presley Blues' – Gillian Welch

'Alex Chilton' – The Replacements

'Frank Sinatra' – Cake

'Mr Wilson' – John Cale (for Brian Wilson and
  The Beach Boys)

'The Day Marty Robbins Died' – The Beasts of Bourbon

'Prince Alone In The Studio' – Smog ('Prince alone in the
  studio / It's two a.m. and all the girls are gone / The girls
  thought they were going to be able to have sex with
  him / They wore their special underwear')

'Hey Hey, My My' – Neil Young (for Johnny Rotten)

'Don Henley Must Die' – Mojo Nixon

Tiny Troubles

Charlie Owen and I are among the last of the cassette men. There aren't many of us left, traders in tapes who cross each other's palms with occasional compilations of cherished tunes. Charlie, son of a painter and a submarine captain, grew up in a lot of different places. His guitar playing, slide and electric, has lit up many terrific bands – The Divinyls; The Beasts of Bourbon; Tex, Don and Charlie; The Dark Horses; The Working Class Ringos, and others.

I discovered the great Brazilian guitarist Baden Powell de Aquino through Charlie, who knows of my fondness for Caetano Veloso,

Milton Nascimento, Gilberto Gil, Jorge Ben, Maria Bethânia and others. They are on tapes I've carried around for years. Brazilian music, at its best, seems to contain all music and reconcile all opposites. It blends the cool with the hot, the atonal with the sweet, the large chorale with the soloist. Dense jazzy chords meet African polyrhythms. It's cerebral, heady music that never forgets the hips. If heaven has a house band – if there *is* a heaven – most of them would be Brazilian.

One dog night of a dog day of a dog week of a dog month late in the twentieth century, I went down to my local music club, The Continental, to see Charlie play with Joel Silbersher under the name of Tendrils. It was just another night in the city – two old friends hunched over their instruments, longish hair flopping, digging deep into their songs. Playing more for themselves than the crowd.

Joel sang the immortal 'I Miss Your Big White Bum'. During another song, Charlie played a strange, harsh run of notes that seemed wrong to me at first. But when I heard them a second time, a verse or two later, they lifted my head clean off my shoulders. Great music does this to you – makes you feel like a wanderer washed up on a seemingly strange island who suddenly realises they've arrived home. Listening to them play that night, all my troubles became tiny things.

CITIES OF TEXAS

I am the wind without a name
I have been blowing since long before you came
I am the wind no one calls
I see your towers rise and fall
Cities of Texas, my lovely ones
Cities of Texas, shining in the sun

I am the wind no one knows
Out from your deserts, down from your melting snows
Over the ocean, right across your land
I turn your high glass back to shifting sand
Cities of Texas, my lovely ones
Cities of Texas, shining in the sun

I am the wind no one sees
I'm gonna cover you by degrees
Cities of Texas, my lovely ones
Cities of Texas, shining in the sun

On The Bus
First tour of America, 1987

The band and crew:
Steve Connolly – guitar
Jon Schofield – bass
Michael Barclay – drums
Peter 'Pedro' Bull – keyboards
Chris Wilson – harmonica and baritone sax
Declan Cooney – sound
Micky Kelly – lights

Washington DC, 8 November

Dear J,

I said I'd write to you after all this, after the drums and the guitars had been packed away for the last time, the last beer drunk, the goodbyes all said and the last hand shook.

I'm at my brother's place in Washington DC now, watching the leaves fall like snow, squadrons of them fluttering noiselessly to the ground. The others all flew home yesterday except for Chris. He's somewhere in Texas – maybe Austin – or heading for Louisiana with a kitbag full of harmonicas. They loved him over here, the Americans, though I think he scared them half to death. Sometimes he looked as if he was going to swallow his harmonica, crunch it up and spit the pieces all over the crowd. Reviewers described him as 'wrestler built', 'intense', 'skinhead' and 'spastic'. People coming backstage often thought he was our bodyguard.

You should've seen him and Declan walking down the street together. If you unravel a wire coathanger and stand it upright, that's the shape of Declan. And just as tough. Sharp-featured with IRA eyes and a scar on his face that looks like a cigar was stubbed out on it, he just looks illegal. People would get jumpy when this pair stopped to ask the time. They stuck out on Hollywood Boulevard and that's saying something.

My brother calls Los Angeles La La Land. Most people call it LA. I like to say 'Los Angeles', the whole thing, I like the way it rolls off the tongue. Perhaps it's my way of giving the place some stress, some weight – a sign of affection. Maybe it's because it's where we started and finished, after eight weeks of being 'out there', that it feels like home. We all felt like that when we rolled back in on the bus down Interstate 5. There was the City of Angels, sprawling in the sun. It was our second home. Our first home, of course, was the bus.

Now, the bus is as much a concept as a motor vehicle. It refers to four different buses – they kept breaking down on us – but all had roughly the same features. A lounge area up the front with a table, video, stereo, fridge and microwave, and beyond this, in the middle of the bus, a sleeping section with twelve bunks in tiers of three. One by one after a show, as the bus rolled down the highway overnight to the next city, we would crawl into our narrow coffins. Eight mammals, layered like Japanese businessmen in a capsule hotel, snickered and snuffled and snored, night after night, in the close dark fug.

The middle bunks were the best, the bottom ones being too noisy and the top ones too high. There was always the risk of falling out of the latter. Declan did one time, when the bus went off the road and almost flipped over in New Mexico, yet somehow he managed to keep on sleeping. (The power of tequila.)

Up the back was a smaller lounge, again with stereo and video. This back lounge became the retreat room. I spent many hours reading there. Occasionally Pedro could be heard in a corner muttering abuse at a small computerised, beeping chessboard. There was music by Howlin' Wolf, Robert Johnson, Skip James, Tom Waits, Miles Davis, stuff like that.

Up the front the music was nearly always in the major keys. AC/DC, Abba, *Exile on Main Street*, *Kill City*, REM, The Beach Boys, and those compilations you always find in truck stops: *Country Legends*, *The Best of Sam and Dave*, *The Motown Sound*, *California Surfin' Safari*. The front lounge was the party room, the public bar, and the site of a highly addictive and totally unskilled dice game called Zilch. It was also the theatre of a two-month run, both on screen and off, of *Spinal Tap*.

Our first bus driver's name was Heavy Duty, a big-bellied bearded fellow from Nashville, Tennessee. He hated country music. Every time we played George Jones he'd start hollering, 'What kinda shit is that?' Luckily he could shut himself off from the rest of us and listen to the heavy-metal radio stations that kept him awake throughout the night.

My head starts spinning in restaurants. The servings are gigantic. Eating becomes a series of multiple choices. How many different ways can a potato be cooked? How many types of salad dressing or bread does a menu need? Chuck Berry says, 'Anything you want they got it right here in the USA.' And he's right, except for one thing: it's virtually impossible to find a decent cup of coffee in this country of coffee drinkers. The ubiquitous brewed coffee-in-a-glass-jug sits on a hotplate everywhere. In restaurants, diners, gas stations, studios, offices, truck stops and hotel lobbies. It's weak and plentiful. Umberto Eco, lover of lists, has observed that no-one in America asks if you want another coffee, they always ask if you want more coffee.

More. I'm trying to describe the more-ness of America. A-more-ica. More seems to have happened here, in myth and in reality. Everywhere you go, the landscapes and the cities throw up multiple associations. Every place seems to have been in a song. Or someone in a movie or a book or a TV show has come from or gone there. Crossing Kansas, for example. We drove clean across it in a day, without stopping, one long flat straight stretch of road – like driving across the Nullarbor except, through the windows, instead of saltbush and spinifex, miles and miles of waving grain. The mind jostles with images of Dorothy being carried off by the twister in *The Wizard of Oz*, John Brown tramping the state making speeches for abolition, Superman growing up in Smallville, *Christina's World* by Andrew Wyeth, Fats Domino singing 'Kansas City, here I come', and the Wichita Indians hunting buffalo on the plains (which in turn brings to mind 'Wichita Lineman' and Glen Campbell, and so it goes on). Hollywood and history, art and rock'n'roll. And Kansas is a so-called empty state, a state of which people say 'Oh, there's nothing out there, there's nothing in Kansas, only wheat.'

So many places seemed deeply familiar. Arizona and New Mexico – the western landscape of John Ford. The first view of San Francisco across the bay from Oakland, grey and mysterious, just like I'd imagined, with its towers peeping through fog. The Chicago Institute of Art on Michigan Avenue and the twin imperial lions guarding the steps. And around every corner in New York the sudden shock of recognition.

This is the strangeness of America – its very familiarity. Everything is exactly as you imagined it, only more so: the way they speak in Texas, the waitresses in truck stops, the first view of the Manhattan skyline, which makes your stomach contract in awe. In San Francisco, on the corner of Haight and Ashbury, a latter-day hippie offered to sell Steven and Michael acid. (I swear this is true).

There's a character in a Wim Wenders film who says, 'America has colonised our subconscious.' This is what's unnerving about being there for the first time. A place that has existed for years in your mind is suddenly before your eyes. Everyone has experienced those feelings of letdown when expectation finally meets reality, but America doesn't let you down. America is a dream and a nightmare. It seems super-real. Even its banality is super-banal.

It makes perfect sense that the man considered America's national poet, Walt Whitman, was a writer of lists. He didn't write short, refined poems. He simply walked and chanted everything he saw. All the things people did, all their different occupations, all the machinery of the cities and towns, all the modes of transport, all the features of the natural world, all the sounds, all the ways people touched. He was the poet of abundance, the poet of profusion, the poet of confidence.

In New York the nations of the world pour into the subway. If everyone in the carriage suddenly began speaking in their mother tongue, you'd hear forty or more different languages. Babel. On the streets of Nashville you can hear the ever-whining strains of country music drifting out from the bars. At the same time, the cruising cars – low-slung, worn Oldsmobiles and Lincolns driven by young black men – are blasting the hard, hostile crack of hip-hop and rap. Both kinds of music are sung in English but they are two distinct languages, diametrically opposed, one sentimental and melodic, the other beat-driven, minimally melodic and tough. Black and white are talking but neither seems to be hearing the other. Babel.

Babel. Babylon. The cities of Texas, built with oil money, appear to the traveller as if in a dream. I woke up on the bus one morning, stumbled to the front lounge, and there was Dallas in the distance, rising mirage-like from the desert, its glass towers holding and reflecting the sky – bold, new, breathtakingly beautiful modern architecture. A day later, Houston seemed to hover in the air as we approached it from the plain.

I've been fooling around with a song for those cities. There's a poem by Shelley about a statue of an ancient king in the desert being slowly erased by time. I remember studying it at school but I've forgotten what it's called. I've been thinking about that and Shakespeare's early sonnets and trying to channel Willie Nelson.

It's just begun to snow outside. It's been dark for a long time now. The snow falls like the leaves – soft and papery. Tomorrow I go back to La La Land, and shortly after that, home. The snow is sending me to sleep.

See you soon. P

It's twenty-three years since I wrote that letter. I've toured the States at least a dozen times by now and have had several extended stays. I've travelled by car, bus, van, train and plane, solo and with others. Touring is repetitious – essentially you do the same thing every night – so after a while places, cities, times and people tend to blur. But I'll never forget that first time, all senses alert, soaking up the sights, sounds, smells and ideas of that bizarre bazaar.

Twenty years on, there's a Starbucks on every block but the coffee's not much better. You can walk into a Starbucks, though, or nearly any chain in any city, with your laptop, get online and Google – another American invention – that poem you can't remember the name of. You type in the only scrap you recall. Just a couple of clicks and there it is, in its entirety, on your screen.

Twenty-odd years ago, I finished 'Cities Of Texas', with the palimpsest of a half-remembered poem in my head, and fifteen months later recorded it. Every few years or so I send it to Willie Nelson, but he hasn't called yet.

> I met a traveller from an antique land
> Who said: Two vast and trunkless legs of stone
> Stand in the desert. Near them on the sand,

Half sunk, a shatter'd visage lies, whose frown
And wrinkled lip and sneer of cold command
Tell that its sculptor well those passions read
Which yet survive, stamp'd on these lifeless things,
The hand that mock'd them and the heart that fed.
And on the pedestal these words appear:
'My name is Ozymandias, king of kings:
Look on my works, ye Mighty, and despair!'
Nothing beside remains: round the decay
Of that colossal wreck, boundless and bare,
The lone and level sands stretch far away.

                         Percy Bysshe Shelley, 'Ozymandias'

COMA

I can hardly stand your touch
I tremble and I shiver
It's been so long since I felt so much
I just came out of a coma

So take it easy, take it slow
Take your time, dear lover
Inch by inch melts the snow
I just came out of a coma

Help me, help me, help me love
Help me, help me, help me love

Sky so blue, walls so white
I'm crying at their colours
Yeah, I know I ain't talking right
I just came out of a coma

Help me, help me, help me love
Help me, help me, help me love
I just came out of a coma

New Year's Resolutions, 1998

Learn more about wine
Practise Spanish
Finish reading the Bible
Do a computer course
Learn a song a week from the Frank
    Sinatra songbook

Read more history
Cook vitello tonnato just once
Take dancing lessons (western
    swing or Latin)
Give up heroin

Me Or It

Heroin was the one for me, the recreational drug of choice. Its molecules and mine seemed made for each other. Forget marijuana, LSD, amphetamines, cocaine, ecstasy, barbiturates and the rest. Heroin was the perfect fit. Pot and acid were too freaky, ecstasy too lovey-dovey, coke too expensive, mandies too messy, and speed just made me want to take heroin.

I had my first hit at twenty-one. An older, worldly friend, T, initiated me. Solemn as a priest, he boiled water, rinsed out the Blue Lady glass fit he'd just used on himself, and dissolved white powder in a spoon above a flame. He then sucked up the solution (the solution!) through a piece of filter from a cigarette, searched out the plump part of my vein in the crook of my arm and tenderly, expertly injected the contents.

Nothing was hurried, no movement wasted. All was accustomed, ceremonious. The pretty, billowing bloom of blood in the glass tube preceded, by a slow second, the nauseous, freight-train flood of pleasure. *Unnnh.* Metamorphosis. Nothing . . . but . . . THIS.

Snorting smack was for dilettantes. A waste of precious substance. The needle was the thing – the breaking of the skin, the alchemy of the body. Acolytes and adepts, initiates into mysteries, seekers of expanded consciousness, we honoured our avatars, De Quincey, Burroughs, Lou Reed and Arthur Rimbaud. Like Arthur, we wanted to taste all poisons and distill their essence.

I visited T around once a week in his North Adelaide apartment.

I had neither the money nor the desire to become a daily communicant. Nor was more offered. After a while T got into primal therapy in a big way, then computers, and ended up moving to South-East Asia. I went to Melbourne to start a rock'n'roll band.

From then on, heroin came and went. There were long periods of absence, then suddenly it would be around again. I fell in love with a face at the Kingston Hotel. The owner of the face gave me her phone number and when I called, her father answered. She was doing rehab at her parents' place after being busted with her drug-dealer boyfriend at a city hotel. The boyfriend went down but she got off with the help of a lawyer named Lazarus.

The rehab went well. She cleaned herself up and I courted her patiently, bringing her home on time at night. Her parents began to trust me and eventually we moved in together. We got married and had a child. We were good for a long time. Then one day one of us said, 'It'd be nice to score again, wouldn't it? Just one taste couldn't hurt now, could it?'

We broke up two years later because we knew each other too well. No words were needed between us for the whisper in our heads to turn to a roar. One turn of the head, one cocked eyebrow, one sly smile and we were off.

I didn't take heroin because I felt bad or because I had an unhappy childhood. I just liked it. It suited me, freed me up inside. There were long nights of funny, dreamy, storytelling sex. Heroin was a lovely secret with a lover. A big warm blanket in winter. Shooting up together was intimate, tender, sacramental.

Later on, when the pictures faded and the hard-ons too, the sex became heightened in a different way. Coming down from a two- or three-day binge, despite its other problems, had one glorious compensation – the sweet ache returning to the body, every nerve alive, the incredibly intense release in each other's arms. Forget Tantra.

Heroin wasn't good for work, though. I knew that right from the start. It cuts a singer's range, making the higher notes unreachable. And when you're trying to write, everything gets done in your head rather than on the page or on tape. Great ideas, images and schemes swell in the mind like clouds in the sky, and then, like clouds in a drought, move on without dropping rain.

So heroin became the reward for hard work. The thing to look forward to at the end of making a record, at the end of a tour, or after a period of writing. On a Sunday. Flick the switch inside and all anxieties would fall away, all problems recede, to be dealt with later. Buy half a gram and eke it out over a few days. Never more than that, never to let a habit form. To keep it as something to want, not to need; a thing of joy rather than necessity. That was the theory, anyway.

There was one kind of work heroin was made for. Housework – or any time-eating chore. Cleaning, vacuuming, doing the dishes, chopping vegetables. Paying the bills. You simply sailed through the now tedium-free day. Making compilation tapes for birthday presents or to take on the road was fun any time, but funner with the poppy in the blood, and you didn't mind taking all day to get the perfect flow.

The long set-up, the shopping and cooking for big, get-together barbecues at home – celebrations, send-offs, birthdays, Christmases – went well with a little late-morning taste. The trick was not to take too much, to get the dose just right so that people wouldn't notice anything different about you. So your voice wouldn't be too draggy, your pupils too pinned, your eyelids too heavy.

Maintaining that balance was its own satisfaction. I'm getting away with this! you said to yourself, purring along. You were warm, funny, a little more loquacious than normal, but not rambling. Alert, unanxious, in control, pouring drinks, looking after people, keeping an eye on the calamari. You were Ray Liotta in *Goodfellas* – buying the gun, crossing town watching the helicopters, giving instructions over the phone on how to make the bolognaise sauce – without the paranoia. Master of the universe.

And later in the evening, when all was convivial, merry and bright, you'd slip away briefly to the bedroom for a little top-up – careful now – to keep you going for the rest of the night, all the way through the music and laughter, the cleaning up and the fond farewells. No worries.

Oh, and maybe just one more when everyone's gone and all is quiet in the house again. To drift across the midnight line and beyond in dozy, waking dreams.

But of course you weren't getting away with it. People knew. Or suspected. 'You're looking tired,' they'd say, not quite coming out with it. 'Yes, I've been really busy,' came your reply. Or, 'I haven't been sleeping that well.' You knew that they knew but you convinced yourself they didn't. Heroin rewires your brain. It's a beautiful brainwasher that makes you believe the dumbest things.

You weren't getting away with it at all. What you thought was your witty charm caused intense annoyance, worry or fear (or all three) in those close to you. You saw friends, long-time recreational users like yourself who'd kept it under control for years, suddenly go under. The black dog was always snapping at your heels. The hangovers got longer, roughly double the period of pleasure. If you had one day on, it took two days of depression to recover. Two days took four. Too many days of dread. Weeks disappeared and lists stayed uncrossed. You felt grooves being made in your brain that you feared would turn into ruts you wouldn't be able to climb out of.

Your children knew when you were acting differently. You and your wife, soon to be divorced, were like two people on opposite shores of a wide river. She was waving but you pretended not to see. You were ashamed of yourself, ashamed of wasting money, sick of deception and alarmed at the shoddiness creeping into your work.

I got lucky. I met a woman who said, 'It's me or it.' She gave me the number of a counsellor who made me write a list. I threw out certain phone numbers, said goodbye to all that. I thought about 'it' every day for a long time. Less now.

'Coma' started life as a bass line written by Steve Hadley, who played with me for a number of years. Steve, along with Bruce Haymes (keyboards) and Peter Luscombe (drums) who were also in my band, had a trio called Les Casuals that held down an occasional residency at The Night Cat in Melbourne when we weren't touring. People came there to dance on Sundays and Les Casuals served up extended versions of mainly instrumental tunes by The Meters, War, Harry J. Allstars and other funk-reggae classics, as well as a few of their own. Now and then they would have guest vocalists, and I sang with them a couple of times.

They were talking about making a record and asked me to write with them. We set up a once-a-week jam session in a rehearsal studio and over nine months, on and off, we built up an album's worth of material. Pete or Steve or Bruce would come in with a riff, a chord progression or a drum pattern and we'd all jump on it, me playing electric rhythm guitar, until it morphed into something interesting. Sometimes I'd sing stuff over the top. We had a little cassette recorder working hard in the middle of the room. I'd take the tapes with me, play them at home or as I drove around, and sing more stuff.

Some of the grooves stayed instrumentals while some slowly turned into songs. Circle songs. Once I had the melodies fairly set, I'd go for long walks around the neighbourhood until I had the words. 'Coma' came this way.

We named ourselves Professor Ratbaggy, after a character from a children's show and in honour of some of the great scientists of dub music – King Tubby, Mad Professor, Lee Perry and co. We cut and pasted, filtered and flanged, echoed, dubbed and delayed until we had eleven tunes that hung together. Not many of the Ratbaggy songs are playable without that particular lineup. But somehow 'Coma' managed to detach itself from its original distinctive bass line – like those tropical vines that wrap themselves around a tree and feed on it 'til the trunk disappears and only the vine's long thriving tendrils remain – and morph again into some nutty klezmerish mutation with Sian Prior, the 'me or it' girl, playing the clarinet.

CRADLE OF LOVE

Well it burned like a ball of fire
When the rebel took a little child bride . . .
Rock the cradle of love
That's me mama
I robbed the devil of love
If you teaze me tonight
If you sleaze me all right
If you appeaze me tonight
And let me ease you . . .

Uh, sorry, wrong words – that's Billy Idol's 'Cradle Of Love'. Here's mine:

Baby, you look tired, baby, you look beat
Seems like you've been working eight days a week
Baby, take a break from all you're thinking of
And come into my cradle of love

Baby, let me hold you and rock your cares away
Put aside your troubles at the ending of the day
'Cause when we lie together I fit you like a glove
Come into my cradle of love

Down in the valley you can lose your name
Your sorrow and your pain
The dark, warm waters can heal you
And make you clean again

So, baby, come on over and lean your head on me
Here in my arms now is where you're meant to be
Baby, take advantage of all I've got to give
And let me be your cradle of love

Icon

I'm not much fond of talking to strangers while I'm having a piss.
Talking to my boon companions, that's fine – especially in the great
outdoors, somewhere between Broome and Port Hedland, say, getting
out of the tour van, standing under the huge starry sky and discussing
the constellations. But at a pub on a Friday night, that's a different
story. It's a matter of temperament. Or upbringing, perhaps. I was
watching one of my favourite bands, King Curly, at the Elsternwick
Hotel a while ago and went to the Men's between sets. The guy next
to me at the urinal spotted me as he was shaking himself dry and said,
'Mate, you're an icon! Let me shake your hand!'

Good grief. What an impasse for a man – I shook it and said nothing – what a comedown for a word. A word that originally meant
a small religious painting to which one prayed, and that changed
over time to mean any object of awe – Ayer's Rock, Sydney Harbour
Bridge, the Statue of Liberty. A word that eventually lost its moorings
altogether, along with its power, and began to be applied to people and
advertising. Now TV soap stars, Australian Idols and cars are icons.

There is one Australian, however, who justifies the label iconic,
embodying the idea of a fixed image of devotion. Born David
Gordon Kirkpatrick, he changed his name when he was eleven to
Slim Dusty – he was already making the painting, he had the picture
in his head – studied Jimmie Rodgers, and made his first commercial
record in 1946 at the age of nineteen. He married Joy McKean, a fine
yodeller and songwriter who penned some of his biggest hits, and
together they raised a family and travelled all over the country with a
tent show for years and years, missing nary a backblock. All in all, he
made one hundred and six albums, the last of which he was working
on when he died in 2003.

People adored Slim – his plain singing, his storytelling, his dusty
hat – especially in the bush. Fads and fashions came and went but
Slim stayed Slim for sixty years. He was huge in Aboriginal commu-
nities. The year he died, I was touring the Northern Territory with

the band. We were in Yuendumu, north-west of Alice Springs, on the footy oval. Standing in the dark by the truck, waiting to go on, I was approached by two lanky old men in faded check shirts, jeans and cowboy hats. 'Play Slim,' one of them said softly. I couldn't see their faces but understood it wasn't a request. Luckily I had a few of his songs in the swag – essential items for travelling out back.

I got to know Slim and Joy in the early 1990s. We were on the same bill a few times. It was always good to be around them, they made you feel like family. One of my most thrilling moments ever onstage was yodelling in harmony with Joy on Slim's song 'The Sunlander' at a tribute concert to him in Tamworth after his death. Yodelling makes you feel good any time but yodelling with Joy, one of the best, took me to another level. I floated off stage.

In 1991 their daughter Anne Kirkpatrick, a country singer in her own right, asked me for a song. I wrote 'Cradle Of Love' for her and she made it her own. Not long afterwards, I became aware of other Love Cradles out and about. It was like when you buy a car you think isn't so common, then drive around and see your 'unusual' car everywhere you go. There's Billy's 'Cradle Of Love', of course. And Gwen McCrae gets funky, as she does, in hers. Freda Payne, who had a big hit with 'Band Of Gold', is out there too, driving hers around, continuing her string of 'of' songs. And there's a whole fleet of others.

'Cradle Of Love' – it's such a popular title, mate, it's gotta be an icon.

DEEPER WATER

On a crowded beach in a distant time
At the height of summer, see a boy of five
At the water's edge, so nimble and free
Jumping over the ripples, looking way out to sea

Now a man comes up from amongst the throng
Takes the young boy's hand and his hand is strong
And the child feels safe, yeah, the child feels brave
As he's carried in those arms up and over the waves

Deeper water, deeper water, deeper water, calling him on

Let's move forward now, the child's seventeen
With a girl in the back seat, tugging at his jeans
And she knows what she wants, she guides with her hand
As a voice cries inside him – I'm a man, I'm a man!

Deeper water, deeper water, deeper water, calling him on

Now the man meets a woman unlike all the rest
He doesn't know it yet but he's out of his depth
And he thinks he can run, it's a matter of pride
But he keeps coming back like a cork on the tide

Well the years hurry by and the woman loves the man
Then one night in the dark she grabs hold of his hand
Says, 'There, can you feel it kicking inside!'
And the man gets a shiver right up and down his spine

Deeper water, deeper water, deeper water, calling him on

So the clock moves around and the child is a joy
But Death doesn't care just who it destroys
Now the woman gets sick, thins down to the bone
She says, 'Where I'm going next, I'm going alone'

On a distant beach lonely and wild
At a later time see a man and a child
And the man takes the child up into his arms
Takes her over the breakers
To where the water is calm

Deeper water, deeper water, deeper water, calling them on

Begat

Into the unknown, out of Ireland in 1852, came Jeremiah and Mary Kelly, landless, leaving behind a disapproving father, the famine years in County Clare, the hungry homeless, and the evangelists who doled soup only to Protestants.

On the good ship *Phoebe Dunbar* they sailed, with their four begotten, two girls and two boys, the youngest, James, still a babe in arms. At Port Adelaide they docked and found a house in town where Jeremiah dealt in cattle until his death. His wife and her fatherless brood headed north then, to the 'new' country being opened up as farmland around 'new' Clare, the older boy strong and ready for work, and relations in the area to lend a hand.

And James, the youngest, down the years grew strong and fierce of mind and moved further north to take up land of his own. And with him into the unknown went his bride, Kate Erwin, a big fine girl from County Wicklow. Eight children they begat, the seven survivors educated all. Frank, the eldest son, worked on the farm, studied then practised law, travelled and met by chance his future bride in an ice-cream shop in a tropical town. From Ballarat she'd come, Sheila Mann, a nurse, and in time she took Frank's hand.

Two thousand miles back from Darwin to Adelaide they journeyed, as the twentieth century got going and geared up for its first terrible war. Six children Frank and Sheila begat, the eldest of whom became a priest. The second-eldest, John, who was reading at the age of three, completed school when he was fourteen. Finishing his law degree too young to practise, he bided his time a full twelve months, studying Ancient Greek and Latin, before joining his father's firm.

From the second terrible war he was spared by a shadow on his lung, finding work with the War Office in the city of Melbourne. There he met Josephine Filippini, daughter of an Italian opera singer and an Irish-Australian musician – a nineteen-year-old dark, curly-haired beauty with an unprecedented taste for garlic. Spaghetti bolognaise was the first meal she cooked him, an exotic dish in Australia in 1942. She broke off with a colonel to marry him and across the border with him she went into the unknown, where she stirred up staid Adelaide with her bare legs, expressive love, and penchant for cooking squid.

Nine children Josephine and John begat, the third of whom died before a year was done and the eldest of whom would become a nun. In love they were bathed and for their talents praised, their faults corrected and expectations raised. And a song she had for each and every one.

And he read to them, as they sat on his knee, French nursery rhymes and tales from *The Odyssey*, Greek letters on the page, English words from his mouth, letting the children drink the froth from the top of his pewter mug of Coopers Ale, brewed yea verily but a mile down the road.

And on Sundays in summer, after mass, came they all to the Norwood pool, young limbs twitching, exploding out of the station wagon, running to the turnstile, hungry for the blue water and thirsty for the special-treat taste of Woodroofe's lemonade.

And straightaway to the deep end went the older ones, accomplished swimmers all, well taught by their father, to do bombs off the diving board, to swim and splash and dunk each other at will. While down in the shallow end the younger ones went through their strokes under his eye, his hand beneath their tummies, widthways across the pool, gaining skill slowly, Sunday after Sunday. All through the long summer they laboured and struggled, and when at rest turned their longing gaze from time to time towards the deep end and the deeper water, mad for it, the sweet, dangerous, dazzling deeper water, the ever-calling unknown.

DESDEMONA

Once I had a life so rare
Beauty lived inside the lair
Desdemona straight and true
Desdemona gold and blue
Well, I lost my Desdemona
With my own hands I destroyed her
Yes, I lost my Desdemona
I fell for lies, I fell for lies

Poison in my ear at night
Took away my appetite
I couldn't hold on to the pain
Something broke inside my brain
Well, I lost my Desdemona
With my own hands I destroyed her
Yes, I lost my Desdemona
I fell for lies, I fell for lies

Never has a man been born
Who can take a woman's scorn
Who's tasted a more bitter wine
Than the brewing of his mind
Yes, I lost my Desdemona
With my own hands I destroyed her
Yes, I lost my Desdemona
I fell for lies, I fell for lies

The Greeks, The Italians, The Scots, The Englishman, The Irishman, The Australian And The Moor

> O, beware, my lord, of jealousy!
> It is the green-eyed monster which doth mock
> The meat it feeds on.
>
> Cassio in *Othello*

Take a traditional Scottish tune, say 'The Wild Mountain Thyme', and change a few notes around. Put some lyrics to it based on the story of a play set in Italy, written by an Englishman, in the course of which a soldier named Iago, unhappy about being overlooked for the position of lieutenant, lays a trap for his general, Othello the Moor. Getting up to hanky-panky with a hanky, Iago convinces him that his beautiful virtuous wife Desdemona has been unfaithful. Othello takes the bait and murders her in a rage. In despair upon realising his mistake, he murders himself and lies down on top of his dead wife.

A lot more happens during the play, including the first entry into the English language of the phrase 'It's neither here nor there'. But that's the guts of it, fulfilling W. B. Yeats's dictum that the only two things any intelligent writer should be concerned with are sex and death.

Call the song 'Desdemona', which is a Greek name meaning 'ill-starred' (from *dys* meaning 'bad', and *daimon* meaning 'divine power' or 'fate' – the great unknown). Sing it in your usual key – G. Sing it in your usual voice – Australian. Sex and death know no borders.

DIFFICULT WOMAN

A difficult woman
Sometimes hurts her friends when she don't mean to
A difficult woman
Makes it hard for the ones she loves
It's easy to do
She's had to be tough all of her life
So she's built herself a wall
She doesn't know how to trust herself
So it's hard for her to trust at all
A difficult woman needs a special kind of friend

A difficult woman
Swings between shame and pride
A difficult woman
Has strong, strong stuff deep inside
And getting to her is no easy affair
It's like working in a mine
You'd better prepare to pay the price
If it's treasure you want to find
A difficult woman needs a special kind of friend

And living with her is better and worse
Than living with anyone else
She can be cruel or so kind
Oh you go from heaven to hell
If she got what she wanted
If she got what she needed
She wouldn't be hard to understand
A difficult woman needs a special kind of man

Twenty Long, Long Seconds

The seven deadly sins – wrath, avarice, sloth, pride, envy, gluttony and lust – were the subject of a TV series devised in 1992. I was invited to participate in the soundtrack with several other singers – Vika Bull, Deborah Conway and Renée Geyer. We sang various songs related to the sins, some solo, some together. The musical director, Martin Armiger, was short one song and asked if I had anything that might be relevant. I drew a long bow, gave him an old song I hadn't recorded called 'Foggy Highway' – a lost-in-the-wilderness song – and suggested Renée sing it.

I didn't know Renée well at that stage but I admired her deep soul singing, ferocious and vulnerable. She'd grown up in Sydney, the daughter of Holocaust survivors who ran a kosher catering business. Her father loved Mahler, but as a young woman Renée fell hard for Aretha Franklin, Donny Hathaway and James Brown, which, she told me later, Dad wasn't too thrilled about. Blonde, leggy and sassy, she put together a seriously funky band in the early seventies and started making records. She has never recorded an Aretha song because, as she says herself, 'You just don't go there, you know. Aretha – she's untouchable.' But she did tackle 'It's A Man's World', by the Godfather of Soul, an undertaking only the brave or foolish would attempt, and reinvented the song. It was her second single and has been part of her show ever since.

I wasn't in the studio when she recorded 'Foggy Highway'. Martin put it in a low key and with the band lay down a late-night-lonesome music track. According to him, she wasn't convinced the song was right for her, but after turning the lights down he coaxed her to the mic. When I heard the finished version a few days later the hairs rose up on the back of my neck.

Not long after those sessions Renée returned to Los Angeles, where she was living, and we promised to keep in touch. She started digging around in some of my old songs and picked a couple more to record. Some time after that I moved to LA for a while myself and looked her up. It was around the time Kate Ceberano's version of 'The Cake And The Candle' came out.

Renée and Kate kept an eye and an ear on each other. One day I got a phone call. That husky voice was on the line: 'How come Kate gets a brand-new song, fresh from the factory, written just for her, and I don't?'

When you get a question like that from Renée you know it's not a question. So I said I'd have a think about it and get back to her. For the next few days I sweated and slaved and hammered and banged and sawed and sang. Finally I rang her up and said, 'I may have something. Can I come over and play it for you?'

'Tell me the words over the phone,' she said.

'Well, I'd rather play it for you. It'll sound better.'

'No, I don't want to wait, just tell me the words now.'

So I spoke all the words to 'Difficult Woman' down the phone line. When I finished there was a silence of maybe twenty seconds. It's hard to remember how long it was exactly, because time seemed to stretch. If it was twenty seconds it may be the longest twenty seconds of my life. Finally she said in a snippy voice, 'Okay then, bring it over, I'll give it a try.'

I took my guitar with me to her rented house in the Hollywood Hills. It was a fine hot day. The pool man was cleaning the pool, bare-topped, wearing a pair of zigzag board shorts. I sat in front of her and played the song, looking down, heart in my mouth, zigzags at the edges of my eyes like a flashing warning.

It all turned out well in the end. I survived. We fiddled with the key, the pool man went home, she took hold of the song and she's still singing it. Now it's her badge of honour. Years later, after biding her time, she took 'The Cake' from Kate too.

DON'T EXPLAIN

Don't explain
It's really not your style
I've had some fun
You really made me smile
Don't look so serious
It doesn't suit your face
Don't explain, don't explain

You sure know
How to use your hands
But you don't have a great attention span
Don't apologise
Or drop your eyes
Don't explain, don't explain

I've seen them come, I've seen them go
Boys like you
Their gangster hearts, their dreamy loads
Boys like you

So take your things
I won't count the days
Sure, you can call on me
If you pass this way
But if one night you're lonely
And I have other company
Don't complain, don't complain

Parallel Universe

Arthur Herzog Jr, a New York jazz musician in the 1930s and '40s, didn't write that many songs but he did write 'God Bless The Child' and 'Don't Explain' with Billie Holiday. That's a pretty good strike rate and something to brag about to the grandkids.

Arthur and Billie's protagonist in 'Don't Explain' seems powerless, stuck with a man who treats her badly. The pleasure outweighs the pain, imply the lyrics, but when Billie sings the words she wrote, the listener can't help but wonder how long it will be before something has to break.

> I cry to hear folks chatter
> And I know you cheat
> Right or wrong, don't matter
> When you're with me, sweet
>
> Hush now, don't explain
> You're my joy and pain
> My life's yours, love
> Don't explain

Lots of people have had a crack at Billie and Arthur's song, most notably Etta James and Nina Simone. Etta breaks out of the claustrophobia of the original with a shuffle beat, thick horns and a playful attitude, letting her piano player stretch out with a longish solo. Nina goes the other way, taking Billie's fragility and ramping it up even further with her skittering vibrato, as a flute, piano and brushes tiptoe behind her.

Billie did some hard living and went with some mean men. She sang like a bruised angel. When she died in hospital in 1959 from drug- and alcohol-related problems, she had seventy cents in the bank. In a parallel universe I dream of sometimes, Billie Holiday finds a good man, gets off the grog and the gear, regains her health and, like Asha

Bhosle, continues to make great records well into her seventies. In this universe, I'm born a little earlier and go to see her play one night in New York City. I'm carrying a cassette of a kiss-off song I've written in which a wry woman farewells a younger man. After the show I slip the cassette to the doorman at the stage door, and sometime the next year, sitting in a café in Melbourne, I hear her singing it through a little distorted radio.

DON'T HARM THE MESSENGER

One day you might hear someone knocking loudly at your door
And you know it must be bad news – absolutely sure
You must realise before you strike the very first blow
He's the one who only tells you what you already know

Lay not a finger on him
Beat not, oh bruise not, his skinny skin skin
No don't ever harm the messenger

Understand he came a long way on a lonely road
Multiplying were his trials, heavy was his load
Understand his heart was breaking, never once did he sleep
And no hollow log kept him warm, no counsel did he keep

Give him food, give him a bed
Touch not one single hair on his head
Don't ever harm the messenger

The Pretendies

The talking interlude has a long history in popular song. And takes
a fair bit of nerve to pull off. The singer has to step out from behind
melody's curtain and act. Elvis's famous talking bit in 'Are You Lonesome Tonight?' stretches Shakespeare's metaphor of the actor on the
stage of life to breaking point. In later years, even Elvis lost his nerve
reciting those bombastic lines. You can hear him on a live recording
falter halfway through, giggle, then lapse into gibberish in a classic
example of the pretendies, the scourge of all performing artists.

The pretendies, a term first coined and defined, to my knowledge,
by songwriter Spencer P. Jones in the back of the band Tarago after

a gig in Geelong, can strike any time. One minute you're putting a song over to the crowd, totally inside what you're doing, everything meshing, then suddenly you're adrift, floating above yourself and wondering what on earth you're doing there. You feel like a complete fake as the thought runs through your head, Whatever made me think I could get away with this?

Anything can set the pretendies off. Maybe a fluffed line or chord which jars you out of the moment. A pretty woman in the audience, or someone in the front row who reminds you of somebody you went to school with. You may be just a fraction overtired. Or overconfident, having done, perhaps, a great show the night before. Without warning you've lost control of what you're doing – like the child who's riding a bike with no hands and going along fine until he calls out, 'Look at me, Mum!'

The pretendies can shudder through a band. You can almost see them ripple across the stage. The guitarist and the drummer sense that the singer's got the existential wobbles and everyone keeps their head down, not daring to look each other in the eye as they try to right the listing ship.

Elvis, though, on that night, once he's taken his turn, doesn't bother trying to get back. He's broken right through the veil of illusion, exposed the working of the hitherto unseen gears and is taking the audience with him. It's painful and thrilling to listen to. He sounds pilled off his head. Unmoored.

Circumventing the perils of the talking bit is mainly a matter of wheel alignment – having the axles of sincerity and slyness in perfect counterbalance. Too much overblown feeling on the one side or too much smirk on the other, and you're swerving all over the road. Lou Reed steers this course beautifully with The Velvet Underground in 'I Found A Reason'. You have to keep both hands firmly on the wheel to get away with a line like 'I've walked down life's lonely highways hand in hand with myself.'

The cadences of southern American speech are particularly suited to spoken interludes. Old-time preaching straddles song and prose and

goes naturally with country music's solid pillars of sentiment, moral-
ity and religion. The Louvin Brothers serve it up straight in 'Satan Is
Real', with not a whiff of the pretendies anywhere. Even if there were, it
would be overpowered by the smell of sulphur. Likewise, Red Simpson
in 'Roll, Truck, Roll', his tale of a trucker missing home, says:

> Mama said little Danny's not doing too good in school
> Said he keeps talkin' about his daddy that he hardly knows
> Teacher said that he just sits at his desk and draws the pictures
> of trucks
> I guess I know what that means and what it shows

Delivered without a shred of irony. And rightly so.

Rose Maddox and Buck Owens get a little more playful, talking
back and forth to each other, in 'Mental Cruelty', despite the serious-
ness of the subject matter. For some reason, Rose speaks in rhyme but
Buck doesn't, which has a slightly odd effect on the listener. (On this
listener, anyway.)

Many years later, Mick Jagger in 'Far Away Eyes' imitated Rose's
vowel-bending drawl with his tongue firmly in his cheek. His reference to driving through Bakersfield, Buck's home town, listening to
the gospel music station, is a sly wink to the aficionados.

The talking bit can turn a song into a nightmare – as in 'The
Leader Of The Pack' – or a dream. In 'Green, Green Grass Of Home'
Tom Jones wakes up in a prison cell the morning of his execution
to realise he'll never ever touch again the gold hair of Mary or kiss
her cherry lips. The padre and the hangman are coming for him at
daybreak. With the bleak spoken reality breaking in on his pastoral
vision, this is the talking bit at its finest and most dramatic.

It's not for everyone, though. Some people run a mile. One has to
be a believer, or at least be prepared to suspend belief, to let the tears
flow or the goose bumps pimple. Some are appalled. Others fancify
their sneer by calling the talking bit wonderful 'kitsch' – a word that
makes my skin crawl.

The beauty and fascination of being human lies in our ability to experience opposing emotions at the one time, to be cynical and moved in concert (crying during schmaltzy, manipulative movies) or to feel blessed and ridiculous simultaneously (sex) and to be able to float above them both, observing, testing out the one then the other, dancing the devilish dance of the pretendies.

He Was A Friend Of Mine

The Go-Betweens were a band blessed with two distinct and complementary songwriters, Grant McLennan and Robert Forster. They had big artistic aims, which, one wiseguy said, included marrying The Monkees with The Velvet Underground.

Grant, allegedly, was the more melodic one – a sweet, romantic, heart-on-the-sleeve writer, at times overreaching. Robert, angular, elliptical and sly, was the perfect counterbalance. Their differences, however, weren't that clear-cut. They became deep friends at a tender age and naturally much flowed between them and mingled – sweetness and slyness, straight-talking and crypticisms, innocence and world ennui.

They made six albums together in the eighties, broke up in 1989 to make solo records, and reformed in 2000. They were more popular in the UK and Europe than at home.

In 1986 I had big artistic plans of my own. I was nearing the end of making *Gossip* at Trafalgar Studios in Sydney. We'd recorded twenty-four songs, one of which, 'Don't Harm The Messenger', had only two verses. The music was down on tape (big thick two-inch tape) in the expectation of a third verse to come. But it never did. I sang my two verses and choruses and mumbled/spoke the second verse again where the third verse was supposed to be, and hoped I would be able to think of something else later.

The Go-Betweens were in town at that time, back from London, doing shows. I was playing their albums *Before Hollywood* and *Liberty*

Belle and the Black Diamond Express a lot at home. One night, when we'd finished recording for the day, I went to see them play at The Graphic Arts Club, where Grant and I got talking afterwards. I didn't know him that well then but sensed he was someone not lacking in self-confidence, someone who could step up to the plate for a talking bit without being overcome by the pretendies.

'I'm a bit stuck with a song,' I told him. 'I wonder if you want to do a speaking part on it, like Robert does on "Cattle And Cane". It's not a big change-up; there's no sudden switch to drama or waking from a dream. No shift in point of view. The truth is, I just don't have a third verse. It needs a little elevation in mood.'

So Grant came down to the studio a couple of days later, full of praise and smiling bonhomie, complimented the band and the engineer on the 'gorgeous track', saying it was 'a joy to speak over', and nailed it in a couple of takes.

We became friends after that and saw a fair bit of each other when The Go-Betweens broke up and he moved to Sydney. We liked to kick the footy together in Rushcutters Bay Park, joined sometimes by Rob Younger from Radio Birdman. We'd play our new songs to each other cagily. Tried writing together once but it didn't work. Once he'd written a line, it wasn't going to change. And I can be stubborn myself. On Oxford Street in summer we'd eat large pizzas, stay up all night with guitars and beer, quote poetry and watch the sun rise over Bondi. He knew more Bob Dylan songs than I did, and that's saying something.

I returned the favour a couple of years later by playing harmonica on his first solo record. He was calling himself G.W. by then. Every record G.W. made was 'the best thing I've ever done'.

Grant died suddenly and shockingly of a heart attack in 2006. He was forty-eight. I carry his voice in my head every time I speak the words to the third verse (same as the second verse) of 'Don't Harm The Messenger', just as I feel the sound of Steve Connolly's Stratocaster chiming in my chest whenever I sing 'Before Too Long'. Those songs haven't fallen away from me. They remain companions on my travels, and my old companions live in them, talking to me from time to time.

DON'T STAND SO CLOSE TO THE WINDOW

Oh my love, how we fell
What we've done now we never can tell
Bottle of wine, then another
Suddenly we fell into each other

Don't stand so close to the window
Somebody out there might see

Then the word on the wire
Would be just like a raging bushfire
Kiss me quick, kiss me warm
Put your dress on and hurry back home

Don't stand so close to the window
Somebody out there might see
And you're not supposed to be here with me

There's a way, there's a track
One false move and there's no turning back
Turn the page, close the book
Walk out the door now with never a look

And don't stand so close to the window
Somebody out there might see
And you're not supposed to be here with me
The walls have ears and the darkness has eyes, don't you see?

Surf And High Singing

Michael Barclay, son of a pilot and nephew to The Hawking Brothers, a successful Australian country band of the sixties and seventies, remembers listening to his parents' record collection, which included The Beatles, The Seekers, and Simon and Garfunkel, and always singing along to the high harmony. He started surfing and playing drums in secondary school. A few years later, he was playing with a band called The Japanese Comix and fraternising in the Melbourne music scene of the early eighties. The Comix, The Leftovers, The Cuban Heels, Little Murders and various lineups of mine all knew and played with each other in inner-city hotels and beer-sodden university refectories.

After moving to Sydney in 1984, Michael and I sang and played together for seven years. His surfboard more often than not came with the band on tour, which made it interesting at times packing the van. Muttered curses followed that board all the way from Cairns to Broome, as thousands of miles of ocean went by without it getting wet.

But one shining day at Seal Rocks on the central New South Wales coast – a day that will never come again – wave after perfect wave peeled onto the beach, and as Michael rode the swell by the rocks, Jon Schofield and I ducked our shoulders into the shore-breakers to be blissfully propelled again and again into the shallows. All afternoon on a rare day off we surfed until exhaustion and a setting sun called us in.

And so the board stayed – wedged into the truck, jammed into the van, strapped to the roof of the rental car – in readiness for the next one-in-a-million brilliant afternoon.

Michael was (and is) a huge fan of The Pogues, The Smiths, Dragon, and REM and could sing any number of their songs at our after-show singalongs – 'A Pair Of Brown Eyes', 'There Is A Light That Never Goes Out', 'April Sun In Cuba', 'Rockville' . . . We kicked a lot of George Jones songs around too. And The Louvin Brothers.

Michael always took the high harmony, in the back rooms, onstage and in the studio.

When we recorded 'Don't Stand So Close To The Window' in 1986 we consciously aped The Louvin's singing style: twinned vocals all the way through the song. Listening back to that original recording, I can't for the life of me understand why we didn't use a real violin instead of a synthesised string sound on a DX7 keyboard. But few bands escaped the eighties unscathed.

I also wonder why I couldn't do better than use the word 'fell' twice in the same verse. It niggled me for a long time but never got changed. Constant usage – singing it repeatedly – smoothed away my concern, like water running over stone. After a while the words simply fitted and felt okay. Art is abandoned, not finished.

Between 1986 and 1991, as The Coloured Girls and then The Messengers, we recorded and released four albums and toured Australia consistently, with occasional trips overseas. Since most Australians live by the sea, we hugged the coast, though every now and then we headed for the interior, often the Northern Territory. The surfboard stayed behind then. We went to a lot of places not many other bands got to – Alice Springs, Tennant Creek, Katherine and, over in the north-west, the Pilbara and the Kimberley.

We played in jails, on dusty football ovals, on the backs of semi-trailers, in circus tents and boxing rings, at speedways, racetracks, in civic halls, town halls, church halls, mechanics institutes, old theatres (all wood and creaky leather chairs), grand theatres (marble and velvet), new theatres (panel and beige), on campuses, at street fairs, in leaky basements, small dingy pubs, huge bright beer barns, chromed night-clubs, garish TV studios (hung-over and too early in the morning), and jammed around one mic in little radio-station control rooms.

And to get there, all the time driving, flying, driving, flying, but mostly driving. The one constant in the van, from first drive 'til last, The Beach Boys – our touchstone, the one band we could all agree on. Singing along to Brian Wilson's aching high falsetto on 'Don't Worry, Baby' – 'the greatest song of all time', we agreed, with 'the greatest solo of all time', because 'nothing happens in it!' And later on, trying to figure out that weird chord at the end of the chorus but never quite getting it right. Not even Steve.

Two decades later, at the Domain in Sydney on a moist summer night, I stood by the side of the stage in the dark next to the monitor desk with my spine tingling as Brian, seated at an electric piano and reading from an autocue, in front of what used to be a Beach Boys covers band, sang and played his hits. He noodled on the keys and talked out of the side of his mouth between songs. And when he couldn't reach the high parts, the big guitarist to his left stepped up and sang like a bird.

The band, though heretical – one of them was a woman – were impeccable, the harmonies flawless. The man who wrote 'God Only Knows' was singing it right before my eyes. I thought to myself, I could die happy now.

And that man Brian – avatar of sun and bliss and girls and surf, who never rode a wave in his life, and probably never will – why, he'll die only when the world dies.

DON'T START ME TALKING

Don't start me talking or I'll tell everything I know
Don't start me talking, I'll spill the beans for sure
Right before your eyes
I'll blow it all open wide
Don't start me talking

Don't start me talking 'cause once I get the itch
Don't start me talking, I just have to scratch
First a little slow
Then I start to flow
Don't start me talking

Cheers, all you, cheers
Help me if I fall
Cheers, all you, cheers
God bless you all

Don't start me talking or I'll have it all my way
Don't start me talking 'cause night will turn to day
Stars will run and hide
Strong men weep a tide
So don't start me talking

Cheers, all you, cheers
Help me find a wall
Cheers, all of you, cheers
God bless you all

Forget Not Hal

Dante, Dickens, Tolstoy and Morrissey knew how to begin. In the middle of the journey of my life I found myself in a dark wood. It was the best of times, it was the worst of times. All happy families are alike, all unhappy families are unhappy in their own way. Sweetness, sweetness I was only joking when I said I'd like to smash every tooth in your head. Morrissey has a real knack – nearly every first line of The Smiths' songs is a killer.

Hal David, who wrote the lyrics to 'Walk On By', 'The Man Who Shot Liberty Valance', '24 Hours From Tulsa' – little movies all – but who curiously seems to get less credit than his musical collaborator Burt Bacharach, knew how to begin too. He often cuts straight to the chase, with the song title included in the first line. 'The look of love is in your eyes.' 'Trains and boats and planes are passing by.' 'I just don't know what to do with myself.' 'What's it all about, Alfie?' When Aretha Franklin sings 'The moment I wake up, before I put on my make-up, I say a little prayer for you' the words sound so tender, so womanly, it's hard to believe a man wrote them.

It's worth sweating on, a good opening line. It can really set you on your way. You've been scratching around with a couple of chords and half a tune and *bang!* – there it is. I love the start of 'What's My Scene?' by The Hoodoo Gurus. Dave Faulkner sings, 'And another thing, I've been wondering lately,' busting in on the listener as if the conversation's already been going a while. You can't help but lean forward on your seat to catch up with what you've missed and what will happen next.

Other songs do something similar. 'I got some bad news this morning, which in turn made my day,' sing Gnarls Barkley in 'Who's Gonna Save My Soul?' 'Some velvet morning when I'm straight, I'm gonna open up your gate,' drawls Lee Hazlewood to Nancy Sinatra in 'Some Velvet Morning', and in both songs we're plunged immediately into a puzzle. Where are we? Where are we being taken?

Sometimes, rather than being a mysterious portal, the first line encapsulates the whole song. Bill Withers sings, 'A man we passed just tried to stare me down, and when I looked at you, you looked at the ground,' at the start of 'Who Is He And What Is He To You' and straightaway the whole story lies unspooled before you, with no revelations to come. He doesn't need to sing another word, but he does of course. The slinky, insistent musical backing of the song demands full honour. Listen to the guitar Bill's playing as he sings. It's truly funky, like smelly cheese – so out of tune and so right, because Billy and his girl are out of tune with each other too.

Once in a while, writing a song, someone else's opening line pops into your head and you go with it. You end up writing your whole song around it and by then you can't take it away. It's the bottom brick – remove it and the whole building comes down. Elvis Costello nicked part of Sonny Boy Williamson's great opening line 'Don't start me talking or I'll tell everything I know' for the start of his song 'Oliver's Army'. It's a good steal. And as Homer well knew, a good steal is worth stealing again.

Don't Start Me Quoting Great Opening Lines To Songs

'The drums rolled off in my forehead, the guns went off in my chest'
'Well, they blew up the chicken man in Philly last night'
'My story is much too sad to be told'
'Watching as some old friends do a line, holding back the want to in my own addicted mind'
'Goddamn you half Japanese girls do it to me every time'
'You've painted up your lips and rolled and curled your tinted hair'
'Jesus died for somebody's sins but not mine'
'Just a little lovin' early in the morning beats a cup of coffee for starting up the day'
'I saw a werewolf with a Chinese menu in his hand, walking through

the streets of Soho in the rain'

'I fell asleep on a tram, Harry Potter in hand, woke up drooling in
the south of Vietnam'

'God said to Abraham, "Kill me a son"'

'The Mississippi Delta was shining like a National guitar'

'Please allow me to introduce myself, I'm a man of wealth and taste'

'It was said of the sheriff to Calhoun Parish not to ever touch his
daughter Emily'

'Hey, Charlie, I'm pregnant and living on 9th Street'

'When I first came to town they called me The Roving Jewel'

'Early this morning – hooo – when you knocked upon my door,
I said: Hello Satan, I believe it's time to go'

'I found her on a night of fire and noise'

'Just before our love got lost, you said I am as constant as a
northern star'

'Well my friends have gone and my hair is grey, I ache in the places
I used to play'

'You walked into the party like you were walking onto a yacht'

'I've been in and out of trouble, mainly in'

'Well, I dreamed I saw the knights in armour coming, saying
something about a queen'

'I walk 47 miles of barbed wire, I use a cobra-snake for a necktie'

'A-wop-bop-a-lu-bop-a-lop-bam-boom'

Match the titles and artists below to the above lines:

'Wishing All These Old Things Were New' – Merle Haggard

'El Scorcho' – Weezer

'Me And The Devil Blues' – Robert Johnson

'Tower Of Song' – Leonard Cohen

'After The Gold Rush' – Neil Young

'Gloria' – Patti Smith

'Who Do You Love' – Bo Diddley

'Just A Little Lovin' – Dusty Springfield

'Werewolves Of London' – Warren Zevon

'Dan Kelly's Dream' – Dan Kelly
'You're So Vain' – Carly Simon
'Highway 61 Revisited' – Bob Dylan
'Graceland' – Paul Simon
'Sympathy For The Devil' – The Rolling Stones
'High Sheriff Of Calhoun Parish' – Tony Joe White
'Wide Open Road' – The Triffids
'Tutti Frutti' – Little Richard
'Do You Love Me?' – Nick Cave
'Christmas Card From A Hooker In Minneapolis' – Tom Waits
'Ruby, Don't Take Your Love To Town' – Kenny Rogers
'Katie Cruel' – Karen Dalton
'Atlantic City' – Bruce Springsteen
'A Case Of You' – Joni Mitchell
'I've Got You Under My Skin' – Cole Porter
'Redheads, Gold Cards & Long Black Limousines' – Tex, Don and
    Charlie

(Answers at back of book)

DOWN TO MY SOUL

We light the dark and lie us down to pray
All night long we keep the dogs at bay
If I had my time over again
You know that I wouldn't change a thing
You touch me down to my soul
Down to my soul

You wake me up, speaking dreams at dawn
I reach and touch the fine lines time has drawn
For all the world I wouldn't trade my place
Your mixed up tears falling on my face
You touch me down to my soul
Down to my soul

No other kiss ever felt like this – such tenderness
Oh, give me one more kiss 'cause every time we kiss
All heaven breaks loose!
You touch me down to my soul
Down to my soul

London Blues

12 November 2001
Dear S,

London was beautiful yesterday. The sky was like a painting, perfectly still, scudded clouds against pale blue, and I walked a long time, pounding out the post-24-hours-on-a-plane blues. Passed by the Royal Academy and saw they had an exhibition called Rembrandt's Women so I went in. It was the perfect antidote. I walked out afterwards in an exalted state – a kind of alchemised melancholy – which

I stayed in all day and all through the gig last night, and which lent a back note to my singing. He paints age and beauty, health and decay, sagging bellies, cellulite thighs, blotches on the skin next to bejewelled fabrics and threaded gold, the dark thread of hair trailing down from the navel to the mound of Venus; a woman peering out of a canopied bed, pulling back the curtain with her large clumpy hand, looking out into the light across three hundred and fifty years to us with a tender, steady gaze that says, We are one. There was a painting of his mistress later in her life when she was beginning to get ill that ripped my heart. I wanted to put my arm around you and stand in front of it together. Instead, in my weird jetlagged state, I just stood there and wept – for her, for him, for you, for us all. I miss you like sleep. P

DUMB THINGS

Welcome, strangers, to the show
I'm the one who should be lying low
Saw the knives out, turned my back
Heard the train coming, stayed out on the track
In the middle, in the middle, in the middle of a dream
I lost my shirt, I pawned my rings
I've done all the dumb things

Caught the fever, heard that old song
Thought I loved her, thought I could do no wrong
Started howling, made no sense
Thought all of my good friends would rush to my defence
In the middle, in the middle, in the middle of a dream
I lost my shirt, I pawned my rings
I've done all the dumb things

And I get all your good advice
Never stops me from going through these things twice
I see the knives out, I turn my back
I hear the train coming, I stay right on that track
In the middle, in the middle, in the middle of a dream
I lost my shirt, I pawned my rings
I've done all the dumb things

Yeah, I melted wax to fix my wings
I've done all the dumb things
I threw my hat into the ring
I've done all the dumb things
I thought that I just had to sing
I've done all the dumb things

The Thing Is . . .

I've been told I have a thing about 'thing' songs. 'Heavy Thing', 'Hidden Things', 'From Little Things Big Things Grow' (a double 'thing' song), 'I Don't Know Anything Anymore', 'I Don't Remember A Thing' and 'You Broke A Beautiful Thing' are some still in the kit.

Maybe it's from reading and rereading *Where the Wild Things Are* to Declan when I was in my twenties and first writing songs. Or maybe it's because 'things' is a great catch-all word and can mean a whole lot of different things. 'Things' also rhymes with good singing words like 'rings', 'wings' and 'sings'.

Raymond Carver, the American short-story writer, likes the word 'thing' in his titles too: 'A Small Good Thing', 'I Could See the Smallest Things', 'The Third Thing That Killed My Father Off', 'One More Thing', 'Little Things', 'Nobody Said Anything'. And for a while there, I had a thing about Carver.

Yahoo Serious, Sydney filmmaker (real name Greg), had a thing about Albert Einstein, and in 1986 was shooting a fantastical version of his life in which Albert is born in Tasmania, ponders the falling of apples (after Newton) and in the process of proving relativity accidentally invents rock'n'roll. The movie was called *Young Einstein* and in it my wife Kaarin played a prostitute. The other prostitute was played by Yahoo's wife Lulu Pinkus (real name).

Yahoo didn't come up through the film-industry ranks in the usual way. As far as I could tell, he had a kind of outsider status, which was a point of pride for him. He wrote, directed and starred in his film, seeing himself in the tradition of Charlie Chaplin and Buster Keaton. He put some people's noses out of joint but had a way of getting things done. Through Lulu, Yahoo heard that I was working on some new songs and asked if I had anything suitable.

At the time, I was in rehearsals with the band prior to recording *Under the Sun*. We'd gone into the studio and put down fourteen songs in a day, to give the record company an idea of what we were up to, and to hear for ourselves what the songs sounded like. Recorded, they always sound different to how they do live. Onstage and in a rehearsal room everything's clanging around, blurring the sound. And hearing songs from inside your head as you sing them is always more forgiving than hearing them back on tape. You can be playing a song live for a year before you notice, for example, that a bass note and guitar part are at odds with each other in a particular section. It can be a rude shock sometimes, but the tape doesn't lie.

I passed on the fourteen-song demo to Yahoo, saying, 'See if there's anything there that fits. They're just roughs. We're going back into the studio next month to record them properly.' I'd been listening to the demos and noticed that some of the tempos weren't quite right. This wasn't unusual with a group of new songs recorded in one hit, no big deal, and I'd made notes to adjust a few of them. 'Dumb Things', for one, was too fast. I'd wanted it to have more of a grind but it sounded a little ahead of itself.

Yahoo rang a week or two later, very excited. 'That song "Dumb Things" is great,' he said. 'It's working beautifully with the pictures.'

'That's good,' I said. 'Glad you like it. We're going to slow it down a little when we record it.'

'No, you don't understand. I've already cut the pictures to it. It's the scene where they're having dinner in the asylum. All the cuts are on the beat. Don't change a thing! Come and have a look.'

I went over to his little editing suite, where he showed me the bit of the movie with the music. It was rocking. So two weeks later, the band and I found ourselves in the studio playing along to our demo pumping through the speakers, in, I imagined, some kind of bizarre world-first. We even mimicked, after some practice, the way the original track sped up and slowed down.

And why didn't we just use the demo? Because the earlier recording had been done in a smaller room with fewer mics. Things were spilling into each other, vocals into the drum mics, and vice versa. And the lead vocal, which I was still getting a handle on, was pretty ratty.

The film had a decent music budget and a musical supervisor who took us into a 'proper' studio with a Very Important Engineer. This was the eighties, when it sometimes seemed 'the sound' was considered more important than the performance. Spill was anathema. Total separation was the holy grail, so that the sound of each instrument could be sculpted and worked on without interference from the others. Certain engineers were little martinets who wouldn't deign to work on an already existing track recorded by another engineer with different mic techniques. 'Now, you, drummer, hit this snare for four hours while I dial up my tremendous drum sound. And you, band, just hang around all day until the life's been sucked out of you.'

One good thing about redoing our original version of 'Dumb Things' was that we didn't have to play to a click track, another scourge of the eighties' clinical approach to recording. Playing along to our imperfect selves was nutty – nutty enough to enjoy and a satisfying technical challenge. And the track turned out well, despite the tremendously gated, filtered and mega-reverbed snare drum. It kept its edge.

Yahoo was very happy with the recording, so happy that he decided to move it to another scene and recut. #@$*! That's the thing about fiddling filmmakers. They say one thing about the music and then they say another. They fiddle until the men in white coats come to take them away, until the gentle tap on the shoulder in the dark room and the kind voice that says, 'Enough now. It's finished. Time to let it go.'

The folks who made the American movie *Look Who's Talking* a couple of years later liked the song too. They used it for the scene where John Travolta takes Kirstie Alley, huffing and puffing in advanced labour, to hospital. It's fast. It's urgent. It's loud. I wanted to jump up in the cinema when I first saw it and yell out, 'That's my song!'

The cheque wasn't bad either.

So here's the thing – there's no such thing as a demo.

EMOTIONAL

The days are getting colder
They stand before me all in a line
Each night gets a little bit longer
And these stars that once were strange, now I call mine
Oh, it's been so long since I saw her face
And I just can't find my way out of this place
I took the law into my hands
You'd do the same from where I stand
But the punishment here is much worse than the crime
I guess I get a little emotional sometimes

Each night I light a candle
And I get down on my knees and I pray
My home in ashes I can handle
But not to see my loved ones losing their way
If my tongue sounds lame please don't turn away
Don't you see I'm losing it a little bit every day
If you let yourself understand
I'll give you my heart and hands
Or else the punishment will be much worse than the crime
I know I get a little emotional sometimes
Do you blame me if I get a little emotional sometimes?
Don't act so surprised if I get a little emotional sometimes

Stale, Mate

If, in the crowd, there's one who's not forgot me,
If there's one, perhaps, who asks how I am,
Say I'm alive, but deny that I am well:
That I'm even alive is a gift from a god.

Ovid (in exile)

In 1947, when the British government set up a rocket-testing area in the desert 500 kilometres north of Adelaide, they named it Woomera, after an Aboriginal word for spear thrower. 'Woomera' was not a local word but came from New South Wales, over a thousand kilometres away. It didn't matter to the British: those blackfella words all sounded pretty much the same anyway. And it had a good ring to it – a kind of a *whoosh*. Unlike anywhere in green crowded England, the site was perfect – so harsh and dry that hardly anybody lived there.

It was perfect too, fifty years later, when the Australian government was looking for somewhere to detain asylum seekers arriving by boat on Australian shores – Iranians, Afghanis, Iraqis, Sri Lankans, most of whom were fleeing war, persecution and torture. Under the policy of mandatory detention, designed to deter 'illegal aliens' – though a large majority were legal under international law – the government funded the building of detention centres in remote areas far from cities, hospitals, lawyers and potential visitors. And then handed them over to private contractors to run.

It was a case of out of sight, out of mind. And Woomera was the out-of-sightest of them all. But not out of mind for long. Inside the compound, built to house four hundred but containing at times up to fifteen hundred people, including many children, things started to turn bad. Disturbing reports of what was going on there began to filter out. Detainees in deep despair over the cruel conditions and the slow processing of their claims slashed their bodies, swallowed poison, sewed their lips, lit fires, went on hunger strikes and went crazy. Violence increased. Riots broke out. Prisoners broke out. Four hundred people escaped in 2000 and walked into the town. But there was nowhere else to go. Two years later, during a thousand-strong protest outside the gates, forty more detainees escaped, most of whom were captured within hours.

The inmates were not the only ones traumatised. After the centre was shut down in 2003, some guards and doctors broke their silence to detail the intense stress of their jobs and to describe the spiralling psychiatric disorders afflicting all parties involved. One doctor who had taken his concerns to government bureaucrats reported that he'd been told: 'That sounds all well and good to us but we don't want to make it so nice for them in detention that they won't want to leave.'

Not long after the 2002 breakout I was on my way to Perth with the band for a week of gigs. Our plane was delayed in Adelaide for several hours, so I decided to get out of the airport and walk towards West Beach, a few kilometres away. I had a melody in my head I'd written recently on piano, with no words yet except for one repeated line: 'I guess I get a little emotional sometimes.' That morning, I'd read a letter in the paper accusing the imprisoned asylum seekers of 'behaving irrationally'. About twenty minutes into my ramble the 'emotional' line fused in my head with the letter. Suddenly I had a picture. And with that picture a first line. Then a second, followed quickly by a third and fourth.

Soon I had a long verse and chorus. I'd forgotten to take a pen or paper with me (breaking the first rule of songwriting) and was getting concerned about my ability to hold all the words in my head. I was on a long street without any shops. I texted Sian, in Melbourne: 'I'm sending you some lyrics. Please save them. I'm nowhere near a pen.' My mobile would only allow me to send a few lines at a time.

Once I had the first verse, the second verse slid out like a baby after it's crowned. I sat on a bench in a windy park and texted over and over again to Sian, who told me later that she was having coffee with a friend and had to turn the phone off it was beeping so much. The third verse was half instrumental and then variations on what was already written. In thirty minutes the song was done.

When we returned from Perth I went to Bruce Haymes's house in Northcote. He'd recently bought some recording gear. We put the song down, just piano and vocal, in an afternoon.

Woomera was in the news every day. I wanted to get the song out as quickly as possible so I spoke to some tech-heads and within a week we had the song up on the website for people to download free. Up to this point the internet for me had just been a way to send emails – wondrous enough, to write a letter in San Francisco and have it read instantly in Melbourne – but this was something else.

Here was a song, its subject – exile – as old as prostitution, its lyrics written on a mobile phone, and its music on one of the great inventions of the eighteenth century, which was being released simultaneously on an unlimited number of computers all around the world.

Interesting times.

A large number of Australians were opposed to the government's refugee policy, and as a result many groups and websites – Rural Australians for Refugees, We Are All Boat People, and a host of others – sprang up to mobilise support. Apart from lobbying, protesting and petitions, people sought to create links between the refugees and the outside world in order to soften the effects of isolation – to establish regular visits where practical, or a pen-pal correspondence.

Via my sister Mary Jo, Sian and I got in touch with one such group that sponsored contact between detainees and citizens. In 2002 we were emailed the names of two people inside Baxter Detention Centre and instructions on how to apply for a visit. Baxter was outside the town of Port Augusta in South Australia, about three and a half hours north of Adelaide and a few hours south of Woomera. In October that year, after a family camping trip to the Flinders Ranges, Sian and I drove to Baxter with my two daughters, Maddy and Memphis, aged eleven and nine respectively.

We pulled up at the prison in the afternoon. There is no other word for it. Two tall rows of barbed-wire fencing, one electrified, with a no-man's land of white pebbles in between, surrounded a compound of low-lying, donga-style buildings, some of which in turn had their own fences. We walked to the first gate, pressed the red button, waited for the giant steel door to open, then walked along a mesh-enclosed corridor to the next steel door, which eventually let us into a reception area buzzing with flies. We presented multiple versions of ID, filled in numerous forms, and were asked to empty our pockets of all personal items and put them in a locker. We'd bought a fresh cream cake in Port Augusta as a gift.

'I'll take that,' said the guard.

'Why?' said Sian.

'Because that's the rule.'

'But what will you do with it?'

'It has to go to property.'

'What will property do with it?'

'They might take it through tomorrow, if they have time.'

'Why not today?'

'Because that's the rule.'

'So our friends won't be able to eat the cake today?'

'No.'

'So if they get the cake at all, it will be stale?'

He gave us a thin smile. Stale, mate.

We were taken into a nondescript meeting room with a few tables and plastic chairs. Glass doors led into a small courtyard. There were a couple of other groups of detainees with visitors. A door opened and a woman and a man walked in and came to us. The woman kissed us on both cheeks and her eyes lit up at the sight of the children. We introduced ourselves. They were both from Iran.

R was in her mid-twenties, beautiful, dark-haired and petite with flashing dark eyes. Though she struggled with English she spoke it better than we spoke Persian. Conversation was halting. She told us her husband was locked in a separate compound and would not be part of our visit. He'd had 'big problems' in Iran and they'd fled for their lives, first to Indonesia where they waited five months for a boat operated by people smugglers. They'd landed on the remote north-west coast of Australia two years before and had been in detention ever since. She couldn't stop touching the girls, stroking their hair, pinching their cheeks.

T, the man with her, wore a white chef's coat that smelt of fried chicken. He was working eight hours a day in the hot kitchen, earning one point an hour, one dollar a point, to buy phone cards. He'd been in detention a year longer than R and her husband. We said we'd brought cake for them but it had been impounded. She smiled and shrugged. He held up his hands and shook his head sadly. Situation normal, all fucked up.

After a while a third person joined us. He was older, carried a white stick and said little. Twenty-eight days on a hunger strike in Curtin detention centre in Western Australia had robbed him of his sight, and possibly his mind. He was from Iraq. The others led him gently into the courtyard so he could sit with us in the afternoon sun.

Our visit lasted a couple of hours. Despite the language barrier, we learnt a little about them and they about us. Hollywood movies and Persian poetry – Rumi, from the thirteenth century – were touched on. Addresses were exchanged. R showed off her cat, a stray she had managed to claim as her own, to the girls.

As we were about to leave, there was a conference of guards at the exit door, followed by an announcement that the centre was shutting down due to security reasons and none of the visitors would be allowed to leave right now.

'What's the problem?' I asked one of the guards.

'It's a security problem.'

'Oh, what kind of security problem?'

'Can't say.'

'Has something happened?'

'We can't give out that information, sir.'

'Where's the problem?'

'I can't say.'

'Any idea how long we have to stay here?'

'No. It's a security matter.'

We went back to our halting chat but this time there was a new edginess in the room. Was it just our imaginations or did the guards seem pretty pleased with themselves?

Half an hour went by. Sian went to speak to a different guard. Same stonewall response. The children were getting apprehensive.

'Are they going to let us out?' asked Memphis anxiously.

'Yes, they'll have to. Maybe they're having a little fun with us. Perhaps they want to discourage visitors. Anyway, I'm sure they'll let us out before dinner. Otherwise they'll have to feed us.'

Twenty minutes later we got the all-clear. We tried not to show our relief, said our goodbyes, kissed cheeks and went out past reception, where we collected our belongings, through the metal gates, down the mesh-grilled corridor and into the late afternoon. The dimming sky never looked so good.

'You know how we felt for that short little period when we didn't know when we'd get out?' said Sian to the girls as we walked to the car. 'That's how they feel all the time.'

On the drive back to Adelaide the children asked a lot of questions. Some of them were hard to answer.

I don't know what happened to T but we stayed in touch with R through letters and a lawyer. Eventually she was granted a temporary protection visa and released. She left her husband and moved to Sydney to be with a fellow refugee who'd been released before her. They moved in together. She had trouble finding work at first but her English kept improving.

We visited them a couple of times in Sydney and they came to one of my shows at The Metro. They looked us up in Melbourne sometime later and we had a picnic in the park around Christmas time. We haven't seen them for a while but every now and then R and Sian text each other.

EVERY FUCKING CITY

We argued on the channel train to Paris
The vin rouge helped us make it sweet again
But by the time that we got down to Lyon
Everything I said was wrong and you cursed me in the rain
We split up for a while in Barcelona
We met up six days later in Madrid
I was hoping that the break would make things go
    a little better for us
And for a little while it almost did

Now I'm in a bar in Copenhagen
Trying hard to forget your name
And I'm staring at the label on a bottle of cerveza
And every fucking city feels the same

You said to call you when I got to London
A French girl told me that you'd left a note
I said to her 'I like your accent' and she thought
    I sounded funny
So we ended up drinking in Soho
Foolishly I followed you to Dublin
Like a ghost I walked the streets of Temple Bar
And all the bright young things were throwing up their
    Guinness in the gutters
And once I thought I saw you from afar

Now I'm in a nightclub in Helsinki
And they're playing 'La Vida Loca' once again
And I can't believe I'm dancing to this crap but I'm
    a chance here
Yeah, every fucking city sounds the same

At a café in the port of Amsterdam
An email from you said you'd gone to Rome
For a minute I thought maybe, but my funds were running low
And anyway it sounded like you weren't alone
So I headed north until I got to Hamburg
A chilly city suits a troubled soul
And on the Reeperbahn I paid a woman far too much
To kick me out before I'd even reached my goal

Now I'm in a restaurant in Stockholm
And the waiter here wants me to know his name
And I can order sandwiches in seven different languages
But every fucking city tastes the same
Arriverderci, au revoir, auf Wiedersehen, hasta la vista, baby
Yeah, every fucking city's just the same

Oh, How The Ancient Legends
Disappear Into The Mist!
UK tour diary, June 2002
(during the soccer World Cup)

The band and crew:
Spencer Jones – guitar
Steve Hadley – bass
Bruce Haymes – keyboards
Peter Luscombe – drums
Greg Weaver – sound, tour manager
Dave Alpress – monitors, stage
Ben Lyons – lights

London, 5–10 June
We leave Melbourne in the blue sunshine of a 20° Celsius winter's

day and arrive here on Thursday morning to England's midsummer. It's colder than at home. When we finally reach the Holiday Inn in Hammersmith, it's twenty-seven hours since I walked out the front door. I manage to stay awake all day walking under grey skies, watching soccer on TV, reading *The Red Tent* (based on Jacob's daughter Dinah, from the Bible), and drag myself out in the evening for a meal and a movie with a friend – *Y Tu Mamá También*, a sexy Mexican coming-of-age film.

On Friday we rehearse in a converted warehouse south of the Thames. Oasis are in the room next door but we don't hear any fighting from the Gallagher brothers. We take a break halfway through to eat fish and chips, drink lager and watch the last fifteen minutes of England v Argentina – we're assimilating.

England triumph against the hated foe, so London is heaving when I go out to meet my two nieces at the pub after work. They both have jobs here for a spell, are both in their early twenties and both exceptionally talkative. They seem very grown up. One of them wears pinstripe pants. The conversation and beer flow incessantly at several locations. (Where *do* these slender young women put all those pints?) At some point we slurp noodles, my heavy head nearly falling into them, and over the course of several hours I manage to slip in the odd sentence here and there.

On Saturday we perform at the Fleadh Festival in Finsbury Park with a whole string of bands. Cornershop and Joe Strummer are the highlights. Joe plays quite a few old Clash songs, including 'Police On My Back', a staple of my own set in the early eighties. His band are all younger than he is – with teddy-boy attitude, tight black jeans and rockabilly quiffs – and huddle with him backstage before they go on.

The next day, at my publisher's request, I go, still sleep deprived, to try to write a song with two pretty blond twenty-year-old Australian twins who are going after the girl-pop thing here in a big way. I like them but their bubbliness makes me feel flat. We get something started but it's a long way from finished yet.

That night we do our own show at The Mean Fiddler. The crowd are roaring. Afterwards hordes of people want to chat. I'm swaying, delirious with tiredness. Tonight's the night, I say to myself back at the hotel. Tonight I'll sleep straight through.

But *bing!* It's way too early in the morning – five o'clock – and after only three and a half hours' sleep I can't go back under. It's already light outside and through the rain-flecked window the sky is lowering over cheerless roofs and ugly office blocks.

> I'm driving north to Aberdeen
> Where it can get quite cold
> It's somewhere that I've never seen
> But hospitable I'm told
>
> I'll drink a pint in Aberdeen
> A drop of whisky, too
> I'll raise my glass in Aberdeen
> And sing a song or two

Aberdeen, 11 June

At this time of year here it's still light at eleven o'clock at night. The sound of seagulls crying in the sky brings back some faint ancient memory of old British films. Peter and I go for a run along the beach, where it's windy, wild and grey – buttressed with concrete walls and strutted with wooden groynes (love that word) to keep the sand from shifting. Not a soul in the water. The taxi driver who takes me to the BBC later says it varies by only one degree from winter to summer and your life expectancy in it is three minutes. He may be pulling the Australian's leg but I don't intend to put it to the test.

After the sound check the venue feeds us spicy minced meat with rice – the kind of meal you might have had as a child in the sixties. All it needs are a few sultanas and pineapple pieces. I think it's Aberdeen curry. Or Scottish chilli con carne. Whatever it is, it hits the spot, but I don't know if I want to eat it again too soon.

The gig is distinguished mainly by a gorgeous-looking girl in orange dancing very badly, Elaine-style – as in Elaine from *Seinfeld* – right up the front. Sometimes you just don't know where to look.

Glasgow, 12 June
The Oasis connection continues. King Tut's, where we are playing, is the place, legend has it, they were discovered and the new wave of Britpop launched ten years ago. The two young bands on the bill before us seem quite overawed by the history of the place. Spencer knows all about it too, from reading rock magazines. It's a small room with a basic sound system and the only access to the stage is from the lane outside in the rain. It's like a million other joints.

King Tut's, as usual, feed us. Mince again. Tomorrow I'm going to try to find a vegetable. Here's a sentence from a travel book called *McCarthy's Bar* I picked up at the airport: 'Next morning the reception desk is staffed by two pallid, grey young women who've had no recent exposure to sunlight or unfried food.'

I think they're following us around.

The show goes well. A good crowd again, as in Aberdeen, and very attentive, but it's hard work, physically and mentally. My voice is tired. I battle the pretendies early on. The others get the jitters by contagion. We wobble a little, then right ourselves. I forget every time about the delayed effects of jetlag. You think you're getting over it, then it strikes again.

The hotel rooms are generally small in Europe and the UK, and even smaller when you're sharing. Most of the time a twin room is two single beds right next to each other, and Bruce, my regular roomie, and I often have to rearrange the furniture to give each other a little breathing space. Peter and Steve are getting quite elaborate, putting mattresses on the floor and making partitions out of the bed bases so that their room resembles a tiny Japanese house. They get more inventive by the day. At each hotel now there is a customary viewing of the room after their makeover. Photos are taken.

We're rigorous about putting the rooms back exactly as we found them, though. We don't want to ruin things for future generations. Those future generations include us. It wouldn't be good to come back here in a few years' time and find these single beds bolted together.

Driving to Cork, 13 June

There's a reason Ireland's so green and that reason is rain. The Belfast show was cancelled, so we're going straight through to Cork. Up at five-thirty to catch a cheap flight from Glasgow to Belfast that we couldn't change, and then a long, slow, stop-start drizzling drive from the airport down the length of the land of Eire.

We crawl around Dublin on the ring road. The trouble with Ireland's recent economic boom, it seems, is that now there are too many cars for the narrow roads to cope with. No use complaining about the traffic, though. We *are* the traffic. I'm glad we don't have to play tonight: a chance to do the washing – critical! – explore the town a little and get a good night's sleep.

Cork, 14 June

The yeasty apple smell of malt drifts in through the window from what must be the local brewery. It's the smell of goodness and a long time ago. The town of Cork is the right size for walking, although being built on two rivers, it can get confusing. A local girl I met in Alice Springs last year takes me out and about. First to a Mexican restaurant with an Elvis theme. Dub reggae music is playing on the stereo. Listening to Linton Kwesi Johnson and talking to an Irish girl in a Mexican restaurant with pictures of Elvis all over the walls kinda sums up the way of the world at this point in history. Every fucking city . . . or as they say around these parts, every fecking city.

Next she takes me to an 'old man's pub' where you get the best Guinness (or Murphy's, which is the preferred drop here). Some musicians are playing in the corner. I'm fond of the tradition in Ireland where the band plays sitting round a table or on couches in a corner. No mics, no PA. If you want to hear the music you go in close to them; if you want to have a conversation you move away. We lean in for a while to six men, three of them quite old, making sweet yearning music on banjo, fiddle, mandolin, Dobro, bass and guitar, with voices straight from heaven.

Some of her friends drop in after a while. We move away from the band. Many hands are shaken, many Murphy's downed and many words spoken. My nieces should come here. They'd get a run for their money, pint-wise and word-wise.

The following day the Irish girl drives me to a little fishing village by the name of Kinsale, where we eat fisherman's pie and walk along the water. The sun even comes out for a while. On the way back she sings me a long song in Gaelic about a wandering goat. Ain't life sweet sometimes.

And yeah, the gig is good too.

Dublin, 15 June

Every taxi driver in Dublin knows Whelan's. It's a famed venue for songwriters and folk musicians. There's a front bar and a back room where the live music happens. On the weekends both rooms pump. We have shows two nights in a row.

The first night is a wrestle. It's a full rowdy house, around three hundred and fifty people. Very chatty. They all seem happy enough but we can hardly hear ourselves play over the din. We're sweating buckets under the lights. Halfway through our set we break the show down to a short acoustic section. It's just Spencer and me onstage now. The crowd sounds even louder without the bass and drums behind us. It seems like all three hundred and fifty of them have just been let out of a Trappist monastery and have to return in the morning. They have so much to catch up on. We decide to mimic the audience and chat to each other off-mic for a while about this and that – the upcoming World Cup match, what we're going to do tomorrow, the girl in the tight red dress standing near the mixing desk, and so on. No-one seems to mind. Then I sing 'If I Could Start Today Again' very softly and make the room quiet for, oh, I'd say two minutes.

Later, with the whole band back on, we get two girls from the front up onstage where they dance appallingly – Elaine-style again, one of them – to 'Tease Me'. The very last song of the night is 'You Broke A Beautiful Thing'. We play it slow and smoochy, like it's the last song of the high-school dance. During the short instrumental I skol a pint of cool creamy Guinness, a gift from the audience. It slides down easy in the heat and brings the house down. Some nights you just have to pull things out of your arse.

Afterwards the large band room upstairs is full of earnest Norwegians, Irish songwriters, Australian pop stars, curly-haired West Country girls and drunk blondes. One of the blondes offers me a tab of ecstasy called a Mitsubishi. I think about taking a drive, but being among mostly strangers at two in the morning with no day off tomorrow doesn't strike me as ideal conditions for taking a euphoria-inducing stimulant. The last thing I need is an attack of the friendlies. And hell, I'm forty-seven.

The Irish songwriters are pretty good and we pass the guitar around for a while. Nick Seymour from Crowded House sings a Hank Williams song. We all jolly out onto the street around three a.m. with a million different plans to watch Ireland v. Spain that afternoon. It's big news here. The Irish team's had a great run, and though they're expected to lose, everyone's excited they've managed to get this far.

We're staying in Temple Bar, the old bohemian quarter of the city, once packed with old man's pubs, little bars and cheap student eateries, and now taken over by Hard Rock Cafés, pulsating chrome discos and hordes of Englishers on stag and hen weekends. Large, all-male and all-female groups stagger through the streets screaming and spewing and losing their shoes until dawn. I weave my way home between them to the hotel; their racket assaults my window above the alley, but a bellyful of six pints of black and several Jamesons sending soporific support up the supply lines to the brain are all the defence I need to secure the fortress of sleep.

16 June

Bloomsday. All the action of James Joyce's *Ulysses* takes place on this day as his main character, Leopold Bloom, perambulates Dublin, and each year in commemoration there are readings and re-enactments from the novel. But today Leo seems overshadowed by the football. Irish flags hang from houses, shops and pubs, and everywhere in the streets people are wearing green, white and orange.

Moving a bit slowly from the night before, I pass on the various invitations to go out and decide to watch the game with Peter at the hotel. It's a terrific match. Ireland go down 1–0 early but get on top in the second half and equalise a minute before the end. We're jumping up and down and hollering like it's an Adelaide–Collingwood Grand Final. The game goes into extra time and with Spain down a man, Ireland have a couple of chances to score. Spain hang on, force the game to a penalty shootout and, courtesy of a couple of heartbreaking Irish errors, sneak through.

There are many who say that a penalty shootout is an inadequate way to decide a match but I think it's perfect. After two sides have wrestled each other for two hours and the scores stand locked together, this classic team game comes down to one man against another in the most elemental of contests. It's pure drama, demanding incredible nerve from the participants. It's unfair, yes. Cruel, yes. But that's one of the reasons we watch sport. Apart from the appreciation of skill, aesthetics and tactics, a longing to merge with a crowd and the chance to think magically, our deep and dirty desire is to witness cruelty, to know that we are to the gods as flies are to wanton boys, to have it brought home to us that our fate is sometimes out of our hands no matter how hard we work and how well we prepare.

Same as life. Every mortal knows this sooner or later.

Not to mention that I can understand the penalty shootout, whereas the rest of soccer is a mystery to me.

Our crowd at Whelan's on the second night is just as big, but much quieter than the night before. Perhaps nursing the loss. The downstairs bar, though, is like Fellini's *Satyricon* with a Van Morrison and U2 soundtrack.

Liverpool to London, 17–19 June
We catch the ferry Monday morning from the port of Dún Laoghaire to Holyhead in Wales. Thhyn wy dhryv alynngh th coast to Liverpool thryggh byghhtyfyll cyhnntrhy.

Liverpool is an impressive city, with its big port on the wide Mersey River and its imposing Victorian and Georgian architecture. We are booked at the famous Cavern, where The Beatles started out, except it's not exactly the same cavern. The original was demolished sometime in the seventies to make way for an underground railway ventilator shaft, and the present-day venue has been faithfully reconstructed, depending on who you speak to, either directly below or just adjacent to the first one.

The Cavern today has two rooms, the one we're in and the replica, which is now a museum piece. Again depending on your source, the back wall of the replica, with the names of the bands of the time written on brick – The Swinging Blue Jeans, The Merseybeats, The Beatles, Gerry and The Pacemakers, and others – is either the original back wall or it isn't.

Oh, how the ancient legends disappear into the mist.

The area outside the club is now a pedestrian mall called Cavern Walks – a tourist precinct with a statue of John Lennon, theme bars, and shops selling Beatles memorabilia. We play to around a hundred and fifty people, much to the pleasant surprise of the club manager, who looks like a boxing promoter. He was hounded into booking us by a Scouse fan of ours, Andy, who's been trying for some time to get us to come and play in his hometown. I suspect Andy is single-handedly responsible for the crowd. We kick off with 'Words And Music', with its reference to 'I Feel Fine'. I think there are a few local bands checking us out: I notice knots of three or four young men watching seriously and taking particular notice when Spencer picks up the lap steel. ('Fret-watchers', Spencer calls them.)

The next morning, our Liverpudlian champion takes us to some of the other sacred sites: the house where John Lennon grew up, the house where Paul McCartney grew up (much smaller and pokier than the working-class hero's and in a poorer area), and Penny Lane (no barber shop any more and no fire engine).

Our last stop is Strawberry Field (not Fields). It takes us a while to find it as our guide has never been there (ain't that the way), though his mother once gave John Lennon the price of a drink. After asking directions a couple of times we eventually succeed in our quest. It's an orphanage set back from the road in a large deserted garden. John used to go to fêtes there as a child and sell lemonade. It looks empty now. The big wrought-iron gates are locked. We all stand looking through them in silence.

A friend of mine once told me that he went to Disneyland for the first time as an adult, taking his children. When he got to the front gates he burst into tears, as all the Sunday nights of his childhood – watching Frontierland, Adventureland, Tomorrowland and Fantasyland on TV – came flooding in on him. I'm feeling about the same.

It's time to go. We all pile into the Tarago, drop Andy home with many thanks and find our way to the London motorway. As we drive I write a postcard to Dave Graney, Melbourne songwriter, iconoclast and dandy, who loves to say The Beatles are overrated. The postcard is a picture of Penny Lane.

Everybody's excited in the van. We're laughing, chatting and taking turns playing DJ. I'm humming down the road with my little band of brothers. One more show then home to loving arms. White fog is nestling in the valleys. Blue sky is breaking in the west.

EVERYBODY WANTS TO TOUCH ME

Everybody wants to touch me
Everybody wants a feel
Everybody wants a piece of something that's real

Everybody wants to touch me
They all love my skin
They all want to take me home
They don't even care where I've been

Everybody wants to touch me
Everybody wants a little pat
They can't wait to tell their friends
How they had themselves a piece of that

Everybody wants to touch me
Everybody wants to touch me
Everybody wants to touch me
Everybody wants to touch me

Everybody's lost their manners
Everybody's in a rush
One starts to push, another starts to shove
Then they all get caught in the crush

Everybody wants to touch me
Everybody wants a slice
Everybody wants to touch me
Want a little magic in their lives

Absolutely Awesome

His heart beneath your heart is a war drum
Mustering force. His parasitical
And ignorant little fists already
Beat at your borders and I know they're cocked
At me across the water.

Seamus Heaney, 'Act of Union'

'Absolutely, a hundred percent no problem!' a waiter once said to me when I asked if I could have a bread roll with my meal. 'Awesome!' says Nephew Dan when I tell him I'm going past his place and can drop off the coat he's left behind the night before. They've lost a lot of power these days, the words 'absolute' and 'awesome', just like 'icon' has. 'Awesome' seems to be going the way of 'terrific', another great old word, which used to mean terrifying but now generally means great or fun.

You can't stop language changing. It's curmudgeonly to complain. I used to correct my children when they said 'Me and so-and-so did this', but like King Canute on the shore, I couldn't stop the tide.

Poor old King Canute. He wanted to make a point about the limited power of kings. He summoned his retinue down to the sea. 'We are not divine. See, I cannot turn back these waves,' he said to them, sitting on his chair while his robes got wet. Now, with his intention washed away by time and only the image of his act remaining to most, he's cited as an example of foolish pride. History is as slippery as language.

A pregnant woman approaching full term is awesome in the original sense of the word. Which is to say, she inspires awe, reverence, wonder. Sometimes fear or revulsion. Conquered by the coloniser within, she has gained through her surrender previously unimaginable power, as mystics and meditators do when, losing their narrow limited selves, they become flooded with a wider force. Me no more. Now she is another kind of being entirely – superhuman – having moved from the realm of the personal towards that of symbol. She is New Life. Creation. Fertility.

She's also a freak, something out of sideshow alley. She no longer belongs to herself. That very private thing she did behind the door, under the sheets in her own home, is now on un-ignorable public display. Strangers in the street think nothing of coming up to her to pat her big belly and dispense advice. Housewives become prophetesses, pronouncing in solemn tones, like the oracle at Delphi: 'It's a boy, for sure.' She has become talismanic, a kind of good-luck charm. Everybody, it seems, wants to touch her. They are drawn to her womb like iron filings to a magnet.

But there are those, she often senses, who are more repelled than attracted. Still, they can't stop looking. She feels the waves of disgust coming at her from teenage boys on the tram. A disgust she shares herself at times. One minute she's a brooding, self-contained goddess charged with a sacred task. A walking power station serving the nation. Next she is nothing but a body and mind out of control – a collection of hormones that surge and ebb, bones and muscles that ache, sacs that leak, flesh that bloats and organs that are being slowly crushed. She can't sleep properly at night, she can't get comfortable sitting or standing, she needs to piss all the time. She's a doll shaken by a dog. There's absolutely nothing she can do but wait.

'Everybody Wants To Touch Me' is sometimes read as a riff on celebrity or desirability. That could be Sydney cabaret singer Paul Capsis's take on it on his album of the same name. Medusa-haired Deborah Conway, Melbourne singer-songwriter and mother of three, knows a little about celebrity and pregnancy both. She fronted a band called Do-Re-Mi in the eighties and had a big hit with a song called 'Man Overboard', featuring the memorable lines 'Your pubic hairs on my pillow, your stubble rings the sink.' Her shapely posterior was also famous, full-framed and proudly bare on big Bluegrass Jeans billboards nationwide, with the tagline 'Get yours into Bluegrass'.

Do-Re-Mi functioned as a collective – a shaky construct in pop music at the best of times – and used language such as 'ideologically unsound' (the predecessor of 'politically incorrect') in their band meetings. Deborah, with her charisma, dark good looks (don't mention the billboard) and songwriting ability, was always an uneasy fit. It wasn't long before she went solo and had great success.

She and her husband Willy cut a lean and sassy, Prince-inspired version of 'Everybody Wants To Touch Me' in 2000 for an album called *The Women at the Well*. She started low then went up the octave, pulling out just the right amount of stops. She brought all her qualifications to bear. I don't like all covers of my songs but I have to say this one's awesome. Absolutely.

EVERYTHING'S TURNING TO WHITE

Late on a Friday my husband went up to the mountains
    with three friends
They took provisions and bottles of bourbon to last them all
    through the weekend
One hundred miles they drove just to fish in a stream
And there's so much water so close to home

When they arrived it was cold and dark; they set up
    their camp quickly
Warmed up with whisky they walked to the river where the water
    flowed past darkly
In the moonlight they saw the body of a girl floating face down
And there's so much water so close to home

When he holds me now I'm pretending
I feel like I'm frozen inside
And behind my eyes, my daily disguise
Everything's turning to white

It was too hard to tell how long she'd been dead, the river was
    that close to freezing
But one thing for sure, the girl hadn't died very well to judge
    from the bruising
They stood there above her all thinking the same thoughts
    at the same time
There's so much water so close to home

They carried her downstream from their fishing
Between two rocks they gently wedged her
After all, they'd come so far, it was late
And the girl would keep, she was going nowhere
They stayed up there fishing for two days

They reported it on Sunday when they came back down
There's so much water so close to home

When he holds me now I'm pretending
Nothing is working inside
And behind my eyes, my daily disguise
Everything's turning to white

The newspapers said that the girl had been strangled to death
    and also molested
On the day of the funeral the radio reported that a young man
    had been arrested
I went to the service a stranger, I drove past the lake out of town
There's so much water so close to home

When he holds me now I'm pretending
I feel like I'm frozen inside
And behind my eyes, my daily disguise
Everything's turning to white

Visitation

I first came across Raymond Carver's stories in the early eighties.
My cousin Alex gave me the collection *What We Talk About When We
Talk About Love.* I was hooked straightaway and read everything of his
I could get my hands on.

My life around that time felt like a Carver story – drinking and
chaos and failure and children and landlords. And through it all, writing and big plans and holding things together, just. There was often
a sense in his stories that something was just about to happen, that
something was just about to break.

Short stories have much in common with songs. Both need to

carry their weight lightly. And Carver's stories in particular are a perfect model for a certain kind of songwriter. They're lean, clipped, mysterious, with a lot happening around the edges. This felt like what I was trying to do. I wanted to write modern love songs, sing all kinds of love – old love, young love, complicated love, happy love, sad love, carnal love, yearning love, hanging-on love, hanging-in love, out-of-control love, love gone wrong, love pretty right, love between friends, love among families, love of home, love of the unknown, love of clan, love of enemies, love of drinking, love of oblivion, love of pain.

It seemed to me that any love story between a man and a woman (or boy and girl) always had more than two people involved. In real life there were exes, rivals, children, stepchildren, siblings, parents, in-laws, friends. My songs began to get crowded.

In 1986 I was asked to perform at a poetry reading in Sydney. I need to impress these poets, I thought, and managed to finish off a tune I'd been working on for some time called 'To Her Door'. A guy is sacked and gets back on the booze again until his wife and children leave him. She moves into her brother's place while he goes into rehab up north. After about a year she sends him the money to catch a bus home. He rides back all day and night across two state borders, not knowing where he'll stand when he gets there. The entire story takes three and a half minutes and ends at the beginning.

I was learning to make words count. I drank my man Carver down in big gulps.

In November 1988 I'd just finished an American tour with The Messengers. We had a deal with A&M records and were booked to record in Los Angeles early the following year. The rest of the band went home for a while but I decided to stay. Kaarin and my son Declan flew in from Melbourne and we planned a month's driving trip across the south-west states. I had cousins in New Mexico, a solo gig in Austin, Texas, and an invitation to stay with my brother and his family in Washington DC for Christmas.

For the first leg we plotted a route through eastern California, Nevada, Arizona, southern Utah and Colorado, aiming for Los Alamos, where the cousins lived. We drove through the Mojave desert and Death Valley, staying in motels by the highway. At The Sands in Las Vegas our eyes boggled as Wayne Newton, wearing a white suit, arrived onstage in a spaceship. He sang 'Dreams Of The Everyday Housewife', which had always made me feel good inside when I was a kid. His performance was funny, warm and beautifully paced. At one point the orchestra had a rest and Wayne played guitar and sang songs based on his Native American heritage. The whole concert was like a dream.

The trip was studded with many other wonders. We stopped at the Painted Desert and the Petrified Forest, where over aeons of time wood has turned to stone, and stayed a night at the Grand Canyon. Awesome. Yes, awesome. We drove through Monument Valley, landscape of a thousand westerns. Giant rock formations and mesas rose from the plains. Ever since we'd left LA the country around us had looked mythic, majestic, at times lunar. There were always mountains in the distance.

We visited the Hopi lands and drove to a town on top of a mesa. At Mesa Verde we took a guided tour of an abandoned city built into the rock. The Anasazi (the ancient ones) had built pueblos and lived, farmed and hunted there for a couple of centuries, until they mysteriously vanished towards the end of the thirteenth (around the time Dante wrote his *Inferno*). We ate at roadside diners and restaurants – hamburgers, tamales, chile relleno, chicken burritos – and slept in Motel 6s. Declan, who turned eight along the way, recorded each day's events and places in his scrapbook diary. We had the greatest time. It still glows in my mind.

One afternoon, driving into Cameron, Arizona, with Kaarin at the wheel and Declan in the front seat, I was messing around in the back with some chords on guitar and a melody that sounded kind of Irish. I started thinking about the Carver story 'So Much Water so Close to Home', which tells of a fishing trip in the mountains that didn't quite go as planned. I don't know why the story came into my head – it had been five years since I read it. Maybe the mountains around us were the trigger. But once it took hold of me it wouldn't let go. I reached for my pen and notebook. Over the next couple of hours the whole song slithered out.

I wish they all came like that, words and tune together in a rush, like a visitation. Most don't, though. They start and then stall. They may get nearly finished and then, like a yacht on a windless day, become becalmed. You may have a tune you like but only scraps of words. You come back to it every few weeks or months or years, hoping for a breakthrough. Or you have the whole structure in your mind and nearly all the words, but despite walking around the neighbourhood for hours you can't crack the last verse.

There's always a moment, though, somewhere in the writing of a song that feels like a rush. Maybe it's the melody coming out of nowhere as you reach for a chord. Maybe it's hearing someone behind you in a bar say, 'I've done all the dumb things,' and you slip away from the round for a minute to borrow a biro from the barmaid. Maybe you've been searching for a rhyme or a couplet, and when you get it the whole intent of the song suddenly shifts. Whatever it is, it's the part that takes you by surprise – and if that doesn't happen, what you have is probably not that good.

And when it does happen, that rush, that visitation? In the immortal words of Del McCoury, you get down on your knees and pray.

A couple of weeks later we arrived in Washington, just before Christmas. I went to a bookshop, found a copy of *What We Talk About When We Talk About Love* and thumbed through it to find 'So Much Water so Close to Home'. I was keen to compare it to my song, expecting to have remembered the story imperfectly and made up some of my own stuff. But I was surprised to read that the details in each were exactly the same – the men, the mountains, the whisky, the cold river, the body – right down to the story being told from the point of view of the wife of one of the men.

Many songwriters, especially American ones on awards nights, talk about their songs coming from God or from somewhere outside themselves. You often hear them say they didn't write them, they were just tuning in, that the song already existed in the air and they were merely fortunate enough to be the vessel receiving the marvellous gift. This kind of talk sends me to the sink. I don't suppose God gets their royalties, either. But the feeling they describe rings true in a way. Writing, though it may involve a lot of thinking, is never entirely under our conscious control. Our cunningly evolved brains are beyond us still. Those men, the mountains, the girl and the river were embalmed for years, all intact, somewhere deep in the folds of my hippocampus, biding their own sweet time before wending their own sweet way along the winding pathways to the prefrontal cortex.

Ye know not the hour when they cometh. If I knew how to write a song I'd write one every day.

We recorded the song, and twelve others, a couple of months later at Ocean Way studios in Los Angeles. It was our third album on A&M Records but the first made in the States. They had big plans and brought in a famous producer, Scott Litt, who was riding high with REM at the time. When we were done we named the record after the story – *So Much Water so Close to Home*. We did an expensive photo shoot in several locations. The graphic designer washed the cover in a watery blue. Lovely. Just as the record came out in the states, Polygram took over the company and many people got the sack. Those who didn't were watching their backs and somehow we got lost in the shuffle. But that's a whole other story, and one told many times before.

How Ray Found Ray

The Australian director Ray Lawrence doesn't make a lot of films – three in twenty-three years. He's reluctant to cede control to the investors so is happy making a living doing ads until he gets the terms he wants. It means that sometimes he works a long time developing a film that falls over at the last moment. These experiences have deepened his already philosophical nature.

Ray and I had never met but he found my number somehow and invited me to lunch in 1989, a few years after his first film *Bliss*, based on Peter Carey's novel, came out. Over Sydney rock oysters and squid, I discovered he'd been listening closely to a couple of my albums. He's the kind of man who, once he's interested, turns his beam on a subject and examines it in every detail. He quoted lines from the songs and asked questions about them. He was particularly interested in 'Everything's Turning To White'. The next day I sent him a collection of Carver stories.

At the time, he was working on a script with Australian author Robert Drewe, based on one of Robert's stories. 'Maybe you'd be interested in writing some music for it,' Ray said.

'I've never written film music before,' I replied, 'but I'd certainly consider it.'

Some time after that I moved back to Melbourne from Sydney and we lost touch. Eleven years later he called again.

'I'm about to shoot a movie called *Lantana*. Do you want to read the script and see if you'd like to do the score?'

The script was based on a play by Andrew Bovell called *Speaking in Tongues*. It was an ensemble piece and looked pretty interesting.

'I've done music for one film since we last met,' I told Ray, 'but I'm not a traditional film composer. I don't read music or write it down. I can't orchestrate.'

'That's okay,' said Ray, 'it feels right. Come and look at the rough cut when I have one and tell me what you think.'

Ray shoots pretty quickly, often using natural light indoors and out, so it wasn't long before he had something to show me. By then I had a plan.

'Do you know a Sydney band called The Necks?' I asked him. 'They did the music for *The Boys*. They're a three-piece – piano, stand-up bass and drums – and their performances are totally improvised. They're famous for turning up onstage with no idea of what they're about to play. Then one of them starts. They have a record called *Sex* which is one long piece that goes for fifty-nine minutes. It's based on a simple riff that anchors the piece all the way through. It's intense, hypnotic and meditative all at once. I'd like to take a leaf from their book. If I can come up with one or two simple melodic motifs that you and I agree on, I'll take them to my band and we could improvise around them at length. We've been doing a lot of jamming lately and would love to stretch out. Then I could cut and paste bits of the recorded jams into the movie wherever we see fit.'

Ray was agog. It seemed like such an off-the-wall idea to him, it so tickled his sense of adventure, that he agreed straightaway. I went home and watched the rough cut and sang and played a few melodies into my little tape recorder. I took them to Ray, hiss and all, and we chose a couple. I booked an afternoon's rehearsal with the band but called it off after five minutes because it seemed like we were about to blow our wad into a shitty little cassette player. 'Let's save it for the big studio,' I said. 'I don't want to have to try and recreate or remember this.'

Ray came down to Melbourne for the proper recording and sat in the control room, shaking his head and smiling – part wonder, part nerves – as the band and I, over six hours, played a series of long, twisting, turning variations on our simple themes. It was a five-piece band and two of them, Bruce on keyboards and Shane on guitar, used a lot of effects – distortion, delays, reverbs, flange and so on. At times the sound built up to a dense, squalling noise.

By the end of the session, Ray was looking green around the gills. 'It's too much, too much. This won't work with the film.'

I asked the engineer to play back one of the loud messy sections.

'You know how every instrument's on a separate track,' I said to Ray. 'Listen, we can do this.' And pulled down three of the faders. Out of the chaos emerged a tremolo guitar floating with an ambient organ. 'Or we can do this.' I muted everything but the drums.

A spy-movie ride cymbal with a distant booming kick-drum skittered across the speakers.

Ray's eyes opened wide as he wiped the sweat from his brow.

The recording session was the easy part. Cutting and pasting was a whole other story. I've been asked if I like scoring for films. It's hard to give a short answer. One of its pleasures is writing music that doesn't need words attached. This is a relief to me: words are the hardest part of writing songs. I have hundreds of cassettes of melodies I've mumbled/sung over the years – not straight humming, aahing or oohing, but a strange, babbling kind of pre-language. Half-sounds, half-words. Gibberish. Songwriting is mostly trying to find words to match those sounds. Only a small fraction of those tunes become songs.

So melodies are easy. I make them up fresh or pick them from the shelf. But film scoring is a painstaking, finicky business. Generally the director wants the music to start at a certain point in the scene and end at another precise point. So you need to write thirty-three seconds here, one minute forty-seven seconds there, place a three-second sting on a cut, and so on. Not only that, the director wants the music to be shifting gears within the scene, in keeping with the action or dialogue. And that's where the fun begins – because film people and music people are like two New Guinean tribes meeting on a highland border, speaking entirely different languages and trying to come to terms.

'Can you make it tense and tender here at the same time?'

'No, I didn't mean choppy literally – I meant emotionally, like a sea.'

Over a month at Shane's place, Shane and Ray and I chipped away at the large ore deposit the band had laid down, slowly extracting slivers of precious metal.

'You don't like this, Ray? Well, how about this?' And Shane would move the mouse across the screen and drag another blob over. 'Too long? We'll give it a little snip. Is that too abrupt now? Wait on, I think there's a hanging chord I can grab from over there. Not long enough? I reckon we can loop this fella a few times.'

Every time we got something to fit it felt like a fluke. A thrilling accident. We clapped our hands and did a little jig. *Eureka*. But sometimes Ray would ring a few days later.

'You know that scene from the other day – I think I've changed my mind. The music needs to be more indirect. Or maybe it doesn't need music at all. I think perhaps we need to have the music in the scene before.'

Lantana turned out well. The music was all in the one key, like *Sex*. The movie did great box-office business in Australia and overseas. Apparently the French loved it. Four years later, Ray called. He was rocketing along now.

'Do you want to do this thing again that we don't understand?' he said. He'd secured the rights to 'So Much Water so Close to Home', developed a script that expanded the range of characters – another ensemble film – and set the story in and around the Snowy Mountains town of Jindabyne (where the old town's buried in the lake).

'You bet!' I said.

Ray had his usual trouble with the money people. Investors dropped in and out. The schedule for shooting kept changing. But through all the twists and turns the lead actors, Laura Linney and Gabriel Byrne, both in big demand, kept themselves available for the film. Actors love Ray because he loves them. He gives them room to move. He's well prepared and organised but he doesn't nail everything down. He lets the actors breathe, rolls the camera and hopes to be surprised. He's looking for the thing he can't see coming.

Like a fisherman out on a lake, like a writer who turns up to his desk each day, he waits for the visitation.

NIG

T

HT

WO

FOGGY FIELDS
FOGGY HIGHWAY
FORTY MILES
FORTY-EIGHT
LITTLE THINGS
ST KILDA
GATHERING STORM
GOD
GIFT
GLORY BE
DAD'S BIZ
GRAVY
MARRIED

I CLOSE MY EYES
I DON'T KNOW
KEEP ON COMING
BLIND
START TODAY
I WASTED TIME
DOG
JANDAMARRA
JUMP TO LOVE
JUST ABOUT TO BREAK
KING OF FOOLS
LATELY
LEAPS

(THE) FOGGY FIELDS OF FRANCE

Green the foggy fields of France today I journey through
Green the singer, Al, who sings the way I feel for you
Green our love so tender yet, a gift each day made new
Green would be the whole wide world if they our secret knew

Blue the little patch of sky peeping through the grey
Blue the colour of your dress the day I went away
Blue the mighty ocean deep keeping us apart
Blue the melody I strum on this old guitar

> I carry you with me wrapped up in my heart
> We are the wonder that keeps the stars apart
> The root of the root and the bud of the bud
> The deepest of the deepest
> The singing in the blood

Gold the feeling that I get as the plane comes in to land
Gold the sinking western sun making fiery bands
Gold the colour of your curls as at the gate you stand
Gold the ring I bring for you to slip on your left hand

I carry you with me wrapped up in my heart
This is the wonder that keeps the stars apart
The root of the root and the bud of the bud
The deepest of the deepest
The singing in the blood

Ye Were Not Born For Death, Immortal Birds

Maddy and Memphis, in their early teens, came home from the video store one day during school holidays with a movie called *In Her Shoes* starring Toni Collette and Cameron Diaz. Their cousins of about the same age were with them. The four girls plopped on the couch and popped the disc into the DVD. I read the blurb on the cover and hovered in the doorway for a while to watch the opening scenes and make sure the movie was suitable. It wasn't long before I was sucked in. I didn't have much on that day. That's the good thing about being a songwriter. No boss.

Towards the end of the movie – a good sister/bad sister redemption flick – the Cameron Diaz character recites a poem by American poet E. E. Cummings called 'i carry your heart'. The poem speaks of roots and buds and stars and took root in me immediately. I did some more digging into E. E. after that. He was born late in the nineteenth century and died in the middle of the twentieth. Self-consciously modernist, he wrote his poems in lower case, eschewed conventional punctuation and grammar, yet wrote a lot of sonnets, a 500-year-old form. In his poetry he sometimes seems to be trying to capture the way our thoughts and conversations move – overlapping, quicksilver and sometimes disconnected. He loves women and women's bodies and God.

I don't suppose he ever met the Australian poet John Shaw Neilson, whose life also straddled the turn of the twentieth century. Neilson liked capital letters and ballad structures, worked as a bush labourer most of his life, and sang in self-consciously archaic style to the land and seasons and trees he loved. But he was a different kind of bird altogether to the other bush poets. At times his poems are hallucinatory and mystical, often shot through with colour. Green flourishes in his verse constantly. He writes lines like 'The world is a woman in velvet, the air is the colour of ale.' He loves God in a pagan way and imagines him as a lover bringing the world into being. He talks to flowers. He loves women too, but where E. E. sings of men 'between the breasts of bestial Marj', Neilson's 'schoolgirls hasten through the light and touch the unknowable Divine'.

Writing songs is a magpie business. You build your nest and fetch and carry to it the bright shiny things that catch your eye. You don't care where they come from just so long as they fit just so.

> Shyly the silver-hatted mushrooms make
>   Soft entrance through,
> And undelivered lovers, half awake,
>   Hear noises in the dew
>
> Yellow in all the earth and in the skies,
>   The world would seem
> Faint as a widow mourning with soft eyes
>   And falling into dream.
>
> Up the long hill I see the slow plough leave
>   Furrows of brown;
> Dim is the day and beautiful: I grieve
>   To see the sun go down.
>
> But there are suns a many for mine eyes
>   Day after day:
> Delightsome in grave greenery they rise,
>   Red oranges in May.
>
> John Shaw Neilson, 'May'

FOGGY HIGHWAY

I'm on a foggy highway
I'm on a lonely road
I can't see the way ahead
I'm on a foggy highway

Don't know just why I'm out here
Don't know just how I strayed
The road behind me is long and dark
I'm on a foggy highway

Cold my heart, cold the ground
And my way is darkest night
Not a word, not a friend
To help or guide me
To walk beside me tonight

I'm on a foggy highway
I'm on a lonely road
I'm not long for this world
I'm just passing through
I'm on a foggy highway

They Don't Make Names Like This Any More

Players of American old-time music, 1920s–50s:
Frank Necessary
Earl Scruggs
Buell Kazee
Red Smiley
Dock Boggs

Lester Flatt
Chubby Wise
Cléoma Breaux
Dick Justice
Cedric Rainwater
Bascom Lamar Lunsford

Bill's Building

You could write a book about The Stanley Brothers' song 'Rank Stranger'. A man returns to his hometown after a long time away and wanders the streets like a ghost. Nobody knows him and no face is familiar. A stranger proclaims that his family and friends have all gone away to a beautiful shore by a bright crystal sea. It's sung in high keening voices full of sorrow, wonder and hope. I hadn't known music could be so weird and beautiful. I could figure out the chords to the song easily but the singing was beyond me.

The Stanley Brothers, my high lonesome companions, travelled around with me on cassette for many years. I fell for their songs hard – 'If I Lose', 'The Darkest Hour Is Just Before the Dawn', 'Little Maggie', 'I'm A Man Of Constant Sorrow', 'Angel Band', 'Little Glass Of Wine'. When I first heard 'Pretty Polly' I thought to myself, I know that tune. Dylan had nicked it wholesale for 'Ballad Of Hollis Brown'.

Pick it up and pass it on. Looking forward, looking back. Nothing new under the sun. The Stanley Brothers eventually led me, as they had to, back in time to Bill.

Bluegrass music, the bastard child of folk and country, evolved out of American old-time rural music but seemed to spring fully formed from the head and fingers of Bill Monroe and His Blue Grass Boys in the mid-1940s. Bebop was being born around the same time with Charlie Parker, Dizzy Gillespie, Thelonious Monk and others pushing innovations in tempo, rhythm and harmony. Frank Sinatra was still crooning, under the sway of Bing Crosby, yet to find his edge.

Bill was making a building in his head. He heard a banjo player, Earl Scruggs, who'd developed a new way of playing his instrument. Ironically, the prototype of the banjo – an instrument long associated with white country music – had come out of Africa. It became a rhythm instrument in Dixieland jazz and made its way via blackface minstrelsy into the hands of hillbillies, who played it in a frailing folk style to accompany songs and comedy. But no-one had ever played it like Earl before. Using his own rolling, three-finger technique he found a way to rip notes at dazzling speed. Bill nabbed him for his band and the final foundation stone was in place.

Bill Monroe and His Blue Grass Boys had a similar effect on country music as bebop had on jazz, or punk on late-seventies rock. Audiences were shocked at what they were hearing. And thrilled. You can hear them gasp on early live recordings. The turbocharged banjo, Bill's fierce mandolin and Chubby Wise's breakneck fiddle rocked them in their seats at the Grand Ole Opry. Guitar player Cleo Davis said, 'We took off fast and furious. People couldn't even think as fast as we played, I believe. There was nobody living who played with the speed that we had.'

Something new was going on, all right. But canny Bill never forgot he was making music for farmers. Despite having left home (as all heroes must), he named his band after the native blue grass of his home state, Kentucky. None of his classic 1946 band came from there and he'd left for lack of opportunities, making his living in neighbouring states, but Kentucky became Bill's idealised motherland, the pure wellspring. He crafted a myth of continuity, of the old mountain home, speaking of 'ancient tones' and presenting his music not as radical innovation but as a return to the source. Mothers await their children, and children their mothers, in heaven. And Jesus is always there to bless them all – the drowned, the poisoned and the stabbed, the sinners and the sinned against. Satan also waits, down below, for those who take the wrong fork in the road.

Bill rehearsed and rehearsed the band 'til they could play blind, tighter than a Prussian army on drill manoeuvres, but the singing stayed high, sweet and raw. The rafters of Bill's building are sturdy with cross-grain, straining with paradox, and made stronger by it. Bluegrass is simple to play but takes years to learn. Wild yet demanding intense discipline. It's joyous and mournful, modern and timeless. No other style of music, to my knowledge, is named after one band. Imagine all mid-sixties pop music being called Beatles music.

Bill guarded his building closely, holding the keys tight in his fist. The Stanley Brothers, The Foggy Mountain Boys, Del McCoury, and many others who served apprenticeships with the big fella had pass keys, but on the understanding that they abide by the rules. Bill lived a long time, four score and five years, and his grip on the keys slowly weakened even as the legend solidified. Then too, it's hard to keep track of pass keys, especially if you never change the lock.

His one-time protégés Lester Flatt and Earl Scruggs added Dobro to their band, and others perpetuated this heresy. Later would come the sacrilege of electric bass, electric guitars, electric fiddles and – horror! – drums. Bluegrass mutated into 'newgrass' and 'progressive bluegrass', sometimes getting too slick and clever for itself. Czechs and Swedes and Japanese took up banjos and mandolins and devoted themselves to serious study of Appalachian mountain singing. Some Australians too.

In 1997 I heard an album by Tim O'Brien, from West Virginia, called *Red on Blonde*. Every track on it was a Bob Dylan song, done in classic bluegrass style. Most of it worked beautifully. It made sense, as a lot of Dylan's tunes come from folk music, and got me thinking I could do something similar with mine. Some old tunes came immediately to mind and I decided to write a few new ones. A bluegrass band in Melbourne, Uncle Bill, had covered a couple of my songs already, so I roped them in and we made a record called *Smoke* in 1999.

That was the year I was working with Professor Ratbaggy, jamming and building up pieces for our eponymously named album. One Saturday, after rehearsing with Ratbaggy in Prahran, I put on a hat and a different shirt before heading across the river to sit in with Uncle Bill at a Fitzroy pub. I needed to change my way of thinking, as the contrast between the two kinds of music couldn't have been more stark. The one was built from the bottom up, around drums and deep bass, with minimal vocals and relying on effects – loops, distortion, reverb and the like – and dissonance. The other was built from the top down – high vocals, lots of harmonies, acoustic instruments only, with no effects or drums.

Smoke and *Professor Ratbaggy* both came out on the same day. I'd switched record labels after fourteen years and these were the first two with the new company, EMI. I'd convinced them of the worth of a simultaneous release, saying they wouldn't get in the way of each other, that in fact record buyers would be more confused going first in one musical direction then another six months or a year later. 'We can let the ground lie fallow for a while before I come again with a "normal" record next year,' I argued.

They bought the argument, agreeing it gave the press an angle. Maybe they were just humouring me, keeping The Artist happy with his weird little side projects. *Smoke* did all right, selling more than *Professor Ratbaggy*, which didn't surprise or bother me. Both covered their costs. The 'normal' record, which came out eighteen months later with a hungry EMI on the hunt for chart success, sold more than the both of them put together.

Six years after *Smoke*, I got the bluegrass itch again and began assembling more songs for the same treatment. I wrote a few freshies I knew would suit and targeted some old songs for revamping. I'd been carrying 'Foggy Highway' since the late eighties but had never successfully recorded it, despite a couple of attempts to get it on tape. Mick Harvey from The Bad Seeds produced a version on which he played guitar, bass and drums: it got close. In truth, I was a bit spooked by

Renée Geyer's 1991 recording. I'd been unsure of the song until she revealed it to me, laying it open as a surgeon does a patient on the operating table. But from then on, though I had confidence in the song, I couldn't get near it myself. I felt clumsy and inadequate each time I approached.

However, I had a hunch this time. I threw it in the swag I took to Terrigal Beach on the central coast of New South Wales, where Rod McCormack, crown prince of Australian country music, had assembled a group of players in his home studio, perched on a hill among trees.

Rod called this group the A-Team. There was baby-faced Simmo, Ian Simpson, from Western Australia, lover and beloved of women, who'd emerged fully formed from his bedroom as a wunderkind banjo player at the age of seventeen and gone on to become a long-term member of Slim Dusty's band. Along the way he'd won Best Instrumentalist awards year after year at the Tamworth Country Music Festival. Simmo, the smiling assassin, was the thrumming motor of the band.

There was Mick Albeck on fiddle, a big square man who looked like a police sergeant, originally from a small town on the western New South Wales/Queensland border. He used to play rugby league before he took up the fiddle at the age of twenty. In his large hands the instrument looked tiny, in danger of being brutalised – until he began to play, and sweet warm bluesiness poured into the air.

On mandolin was Trev Warner, in his 'late fifties' (that's as definite as he wanted to be), the old man of the band, steeped in folk and country, and one of the pioneers of Australian bluegrass. Every morning in our motel by the sea, I'd hear him picking and singing out the back of his room a few doors down. He could sing old-time songs from dawn 'til dusk, until the end of time if you asked him to. Rawer and rougher in his playing than the others, he was the grit in the machine.

James Gillard played double bass. Curly-haired, wiry, boyish, hyperkinetic, often clowning, sometimes happy as a puppy, other times fretful and hard on himself. Another transplanted West

Australian, who'd toured with everybody, including Dinah Shore in the seventies, he usually took the high harmony.

Young Ted Howard, the engineer, positioned the mics, worked the board, and listened with wide ears to the sounds and the stories. Some mornings before work he'd catch a bonito off the rocks and we'd slice it up raw for lunch. (Not really Trev's cup of tea.)

And lightly in command, overseeing all, was Rod, who as a young man had financed his travels through the American south by winning banjo and flat-picking competitions. He was a multi-instrumentalist and a smooth tenor singer; every time he picked up an instrument grace flowed from him. He directed the band and played guitar, Lester Flatt-style, leaving me free to sing without distraction.

It was a different experience for me. Arranging and recording with my electric bands is an experimental process. We grope our way along, searching for sounds or a groove, stopping and starting, trying to find a way into the song. A lot of the time we're not quite sure what we're doing. But in country music the path is clearer, in bluegrass even more so. The road has been built and tamped down hard by thousands of travellers.

Pop music, the kind I like, feeds on the new. It seeks the unusual sound, the fresh angle, the strange combination, whereas country music generally aims for classicism and timelessness. The older it sounds, the better. So the songs got sorted out quickly, without fuss. The band, which we christened The Stormwater Boys in honour of Cedric Rainwater, one-time member of Monroe's band, and of the late summer storm that pummelled the studio roof one night, all had charts. Instead of writing out chords, they wrote numbers. 'The chorus is four, one, five. The verse goes to a six. I'll play a two over a five on the third bar.'

With the structure nailed down and the arrangement sturdy, every man was freed by the certainty of maths to swing, dance, cruise and coax the music from their bodies. We hunkered down, straining nerve, brain and sinew, to squeeze out three songs a day through steel, gut and old wood – songs of stumbling blocks, tent-boxers, ghosts, angels of death, old men by the fire, lost souls, floating Jesuses and talking spirits. In the evenings we downed tools and drank beer. On the seventh day, we rested and looked upon our labours and were pleased.

'Foggy Highway' passed through the assembly line on day four and came out careening now, not creeping down the road. It had always been a song but now I was someone who could sing it. The horse had come for the hay. After listening to the playback I went for a walk in the early evening, heading down the hill towards the sea. A warm wet wind blew in my face. Heavy clouds massed above the ocean, purple and gold, the colour of a three-day-old bruise. The key to some of these bluegrass interpretations, I was thinking, seemed to be simply playing the song faster and higher. We'd take an old song of mine – if it was in G, say, we'd crank it up to B, a popular bluegrass key. I'd be singing at the limit of my range, starting to sound like a mountain man. We'd notch the tempo up a few clicks too. More often than not it worked. And singing high and loud gives you a nice little buzz in the head.

Kasey Chambers, who lived down the road at Avoca Beach, came to work on day five. The first time I'd seen Kasey she was in a tent singing 'Up On Cripple Creek' to a bunch of muddy, bearded bikers. She had a ring in her nose and wore a long black dress. This is something, I thought. I didn't meet her then but a few months later she came to a show of mine at The Basement, a dark underground club in Sydney. Afterwards we sat around with a gang in the band room singing Carter Family, George Jones, Gram Parsons and Louvin Brothers songs.

I'd always had a yen to record The Louvin Brothers' 'You're Learning', a sublime and dippy song, not as well known as some of their others. Kasey was perfect for it. Once we'd worked out the key and the harmony, it played and sang itself. 'Rank Stranger', written by Albert E. Brumley, who also wrote 'I'll Fly Away', was the other cover we recorded that week. After thirty years of circling the song, singing it in back rooms and around kitchen tables, I finally summoned up the courage to sing it to tape. But it still didn't make the cut. The original is too awesome and just can't be touched.

FORTY MILES TO SATURDAY NIGHT

Well I rubbed the dirt all down
And I washed away six aching days
And my shoes all slick and spit
And my singlet fresh and my sideburns shaved
As I turn from the mirror
And I open my first beer since yesterday

Danny brings the Bedford round
A three-ton girl with a ten-foot tray
And she knows the way to town
So we kiss goodbye to two weeks' pay
Now the leaves are shaking
And the stars are all waking from the day

Big wheel turning (turning all night)
Big light burning (burning so bright)
Downright foolish but that's alright
It's only forty miles to Saturday night!

There's a place on Fortune Street
And a band down there called Gunga Din
And Joanne from Miner's Creek
She said that she'd be back again
She lives out on the station
And she works on my imagination

Big wheel turning (turning all night)
Big light burning (burning so bright)
Downright foolish but that's alright
It's only forty miles to Saturday night!

Five Hombres

'Forty Days And Forty Nights' – Muddy Waters
'Forty Days' – Ronnie Hawkins
'Forty Shades Of Green' – Johnny Cash
'Forty Four' – Howlin' Wolf
'Forty Miles Of Bad Road' – Duane Eddy

The Governor's Palace

On my first trip to America, in 1987, I visited the old governor's palace in Santa Fe, New Mexico. It's now an art gallery and museum. I saw a painting there of several men on horseback riding along a ridge, one of whom carried a fiddle under his arm. The painting was called *Ten Miles to Saturday Night*. Some time later I came up with a tune for the title, but was short a syllable so I turned the ten miles into forty and put the guys in a truck. They wouldn't have got there in time otherwise.

FORTY-EIGHT ANGELS

Twelve angels from the north
Twelve angels from the east
Twelve angels from the south
Twelve angels from the west
Coming for to carry me away

Angels shooting from your brow
Angels leaping from your mouth
Angels lighting on your shoulders
East and west and north and south
Coming for to carry me away

Angels flying from your fingers
Angels dancing on your breast
Angels happy just to linger
North and south and east and west
Coming for to carry me away

Angels sleeping in your hair
Angels resting at your feet
Angels singing on your stairs
South and north and west and east
Coming for to carry me away

Angels in the inky night
Angels when the day breaks forth
Angels at the noonday table
West and east and south and north
Coming for to carry me away

Me no more, me no more, me no more

Swing Low, Sweet Chariot

We had a lot of old art books around the house when we were grow-ing up. I liked to look at them on rainy days. My father's Aunt Gwen had travelled in Europe as a young woman in the early twentieth century and visited a lot of galleries, especially in Italy. She must have had spending money and a big suitcase, because she brought home some beautiful books. Somehow Dad, one of six children, inherited them.

Gwen also collected art postcards and arranged them in small photo albums. She never married or had children, though nearly every postcard features the Madonna either with a child or being visited by a child-announcing angel. I wish I'd known this mysteri-ous, perhaps melancholy, great-aunt who died when I was five. She travelled as a companion to her own aunt, a benefactress of the Church, and I've heard she was bored a lot of the time, sitting in drawing rooms with bishops and prelates. Later in life she made exquisite pieces out of wrought metal – bowls, pots, trays and let-ter holders in brass and copper, a couple of which have come down to me.

The Italian painters of the fourteenth and fifteenth centuries loved to paint angels. They often float symmetrically in the top corners of the frame, looking down on Mary and her plump little baby Jesus. In other works armies of them mass in the sky. The Annunciation is a very popular theme – the angel bearing the news to Mary that she is pregnant with the Saviour of the World. Most of the reproductions in Gwen's books were black and white, due to the prohibitive cost of colour printing at the time. But one, by Fra Angelico, in full col-our transfixed me as a teenager. The angel's robe is pink and her one visible wing is layered with bands of blue, purple, russet, aqua-grey, yellow, bone and cream. Her halo is gold.

At the age of forty I went to Italy for the first time, on tour as the opening act for Joe Jackson, and visited the monastery of San Marco in Florence, built in the thirteenth century. In each and every monk's cell was a Fra Angelico mural, including the one from my youth. I thought I'd wandered into heaven.

Some time in the late seventies I was doodling a tune on piano. It had a processional feeling and with it came words about angels from the four corners of the compass. They sounded kind of familiar. Years later, watching a documentary, I saw Elvis warming up backstage with a gospel song called 'I, John'. Those angels again, straight from the Book of Revelations. Had I heard Elvis, or someone else, singing that song before? Or had they entered me way back during my ten years of Sunday mass, as I kneeled and stood in front of the wooden benches of St Ignatius?

They sounded good with the piano chords, those repetitive angels, but I didn't particularly want to write a gospel song using them. That had been done. If I'd stolen these angels, I needed to put them to some different service. But what? Should I make them flesh? Dress them in colours? De-wing them and disguise them as men? Perhaps I could have them roam as shadowy agents of good and evil.

Those angels were a stumbling block for twenty-five years. Lord knows, there were enough angel songs written already, a lot of them mawkish. Why add to the choir? Often I sought to push them away and try other words to the tune, but they wouldn't move. I couldn't get around them, these heavy solid beings.

'How many angels can dance on the point of a needle?' medieval theologians reportedly asked when discussing whether angels had bodies or not. 'An infinite number,' said the metaphysicians, 'because they don't take up any space.' (Oh yes, they do.)

The discussion is perhaps apocryphal. D'Israeli, a nineteenth-century British scholar, refers to it but he was possibly taking the micky out of Thomas Aquinas, the renowned Catholic philosopher who thought and wrote painstakingly about form, substance, angels, existence, essence and other similar matters. He's still read and discussed today, although not long before his death he told a friend,

'Such secrets have been revealed to me that all I have written appears of little value.'

Thomas, born in Sicily in 1225, shocked his family as a young man when he decided to join the Dominicans, a new order at the time (and Fra's future brethren), considered too radical by the established Church. So his brothers kidnapped him and imprisoned him in a fortress for two years in an attempt to change his mind. He proved so obstinate they brought in a prostitute to tempt him but he drove her from his cell with a brand snatched from the fire. He then got down on his knees to pray, imploring God to keep him from temptation. The story goes that he fell asleep and was woken up by two angels who put a white girdle around him, saying, 'We gird thee with the girdle of perpetual virginity.' And from that day forward 'he never felt the slightest motions of concupiscence'. I find this hard to believe.

In 2003 I had a breakthrough at last with my angels. Turning them into invisible imps of pleasure, I came up with a set of words and took the song into the studio with the band. At the time, I was listening to Serge Gainsbourg and Brigitte Bardot's duet 'Je T'Aime . . . Moi Non Plus', which Serge had written especially for her. During the song she and Serge breathe heavily as Serge comes and goes lyrically between her loins. He is the wave and she is the naked island. She sighs and moans orgasmically in between verses and on the playout.

Apparently the immortal B.B. got cold feet on hearing the finished song and, worried about her German husband of the time, begged Serge not to release it. So he re-recorded it with his girlfriend, English actress Jane Birkin. With Jane following B.B.'s template to a T, half singing, half talking, she and Serge had a worldwide hit. (B.B. may have had her regrets. She released 'Je T'Aime' herself some time later and it's now on all her collected musical works. I prefer her version to Jane's. The mix is murky and mysterious, and she sounds inside her own skin. Jane is less believable and seems to be singing above her range.)

Listening to Serge and B.B. getting it on, I wondered at Serge's interjection '*moi non plus*' each time Brigitte says '*Je t'aime*' ('I love you'). Mustering my schoolboy French, I translated it as 'me no more', which made perfect sense in the context of the song – the obliteration of the self-drop in the ocean of love, the dissolving of the walls of the ego, the joining with the other. Definitely worth nicking, I thought, and slipped it in on the playout of 'Forty-Eight Angels'– a sly little tribute to Serge and his women.

Later on, someone told me '*moi non plus*' actually means 'me neither'. But I don't understand why, when Brigitte says to Serge, 'I love you,' he says, 'Me neither.' I'd rather stick with 'me no more', along with 'Hello Douglas, my old friend' and 'Excuse me, while I kiss this guy.'

And Thomas the Dominican? If he walked among us today and listened to classic French pop, what would he make of 'Je T'Aime'? 'Me no more' sounds like something he could have uttered during one of his famous late-life ecstasies. It's rumoured he was levitating in bliss once when the voice of God issued from the crucifix before him.

'Thou hast served me well, Thomas. What reward wilt thou have?'

'None other than thyself, Lord.'

I suspect Tom and Serge have much in common. In 'Je T'Aime' Serge sings, '*L'amour physique est sans issue*,' which translates as 'Physical love is a dead end.' If he's made it to heaven yet – and it's doubtful, as he may still be in purgatory for his many sins of excess, which include telling a young Whitney Houston on live TV he'd like to fuck her – I hope they've met. I'm taking it as given Tom's already there – they canonised him lickety-split after he died. I can see the two of them, wings folded, sitting on a cloud in earnest discussion – partly in French, partly Italian – ruminating over a glass or two of red wine on the material world, its wonders and illusions.

FROM LITTLE THINGS BIG THINGS GROW
(written with Kev Carmody)

Gather round people, I'll tell you a story
An eight-year long story of power and pride
British Lord Vestey and Vincent Lingiari
Were opposite men on opposite sides

Vestey was fat with money and muscle
Beef was his business, broad was his door
Vincent was lean and spoke very little
He had no bank balance, hard dirt was his floor

From little things big things grow
From little things big things grow

Gurindji were working for nothing but rations
Where once they had gathered the wealth of the land
Daily the pressure got tighter and tighter
Gurindji decided they must make a stand

They picked up their swags and started off walking
At Wattie Creek they sat themselves down
Now it don't sound like much but it sure got tongues talking
Back at the homestead and then in the town

From little things big things grow
From little things big things grow

Vestey man said 'I'll double your wages
Seven quid a week you'll have in your hand'
Vincent said 'Uh-uh we're not talking about wages
We're sitting right here 'til we get our land'
Vestey man roared and Vestey man thundered

'You don't stand the chance of a cinder in snow!'
Vince said 'If we fall others are rising'

From little things big things grow
From little things big things grow

Then Vincent Lingiari boarded an airplane
Landed in Sydney, big city of lights
And daily he went round softly speaking his story
To all kinds of men from all walks of life

And Vincent sat down with big politicians
'This affair,' they told him, 'it's a matter of state
Let us sort it out, your people are hungry'
Vincent said 'No thanks, we know how to wait'

From little things big things grow
From little things big things grow

Then Vincent Lingiari returned in an airplane
Back to his country once more to sit down
And he told his people 'Let the stars keep on turning
We have friends in the south, in the cities and towns'

Eight years went by, eight long years of waiting
'Til one day a tall stranger appeared in the land
And he came with lawyers and he came with great ceremony
And through Vincent's fingers he poured a handful of sand

From little things big things grow
From little things big things grow

That was the story of Vincent Lingiari
But this is the story of something much more

How power and privilege cannot move a people
Who know where they stand and stand in the law

From little things big things grow
From little things big things grow

Big Boss Man

In 1966 a group of Gurindji stockmen, house servants and their families walked off Wave Hill, a cattle station in the Northern Territory leased by British peer Lord Vestey. Initially it appeared to be a dispute over wages and conditions – black workers at that time were paid less than white – but it soon turned into a land claim, one of the first in the country. Following on from the bark petition sent to the federal government by the Yolngu people in 1963, demanding sovereignty over their ancestral home further to the north, the strike spearheaded the land rights movement in Australia.

The stockmen, around 200-strong, based themselves at Daguragu, also known as Wattie Creek. Their main spokesperson, Vincent Lingiari, said, 'What was before Lord Vestey born and I born? It was blackfella country.' Over the years, Vincent and the Gurindji gradually gathered support. The novelist Frank Hardy got involved and wrote a book about their struggle called *The Unlucky Australians*. Vincent travelled to the southern states and drew unionists and students to his cause.

Despite bribes and threats the Gurindji stood their ground. The longer they waited, the stronger they became. What many outsiders had thought unthinkable at first came to pass almost nine years later, when the Labor government of the day agreed to give them back their land.

The Prime Minister himself, Gough Whitlam, came out to Gurindji country to officiate at the handover ceremony and said, 'I want this to acknowledge that we Australians have still much to do to redress the injustice and oppression that has for so long been the lot of Black Australians. Vincent Lingiari, I solemnly hand to you these deeds as proof, in Australian law, that these lands belong to the Gurindji people and I put into your hands part of the earth itself as a sign that this land will be the possession of you and your children forever.'

I was twenty years old at that time, moving around from place to place. I may have seen the picture, now famous, of Gough pouring dirt into Vincent's hands, or seen some film footage on the TV news, but I pretty much missed the whole affair. It wasn't until years later that I tuned in.

Kev Carmody didn't miss it, though. He was twenty-eight years old and it was big news in his world. Kev had grown up in a droving family. His dad was second-generation Irish Australian, his mother a Bunjalung woman, her father a traditional man from Cape York in the far north. Kev's first language was a kind of creole. As a child he spent a lot of time in mustering and droving camps throughout the great plains of western Queensland and the Darling Downs; slept in a swag under stars that went forever. At the age of ten he went to school and learnt proper English, and as a young man he moved to the large town of Toowoomba, became a welder and played rugby union for the Queensland Country team. He found his way to university, studied politics and devoured books, started writing songs for his thesis as a form of oral history.

When I first met Kev in the late 1980s he was a full-grown bull of a man who looked like he was carved out of stone, with a thick unruly head of hair only partly tamed by a red, black and gold headband. We were on the same bill at a Rock for Land Rights concert in Sydney. His first record, *Pillars of Society*, had just come out and he sang a song called 'Thou Shalt Not Steal' which began with the lines:

> In 1788 down Sydney Cove
> The first boat-people land

> Said sorry boys, our gain's your loss
> We gonna steal your land

He also sang a song called 'Black Deaths In Custody', and another one, 'White Bourgeois Woman'. He played his guitar like a machine gun and howled, curled and hurled his words into the air. He meant business. After the show we kicked on here and there and ended up sitting around his kitchen table in Marrickville with Crown Lagers and a bottle of Johnnie Walker Red, playing songs to each other.

I soon found out, as our friendship developed, that he had a whole swag of songs written over twenty years – stories of drovers and their wives, miners, drifters, warriors, junkies and brothel madams. Stinging polemics too, that tore strips off the establishment. And hymns, paeans of praise to the land, the natural world and its wonders. One song, 'Cannot Buy My Soul', was politics and prayer combined. Another, 'Eulogy For A Black Man', was his will in musical form. The whole was stitched together with rich, poetic language: 'Make no monuments or mortal crowns or speak my name again when you lay me down.'

Steve Connolly produced Kev's second album, *Eulogy*, and I played harmonica on a few tracks. Not long after that Kev and I and Declan went camping for a few days at Lake Wivenhoe, a huge dam supplying Brisbane, eighty kilometres to the east.

We walked and fished, kayaked and cooked, and played guitars around the campfire. One night we got to talking about Vincent Lingiari and the Gurindji walkout. I knew more of the story by then: 1988 had just passed, the 200th anniversary of white settlement. There had been big demonstrations by Indigenous and non-Indigenous Australians. Aboriginal land councils, which traced their origins back to the Wave Hill walk-off, were active and vocal. Self-determination for Aboriginal Australia was in the air, and Prime Minister Bob Hawke had raised the possibility of a treaty between black and white Australia. Nineteen eighty-eight was also the year 'that old man', Vincent, died. For many people, by then, he was a hero.

I knew the broad outlines of the fabled, unfathomably long strike, and Kev had a few more details. My notebook contained a line I'd jotted down a few months before, a line I'd picked up from a Bruce Springsteen song: 'From small things, Mama/Big things one day come.' The song was about a former hamburger waitress who leaves her husband and two baby children to head to Florida with a real-estate man. She shoots her lover dead on the road because she 'can't stand the way he drives', and winds up in jail.

I'd tightened the line up to 'From Little Things Big Things Grow' (the Boss, God love him, can be a bit prolix at times), thinking it might be the perfect title for a love song along the lines of 'It's Grow-ing' by The Temptations. But when Kev said, 'Let's write a song about that old man, about the strike,' I replied straightaway, my mind fizz-ing, 'I think I've got something to throw in the pot.'

With Kev doodling a few chords on the mandolin, me playing a capoed guitar, Declan poking the fire, and the ghosts of 'Hattie Carroll' and Woody Guthrie's 'Deportees' hovering overhead, we con-jured most of the song over a couple of hours under the bright, bright stars. We were both a little hazy about some of the facts, so when I got home I found a copy of Hardy's book, read it, and finished off the lyrics with Kev over the phone.

The first time I sang the song in public was at a concert on Bondi Beach put on by Building Bridges, an organisation dedicated to reconciliation between Aboriginal and white Australians. I thought reconciliation was an odd choice of word – when was the original conciliation? – but they seemed like good people.

I was nervous about singing a new, long song still wet with paint. Would I remember all the words? Luckily the chords stayed the same all the way through – a circle song – so I didn't have to worry about them. I wrote myself a cheat sheet in big block letters on a couple of pages of paper – MUSCLE, RATIONS, SWAGS, WAGES, SNOW, AIRPLANE, POLITICIANS, STARS, STRANGER – laying them on the stage at my feet, and managed to get through all the lyrics without stumbling. Someone came up to me afterwards and said,

'I don't know what that song was about but I really loved the imagery.'

When we recorded it Michael Barclay used an old tape box as a drum, playing it with his fingers. We invited Ernie Dingo to play didgeridoo. Ernie, actor and TV presenter, is a Yamatji man from Western Australia. He didn't have a didge in the right key so he asked his neighbour, a seamstress, for some cardboard tubes. She had a whole stack that had held cloth, six of which he brought into the studio. None of them was exactly the right note but we found one that was close and cut it a couple of times with a Stanley knife until it matched the song key. The tube was probably a few months old. On the record it sounds thirty thousand years ancient.

Kev recorded his own version of the song and released it around the same time. Neither version ever got played on commercial radio. Neither of us made a video. In February 2008, Prime Minister Kevin Rudd, not long after being elected, made an official apology from the government to Indigenous Australia for the removal of their children under policies of assimilation. Immediately afterwards, members of the hip-hop group The Herd combined the chorus of 'Little Things' with parts of the PM's speech and a sixteen-year-old speech by former prime minister Paul Keating – who once called himself the Placido Domingo of Australian politics – to make a single that went to number four on the national Top Forty chart. After thirty years in show business it was the first time I'd been involved in a Top Ten single.

It's a creaky song with a Sunday-school melody that makes me cringe sometimes. But it just keeps on going, like an old buggy bumping on down the road.

FROM ST KILDA TO KINGS CROSS

From St Kilda to Kings Cross is thirteen hours on a bus
I pressed my face against the glass and watched the white lines
   rushing past
And all around me felt like all inside me
And my body left me and my soul went running

Have you ever seen Kings Cross when the rain is falling soft?
I came in on the evening bus, from Oxford Street I cut across
And if the rain don't fall too hard everything shines
   just like a postcard
Everything goes on just the same

Fair-weather friends are the hungriest friends
I keep my mouth well shut, I cross their open hands

I want to see the sun go down from St Kilda Esplanade
Where the beach needs reconstruction, where the palm trees
   have it hard
I'd give you all of Sydney Harbour (all that land, all that water)
For that one sweet promenade

So Much Water So Close To Home

So many Australian place names are British in origin. Understand-
ably so. You come to a new world, you bring your old names with
you. Nearly all our capital cities are named after famous person-
ages. Some figures who once loomed large diminish as the cities
commemorating them expand. You don't hear much about Queen
Adelaide these days. And what was it exactly that Lord Sydney
did? Other towering figures are attached to backwaters. Australia's

smallest capital, Darwin, takes its name from a man whose shadow gets longer and longer as time goes on.

St Kilda is a small group of islands off the coast of Scotland, and also the name of a British ship. Kings Cross, a railway station in London, is one of four I remember from the Monopoly board. (The others, Fenchurch, Marylebone and Liverpool, are engraved in my brain from all-day games during the winter school holidays.) St Kilda, Melbourne, named after the ship, became a seaside resort for the wealthy in the nineteenth century. Now it's considered an inner-city suburb. The grand old mansions and Edwardian houses became boarding houses and apartments. Prostitutes have plied their trade there for a hundred years but rents keep rising.

All up, over several stints, I've lived in St Kilda longer than I've lived anywhere else. I like living by the sea, where you can look down a street near the shore and see a horizon of water and sky. You can breathe; jump on your bike and in a couple of minutes be on a track along the bay. It's like living next door to a huge liquid national park. You can smell the sea – salt, seaweed, fish. There's never a body wave, but in the summertime you can swim a couple of hundred metres out to the yellow buoy and back. You have to give it a few days before swimming after rain because a whole lot of junk comes down the stormwater drains. But it doesn't seem to rain so much any more.

Don Walker, of 'Harry' fame, lived in Kings Cross, Sydney's famous red-light and nightclub district, for many years. His place was tucked away down a hill, just off the action, but he could walk up to the bright lights any time he wanted. That's the way he liked it. He wrote a song about a breakfast place on the strip called Sweethearts – 'the coffee's hot and the toast is brown'. And the records he made with Cold Chisel sold like toast and coffee.

Don was sort of related to me for a little while when he was living with the sister of my first wife, Hilary. I played him some songs in the early eighties. The songs didn't last but what Don said did. Not that he said much – he's a man who chooses his words – just told me to keep writing. He couldn't have said a better thing. A few years later he put me up when I got off the bus broke from Melbourne and didn't have a place to stay.

Don had a white grand piano in the front room of his double-storey terrace house. I wrote a few songs on it, including 'Adelaide', inspired by the tune of John Cale's 'Chorale'. I also had some lyrics from a Robert Johnson song in my head – 'From Memphis To Norfolk Is A 36-hour Ride' – which I'd adapted some. I was planning to write a blues. But that beautiful white piano took me somewhere else, took me to The Lovin' Spoonful's 'Never Going Back', a gorgeous tune which mutated into something else via Don's piano. The mutation was pretty infectious. The day it came I couldn't stop humming it and by sunset a set of words was attached. When Don came home I said, 'Can I play you something?' He listened and said, 'You've got your own thing now.'

Not long afterwards I was offered a room in an apartment around the corner by Paul Hewson (same name as Bono), the piano player and songwriter for Dragon. Dragon were huge at the time, all over the radio, the notorious bad boys of Australian pop. When they came to town they laid everything to waste. Two big New Zealand brothers dominated the stage. Todd stood as still as an Easter Island statue, pumping out the bass, while Marc, the lead singer, prowled from side to side. Marc would get girls up from the audience and dry-hump them onstage. Paul, the soulful, rake-thin wizard at the keyboard, hiding behind his long lank hair, wrote the hits – songs like 'Are You Old Enough?', 'I'm Still In Love With You'. They were all smart, ironic, savvy – knew how the levers worked.

Paul and I played songs to and with each other in our little flat. Went out and scored from time to time. During the 1984 Olympics we wrote a song together in an afternoon, about Dean Lukin, the weightlifter and tuna fisherman from Port Lincoln who won a gold medal.

They gave me confidence, Paul and Don. A lot of things in my life were shaky but here were these two guys with heavy reputations, rulers of the roost, giving me their quiet imprimatur. It wasn't that they trumpeted my praises, but when I was with them I felt I was holding my own.

After a while my Melbourne allies Steve and Michael came up to Sydney. Soon I had eleven songs that hung together, songs unlike any I'd written before. I'd found my own little patch of ground, was hoeing a row nobody else was.

Clive Shakespeare, another luminary of the Australian pop scene, retired from the chart-topping group Sherbet, had a home studio in the leafy northern suburbs on the other side of the Harbour Bridge. He was a friendly guy, a good engineer and musician, and charged a decent rate. After two poor-selling albums I was out of favour with record companies and so borrowed the money for the recording sessions from a few friends. We hunkered down at Clive's for a fortnight and cut the songs without drums. Most of it was two instruments – acoustic and electric guitar – and three voices.

I sang 'From St Kilda' late at night in the second week with a heavy cold. It seemed to suit the track. I can't listen to that version now without going all prickly but at the time we thought we were off to the races. By then Paul and I had disbanded the flat in Elizabeth Bay and he'd gone back home to New Zealand to get straight. He took his new-world ways with him. One day I got a phone call from Don with some bad news. Paul, that sweet, elegantly scruffy, melody-leaking man, had died accidentally from an overdose.

Not long afterwards, our record came out. We named it *Post*, and at the suggestion of melody-loving Steve, dedicated it to Paul. This was in 1985. The album slowly recovered its costs and by the end of 1986 I'd paid back my friends.

I still hear Paul's piano on the radio from time to time, Steve's guitar too.

GATHERING STORM

I had a dream
I saw you walking down a road
In a gathering storm

Wind on the rise
A black crow was flying
You alone in a gathering storm

I wake up alone in my bed
There's nothing before my eyes
And outside the door
Only the sighing
And you out there in a gathering storm

So cover your head
Keep your eyes open
Make speed in the gathering storm

I rise up and turn on the light
Now it's shining in my window
My walls are strong
My chimney's smoking
God speed you
In the gathering storm

Fire, Pipe And Ale

As well as art books, there were quite a few paintings in the house of
my childhood. One, a print of a landscape by Dutch artist Meindert
Hobbema, I stared at for many hours growing up. Every night after

dinner we all got down on our knees and said the rosary as a family. The full rosary consists of one Our Father, ten Hail Marys and one Glory Be, and then the whole thing repeated four times. We would do this, unorthodoxly, over two nights – the glorious mysteries, the joyful mysteries, the sorrowful mysteries. If I looked up, the painting was often in my eye line as we droned on, running the words of the prayer together until they were no longer words but one long slurred breath: hailmaryfullofgracethelordiswiththeeblessedart thouamongwomenandblessedisthefruitofthywombjesus . . . (collective inwards rasp) . . . holymarymotherofgodprayforus sinnersnowandatthehourofourdeathamen.

The Hobbema painting that hung in our house was *The Avenue at Middelharnis*. In it a man and a dog walk down a deserted country road. They're in the distance, walking towards the viewer, and the dirt road is colonnaded by straight lines of tall skinny trees. They are sparse and spindly, like gum trees without branches. There's a building – barn? house? – on the right, fields on either side and a steeple far off to the left. The man and the dog look very small. Most of the picture is sky and most of the sky is clouds. Looking at it made me sweetly melancholy as I mumble-chanted with the others. I thought about that smudged man and dog and wondered if they made it home before dark, to a cosy fire, pipe and ale.

Years later I saw the original painting at the National Gallery in London. The sky looked brighter, the clouds billowy and benign. The man and the dog appeared to be walking in the middle of the day. They could have been heading home to lunch, or simply taking a stroll. I'd always thought they were alone but now I noticed other figures in the painting – a couple chatting, a man pruning small trees. Everyone seemed happy. Still, I couldn't quite shake the immanence of our gloomy old print above the bookshelf and its sense of impending doom.

'Gathering Storm' was written for the Bull sisters, Vika and Linda. I always like writing songs for them. Their voices combined sound salty-sweet and have that elusive twinned quality you only get when siblings sing together – two swallows swooping and spiralling in the air as if invisibly girded. Vika has great cut and articulation and can really open up the throttle. Linda is warm and mellow like honey. But they can switch roles. They can both be tough and tender.

I produced their first record, in 1993. During rehearsals their piano player, Jex Saarelaht, gave me a piece of music he thought would suit the girls and asked if I could put lyrics to it. Hobbema's lonely avenue, darkly remembered, hovered above me for a few days. Someone was coming home but not for lunch, and the hour of their coming was known not.

The girls liked the song and we worked hard at it. It was sounding good at rehearsals. We brought in some extra singers for the recording, to give it a gospel flavour. The band played well and the singers sang beautifully. We had all the parts but for some reason we could never quite make the whole. The performance didn't make the cut, so after we were done I picked the song off the cutting-room floor and put it in my pocket to travel. It's been a stayer over the years, a good way to close the show. Sometimes I sing it at the end of an encore to send people home with a sweet melancholy feeling.

She Hears The Storm

There was a time in former years—
While my roof-tree was his—
When I should have been distressed by fears
At such a night as this!

I should have murmured anxiously,
'The prickling rain strikes cold;
His road is bare of hedge or tree,
And he is getting old.'

But now the fitful chimney-roar,
The drone of Thorncombe trees,
The Froom in flood upon the moor,
The mud of Mellstock Leaze,

The candle slanting sooty-wick'd,
The thuds upon the thatch,
The eaves drops on the window flicked,
The clanking garden-hatch,

And what they mean to wayfarers,
I scarcely heed or mind;
He has won that storm-tight roof of hers
Which Earth grants all her kind.

Thomas Hardy

GOD TOLD ME TO

My name is John Johanna, I am misunderstood
Lately I have been accused of grievous murder in cold blood
My mission is most righteous, my cause is true and just
The wicked need chastisement, you know it's either them or us
>God told me to
>I did what I had to do
>God told me to

All around me empty chatter, the old men wring their hands,
Meanwhile in broad daylight Satan gathers his unholy bands
The mighty strength of angels carries me on my seeking flight
My anger is a hammer – you know not its power or the hour
>it strikes!
>>God told me to
>>I answer not to them or you
>>God told me to

Seven golden candles flaming bring forth the Son of Man
In his mouth a two-edged sword, seven stars shining in
>his right hand
The beast has eyes before him, the beast has eyes behind
Those not with me are against me, they're surely gonna feel
>my holy fire
>>· God told me to
>>To thine own self be true
>>God told me to
>>I'm just doing what I have to do
>>God told me to

There Is A Light

Thank God for the Gideons. In most hotel rooms today you can still find a copy of the Bible, more than a hundred years since two travelling salesmen met in a Wisconsin hotel and came up with the idea of God's word being available to wayfarers. They prayed together and made good their word as well as God's. The Gideons, named after a man in the Book of Judges who, like Abraham, was willing to do whatever God asked him, claim they now distribute more than 75 million copies of the holy book each year. That's around 140 a minute.

Fair play to them. Many times I've had cause to give them thanks. Much of what goes on in hotel rooms after gigs would not be called godly by some, but having a bible within reach is very handy when you've run out of things to read, or the book you've brought on tour is a dud.

The Bible has it all – Fellini and Tarantino don't get close. A woman grows out of a man's rib. A serpent speaks and schemes in a garden. A man murders his brother. Ten brothers – sons of Jacob, who swindled his only brother out of his inheritance – sell their eleventh brother, Joseph, into slavery, cover his coat in blood and tell their father he was eaten by a wild animal.

Abraham, the founding father of three major religions, gives his wife to Pharaoh to save his own skin. Later on he hears a voice in his head and sharpens his knife to slaughter his son; takes him to a lonely place and puts his head on the chopping block. Abe's kinsman Lot, another one of the good guys, offers his virgin daughters to a group of men trying to break into his house. 'Do to them as you please,' he says. The men reject them and are blinded by angels. Lot and his daughters then escape the city of Sodom just before it gets holocausted by divine fire. They hole up in a cave, where both his daughters have sex with him while he's drunk. This is after his wife has turned into a pillar of salt.

All this and more and we haven't finished Book One.

Thereafter a country suffers a series of plagues – frogs, gnats, flies, locusts, to name a few – and the whole population breaks out in boils. The firstborn of every house drops dead. The man who brings these curses down from God eventually leads his chosen people to the promised land, the land of milk and honey. There's only one little problem with the promised land: other people live there. That's okay, though, because God's on the side of the chosen people and He's told them what to do. Pity the Canaanites, the Jebusites and the Hittites. They are driven from their homes. Those who are too slow to leave – men, women, children – are exterminated.

The early pages of the Bible are not all treachery and mayhem. Abraham stays the knife and does not slay his son. Joseph reconciles with his brothers in passages of testing tenderness – they end up weeping on each other's necks. But as a moral code and a guide to living, the Bible is largely incoherent. Should one take an eye for an eye and a tooth for a tooth, or turn the other cheek? (Those arguing proverbs again.) You shouldn't compare the loving, caring New Testament with the stern harsh old one, some people say.

But the Old Testament itself is all over the place. It was written by many people at different times for different societies. Millions, though, claim it as the direct word of God. If this is so then God is often angry, petulant and confused (like a cranky old man with Alzheimer's). He repeats himself and gets his facts mixed up. He can't remember whether Moses is allowed to look upon His face or not. He gets so fed up with His chosen people He wants to wipe out every last one of them, until Moses convinces Him it's not such a smart idea (because who, then, would fulfill his covenant?).

The New Testament, supposedly gentler and more modern, ends with the raving, psychotic Book of Revelations, with its avenging angels, the whore of babylon, the beast with eyes fore and aft, Armageddon and the fiery pit. Not to mention sweet Jesus in the Gospels upending tables in the temple, bringing 'the sword not peace' and refusing to recognise his own mother.

Overall, the holy book is a strange brew of pettiness and grandeur, whim and wisdom. Deep inside Leviticus – after struggling through a thicket of oppressive, obsessive taboos, restrictions and laws on animal sacrifice, the treatment of slaves, diet, crossbreeding, cleanliness, boils, bald spots, homosexuality, menstruating women, and the mixing of fabrics – you suddenly find yourself in a clear sunlit glade of ringing generosity:

> You shall not pick your vineyard bare, or gather the fallen fruit of your vineyard; you shall leave them for the poor and the stranger . . .
> You shall not steal; you shall not deal deceitfully or falsely with one another . . .
> You shall not defraud your fellow. You shall not commit robbery. The wages of a laborer shall not remain with you until morning.
> You shall not insult the deaf, or place a stumbling block before the blind . . .
> You shall not render an unfair decision; do not favor the poor or show deference to the rich; judge your kinsman fairly. Do not deal basely with your countrymen. Do not profit by the blood of your fellow . . .
> You shall not hate your kinsfolk in your heart. Reprove your kinsman but incur no guilt because of him. You shall not take vengeance or bear a grudge against your countrymen. Love your fellow as yourself . . .

This stands tall with the Ten Commandments. The language beautiful and direct. And just a few verses on there's more: 'If a stranger sojourn with you on your land you shall not vex him. But the stranger that dwells with you shall be unto you as one born unto you. And you shall love him as yourself. For you were strangers in the land of Egypt.'

Here is a handbook for moral living. Here, clearly expressed, is the importance of charity, tolerance, fair dealing; the rights of workers, refugees and the disabled, and the fight against corruption and war profiteering. Let it be printed in bold letters on a big board and hung in every government office across the land.

The Bible will always surprise you. Out of its pages come heroes that ring true as real people, deeply flawed. Abraham, Moses and David get angry, depressed, scared, and do things they are ashamed of.

Lying on your bed in a hotel room, waiting to go to sound check, idly browsing, you find a passage that stops your heart. 'Before God, I'm a dancer!' says King David, boogying before the multitude and embarrassing his wife. Yea, verily, it is the gift that keeps on giving. Those early-seventeenth-century bishops, under orders from King James to produce a new bible, translating from the Hebrew via Greek and Latin, gave us our highest and best English. Gave us cadence, strength and song. If I reach for the good book as I lie dying it won't be to pander to the priest, nor because (like Pascal with his wager) I'd rather believe in a God that doesn't exist than not believe in a God that does. It will be to read The Song of Songs one more time.

Then again, who's to say I'll get the chance to lie dying? A ten-tonne truck or a double-decker bus may crash into me. A heart attack or stroke may drop this body standing. All that's out of my hands. And God's too, for that matter.

(THE) GIFT THAT KEEPS ON GIVING

The gift that keeps on giving
Has come into my house
Like a wild deer at my doorway
He was suddenly so close
My beams are made of cedar wood
My rafters made of fir
My garden holds a fountain, honeycomb and myrrh

I went along the broad ways
Searching for my love
I asked among the watchmen
'Have you seen my love?'
Oh, promise not to wake him, sisters
Let him sleep his time
He comforts me with apples and succours me with wine

Holy night! Blessed daylight!
You are my true delight

I sought whom my soul loveth
I sought him on my bed
His right hand doth embrace me
His left under my head
He brought me to the banquet house
And when I looked above
Then I saw his banner over me was love

Cut And Paste

As children we used to throw a series of jokey insults around: Your eyes are like pools – mud pools. Your ears are like flowers – cauliflowers. Your teeth are like stars – they come out at night . . .

I didn't realise until years later that this litany was a parody of The Song of Solomon, also known as The Song of Songs, from the Old Testament, a love poem in which King Solomon (supposedly) and his beloved – the Rose of Sharon – declare their love to each other and the world.

Thy teeth are like a flock of sheep that are even shorn . . . thy belly is like an heap of wheat set about with lilies . . . thy two breasts are like two young roes that are twins, which feed among the lilies . . . thy navel is like a round goblet, which wanteth not liquor . . . thine eyes like the fishpools in Heshbon . . . thy nose is as the tower of Lebanon which looketh toward Damascus . . .

I don't remember hearing these words at Sunday mass, though I heard a lot of passages from the Bible over the years. Perhaps the priests avoided them, discomforted by their frank sensuality. They may have felt they were dangerous falling on fresh young ears, giving rise to lustful thoughts. Because The Song of Solomon, written at high pitch in the language of intoxication, drips with sex.

Let him kiss me with the kisses of his mouth: for thy love is better than wine . . . A bundle of myrrh is my well-beloved unto me; he shall lie all night betwixt my breasts . . . I sat down under his shadow with great delight, and his fruit was sweet to my taste . . .

My beloved put in his hand by the hole of the door, and my bowels were moved for him . . . my hands dropped with myrrh . . . I opened to my beloved . . . His mouth is most sweet: yea, he is altogether lovely . . . How fair and how pleasant art thou, O love, for delights!

Some Bible commentators suggest that the poem is an allegory of Christ and the Church, with the Church as the bride. Er . . . yeah, right. Spin on. A scholar friend of mine tells me that when the different texts were being collated for the collection that became the Bible, The Song of Songs, famous already, was just too good to leave out. The attribution to Solomon came later. Whoever he is, he loves Sharon and Sharon loves him. This is a man and a woman speaking boldly to each other, aching for each other, high on each other's love. It's one of the shortest books in the Bible but as a poem it's long. Too long for a pop song. So I ended up telling Shazza's side of the story only, cutting and pasting some of her lines and giving her a couple of new ones.

New Zealand singer Bic Runga had first bite at 'The Gift', recording it in 2002. She dropped the third verse. Was it the 'loveth' and the 'doth'? I asked her. Too tangling for the tongue? No, it wasn't that, she said, it was just that she felt no more needed to be said after 'You are my true delight.' Fair enough. I missed the third verse, but as far as I'm concerned Bic can do what she likes. She's an exotic queen, the Rose of Aotearoa, a *tour de force* songwriter and a performer you lean into.

Dan Kelly and I sang 'The Gift' together for the first time in public at the 2004 A–Z shows in the Spiegeltent. It was a warm summer night. Steam was rising from the audience, who'd got wet under a sudden downpour while waiting to enter. We sang it soft, on eggshells, feeling it come out of our mouths like a trembling newborn turtledove. We'll never be able to sing it that way again.

GLORY BE TO GOD

Here comes the one that I adore – glory be to God!
And I'm the one she's come here for – glory be to God!
Throws her arms around my neck, oh glory be to God!
Presses in against my chest – glory be to God!
Glory be to God! Glory be to God!

She's got a smile that shames the sun – glory be to God!
Undoes her buttons one by one – glory be to God!
On my knees before her splendour, oh glory be to God!
She knows she's a natural wonder – glory be to God!
Glory be to God! Glory be to God!

Her eyes closed in trust above me – glory be to God!
We both start shaking like a leaf on a tree, oh glory be to God!
Glory be to God! Glory be to God! Glory be to God!

Ad Majorem Dei Gloriam

I don't think of God as a he or a listener or a she . . . I just
love the word. I love using it. It sings, you know? It's sweet.
It's a sweet word. I'm at ease with it. My ancestors used it.
Some wonderful musicians and composers and poets used
it. They must have been talking about something.

Michael Leunig, talking to
Andrew Denton on *Enough Rope*

'There! No – there! Right . . . there! There! There! There! Yes!
There!' Their ecstatic machinery would have dazzled Aquinas
had his senses experienced its economy. If anything served as

an argument for the existence of God, if anything marked creation with God's essence, it was the thousands and thousands of orgasms dancing on the head of that pin. The mother of the microchip, the triumph of evolution, right up with the retina and the tympanic membrane. Why do they need jewelry, when they have that? What's a ruby next to that? There for no reason other than the reason it's there for. Not to run water through, not to spread seed, but included in the package like the toy at the bottom of the old Cracker Jack box, a gift to each and every little girl from God. All hail the maker, a generous wonderful fun-loving guy with a real soft spot for women.

Philip Roth, from *Sabbath's Theater*

GOING ABOUT MY FATHER'S BUSINESS

Standing in the darkness watching while you sleep
I can hear you softly breathing while I creep
Going about my father's business
Doing my father's time
What's done to me I'll do to mine

I woke up one summer morning – he was gone
Soft light through the window breaking for my son
Going about my father's business
Doing my father's time
What's done to me I'll do to mine

Know them by what they do
Let no one speak for you
Just this I beg of you
Forgive me, forgive me

Someday when we sign the treaty I'll be home
War is long and lasts forever and I'm your own
Going about my father's business
Doing my father's time
What's done to me I'll do to mine
What's done to me I'll do to mine

Gloaming

I had a terrible temper as a child. I once tried to maim my brother
John with a cricket ball, throwing it at him with full force from just
feet away, aiming for his head. I'm glad I missed. And so is he.

That was the one and only time my father struck me. I must have been about ten or eleven and John two and a half years older. We had a big backyard with a gravel tennis court which was the venue for all our games, football, cricket, Romans and Christians. In the latter the court became the Colosseum, those of us riding bikes the Romans in chariots, and those on foot, usually the younger children, the poor Christians, trying to avoid getting run over and crushed beneath the wheels. Sometimes we even played tennis.

On this particular occasion, as on many, the court had become the Adelaide Oval. We were in the gloaming, at the end of one of our test cricket games, England versus Australia. Not the end of the match – they were endless – but the end of that day's play. Stumps was called when the light died, and unlike the precious professionals of today, we walked off only when the last pigments of sunset had finally drained away. That's probably why I was so close to John when I attempted the murder on my boiling mind. Any further away and I wouldn't have seen him.

Maybe subconsciously I meant to miss – it should have been easy to nail him – but Mum didn't miss a thing. On the back verandah, unnoticed by us, she saw, with a mother's all-seeing, gloom-penetrating eyes, the climax of the drama, and from the tone of her voice as she called us in I knew I was in for more than a scolding.

Dad was duly informed and I was summoned to the boys' bedroom. I remember there was some delay between the incident and the sentence. The crime was carefully weighed, judgement fully considered, and the criminal given plenty of time to reflect on the gravity of his most serious offence.

Punishment, as those old Italians knew, is a dish best served cold. The waiting was the worst part. Finally Dad entered the room. He was a tender, gentle father, which made what he was about to do more terrible. He moved calmly, kept his voice low and commanded me to lie across his lap, belly down. I must never, ever do such a thing again, he told me, and then struck three controlled blows on the seat of my pants with his open hand. Never was a son so chastened.

And brother John, where was he? Hiding and listening somewhere?

Relieved or scared? Perhaps he got a spanking too, under the Where There's Smoke There's Fire principle. I can't recall why I'd been so mad at him – maybe he'd been gloating over a caught-behind on the last ball of the day (caught by the back fence), or perhaps there was a disputed decision in the dusk – but I was deeply shocked at what I'd done. Five decades on I can still see the whites of his eyes.

We did a lot of fighting in those days. It seems that's all we ever did, us kids – one big brawling mob. And now we're like old soldiers with an undying bond from a long campaign. The blood spilt on the soil of childhood has bound us together forever.

Coming from a large family gives you a feeling of being safe in the world – knowing that there are people who will always love you and take you in, no matter how much you fuck up or get fucked over. Rubbing up against brothers and sisters teaches you when to stand up for yourself and when to give ground. You learn to try to allow the space to fight, to create a place – at work, among friends, within the families you make – where everyone feels they can say what's on their mind, argue their case strongly, suggest a different way of thinking, and where, if you don't get your own way, you don't pick up the red rock-hard cricket ball and throw it straight at the whites of the eyes.

HOW TO MAKE GRAVY

Hello Dan, it's Joe here, I hope you're keeping well
It's the 21st of December, and now they're ringing the last bells
If I get good behaviour, I'll be out of here by July
Won't you kiss my kids on Christmas Day, please don't let 'em cry
    for me
I guess the brothers are driving down from Queensland and Stella's
    flying in from the coast
They say it's gonna be a hundred degrees, even more maybe, but
    that won't stop the roast
Who's gonna make the gravy now? I bet it won't taste the same
Just add flour, salt, a little red wine and don't forget a dollop of
    tomato sauce for sweetness and that extra tang
And give my love to Angus and to Frank and Dolly
Tell 'em all I'm sorry I screwed up this time
And look after Rita, I'll be thinking of her early Christmas morning
When I'm standing in line

I hear Mary's got a new boyfriend, I hope he can hold his own
Do you remember the last one? What was his name again?
What was his problem? He never did get Nina Simone
And Roger, you know I'm even gonna miss Roger
'Cause there's sure as hell no one in here I want to fight
Oh praise the Baby Jesus, have a Merry Christmas
I'm really gonna miss it, all the treasure and the trash
And later in the evening, I can just imagine,
You'll put on Junior Murvin and push the tables back
And you'll dance with Rita, I know you really like her
Just don't hold her too close, oh brother please don't stab me
    in the back
I didn't mean to say that, it's just my mind it plays up
Multiplies each matter, turns imagination into fact
You know I love her badly, she's the one to save me

I'm gonna make some gravy, I'm gonna taste the fat
Tell her that I'm sorry, yeah I love her badly, tell 'em all I'm sorry
And kiss the sleepy children for me
You know one of these days, I'll be making gravy
I'll be making plenty, I'm gonna pay 'em all back

Nativity

Immensity cloistered in thy dear womb,
Now leaves His well-belov'd imprisonment,
There He hath made Himself to His intent
Weak enough, now into the world to come;
But O, for thee, for Him, hath the inn no room?
Yet lay Him in this stall, and from the Orient,
Stars and wise men will travel to prevent
The effect of Herod's jealous general doom.
Seest thou, my soul, with thy faith's eyes, how He
Which fills all place, yet none holds Him, doth lie?
Was not His pity towards thee wondrous high,
That would have need to be pitied by thee?
Kiss Him, and with Him into Egypt go,
With His kind mother, who partakes thy woe.

John Donne

Something In The Air

Jesus was born at Christmas and died at Easter. What are the odds of that?

Captain Frodo from La Clique

In 1996 I was approached to take part in a Christmas charity record organised by Lindsay Fields, guitar player and backing singer for John Farnham's band. It's an annual project of his. Various artists sing carols and Christmas-themed songs to raise money for the Salvation Army.

I chose 'Christmas Must Be Tonight', written by Robbie Robertson and recorded by The Band, but the song had already been claimed by country singer James Blundell. 'Okay,' I said to Lindsay, 'maybe I could have a go at writing my own Christmas song.'

'All right,' he said. 'I'll give you a call in a few weeks.'

I had a rough tune I'd been kicking around with the band at sound check, but was having trouble getting started on the words. Christmas has been pretty well covered over the years. For inspiration I went to one of my all-time favourite records, *A Christmas Gift for You from Phil Spector,* featuring The Crystals, The Ronettes and others. I play this record loud every Christmas morning. Darlene Love comes right out of the blocks with a jaw-dropping rendition of 'White Christmas', written by Irving Berlin and first recorded by Bing Crosby.

For a long time 'White Christmas' – Bing's version – was the greatest-selling record of all time, until Princess Diana died and Elton John's 'Candle In The Wind' went viral. I wouldn't be surprised if Bing regains the lead at some stage. There's something about 'White Christmas' that rings down the ages – a longing for home, for childhood, warm safety and the way things used to be. Irving Berlin, the grand old man of American music, who lived to a hundred and one, cleverly sets the song a world away from the Christmas snow scene he describes. In the rarely performed talking bit, Darlene tells us:

> The sun is shining, the grass is green,
> The orange and palm trees sway.
> There's never been such a day in old LA,
> But it's December the 24th,
> And I am longing to be up north.

Irving intensifies the feeling of Christmas by writing about not being there.

There's a clue, I thought.

Once I turned that key, my carol wrote itself. I made most of it up as usual, though the general atmosphere is a lot like our Kelly Christmas gatherings, where there's generally a large and diverse cast, the odd stray, new and old flames, gossip, singing, and much discussion and planning of food before, during and after the celebrations. The gravy recipe comes direct from my first father-in-law.

I rang Lindsay. 'I have a Christmas song,' I said, 'but it doesn't have a chorus and it's set in prison.'

'I better come over and have a listen.'

The next day he sat in my small back shed while I played it to him, my head down, partly from nerves but also to read the fresh-scratched lyrics in my notebook on the floor. When I looked up at the end he was holding his hanky.

'It's supposed to be a comedy,' I said.

'I know,' he replied, wiping his eyes. He said he loved the song but still had to take it to the board (who were more inclined towards 'Little Drummer Boy', 'Good King Wenceslas' and such) for approval. He did so and got it over the line, God bless him. I've been playing it ever since – Lent, Easter, midyear, All Souls' Day, Advent, whenever.

A few years later Lindsay approached me again for the Salvos. This time I got in early and put in my dibs for 'Christmas Must Be Tonight'. That's the great thing about Christmas. It comes around every year so you always get another shot.

Some Other Christmas Humdingers

'Santa Baby' – Eartha Kitt

'Fairytale Of New York' – The Pogues with Kirsty MacColl

'Christmas Is A Joyful Day' – Lord Executor

'River' – Joni Mitchell

'What Will Santa Claus Say (When He Finds Everybody
  Swingin'?)' – Louis Prima

'Lady Gay' – Buell Kazee'

'Christmas Just Ain't Christmas Without The One You Love' –
  The O'Jays

'Holy Babe' – Kelly Pace, Aaron Brown, Joe Green, Paul Hayes and
  Matthew Johnson

'The Christmas Song (Chestnuts Roasting On An Open Fire)' –
  Mel Tormé

'The Christmas Song' – The Raveonettes

'At The Christmas Ball' – Bessie Smith

'Joy To The World' – Aaron Neville and The Blind Boys of Alabama

'2000 Miles' – The Pretenders

'Who Took The Merry Out Of Christmas?' – The Staple Singers

'Fiesta De Navidad' – Celia Cruz

'Jesus Christ' – Big Star

'Just Like Christmas' – Low

'On A Christmas Day' – C. W. Stoneking

I CAN'T BELIEVE WE WERE MARRIED

We danced in the kitchen on Boxing Day
I held you swaying in my arms to Marvin Gaye
Our Christmas ham turned green by New Year's Eve
We weren't hungry anyway
Now sometimes we see each other on the street
Maybe at a hotel or some party
We say hello then we have to go
I can't believe we were married
That we were wed

Our houses were a shambles, our love conspiracy
Your hand was always down my pants
Before our guests could leave
They didn't like our drugs, our children or our dogs
The way we made it up each day
Now the kids have grown we talk on the phone
If one of them is sick or needs some money
Our words are dry, so measured and polite
I can't believe we were married
That we were wed

Now maybe if I'm with someone you come into my mind
The one I knew with your certain little cries
You're not the only one to come rushing in
It's like a party line
Yeah sometimes we see each other on the street
Maybe at a concert or some party
We say hello talk about the show
I can't believe we were married
Yeah we say hello then we have to go
You send your regards to all my family

And the years have changed even the sound of your name
I can't believe that we were married
That we were wed

Christmas Lunch In St Kilda Early In The New Millennium

(a small one without the whole mob)

Who came:
My sister and her ex-husband
Their children
My brother and his wife
Their children
My first wife and her new partner
Our son
Our son's girlfriend
My first wife's son to her ex-partner (half-brother to our son)
My second wife
Our two daughters
My second wife's stepmother and her daughter, who is the
    half-sister of my second wife
My second wife's mother and her partner
My second wife's brother and his new fiancé
My girlfriend
My nephew (a very good cook)

I CLOSE MY EYES AND THINK OF YOU

When another day has ended
And everything's been said and done
And the lights across the valley
All go out one by one
I close my eyes
I close my eyes and think of you
I close my heavy eyes
That's all I need to do

Sometimes when I get a moment
In the middle of the day
And nothing else needs my attention
I take my chance and slip away
I close my eyes
I close my eyes and think of you
I close my weary eyes
That's all I need to do

I hear the big trucks changing gears
As they go rolling by my door
The driver counts his days 'til he gets home
If I could only count my days
But I just don't know what's in store
I've been so long on my own

I know there's a singing river
I've heard about the golden shore
But I would pass by all that beauty
Just to be with you once more
I close my eyes
I close my eyes and think of you

I close my heavy eyes
And that's all I need to do
I close my weary eyes
And that's when I think of you

Return, Beloved Ideal

When my grandfather was born he had such a big baby chest he was named Ercole, Italian for Hercules. It was the year 1885 and his Italian parents were visiting their relatives in Buenos Aires. His mother died in childbirth and his father not long after in a train crash, so he was brought up in Argentina by his childless uncle and aunt, Count Michelangelo Tonti and his wife Giuseppina.

Ercole discovered, as a stocky young man, that he had a strong baritone voice, and so put aside his medical ambitions in order to study operatic singing. He became a big success in Buenos Aires, which led to his being offered a three-year contract at Milan's renowned opera house, La Scala. It was there he first sang the part of Rigoletto, the hunchbacked jester in Verdi's great opera.

There is an old picture in my house of Ercole in costume for the role. In mid-gesture, with arms waving and dark eyes flashing, he looks the dead spit of my eldest brother Martin, though I've never seen Martin in striped leggings, ruffled sleeves and a three-cornered hat.

Rigoletto became Ercole's signature role. As with most operas, the story is too intricate to tell in brief, but gives a singer/actor the chance to display the full range of histrionics. The jester, labouring under a curse, is both mocker and mocked, schemer and schemed against. The story has many of the staple operatic ingredients – cross-dressing, a vendetta, a mis-stabbing, and a man singing about the inconstancy and interchangeability of women. It ends with Rigoletto in the dark by the river, opening a sack, expecting to see the dead body of his enemy but discovering instead his dying daughter.

Ercole was born for the part – he had the build, the voice and the gusto. There was never a dry eye in the house.

During World War I, when the opera houses of Europe closed, two Spanish entrepreneurs, the Gonzales Brothers, formed a stable of Italian singers who weren't eligible for military call-up to tour India, New Zealand and Australia. Ercole joined them, having already completed his army training in Argentina. At the tour's end, he and several others decided to stay in Australia rather than return to war-torn Europe.

Ercole opened a singing school in a warehouse down a laneway off George Street, in the centre of Sydney. Among his students was a tall redhead named Anne McParland, the only child of Irish immigrants. Her mother was from a well-known Dublin musical family. Her father, from Newry in the north, too young to inherit the family farm, had sailed to the colony of New South Wales to seek his fortune. Anne had a bachelor of arts degree, was attending choral and music classes at the Sydney Conservatorium, and wanted to take her singing further. She'd already seen Count Ercole Tonti-Filippini in concert – the double-barrelled name came from his father and uncle, with the title handed down by his uncle in the hope of advancing his musical career – and had been quite smitten.

As well as giving lessons, Ercole would sometimes put on concerts featuring his students and other Italian singers. At one of these Anne, now studying with Ercole, was to sing two songs by the nineteenth-century composer Paolo Tosti. During a lesson, after she'd rehearsed one of them, 'Ideale', *il maestro* said to *la studentessa*, 'Now I sing for you.' As he sang it dawned on her that he was singing to her as a suitor, not a teacher.

Outside in the gathering dusk, the sounds of the young city – the cries of the street sellers, the jangle and clop of the horse-drawn carriages, the evening birds – faded away. Years later Anne recalled leaving the studio 'walking on air'. On Armistice Day 1918 they announced their engagement, and shortly afterwards were married.

Ideale

Io ti seguii come 'iride di pace
Lungo le vie del cielo;
Io ti seguii come un'amica face
De la notte nel velo.
E ti senti ne la luce, ne l'aria,
Nel profumo dei fiori;
E fu piena la stanza solitaria di te,
Dei tuoi splendori.
In te rapito,
Al suon de la tua voce
Lungamente sognai,
E de la terra ogni affanno, ogni croce
In quel giorno scordai.
Torna, caro ideal,
Torna un istante
A sorridermi ancora,
E a me risplenderà nel tuo sembiante
*   una novell'aurora.*
*   una novell'aurora.*
Torna, caro ideal, torna, torna!

Carmelo Errico

I followed you like a rainbow of peace
A long way across the sky;
I followed you like a friendly face
    of the night under a veil.
And you feel it in the light, in the air,
In the scent of the flowers;
And the solitary room was full of you,
    of your splendours.
Captivated by you, by the sound of your voice
A long time I dreamed,

And all the worry of the earth, every cross
In that day is forgotten.
Return, beloved ideal,
Return for an instant.
Give me a smile again,
And to me the sparkle of your countenance
    will be a new dawn.
. . . a new dawn.
Return, beloved ideal, return, return!

Laugh, Ugly Cow, Laugh!

The saga of our grandparents, Nonna and Nonno, was told and retold in our family over the years, becoming burnished myth. Nonna lived 'til the age of ninety-one and had a vivid recollection of her adventures as Contessa Filippini. (How she loved that title.) Throughout the 1920s she and Ercole formed a series of opera companies around Australia. They were the first to stage live opera in Adelaide and Perth, setting up a base in those cities for a couple of years at a time.

In 1921 they toured Queensland, going as far north as Cairns and as far west as Longreach and Winton. Along the coast there were many Italians working in the cane fields who were thrilled to see and hear excerpts from *Cavalleria Rusticana*, *La Traviata*, *Rigoletto* and *Pagliacci*. The company on that tour consisted of eight principal singers, a chorus of ten, a pianist, two violinists, a manager and an advance agent. All the male principals were Italian, and the leading tenor, Balboni, in true operatic tradition, was temperamental, jealous and crazy. In her self-published memoirs, which she wrote when she was eighty-seven, Nonna tells the story:

In Rockhampton, Balboni was singing the famous clown's song 'Ridi, Pagliaccio' ('Laugh, clown, laugh'). He always sang and acted the aria with great emotion and invariably had the audience spellbound as he turned on the tears. A very stout lady in the front row of the audience was so affected that she became hysterical. Balboni thought that she was laughing at him and, approaching the footlights in front of her, instead of singing the words '*Ridi, Pagliaccio*', he bellowed at her: '*Ridi, brutta vaca!*' ('Laugh, you ugly old cow, you!') Luckily, the act's ending brought the curtain down on further abuse.

The prolific Australian author Frank Clune was one of the choristers, and he too wrote about that tour, in his first book *Try Anything Once*, detailing the trials and tribulations of the company – the heat, the snafus, late trains, factions, intrigues, dissatisfactions and financial problems.

Nearly ninety years later, I tour many of the same cities and towns and do it, I'm sure, a lot easier: in air-conditioned hire cars, with hotels booked and tickets sold in advance, a professional crew, a diligent management team, mobile phones, balanced budgets and a generally happy band. Occasionally I've sung in some of the same theatres, trod the same wooden stages. Every time I play at Her Majesty's in Adelaide, the home of Nonna and Nonno's South Australian Grand Opera Company throughout 1924–25, I hear in my mind those ghostly bel canto voices and see poor misshapen Rigoletto sobbing over his only daughter as the curtain comes down. I think of Balboni, who jumped off the train in Toowoomba and went back to Sydney, where he tried to commit suicide by cutting his throat, was certified insane and died soon after in an asylum. And sometimes during 'How To Make Gravy' or 'Every Fucking City' I want to lean over to the person looking glum and vacant in the front row and yell 'Laugh, you stupid stone, laugh!'

Nancy, Take The Stick!

My grandmother Anne was Nancy or Nance by now. Ercole, who had definite ideas, didn't believe his wife should sing lead roles onstage, though she had a fine voice. Nor should she be mixing it with the chorus. Her role as his wife and partner was to look after the administrative and financial details, and run rehearsals for the singers. This she did very well.

In Adelaide a Russian conductor named Stempinski was engaged for the 1924 season at Her Majesty's. He had a great reputation in Europe, supposedly, but was soon struggling at rehearsals because of his poor command of English. He kept calling out a word in Russian which sounded like 'Brass', perplexing the French horn and trumpet players waiting to come in. Utter confusion ensued, at which point Ercole stepped up to the footlights and called to his wife, 'Nancy, *prend' il bastone!*' ('Nancy, take the stick!')

Nonna took the baton and kept it, and conducted that season and seven others thereafter in various capital cites. And so became the first woman ever to conduct an orchestra in Australia.

Over twelve years, Ercole and Nance spread the gospel of Grand Opera, pulling up stakes in one city and putting them down in another for six months or a year or more. They had two children, Michelangelo and Giuseppina, named after his adopted parents. Giuseppina became my mother, Josephine, and Michelangelo my Uncle Nino.

Nance's widowed mother Mary lived and moved with them all this time, helping out with the children. She and Ercole were very fond of each other, though she spoke no Italian and he never learnt English, claiming that to do so would ruin his singing voice. Nance translated for them. He loved to play little jokes. His most elaborate, which rings down the years, occurred not long after they'd moved into a house in Sydney's Chatswood. The house had a fowl run so they bought laying hens, of which Nonna Mary was very proud. Somehow Ercole managed to suck out the contents of several eggs and replace them with flour. He placed the doctored eggs on top of the bowl of fresh ones. Mary was dumbstruck one morning when, on breaking one egg after another, out came nothing but white powder. She turned to Ercole, who had been watching with apparent indifference, secretly revelling in her bewilderment.

'Oh, Nonna, you'll have to stop feeding those fowls on spaghetti!' he exclaimed, before she chased him out of the kitchen.

This oft-told story has always fascinated me. How did he get the flour into the eggs? One day I decided to put the story to the test. With a drawing pin, I made a tiny hole at one end of the egg, widened it a little, then sucked out the contents. That was the easy part. Getting the flour in was a whole other story. Maybe there's a secret Italian technique that needs to be passed on, perhaps the very same knowledge that lies hidden beneath the phrase 'Don't teach your grandmother how to suck eggs.' But unfortunately any such secrets remained hidden from me. Instead I reinvented the wheel over the course of several days while listening to music or watching the cricket.

When it was done at last and I'd dusted off little trails of flour all around the house, the egg seemed suspiciously light. And that was merely one egg. According to the story there were several on top of the pile. The patience, cunning and determination required to make such a trick succeed are truly impressive. But my grandfather came from the country with multiple proverbs on the plotting of revenge. You hatch your plans, you bide your time and then – you make a scene that astounds.

In 1934, after twelve years of peripatetic existence, the tight little three-generation family – Mary, Ercole, Nance and the two children – were back in Melbourne when Nonna Mary died suddenly at home from a heart attack. She was found on the floor by her granddaughter Josephine. Ercole, around that time, was also becoming unwell. He had trouble walking, fell several times and began to use a stick. His

doctor was puzzled, though later he told Nance that her husband suffered from peripheral neuritis, complicated by a gastric ulcer.

In order to be able to sing comfortably, Ercole didn't eat before his
concerts, so would have a big meal when he came home. He became
particularly ill one night after Nance made him his favourite dish of
'salted ling fish in a sauce of onions, tomato paste, parsley, almonds,
raisins and claret'. Five weeks after his mother-in-law died he went
into hospital, and five days later, shockingly, he too was dead. Nance
worried for years afterwards that the spicy late-night meals she cooked
him may have exacerbated his condition.

Nonna Nance was now suddenly an orphan and a single mother
at the age of thirty-eight. She had skills, though, fierce drive and a
strong religious faith. She picked herself up and went to work for
wages. My mother remembers being in and out of boarding schools
as Nance did the rounds of the Catholic schools, teaching singing,
conducting choirs and putting on pageants. She became the darling
of Dr Mannix, the long-serving, charismatic and controversial Arch-
bishop of Melbourne. Originally from Ireland, he especially loved her
spectacular St Patrick's Day parades, and the huge massed concerts
she staged with combined school choirs.

Still known as the Contessa, she lunched with governors, escorted
war chiefs to dinner, and had tea several times with Dame Nellie
Melba. Despite her devout Catholicism, Nonna maintained a lifelong
friendship with Australian author and communist Katharine Susannah
Prichard, whom she'd first met in Perth. According to Nonna, Katharine
tried to convert her, but although they agreed on the 'universal brother-
hood of man', Nonna felt that 'Christmases' spent at Katharine's home
in Kalamunda – a get-together of family and friends to celebrate the
summer solstice – were empty of meaning.

Some of the scenes from the film *Shine* were set in Katharine's house.
When my mother watched the film in her seventies she had flashbacks
to her childhood visits, so faithful was the recreation of the rooms
within.

John First, God Second

Josephine Alisa Tonti Filippini grew up bilingual until the age of ten, speaking only Italian to her father until his death. As well as her school subjects, which included French and German, she studied singing and piano. When World War II began she was sixteen. By 1942, three years into the war, she'd been engaged several times. One engagement only lasted overnight. She broke it off in the morning. 'It must have been the moonlight,' she told us later. 'And the war. It created a kind of fever.'

We liked to tease Mum from time to time about all her boy-friends before Dad. But everything was above board, she told us. An American colonel, Harry Hannigan, who was in charge of a company of marines on leave from Guadalcanal, took a particular shine to her. He would send her flowers, pick her up in his car with a driver and take her out to dinner and a dance. He was more than twice her age, and married. Nance trusted him, though, and on the nights they went out would leave a cold supper and a warm fire for when he brought her home. 'Look after my girl,' she said to Harry. And by all accounts he did.

Jo became very popular with her girlfriends. With so many Australian men away fighting or on army bases, the Americans had the field to themselves. They also had glamour, gifts and good manners. Whenever Jo and her pals wanted to have a party or go out dancing, all she had to do was call the colonel, who'd round up his men.

Around this time John Kelly, a young Adelaide lawyer, came on the scene. He'd had tuberculosis when he was younger and was ineligible for military service, so had come to Melbourne to work for the Rationing Commission division of the War Office. He met Nance and Jo through a cousin of his who used to play piano for Ercole, and soon became a regular visitor. The house was a haven to him. He loved the music, the interesting cooking and the in-demand, dark-eyed beauty. And Nance adored him – his brain, his gentle teasing and his steadiness.

The colonel's late-night suppers with Jo grew longer and longer, as his driver dozed outside in the Packard. Nance grew anxious. One night John came calling only to find that Jo was out at an officers' party. Nance told him of her concern at the colonel's increasing attentions. The next night, John took Jo out to dinner at the Latin Café in the city and proposed to her. There was no bended knee, no 'Will you marry me?' The only question popped was 'What are we going to call our children?'

His confidence was well placed, despite his lack of ceremony, and soon Colonel Harry was out of the picture. John and Josephine married in 1942, she and the bridesmaids in borrowed dresses – fabric was scarce – and he in his best suit. Not long before the end of the war they moved to his hometown, where he rejoined his father's law firm and she charmed and challenged his family, teaching them new ways to cook – minestrone, osso bucco, garlic squid, tripe in onions and wine. They wanted children straightaway but, frustratingly, it didn't happen. After five years with no success they had the whole town praying for them – the congregation of the church, their families and friends. Jo went to Melbourne for an operation. It was her first time away from her husband. She wrote to him saying she was so miserable she just wanted to 'go out to the garden and eat worms'. On her return home she became pregnant. Hallelujah!

The child was named Anne, after her grandmother. A year and a day later came Sheila. From then on the children didn't stop coming. They had nine in thirteen years. They could turn the prayers on but they couldn't turn them off. Not that they wanted to.

Being Catholic in Adelaide in the forties, fifties and sixties, according to Mum, was the same as being a second-class citizen. Protestant prejudice, both blatant and subtle, was all-pervasive. In the professions, Catholics could only go so far. It was almost impossible to become a judge or government minister. A lot of Dad's friends from his university days were Anglican, educated at the prestigious St Peters and

Prince Alfred private schools. Mum recalls one of the wives saying to her at a party, 'Jo, I keep forgetting you're a Catholic. You're so normal!'

Catholics did a pretty good line in superiority themselves. The Proddies might pull the levers of state but we had the keys to the kingdom. A friend of mine once asked his grandmother what the difference was between Protestants and Catholics.

'Well, it's simple really,' came her reply. 'The Protestants think they're right but we *know* we're right.'

All four of my brothers and I served as altar boys, assisting the priest at mass, ringing the bells for the offertory and the sanctus, handing him the wine. Down the years, the whole family, boys and girls, went through the coming-of-age ceremonies, the first being holy communion, around the age of seven, when you became eligible to receive the holy host – the thin round consecrated wafer representing the body of Christ. Now we could join the snaking queue to the priest on Sundays, kneel down before him and the hovering altar boy, close our eyes and put out our tongues to take the melting bread, after which we'd walk back to the pew feeling ourselves filling up with grace.

Preparing for your first communion meant having your first confession, because you couldn't take Christ's body into yours unless you'd been washed clean of your sins. After that you could confess any time you felt the need. And you were expected to feel the need regularly. The confessional booths were set in the walls of the church on either side of the altar. Inside, the priest sat in darkness. You spoke through a window to a hidden presence.

'Bless me, Father, for I have sinned. It's been two weeks since my last confession.'

'And what is it you wish to confess?' would come the disembodied voice, floating on a tang of soap and smoke.

'Um . . . I told a lie . . . er . . . I fought with my brothers . . . um . . . *[squirm]* I had impure thoughts . . .'

'I absolve you from your sins. Your penance is five Hail Marys and three Our Fathers. Now go in peace.'

Confession was a brand-new start, a wiping of the slate. If you happened to die straight afterwards you were a good chance to chop heaps of time off your purgatory sentence.

The other big ritual was confirmation. This happened around puberty and initiated young Catholics as soldiers of Christ. You chose a confirmation name, which had to be the name of a saint. I chose St Christopher. He was a big strong man who helped carry Jesus across a river and asked for nothing in return. He must have had a different name before that, which nobody remembers, because the name we know him by now describes exactly his deed as bearer of Christ. He's the Christ-ferry-er. Following on from that, he's the patron saint of travellers, sailors and storms. More mysteriously he's the patron saint of bachelors too.

The saints were familiar presences to us, part of our everyday lives. In our pyjamas, on Dad's lap before bed, we drank down their stories from books called *The Lives of the Saints* and *Six O'Clock Saints* – tales of martyrs and miracles; statues weeping blood; ecstatics and good Samaritans; St Theresa, the Little Flower and her visions; Our Lady of Fatima, seen only by those who had eyes to see.

It's part of the reason, I suppose, the Protestants abhorred us so. Deep down we were pagans and idol worshippers. We mouthed our creed, declaring our belief in the One True God, but if you needed something done you didn't go to Him direct. God had important things on his mind, overseeing creation and all that, maintaining His perfection. You were better off going to Our Lady. She was always sympathetic and had effective womanly ways. She knew how to get around God. After all, she was His mother, and what good son can deny a mother's plea?

We Kellys had the double Catholic whammy, being of Irish-Italian stock – both ancient, superstitious cultures. If you'd lost something and couldn't find it, St Anthony was your man. St Francis of Assisi was the patron saint of animals. St John of Bosco helped students, quite useful in exams. For illness, check in with St Bernadette, whose visions at Lourdes in France two centuries ago have made it one of the main pilgrim centres of the Catholic world. For desperate situations, call St Cajetan. If your cause is hopeless, dial St Jude. And so on.

For Mum these saints were not merely ideas or moral exemplars, they weren't out of reach – they were real people, only invisible. You could contact them any time. At the start of Advent, four weeks before Christmas, she would set up a small empty crib in the fireplace by the tree and place around it statuettes of Joseph, Mary and the shepherds. She'd place a box of straw in a nearby cupboard, and whenever we did a good deed or made a little sacrifice we were supposed to go to the cupboard (without drawing attention to ourselves), take a piece of straw and put it in the crib, the idea being to fill it with straw by Christmas Day so the baby Jesus would have a nice soft bed.

On Christmas morning a statue of Jesus would be laid in the crib, so completing the tableau of the holy family, and on that evening figurines of the Three Wise Men would appear on a mantelpiece a couple of rooms away. Over the following twelve days of Christmas they would creep along bookshelves, windowsills, tables and other mantelpieces until they reached the holy infant, still in his swaddling clothes, on January 6, the feast of the Epiphany. This day celebrates the coming out of Jesus – the revelation of his godliness to the world. After that, the Christmas tree would be stripped of its decorations and taken to the backyard woodpile, the baubles and the ribbons and the glittering star packed up in a box and put away for another year.

All these saints and sacraments and creeping magi seem to suggest that we were raised in a cult by raving fanatics. This is far from the case. It was just normal Catholicism in the sixties, and may still be normal for all I know. Unlike those dull Proddies, the Micks had a sense of theatre. For wide-eyed children, the crib and the pieces of straw and the moving statues were fun. It was clever parenting too. I checked on those wise men every morning, and the crib was always overflowing by Christmas Day.

Our parents had a strong faith in God but hated piety. We were not brought up sternly. We were praised and encouraged much more than forbidden; told we were talented and bright, fortunate to have opportunities denied to others, and that the biggest sin would be to squander them; we were taught to respect everyone we met, to help those in need and to judge people by their actions, not their words. The Irish-Italian tradition of hospitality meant that our house was always open, our friends always welcome, and there was always enough for an extra mouth at dinner at short notice, a fact which didn't escape the notice of the popping-in parish priests over the years. And although we children fought like cats and dogs, I never saw my parents fight, nor heard them raise their voices to each other.

In his late forties Dad, like his father-in-law whom he'd never met, began to have trouble walking. I noticed his handwriting, when he signed my homework, getting shakier. His face became stiller. In 1965 he was diagnosed with Parkinson's disease, an even more mysterious illness then than it is now. His motor skills continued to deteriorate. Again like his father-in-law before him, he fell down in the street on his way to work and strangers assumed he was drunk.

Not long after that Nonna, who'd remarried eleven years after Ercole's death, moved to Adelaide with her husband Fred (from Ercole to Fred!), to be with her daughter and her large young family. They moved in close by. It was time to mobilise those prayers once more. Dad, accompanied by Mum, went to Sydney for a tricky operation on his brain during which he had to be awake throughout so he could describe his sensations to the doctors. When he came home his head was shaved and displaying a scary scar.

This time the target of the prayers was Sister Mary MacKillop, the Irish nun who'd come to Australia and set up schools for the poor in the nineteenth century and who, coincidentally, had once employed Nonna's mother as a teacher. The push to have her canonised as a saint was on, a long process, and her fitness for sainthood had to be proved by miracles invoked in her name. Sister Mary needed a miracle. And so did Dad. We all got praying again – the church, the school, the family – asking the ghostly Mary MacKillop to fiddle with the physical world.

My room at home was the cellar, to which I'd recently graduated from the bunk-bed room I'd been sharing with my younger brothers. In this case, graduating meant going down, not up. The cellar had been converted into a bedroom – lovely and cool in summer, and snug enough with the heater on in winter, though a little salt-dampy. It was directly under my parents' room.

One morning in December 1968, lying awake before having to get up for school, I heard Mum talking on the phone upstairs. She asked to speak to Father Peter Kelly, Dad's brother, a Jesuit priest who lived in Melbourne. He wasn't in and I heard her say, 'I'd like to leave a message for him please. It's Jo Kelly calling. Can you tell him that his brother John died of a heart attack last night. He can call me or I'll try him again later.'

She sounded calm and matter-of-fact. Then she went off to mass.

I lay in bed stunned, got up after a while and put on my school clothes. I went to my younger brothers' room – David and Tony – and loitered there as they got dressed, not letting on, waiting for Mum to come home and break the news.

We all went to school that day. This was the sixties – no point moping round the house. Some of us had exams and Mum had things to do. The school had been told and the teacher made an announcement at the start of the first class. I don't recall a single thing after that about the school day. When we got home there were lots of people in the house.

Dad lay in an open coffin in the study for a day or so and the crowds came and went. People brought food. Tony, the youngest at seven years old, remembers that time as one big party, everyone making a fuss over him. I don't remember much at all, but a few days later Dad was given a big funeral mass before being buried. At the graveside Tony cried out, 'Why are they putting Daddy in the hole?' In the church the middle brothers – John and I – rang the bells.

Nonna and Mum both lost their husbands young. Nonna was thirty-eight and Mum forty-five. Unlike Nonna, Mum never remarried. Both of them, by the end of their lives – they died thirteen years apart – were sick of their ailing bodies and wanted nothing more than to be done with them. Jo would tease her mother about her two husbands in heaven and how tricky that was going to be. Ercole and Fred – 'a dear man but dull' – were chalk and cheese and bound to be jealous of each other.

Jo never stopped loving her one true love, John. She talked to him every day for thirty-two years after his death, never doubting his place in heaven. He was first among the saints. During her final years, she lived in a unit in a retirement village just off the Gold Coast Highway, with the big trucks rolling by. She had diabetes and heart problems, and about eighteen months before she died, underwent a quadruple bypass, which knocked her around badly. She never really recovered after that. Her body was hanging on but her mind was ready to go. She spoke more and more about wanting only to meet up with her husband again. She missed him all the time. She used to say, 'If I get to heaven, it's John first, God second.'

I DON'T KNOW ANYTHING ANYMORE

Once I knew how the world worked
You earned your bread, said your prayers well
You loved your own, helped your neighbour
Now I don't know anything anymore

Once I knew what was wrong and right
God was good, black was never white
Once I knew what I was living for
Now I don't know anything anymore

I see her face everywhere
I hear her voice across the air
I drove all kindness from my door
Now I don't know anything anymore

Mind The Furniture

It's a Sunday morning in June, 2000. I'm trying to get out of bed but I can hardly walk. The insides of my legs are posting parcels of pain to my brain whenever I try to move. Yesterday I sat astride a horse for three hours in the Yarra Valley, learning how to look natural in a saddle. It was the first in a series of horse-riding lessons I've agreed to take over the next eight weeks, in preparation for a role in a film in which I'm supposed to be able to ride while lip-synching a song and carrying a .303 rifle. I also need to be able to mount and dismount as naturally as John Wayne or the Man from Snowy River.

My physical anguish is nothing compared to my mental. Who wants to fall off a horse in front of a dozen or more hard-bitten film crew and a couple of harder-bitten horse wranglers? I also have to act out a scene in which I'm presented with the bones of my dead daughter, who is to be played in the film by my real daughter. And then shoot myself with the aforementioned .303. How on earth did I get myself into this?

Once there was a band in Melbourne called Friends and Relations, whose members included three sisters who sang Irish traditional songs in beautiful harmony. They sang on the chorus of the original record- ing of 'From Little Things Big Things Grow'. When Friends and Relations ran its course, the three sisters, who spoke and sang Irish Gaelic and Greek, started up a band called The Xylouris Ensemble with Melbourne-based Greek and Cretan musicians.

Late in 1998 one of the sisters, Mairead Hannan, rang me with a proposition. ABC TV were calling for submissions to make a series of one-hour films that told stories through music. She had recently seen a documentary by Michael Riley called *Blacktracker*, based on the life of Michael's grandfather, Alexander Riley, and thought the story of Tracker Riley could be told as a musical drama. She asked me to join the creative team of playwright John Romeril, songwriter Kev Carmody and herself to develop a kind of mini-opera. I said yes straightaway.

Tracker Riley, who came from the area around Dubbo in western New South Wales, worked as a police tracker between 1911 and 1950, and at the time of his death was the only Aboriginal person in the state to have attained the rank of sergeant. He was instrumental in solving some of the state's most notorious crimes, including the Moss Murders, a huge, serial-murder case in the 1930s, and in 1943 he was awarded the King's Medal, the highest police award. When he died he was given a state funeral.

The story Mairead wanted to tell centred on an incident, touched on in the doco, which had haunted Riley to the end of his days. A child had gone missing on an outback station and a search party assembled. Riley, who would normally have led the search, was excluded because the father refused to allow Aboriginal people on his land. The child was never found alive. Many years later, after the father had died in World War II, the mother invited the tracker onto the property, where he discovered their child's remains.

Knowledge offered, knowledge rejected, unhappy consequences – a simple story which, to my mind, resonated strongly with the wider story of black–white relations in Australia, from the arrival of the first ships to the present day.

Mairead's rough plan, after consulting with Michael Riley, was to fictionalise the story. John would develop characters and plot, Kev and I the songs, and she the score, with all of us mucking in together. This is pretty much what happened. The first song written, 'This Land Is Mine', was a collaboration between Kev and me and gave John a bead on two of the main characters, the farmer and the tracker, with their contrasting concepts of country. Mairead gave me the tune and the idea for the song 'Little Bones', in which the mother sings to her dead child. And John wrote a set of lyrics that I turned into a song called 'One Night The Moon', the eventual title of the film.

Over the course of a year and a half, meeting every once in a while as each stage of funding came through, we thrashed out the screenplay, which was mostly to be sung. Meanwhile Mairead and members of the Xylouris Ensemble developed musical soundscapes and arrangements for the songs. The music was mournful and rich, at times urgent, at times elegiac.

When the ABC eventually gave us the green light to film we approached Rachel Perkins (*Radiance*, *The First Australians*, *Bran Nue Dae*) to direct. She set about choosing her actors. They had to be able to sing. After screen-testing, she cast me as the farmer, Kaarin as the farmer's wife, and our youngest daughter Memphis as the child who goes missing. Kelton Pel, a powerful actor from Western Australia, was the tracker, and singer Ruby Hunter his wife.

Rachel brought her own ideas to the story and the vigorous discussions continued, eventually tilting the screenplay more towards the mother's viewpoint. At some point it was decided that the farmer, rather than going off to war, would kill himself. One of the last songs written for the film, 'I Don't Know Anything Anymore', was his suicide note in rhyme, and it ended up being the opening scene.

The shoot was scheduled for August 2000 in and around South Australia's rugged Flinders Ranges. Cameraman Kim Batterham was director of photography, and his vision, framing and use of colour would result in the finished film having a haunted, dreamlike intensity.

We were all set. I'd had a few more riding lessons and wasn't waking up so sore in the mornings. Kaarin and I pulled our two daughters out of school for a month and drove to the town of Hawker, our base of operations, to join the rest of the cast and crew. Along the way we passed through the Clare Valley, home of the Kelly ancestors. Further north, beyond the south-creeping Goyder's Line, crumbling homestead ruins – emblems of defeat – dotted the landscape, and every colour was in the hills. Now all my normal worries were behind me. Only new ones ahead. All I had to do was sing on a horse, cause my daughter's death through my own stupidity, and shoot myself in the head.

Drummer Charlie Watts famously said that being in The Rolling Stones is mostly hanging around. Being on a film set is even more so. It's a bitty, stop-start business. There's so much preparation to be done before the camera rolls for each scene. Costumes to be put on just right, makeup applied, lights set up, director and crew discussions to be had, camera moves practised, external conditions – light, noise – waited upon, and so on. One day I was driven 35 kilometres to the location, where, after hanging around for four hours, I walked out the front door of our 'house' as the cameras rolled, and put my arm around Kaarin, who shrank from my touch. Rachel called, 'Cut,' I waited around some more for Kaarin to finish the scene on her own, and then we were both driven home. A good day's work.

Apart from pretending to be somebody else, which was difficult enough, I found there was so much more to keep in mind – what Spencer Tracy described as 'not bumping into the furniture'. I enjoyed this technical aspect of acting – being part of a machine made up of around a dozen people who each perform their small, specific roles before and after the director calls 'action.' The makeup person pats down your upper lip to remove the sweat built up as you've waited under lights. The continuity person makes sure the beer bottle gets set down on exactly the same spot as before, the wardrobe person adjusts your collar or untucks your shirt. The sound-recordist presses the red button on the Nagra to 'roll sound'. The clapperboard operator 'claps' the slate in front of the camera – between the director's commands of 'roll camera' and 'action' – to synchronise sound and vision. The dolly operators, matching their movement with the actors', keep the big camera running smoothly on the tracks as the DOP looks through the viewer. The focus puller adjusts the lens midway through the shot at just the right time.

Meanwhile the director is signalling, or quietly talking the crew and actors through their paces, or is still and silent, confident that everyone has their moves down. Silent too but watchful, the gaffer and the best boy, making sure their light is falling in the right places, hope that the actor gets to the perfect spot for the shadow to hit the face just so.

The deep group concentration is a kind of prayer. That first take was good but the camera was a little late panning. The second take had a fluffed line. Start again. Take three was good but the director thinks there's a better one. She likes the little accident just now between the actors that she hasn't seen before in rehearsal. Can you do that again? she says. Take four – hold on, we have to wait 'til that plane finishes passing overhead. Take five, pretty good, we're very close now, but the lip sync's a bit off. And watch that boom mic, it's starting to peek into the shot. Take six – no, wait, we need to change the magazine. Let's have a five-minute break. Okay, take seven – that's it! That's beautiful, that's the one! Thank you, everybody.

At worst, it's grinding tedium, but at best a kind of dance. A few hours of intense focus and something else takes over. Work becomes ceremony. You lose the sense of your separate self and become one moving part among many, meshing together to make something intricate and potent. Deep down, this merging is what most humans yearn for. It's the basis of religion – why people go to church, join a club, play sport, make music, start families, help their neighbour, volunteer, go into politics, do all the things we do that make us part of something larger than ourselves.

One scene called for me to have a breakdown on a hillside after several days' fruitless search for my daughter – at the moment when I realise I'm not going to find her, that she has come to a dreadful end and my pigheadedness has been the causing of it all. I'd been dreading doing this scene for days. The best advice I'd ever had about acting I'd received from Kaarin several years before, when I was in a play. 'Listen to the other actors,' she said. It sounds obvious and simple but I'd found it very useful. An actor can get so caught up in what they have to do – remembering their lines, expressing certain emotions, avoiding the furniture – that they can forget to stay in the moment with their fellow travellers. 'Listen to the other actors' had become a mantra for me. But there were no other actors in the scene I was about to do. I was on my own. And it was a crucial scene in the movie.

We drove to the hillside, far away from the town, where the light was beginning to dim. The sun waits for no-one. I was assisted in the putting on of my garments, anointed with sweat and grime. Director and crew stood solemnly by, ready for the rite.

I'll never forget the tenderness surrounding me that day. I'll never think lightly of an actor's work again. To get into the right state I had to imagine some awful things, things that put me in a place I couldn't return from easily. I was shaky for hours afterwards and strangely disconnected the next morning.

I fell on my knees on stony ground and scrabbled my way up a slope, clawing at the dirt. It was a tricky technical shot for the camera crew, tracking back up the hill as I flailed my way towards them, and we needed a few takes to get it right. Everyone was solicitous and patient with me as I snivelled and sniffed and sobbed. My nose was running like a tap, which told me I was in the right zone emotionally.

The hard part was maintaining it as I was lightly cleaned up between takes before going down the hill to start again.

The sun sank lower and my head began to throb. Kim, on the camera, spoke softly all the while, checking on me and letting me know I was doing all right. We nailed the take in the nick of time and suddenly I was being held, comforted, tended. Someone wrapped me in a blanket, took me to the car and put a beer in my hand. The crew knew I was still in a dark, private place and were careful not to intrude. Still, they let me know one by one that I had their support by a pat, a nod, a quiet word.

I loved them all very, very much.

We finished the shoot a week later. Kaarin sang her song to the bones. She needed some TLC after that too. I sang my suicide song, which comparatively speaking was a breeze. Melody's zephyr makes for a gentler landing. And I didn't have to shoot myself in front of everybody. All I had to do was walk away from the camera towards the horizon with a rifle over my shoulder. They held the shot 'til I was a tiny, shimmering silhouette. Then, 'Cut!' Thanks to the sleight of film, the audience does the rest.

Money had got tight during filming, so the singing-on-the-horse scene was dropped too, because it required an extra day's pay for the horse wranglers. That was a relief. The desperate midnight ride for help remained, though. A wrangler stunt-doubled the galloping bits, and all I had to do was look like I'd just pulled up – they have camera angles for that – dismount in a hurry and race to the front door of the neighbour's place. I concentrated hard on not getting my foot caught in the stirrups. The first take was okay. The second perfect. I didn't fall off the horse in either.

I KEEP ON COMING BACK FOR MORE

Won't somebody help me please
I'm afflicted with a strange disease
No doctor can help me, neither can the nurse
'Cause the cure I crave is just making me worse
And I keep on coming back for more

Every morning I wake up with a promise to keep
Then that old sun begins to creep
In my mind a whisper turns to a roar
And here I am again now baby, knocking at your door
I keep on coming back for more

All my friends keep shaking their heads
You don't care for me, you never did
I'm so tangled up inside your spell
And the gates of your heaven now, baby, lead straight to hell
Oh, I keep on coming back for more

I know, I know, I know what I should not and what I should
But, oooh, you know, you know, you know sometimes it feels
    so good

Like a sick dog licking at his spew
I keep on turning back to you
First my mind's a preacher, then it's turning tricks
Like a drunk to a bottle, baby, like a junkie to a fix
I keep on coming back for more
I keep on coming back for more

Sonnet 147

My love is as a fever, longing still
For that which longer nurseth the disease;
Feeding on that which doth preserve the ill,
The uncertain sickly appetite to please.
My reason, the physician to my love,
Angry that his prescriptions are not kept,
Hath left me, and I desperate now approve
Desire is death, which physic did except.
Past cure I am, now Reason is past care,
And frantic-mad with evermore unrest;
My thoughts and my discourse as madmen's are,
At random from the truth vainly expressed;
For I have sworn thee fair, and thought thee bright,
Who art as black as hell, as dark as night.

William Shakespeare

Pith And Kin

No-one ever did themselves any favours putting their lyrics next to Shakespeare's. But it's you, sweet reader, not me I'm doing the favour for. Songs often remind me of other things after I've written them. You don't start with somebody else's poem or song and try to rewrite it, but years later, maybe, you come across some lines that bear a resemblance. Had you been carrying them unknowingly? Or are there only so many themes and only so many ways to arrange words and images? Anything you write of any pith you can be sure to find in Shakespeare eventually. If I could be re-incarnated backwards – if one's solid flesh could melt and resolve into something old/new – I'd gladly re-fledge with those upstart feathers.

I'D RATHER GO BLIND

I suppose I should get over this
I'm not the first and not the last
To ever wake up with a hurt inside
But it just won't go away
It's getting worse now every day
And I can't find a hole that's big enough for me to crawl
    and hide

I'd rather go blind, I'd rather go blind
Than see you with another guy

You made a special tape for me
With songs from all your favourite CDs
I put it on today then I had to turn it off
From Junior Brown to Dr Dre
And You Am I along the way
The music only made me want to get inside your touch

I'd rather go blind, I'd rather go blind
Than see you with another guy

You robbed me of my peace of mind
Stole the taste out of the wine
You left with nothing but you took it all
Now if you sleep with someone else
I just hope it's with another girl
You know I can't compete with that at all

I'd rather go blind, I'd rather go blind
Than see you with another guy

C90

In my last year of high school, 1971, the two coolest records were *Hot Rats* by Frank Zappa and *Gasoline Alley* by Rod Stewart. (Yes, once there was a time when Rod Stewart was 'underground'.) I wasn't in the hipster gang myself but I knew what they were listening to. I managed to get myself copies on cassette – Frank on one side, Rod on the other. This was the beauty of the C90 tape. You could always fit two albums on it because they didn't make vinyl records longer than forty-five minutes.

On the move after finishing school and never in one place very long, I didn't own a record player and so became a maker of tapes, feeding off other people's record collections. A friend of mine had a lot of blues albums, and I taped Sonny Boy Williamson, Sleepy John Estes, Little Walter, and Blind Willie McTell, writing the titles in small script on the case covers. Someone else had a stack of Bob Dylan bootlegs in plain sleeves. *Great White Wonder* was one. I sucked up the lot and learned how to play 'I'll Keep It With Mine' and 'Quit Your Low Down Ways', rewinding the tape over and again to catch the lyrics and figure out the chords. I taped *Blue* and *For the Roses* by Joni Mitchell; old-time and folk music from the Vanguard and Rounder labels – New Lost City Ramblers, Eric Von Schmidt, Woody Guthrie and heaps more. I was hungry for all kinds of music, plundered wherever I could. Close to forty years later, I still have some of those tapes.

Cassettes were convenient: nice and small, good to travel with. And when I started writing songs, a portable cassette player was all I needed. Just press *play* and *record* at the same time – one action – and sing your idea into the inbuilt mic. I still use that method today – there's no quicker one – though it's getting harder to find decent little tape recorders that don't break down after a year.

Friends made tapes for me, and I in turn for them. Nick Hornby, in his novel *High Fidelity*, talks about the rules of making compilation tapes – never two songs in a row by the same artist, and so on – but everyone has their own rules. It's all about the flow. Your friend Clare has tragically gone through life not knowing the music of John Cale (who you discovered years ago on a tape Phil gave you), so you go through your collection, which you have on CD now. You focus on the early records – *Fear*, *Vintage Violence*, *Slow Dazzle*, *Paris 1919* – and make a J.C. best-of. But how do you fillet *Paris 1919*, the greatest record of all time (at one time in your life)? Hard decisions have to be made in the interests of the overview, but 'Andalucia', 'Half Past France' and 'Hanky Panky Nohow' are walkup starts.

Rich, living in New York through the late eighties and the early nineties, makes you hip-hop compilations from tapes he records off the radio – A Tribe Called Quest, Eric B and Rakim, N.W.A., De La Soul, Biz Markie, EPMD, Boo-Yaa T.R.I.B.E., and those mighty women Queen Latifah, Roxanne, Salt'n'Pepa, and Monie Love. Tapes from tapes. Years later, when your niece turns eighteen, you make her an old-school hip-hop tape from that golden era (it's the golden era to you), picking the eyes out of those tapes. Tapes from tapes from tapes. 'The hiss is important,' you tell her.

A lot of time goes into making a cassette compilation. Unlike making one on CD. You don't just drag and drop into a playlist then press *burn disc*. You have to listen to the music as you do it. You might be doing other things at the same time – housework, cooking, writing letters – but you need to be on hand. When the song stops you have to press *pause* straightaway, then cue up the next track. Press *play* on one deck then *record* on the other – get your timing right so the gap between songs is the right length. You have to make sure the song doesn't get cut off when the tape runs out. If you make a mistake – accidentally erase part of a track, miss the start or change your mind about the order – you have to go back and start again.

So whenever you make a tape for someone, you make a copy for yourself as well. You want some return for the work you've put in. These tapes are for you, anyway. Making them for others is just an excuse. Of course, you give them the 'high quality' copy and keep the dub for yourself. So, in the case of the hip-hop tape, your copy is now fourth-generation. It lives in the car for a while, which is where you rotate a lot of your old tapes. Dust and the years do their work too. Your nephew borrows the car from time to time. Returning it one day, he says, 'I love that old-school tape but, man, it's *muddy*.'

'Yeah, they use a lot of samples.'

Your niece loves her birthday present, so next year you do her another one. She sang Patsy Cline's version of 'Crazy' at the last family Christmas, so you decide to make women singers the theme. Your starting point is Aretha Franklin singing 'Sweet Bitter Love', which you taped off a CD Renée lent you. You've been playing it every day for a month. It's been your get-up-and-go song in the morning, your chopping-vegetables song, your glass-of-wine-in-the-evening song. You've figured out the chords – the B moving up a semitone to the C *kills* you – but the singing you can't touch. It's pain turned to glory, it's the walls of Jericho tumbling down, it's pure Aretha. You know *Sweet Bitter Love* has to be the title of the compilation but you don't want to open with that song. You need to build up to it, lead the listener along the path, then *wham!*

Beginnings are as important as titles. You decide to start way back with Adelaide Hall singing 'Creole Love Call' with The Duke Ellington Orchestra. She's imitating a horn. No words, so it's like an overture. Then you set the scene with Etta James's aching 'I'd Rather Go Blind', her first, stretched-out phrase – 'Something to-o-old me' – sounding like a bell tolling, the oldest bell in the world, the bell that says 'You don't love me any more.' You bring in The Staple Singers after that – for a little release, and to get things on a groovy track – 'I'll Take You There'. Mavis is singing about heaven but she makes it sound like a place of eternal fucking (or taking a really satisfying shit). Now you're off and running. You slip in Nellie Lutcher with her 'Fine Brown Frame' to keep things sweet and tight, then Big Mama Thornton who, like Mavis, sings below the waist. You're on a roll now, pulling out CDs and cassettes from the shelves, making a clutter, jumping around in time. Billie Holiday has to be in there, of course, also Irma Thomas and Nancy Wilson.

I'd Rather Go Blind****
You're pretty pleased with yourself halfway through Side B, after sequencing a run of three Bacharach/David tunes (a sub-theme within a theme) sung by Dusty Springfield, Dionne Warwick and Aretha (again). It's within the rules to bring someone back on the second side. So here comes Etta one more time, happier now, luxuriating in the pleasure of 'At Last'. You bring it on home with Ruth Brown and the returning Staple Singers. Mavis was always gonna have the last word: 'Mmmnph! . . . oaa . . . unhhh . . . mmnh . . . oaaahh . . . uuunnhh!'

Quentin Tarantino made a movie in 2006 called *Death Proof.* There are lots of car stunts and menace and mayhem in it, and, true to form, also a couple of long non-action scenes with people just talking. There's one in the back of a car where four women are chatting about men, sex and dating. They're tough, savvy, working girls – starlets and stunt drivers – trash talking, shooting the shit, serving it up. They've been there, done that. Not long before all four go out to hunt a bad guy and bash him to death, one mentions a boyfriend who made her a tape. 'He made you a tape?' the others softly chime. 'Not a CD?' 'Yeah, a tape!' 'Aawww.' And their faces go all soft.

Early in the millennium, you're going out with a woman who's a writer, a radio presenter and a trained musician. She can play piano and clarinet and sing Ella Fitzgerald. You like her a lot, though in those first courting days she confesses she doesn't much like football or country music. You brood upon this and start writing a list, taking your time like your grandfather did with the eggs.

You start with the heading *She Don't Like Country.* You're gonna have to pull out some big guns. George Jones, from East Texas, is definitely in the team. 'The Race Is On' is one long metaphor, loaded to brilliant breaking point – she's a wordie, she'll appreciate that. And she loves soul music. George is a soul singer to his bootstraps. Lefty Frizzell, too, is a must. He taught George most of what he knows. Lefty came to you via a tape slipped to you backstage by a fan a hundred years ago and he's travelled with you ever since. Experience counts.

Your tall, Ella-singing blonde likes to go to Bennetts Lane and other Melbourne jazz clubs, so she's bound to hear the jazz in Willie Nelson. He's cool in the clinches. She also has Manu Chao and Youssou N'Dour in her record collection and loves to dance. Bob Wills and His Texas Playboys were making world music fifty years before the term was invented, blending Hawaiian, African, South American, jazz, blues and country in a nutty joyful brew you could dance your socks off to. So they're an automatic selection – plenty of flair, those boys.

You set to work one long rainy afternoon, assembling your squad. Buck Owens is a natural choice for captain – you'll start him up forward and put him down back later. He leads the team on with 'Above And Beyond'. It's a bold statement of intent – a high, ringing declaration of love. And it swings like hell, aiming straight for the middle of the big sticks.

She returns the favour. Driving out to a B&B on the west coast one summer weekend, she slips the third act of *Der Rosenkavalier* by Richard Strauss into the car stereo. Three sopranos, intertwined, squeeze out honour, grief, sex and ecstasy through the small speakers, as outside, sunlight and spray dance above a swelling sea.

Nine years later you're still together. You've been shacked up for a while now. Sometimes on a Sunday afternoon she'll play a Gillian Welch record in the back room, lying down to listen with her eyes closed. Occasionally on a Sunday morning you'll put on a Renée Fleming CD, then come back to bed where you can both hear it drifting down the hall. And once in a while on a Saturday, if there's a close game of football on the telly, she'll come and snuggle up on the couch and watch a quarter or two.

IF I COULD START TODAY AGAIN

All the kings and queens in the bible
They could not turn back time
So what chance have I of a miracle
In this life of mine?
I only want one day
To unsay the things I said
Undo the thing I did
Twenty-four little hours
Oh God! Please wipe them all away
And I promise I will change
If I could start today again

I know I'm not the milk and honey kind
Today I proved it true
When the red mist falls around my eyes
I know not what I do
Please give me back today
And I won't say the things I said
Or do that thing I did
Every minute, every hour
The replay's just the same
And I can't stand the shame
Oh, let me start today again

I only want one day
One lousy day, that's all
Out of every day that's been before
Since time began
I know my prayer's in vain
But for a second I'll pretend
That I can start today again

Magical Thinking

> Does the heart know no better than to pray
> That time unwind its coil, the bone unbuild
> Till that lost world sit like a fruit in the hand –
> Till the felled trees rise upright where they lay
> And leaves and birds spring on them as they stand?
>
> Judith Wright, 'The Moving Image'

I grew up barracking for the Norwood football team. I had no choice in the matter. I inherited them along with brown eyes, curly black hair, and the ability to remember phone numbers. My paternal grandparents and their children barracked for Norwood; my parents, my older brothers and sisters and my cousins too. Dad's second cousin Kieran Kelly played for them in the sixties.

Every Saturday afternoon in winter, the Redlegs, eighteen men in red and blue, held my happiness in their hands. My brothers and I would go and see them play at the Parade Oval, their home ground, a couple of miles from our place. Or we'd venture into the enemy territory of other suburban grounds. Alberton Oval, at the other end of the world down by the port, was the worst, where even the grannies in their beanies with their knitting needles and thermoses were scary. I never saw us win one game there. Every time we ran out of the race in white shorts – the required 'away' colour – we looked weak. We might as well have forfeited then and there.

If I wasn't at the game I'd listen to it on the radio at home, guts in a knot, unless it was too close in the last quarter. Then I'd switch the radio off, go out to the backyard, kick the football to myself for a few minutes, run back inside, turn the radio on, and if it was still too close, outside I'd go again. And so on and so on, until the final siren ended my agony.

One Saturday night, after the Redlegs had lost by a kick in the last round of the season, thus missing out on the finals, I went to bed fantasising – praying – that a decision by the goal umpire had been reviewed, or the score recounted, and as a result the game had been awarded retrospectively to Norwood. I imagined a panel of football officials meeting in secret, downtown, that very moment, as I tucked myself in under the blankets. I'd wake up in the morning and – Glory be! – we'd be in the finals.

Eventually I fell asleep. Night's dark forge heated and hammered my hot wish into fierce, unbending will. The will that turns water into wine and the lame into jumping fools. When I woke up Sunday morning I knew it was a freshly made day unlike any other. Yesterday had been a dream, something I'd only imagined, one long hallucination. There would be a headline for sure on the front page of the paper. AMAZING FOOTBALL REVERSAL! The opposing team had had nineteen men on the ground during the last quarter, and as a consequence their score had been declared invalid. The Redlegs were in the finals!

I went out into the front yard, feet chilled in the wet grass, wiped the dew off the paper, tore off the rubber band and unfurled the fat *Sunday Mail*. Nothing on the front page. Nothing on the back page. It couldn't be true, could it? Yesterday *couldn't* have happened. But inside, sure enough, there lurked the shocking report, though I knew it already: REDLEGS MISS OUT!

I trudged back inside to the parallel world, to the 7.45 ABC news theme (same music then, almost half a century ago, as now) and the big teapot steaming in the centre of the table. I passed the paper on and sat down without a word, numb, glum and gutted by the dull toll of irreversible time.

Many years later, I live eight hundred kilometres away from those scenes of early sorrows. The expansion of Australian Rules into a national competition has created new state teams and weakened local footy. Norwood still play in Adelaide but their team is made up of more boys than men (and it's not merely that my perspective has changed from a boy's to a man's). In Victoria, if I care to, I can look up their results in the paper. But I have to put my strong reading glasses on and wade through the fine print at the back of the sports pages.

My team now is the Adelaide Crows, who began in 1991 and have already won two premierships. I saw one of their Grand Final wins at the MCG and walked home for miles, very happy. But they're not Norwood. Football doesn't hurt me any more, though I get twitchy watching Adelaide play on TV. I'm not aware of it myself but the tall blonde, if she's next to me on the couch, notices my little jerks. She says I'm playing the game by remote, as if I think I can change the course of the players and the match by my tiny twists and turns, flinches and clenches; as if, after all these years, my cellular being still believes in voodoo.

Most songs are rough-hewn things. You knock them together with this and that, like the old bitsers you made as a kid – go-karts to get you through the holidays. If they're good they keep on going. 'If I Could Start Today Again' is the most precise song I've written. When I sing it I think of a watch. It's compact and in perfect proportion. All the parts move nicely. The chords are locked tight together and rotate smoothly through the picking. As you go deeper into the mechanism, the lyrical units get smaller and smaller, starting from a whole life in the first verse and concentrating down, through the shrinking measures of time, to a day, an hour, a minute and, finally, to a second. I have no idea how I wrote it. It came without thought or struggle, like it had already been made, straight from the jeweller. The song asks for a miracle. To me it is one.

I WASTED TIME

I wasted time, now time is wasting me
One question left – to be or not to be?
I cheated time and now it's time to pay
All out of change and less and less to say

I was a handsome raver in my time
Oh girl, you should have seen me in my prime
I see old friends at funerals now and then
It's down to this – it's either me or them

Yeah, I wasted time
Now time is wasting me
Soon it's closing time
Won't you stay with me?

Molly took my hand and led the way
Now Molly's yellow hair is silver-grey
She wore a red dress she let me undo
But Molly swears that day her dress was blue

Yeah, I wasted time
I thought it came for free
Now it's closing time
Won't you pray for me?

I tell you there's no failure like success
And no success like failure too, I guess

Fermata

Shakespeare was obsessed with time. It saturates his sonnets and many of the speeches in his plays. Tomorrow, and tomorrow, and tomorrow, creeps in this petty pace from day to day. I wasted time, and now doth time waste me. The seven ages of man. And so on.

All the great poets are similarly obsessed – Yeats, Donne, Milosz, Szymborska, Akhmatova, Hardy, Keats and the rest. Their lines are filled with birds and beasts and beds, oranges and kings and wars and rivers and the like, but the very act of writing a poem gives the game away. They all want to make the thing that floats above time, that belongs not to the seconds, minutes, hours, days or centuries but to the ages. They all want to be like Ovid, who wrote in the final lines of his monumental *Metamorphoses*:

> And now the work is done, that Jupiter's anger, fire or sword cannot erase, nor the gnawing tooth of time. Let that day, that only has power over my body, end, when it will, my uncertain span of years: yet the best part of me will be borne, immortal, beyond the distant stars. Wherever Rome's influence extends, over the lands it has civilised, I will be spoken, on people's lips: and, famous through all the ages, if there is truth in poet's prophecies, vivam – I shall live.

And his wish came true.

Modern-day chronanist Nicholson Baker published a novel in 1994 called *The Fermata*, whose main character has the trick of being able to stop and start time at will. He can make the whole world freeze while he doesn't. Once this happens he gets up to all sorts of sex mischief. It gets a little creepy at times and mostly involves him writing and recording reams of porn, dropping it strategically here and there, and messing with people's minds. It's one of those funny, filthy books that do the rounds of the band on tour.

Fermata is the term he uses for the periods he spends outside time, when he 'drops into The Fold'. He makes it happen usually by some small action such as rubbing his spectacles up and down the bridge of his nose. Then everything and everyone around him – clocks, wind, people – stops and there is only stillness and silence, but for him. When he returns from the fermata by performing his little tic again, time restarts exactly where it left off. In the in-between 'no-time' he prowls around doing his porn business.

At the end of *The Fermata* our protagonist loses the knack, accidentally passing it on to someone else. It's as if Baker is setting us up for the sequel. His previous book, *Vox*, is one long phone-sex conversation, so he has form.

To date there hasn't been a follow-up, though. Sometimes I think of writing Mr Baker a letter, asking him to take up the story again on behalf of all bored rock musicians riding on the bus. Other times, writing to the one I love, laptop on my knees, the miles gliding by, I channel nutty Nicholson as I tap away.

Imagine if two people could be in The Fold at the same time. Imagine you and your sweetheart stopping time at will, for everyone but yourselves. Getting the itch in the middle of the family Christmas lunch or a picnic in the park. Halfway through a play or at the cricket. Doing the little spectacles-on-the-nose trick, freezing the mob – the family at the groaning table, the actor mid-declamation, the batsman in his crouch – and laying each other down in the aisles or on the soft green grass.

But that's another book, not this one.

I WON'T BE YOUR DOG

I've been drinking muddy water and it tastes like turpentine
I've been leaving muddy footprints up and down the Morgan line
Crows are crying all around me in a sky where the sun
    refuse to shine

I've been taking scraps from back doors, I've been hiding in the cane
I've been fighting over morsels and I've been slinking back again
I've been building up a reputation on the levee, all across the plain

No I won't be your dog
Your low riding dog anymore

Now the mangrove sun is sinking and the moon is bloody red
Every gun is clean and loaded, lying by a feather bed
Far and wide goes my description and the price is rising on my head

No I won't be your dog
Your low riding dog anymore

I've been drinking muddy water, I've been keeping way down low
All I hear is my own breathing, all I see is a distant glow
All I have is tearing me up, wearing me down, just won't let me go

No I won't be your dog
Your low riding dog anymore
No I won't be your dog
Your skinny little dog anymore

Heavy

And what rough beast, its hour come at last,
Slouches towards Bethlehem to be born?

W. B. Yeats

After Dad died, Mum had her hands full. Anne, the eldest, was in Sydney doing her novitiate, studying to be a Loreto nun. She had to have special dispensation to come home for the funeral. The rules of the order were very strict then: she wasn't allowed any other contact with the family for a year, except by mail. The rest of us were at home, six still at school.

Nineteen sixty-nine rolled around. Big changes were going on everywhere for young people. Martin went off to university and John followed him a year later. First one then the other began to grow their hair long. They shared a converted garage in the backyard and could come and go without going through the house. Long-haired friends started to drop around. Strange-smelling smoke wafted from the shed, and even stranger sounds – music from LPs with mysterious covers by bands with mysterious names: Pink Floyd, Iron Butterfly, The Moody Blues. Records called *The Piper at the Gates of Dawn*, *A Saucerful of Secrets*, *Ummagumma*, *In-a-Gadda-Da-Vida*, *Days of Future Passed*. Even the titles made your head spin.

I'd sneak out the back sometimes and sit in with them after homework, freaking out quietly to 'Careful With That Axe, Eugene', or drifting off to 'Nights In White Satin'. Later came *Aqualung* by Jethro Tull and their follow-up, *Thick as a Brick*, which was one long song. Heavy!

From campus each day came Martin trailing revolution behind him. New books entered the house. Kurt Vonnegut's *Slaughterhouse-Five* skewered the immorality and insanity of war. *Summerhill*, by A. S. Neil, proclaimed that students were better off directing themselves than being imposed upon by teachers. 'Teachers and students' was a false paradigm, anyway. Kahlil Gibran's *The Prophet* said to parents: 'Your children are not your children . . . They come through you but not from you . . . You may house their bodies but not their souls, For their souls dwell in the house of tomorrow, which you cannot visit, not even in your dreams.'

The younger generation chanted to the older – Back off! You've made a mess. Leave the field to us. There were big demonstrations against the Vietnam War. Martin and John went on a weeklong hunger strike at Flinders Uni in protest.

Picking up their cue, in my last year of school a friend and I started a student newspaper, lobbied the teachers to allow students the day off to attend the 1971 moratorium, and campaigned against the prefect system and the compulsory wearing of school caps. (*Heavy*.) I began composing poems in the style of Gibran, wrote them out neatly on lined paper and passed them around shy-proudfully to my mother, my siblings and their friends. I discovered *Blonde on Blonde* and *Highway 61 Revisited*, which had already been in the house for a few years, and bombs went off in my head.

Mum had enrolled in a librarian course after Dad died and was working now in the library at Loreto Convent, which Mary Jo, the next one down from me, attended. She was raising hell, back-chatting teachers, skipping classes. Eventually she got expelled, much to Mum's embarrassment, who had to deal with all this – negotiate with her children, hold the line, try to find an agreed path – without the support and counsel of her life companion and helpmeet who'd been so suddenly snatched away from her. The old rules of parenting didn't apply and there was no-one to talk things over with at the end of the day. She talked to John in her head but it wasn't the same.

Some time later Sheila, the second eldest, started an affair with the doctor she'd been working with for years. He was much older than her, and his wife had recently died. Sheila moved in with him and his teenage children, who were closer to her age than his. Tongues clucked all over the place. By then I'd dropped out of uni after one term, saying I wanted to be a writer, to choose and read books in my own time, outside the trammels of an official course. A few of us turned vegetarian. Whispers, not so soft, came back to Mum that people, so-called friends, were saying the Kelly children were running wild and were a bad influence on their own children.

Mum backed us to the hilt against our (and her) critics. She argued with us, she worried about us, but she stood up for us before the gossips. She helped Mary Jo find another school that better suited her fierce independence. She was proud of Martin and John's courage in their convictions. She understood the dark, chaotic root of Sheila's love; that logic had nothing to do with it. She was unhappy that I, who'd done well at school, was turning my back on study, but after reminding me once again of the parable of the servants and their talents, she gave me her blessing.

And she learned how to cook soya beans.

I started travelling – north, south, east, west. In the early seventies you could arrive anyplace and get a job straightaway. Walk into Rockhampton dole office in the morning and by the afternoon start working for the Queensland railways, fettling on the Midlander line. Hitchhike to Esperance and begin work as a brickie's labourer the next day. Land in Darwin, make a couple of calls, fill in a form, and before you know it be working at Stokes Hill power station as a tradesman's assistant.

In between I'd come back to Adelaide. I'd fallen in with a gang that played guitar and sang songs by The Ozark Mountain Daredevils, Commander Cody and His Lost Planet Airmen, The Ormond Brothers, Gram Parsons, and Neil Young. I watched their fingers and decided to graduate from tapping along on the bongos, because girls seemed to like singer/guitar players quite a lot.

Armed with the chords to 'Big Blue Frog', I acquired a guitar and bought myself a harmonica holder. 'No, I'm not copying Bob or Neil,' I'd say coolly to non-aficionados. 'This method of getting a song over goes back to Jimmy Reed, the king of the first position harp.' I went to folk clubs and listened in the dark. Listened especially closely to Dave Clarke, one of the lions of the Adelaide scene. He sang traditional songs – Australian, Irish, English – in a way that I liked, straight-shooting, no hand-over-the-ear affectation like some of the others. I saw him play in a dimly lit underground club called The Catacombs, and he showed me how to play 'Streets Of Forbes' and a few other things.

I used to visit Nonna from time to time when I was in town. She was widowed again and in her seventies. She took an interest in my singing. I sat down and played her 'Streets Of Forbes' and an old blues song about women, water and turpentine. She listened politely, secretly appalled I suspect.

She was worried that I wasn't producing my voice in the right way. 'Your throat sounds too tight. You need to make your voice resonate in your head.' And then she'd show me, standing straight with head held up, as a series of pure, bel canto notes issued silverly from her throat.

'I love your kind of singing,' I told her. 'It sends shivers up my spine. But my kind's different.' Hers came from a place of order, training and heavenly perfection. Mine from the ground, from dirt, from swamps, from hollers and moans, from crying, keening, pleading, screaming, from cajoling and conversation – seeking not purity, rounded tones or smooth phrasing, but grain and grit.

She remained dubious. 'You'd better be careful or you'll ruin your voice. You won't be able to sing like I can still, at my age.' And she'd give me a few breathing exercises, holding my diaphragm to make sure it was pushing out correctly.

Mum didn't like my singing much either. She thought Bob Dylan wrote some good songs but Peter, Paul and Mary sang them better. I played her The Stanley Brothers once but she shuddered as if I'd scratched nails on a blackboard. Too crude. I didn't bother with Dock Boggs or Roscoe Holcomb.

Nonna gave me a great piece of advice. She told me to breathe in and out slowly and deeply if I was nervous before going onstage. I use this all the time. So far my voice has held up well, though I still have a ways to go yet. Nonna was knocking 'em dead in the nursing home with 'Ave Maria' in her nineties. She was practically running the place by then. I suppose one shouldn't say 'knocking 'em dead in the nursing home'. But that just about sums it up.

Strange to say, over the years I've become a bit of a crooner.

Nonna suffered quite badly from asthma and the Adelaide winters also began to take their toll. In the late seventies Mum decided to move all the remaining family – Nonna and the younger children still at home, Mary, David and Tony – to Queensland. She said later that she also felt herself to be in a bit of a rut, seeing the same faces, doing the same things – Thursday bridge, Wednesday tennis, Sunday mass. And maybe she never quite forgave certain people.

Martin, now married with a young family and always up for an adventure, joined the caravan to the north. They scoped out southern Queensland and found a two-storey house on eight hectares overlooking a valley, halfway between Brisbane and the Gold Coast. The area was called Ormeau and their block was in cane country, between the highway and the mangroves. Martin took four hectares and began building another house, an A-frame, two hundred metres up the dirt track from the main house. He moved in before it was finished and spent many more years building around his rapidly growing family. He and his wife Rosie had two sets of twins within two years of each other. At that stage they had six children, four under the age of two and no inside toilet.

Ormeau became family headquarters. The rest of us were scattered at various times between America, Africa and the southern Australian states and would gather there for Christmas and the holidays. The weather was often hot and muggy. From the balcony at Mum's place, after smothering yourself with mosquito repellent, you could sit and watch electrical storms jag and flicker across the wide, brooding sky – God's light show.

Whenever I visited I liked to walk along the back roads behind

Martin's house. Much of the country was reclaimed swamp and flattened out towards the coast. Scattered farmhouses stood dwarfed by
the big sky and menaced by thick stands of full-grown cane, which
sometimes reached right up to the back porch. On both sides of the
lonely road, pools of water drowned black, oppressive clouds. Sometimes in the afternoon, before a storm, the air would turn yellow
and crackly. Down towards the water, past faded signs for bait and
tackle, towards the old wooden jetty and the strangling mangroves,
everything smelt mossy and fetid. No-one ever seemed to be around.
Whoever was, was skulking indoors. Time hung heavy. I'd turn back
after a while and slouch home, hoping to beat the storm but not
minding if I didn't.

The younger children left the Ormeau house one by one, but for
many years afterwards it remained our haven. During Queensland
tours, the band and I would drop in on our way to a gig at the
Beenleigh Tavern, just up the road. There was always a casserole or,
on a day off, a barbecue on the grass. If the tour ended in Queensland
I might hole up there for a couple of days – wasted, worn, wrecked –
gathering myself, sleeping 'til noon, as I slowly returned to the land
of the liver-functioning.

Mum eventually moved into a smaller place when the stairs
became too much for her. The railway line came through and Martin
sold up. Over the years, houses thickened on the hillsides. The fields
are disappearing now and the suburbs are creeping steadily to the sea.
Every dog has its tag. (A pun for the Huns.) But every time I sing
'I Won't Be Your Dog' and suck those guttural sounds out of my
throat through a small set of reeds, I see that old back country in all
its lurid light and sombre glory.

JANDAMARRA / PIGEON

My name is Officer O'Malley
My job is hunting Pigeon down
I don't like this kind of work much
I'm sick of sleeping on the ground
Pigeon – that's the name we gave him
Pigeon used to be so tame
'Til one day he turned against his master
Killed him, broke his brother's chains

Now Pigeon could track the Holy Spirit
But he don't leave no tracks at all
I've been running round in circles
I've been feeling like a fool
Pigeon – that's the name we gave him
But he's got another name
It's spreading all across the valleys
Jandamarra! – like a burning flame

One time we had him in a gully
One time we had him in a cave
Each time we closed in on our quarry
He disappeared like smoke into a haze
Pigeon – that's the name we gave him
Pigeon – putting me to shame
I do this job because I have to
I don't say that he's to blame
Jandamarra! – how I hate that name

Slouching Towards Windjana

On 25 April 1915, when Australian and New Zealand troops landed on a Turkish beach in an attempt to capture the Gallipoli peninsula, a key location in Britain's strategy during World War I, hundreds of young men were mown down by well-fortified Turks shooting from the cliffs. We commemorate this slaughter every Anzac Day. We also commemorate the end of that war, with a minute's silence at eleven a.m. on 11 November, Armistice Day. But we don't have a day to commemorate all those Australians who died not in distant countries fighting the battles of others, but on their own soil, defending the country of their ancestors.

At school we learnt about Burke and Wills, Leichhardt, Eyre, Wentworth, Blaxland and Lawson – brave and sometimes blinkered explorers who 'opened up' the country for cattle, sheep, crops and the telegraph. We didn't learn about the massacres, poisonings and battles that occurred as the country was 'settled'. Nor did we learn about the Aboriginal resistance fighters – Pemulwuy, Jandamarra, Windradyne, Yagan, Calyute, Dundalli and others. The natives were 'subdued', or somehow vanished, we were taught, yielding passively to a more advanced civilisation. It was simply 'inevitable'. Today many people still say that Australia became a nation without bloodshed.

In the early eighties I came across a book called *The Other Side of the Frontier*, written by historian Henry Reynolds, which painted a picture of Australian history I hadn't seen before. In it he demonstrated that the first Australians responded in many varied and creative ways to the coming of the Europeans. Sometimes accommodating, sometimes resisting. He made the case that, wherever the terrain allowed it, they had fought fiercely for their land. Guerrilla warfare, naturally, was more effective and prolonged in hilly country than on the plains. He also argued that because the early colonial governors were under clear instructions to 'treat the natives peaceably', they omitted detailed descriptions of hostilities, punitive expeditions and battles from the official record. They couldn't say they were at war.

In this manner, Australian history developed amnesia – what anthropologist W. H. Stanner called 'the great Australian silence'. America had its Geronimos and Sitting Bulls. New Zealand had reams of scholarship on the Maori wars. But in Australia, the blacks who used to live where our cities now stand simply 'melted away'.

Reynolds' book shook the scales from my eyes. Reading it, I remembered my brother Tony's best friend growing up, Jonathan Brown, who lived across the road. His skin was as black as night but his parents were white. Jonathan had exceptionally good manners and spoke in a toffy English accent which we used to make fun of, but apart from that I didn't take much notice of him. Tony, being seven years younger than I was, didn't occupy a lot of my attention and neither did his friends. Jonathan was on the scene for a few years in my peripheral vision and then disappeared when his parents moved interstate.

Around the time that I read *The Other Side of the Frontier* I went to see No Fixed Address, Australia's first Indigenous electric band, play at the Duke of Edinburgh Hotel, around the corner from my house in Melbourne. Their big song was 'We Have Survived'. Afterwards the band and a gang of us went back to my place, where the guitars and the didge came out. We were all into reggae and started jamming. Bart Willoughby, the singer and songwriter for the band, reckoned I wasn't playing the chords the right way. I needed to choke the strings more to make the chops sound tighter. It was good advice.

I picked up other things besides guitar tips. From Bart, Kev Carmody, Lily Sansbury, Yami Lester, Rachel Perkins, June Oscar, Archie Roach, Ruby Hunter, Roger Bennett, Kutcha Edwards and many others I met on my travels over the years, I learnt a whole other view of the world. Of growing up not knowing who or where your parents were, of massacre sites remembered and avoided, of brothers who drank themselves to death, of sisters gone missing, of nephews hanging from a rope, of a thousand little slights, of not being able to get a taxi to stop at night, of pride in survival, of deep and abiding ties to country, of songs going back thousands of years, and of celebration of heroes past and present.

I read other books. Eric Wilmot wrote a novel based on the life of Pemulwuy, who fought on behalf of the Eora people around Sydney. One phrase in that book has always stayed with me – 'a strange hissing tongue'. This is how the English language first strikes Pemulwuy, whose language didn't use 's'.

I learnt more about Jandamarra, whom I'd first encountered through Reynolds. Someone put me onto a novel called *Long Live Sandawarra*, written by Colin Johnson in the seventies. It's set in Perth where the protagonist is in and out of trouble with the law. He draws inspiration and validation from stories about a mythical warrior from the Kimberley named Sandawarra, based on the real-life Jandamarra, who fought a war of resistance against the white settlers and pastoralists of the late nineteenth century. Jandamarra, a Bunuba man whose whitefella name was Pigeon, used to work as a tracker for the Derby police and was considered a model black, highly skilled as both tracker and horseman. His partnership with a man named Richardson, a rough and ready freelance police officer, was renowned. Between them they rounded up many of Jandamarra's countrymen – seen by the settlers as 'wild' blacks committing 'outrages' on the new pastoral leases. They spent a lot of time out bush together, just the two of them, Jandamarra taking Richardson deep into the heart of his country, and formed a close bond.

On one of these trips, Jandamarra had a Road to Damascus conversion. He and Richardson had tracked and captured a large number of important Bunuba warriors, including Ellemarra, Jandamarra's relation, the most wanted man in the Kimberley, for his ravages against the stock, property and people of the new cattle stations. The two men were bringing Ellemarra and the others in 'on the chain' to Derby, all shackled together. Along the way they stopped at Lillimooloora homestead, which had become a makeshift police station, because Richardson wanted to use up extra days in order to claim meal money for his prisoners. This was a rort commonly practised by the West Australian police for more than a century.

Sixteen chained men and women waited at Richardson's pleasure for a week. All during this time Ellemarra kept talking and singing quietly to Jandamarra, urging him to change sides. Richardson never had the chance to regret his dalliance because Jandamarra, after long brooding, shot and killed him in his sleep. The man formerly known as Pigeon then unshackled his countrymen and took to the ranges, where he organised his people into a fighting force against the invaders of his country.

Between 1894 and 1897 he was the Kimberley's public enemy number one – black terror and bogeyman. His surprise raids and clever guerrilla tactics, his ability to evade capture even when seemingly trapped – he had intimate knowledge of secret caves and tunnels in the limestone ranges – and his miraculous recovery from serious wounds earned him a mythical, supernatural reputation. His magic-man status remains central to the Bunuba oral tradition today.

He was eventually cornered by another tracker from further south, a Pilbara man with no ties to Jandamarra's country or kin, and was shot dead on 1 April 1897. The police chopped his head off and carried it in triumph to Derby. There were many precedents for this on the frontier. Yagan, a Noongar warrior of Perth, had had his head chopped off in the 1830s. Like Yagan's, Jandamarra's head was later sent to England as a trophy.

Jandamarra's story fascinated me on many levels, in particular his moving between two worlds and his violent betrayal of his friend and mentor. Had he been biding his time all along, waiting for his moment to strike? Did he have a strategy in place from early on – to join the police force in order to know his enemy? To learn how to shoot and ride horses and to gain access to guns and ammunition? Or was he just reacting to events as they happened, attracted to and fearful of white power, confused and unsure of where he belonged until he struck his fateful blow?

I was also amazed at how recent the story was, and how little it seemed to be known. Jandamarra's 'outbreak' occurred seventeen years after Ned Kelly's, his death only eighteen years before Gallipoli. Yet though the memory of Ned and the Anzacs has continued to shine down the years, their honour, sacrifice and glory invoked and debated, Jandamarra's story seemed shut up and buried, part of a history that was deemed best forgotten. 'All that happened a long time ago' was, and is, the constant refrain of those who oppose the so-called black-armband view of history. 'Why rake over a past that has nothing to do with us now? It's time to move on.'

I wrote a song imagining a hot, bothered and bewildered police officer trying to track Pigeon down, and recorded it in 1989. A couple of years later I was doing a solo tour of Western Australia, which included some shows in the Kimberley, and was given the number of a Bunuba woman in Fitzroy Crossing, a town built on Bunuba land not far from Jandamarra's beloved Napier and Leopold ranges. Her name was June Oscar and she ran a language and cultural centre. June had heard the song and when I came to town she took me out with a couple of old men to places where important incidents in the Jandamarra story happened – Windjana Gorge, the site of a big battle where he was badly wounded, and Tunnel Creek, where he lay low for months, recovering and being nursed by his mother and his wife. These places are now on the official tourist trail.

Three years later, in 1995, the most thorough account yet of Jandamarra and his times appeared. A small publishing company in Broome, Magabala Books, released *Jandamarra and the Bunuba Resistance*, written by Howard Pedersen and Banjo Woorunmurra. This book, based on archival research and oral history, should be on every school syllabus. I learnt in its pages that Jandamarra's campaign had been so effective that the government had given serious consideration at one stage to abandoning the north-west pastoral push all together. The moment passed, however, and police resources were poured into the area, freed from legal restraint. The slaughter of the Bunuba – men, women and children – during this period far outnumbered the few lives taken by Jandamarra and his men. The police made a broad sweep up and down both sides of the Fitzroy River and soaked the ground in blood.

From the book I learnt also that Jandamarra's wife Mayannie had had a child to Richardson, who slept with her occasionally, and Jandamarra brought up the child as his own. The story had everything – blood, betrayal, sex, war, family, mateship and magic. History that speaks to the present day. And all of it taking place in a majestic landscape. This could be the Great Australian Western, I thought. I wasn't the only one. Writer Steve Hawke, a friend of June's, was chipping away at a film script based on Howard and Banjo's book and conversations with present-day Bunuba, who still tell parts of the story in song.

Steve and I corresponded over the years as he sought backers. He formed a company called Bunuba Films with June and the mob at Fitzroy, found development money and made a trailer to attract investors. He talked to producers and script editors, who asked for changes to the screenplay. The money people were naturally wary of the cost of shooting an epic in a remote location, and wanted more control than Steve and Bunuba Films were comfortable with. They got close to a deal several times but things always stalled.

Eventually, in 2005, Tom Gutteridge, director of the Black Swan Theatre Company in Perth, saw the script and said to Steve, 'We can make a play from this.' They put their heads together, started adapting the script for the stage, and invited me in. They also found funding to run workshops in Fitzroy Crossing, the aim being to discover and develop Indigenous actors, to source local music and design, and provide a basic education in country for the non-Bunuba cast and crew.

What evolved throughout 2006 and '07 was a complex beast, a play written in three languages – Bunuba, English and Kriol – with a three-level set and projected animation. June, with another Fitzroy Crossing woman, Patsy Bedford, was in charge of translation and pronunciation for the actors and I was in charge of music and sound.

It was a long hard struggle getting the play into shape for its premiere at the 2008 Perth Festival. An epic process. Every challenge to staging a show you can think of was ours. Cross-cultural collaboration. A large cast. Some had never acted before and many were delivering lines in languages they'd just learnt. There were lots of complicated technical feats, Jandamarra levitating in a cave and turning into a bird being one. The actors had to climb and sometimes fall from high narrow stages, representing the ranges and cliffs. This had to be done in harnesses, with specialist crew manning the ropes in the darkness backstage. There were intricate lighting cues with many short scenes, and English surtitles and animation projected onto a cliff face. And because Tom and I wanted a rawness to the sound that prerecording doesn't allow, all sound effects and music were performed live.

The effects were a mixture of naturalism (bush and wet-season sounds, birdcalls, battles) and abstraction (drones, spirit noises) blended with existing music (a contemporary song cycle sung by a senior Bunuba man, George Brooking, who functioned as a solo Greek chorus on the side of the stage. The actors also sang it at various times.) Much of the sound was based on old radio-play techniques – flapping gloves for birds' wings, rubbing steel balls together for night-time frogs, crunching cellophane around a mic for fire, and making animal, bird and cricket noises vocally. To summon Yilimbirri Unggud, the great Rainbow Serpent, the cast layered drones with their voices and whirled plastic tubes of various lengths. Rehearsals were rowdy fun at times.

'Okay, Kevin, you've got the best dingo, but Dennis, can you do the campfire dog? Geoff, you're on crows. Just Geoff, we don't need a murder of them. Now, all of you offstage are on cattle sounds when they come through the gorge. And Peter, Ningali, hit it right on the change of scene with the frogs after the rain.'

We ground along in the high January heat, wrestling our leviathan onto shore. It was an exhausting job for Tom, in charge of the whole thing, who carried himself throughout with good humour, patience and grace. Long days of tech rehearsal dragged on 'til late at night. And some nights some of the actors had trouble getting a taxi home.

Not being in the play myself, my job was over by opening night. From then, as always in theatre, the show was in the actors' hands. We'd been struggling during dress rehearsals to trim its length, but the première ran for three hours and five minutes, still too long, I thought. The sympathetic audience applauded strongly at the end and there were some cheers, but I sensed they were as much worn down as exhilarated.

The following morning was the morning of Kevin Rudd's apology to the stolen generations, one of his first public utterances as Prime Minister. I wandered down to the river at dawn to watch the telecast from Canberra on the big screen. There were a few thousand people there, roughly half Noongahs (blackfellas) and half Wadjalas (whitefellas). The atmosphere was charged, a strange mixture of sombreness and festivity. At the end of Rudd's good but longwinded speech – a bit like the play – all those sitting down stood up and clapped and clapped. Many wept.

I left the riverbank and headed straight to the airport to fly home. Over the next fortnight, Black Swan Theatre sent me daily reports from the stage manager. The play's running time came down a little during the season, as Tom and Steve worked on cuts and tightened the nuts and bolts of the staging. Attendances were good, though reviews were mixed. There was a hope the production might be picked up by a company over east, or that funding could be obtained to tour it through the Kimberley, but the staging cost is high and so far has proved prohibitive.

Jandamarra the play was a brave and ambitious experiment. It had moments of great power and beauty, and Jimi Bani from Thursday Island was charismatic in the lead role. To see the legendary warrior live in him and hear the Bunuba language onstage was an achievement in itself. You don't often get two chances at this kind of thing. Only time will tell if *Jandamarra* the movie will emerge from the play's chrysalis, as Jandamarra the man once did into the light from the healing cave of Tunnel Creek.

I see him at Lillimooloora in the dead of night, holding his rifle above the sleeping Richardson as his chained brothers sit on the ground softly singing. I see him and his countrymen crouched on the ledges of Windjana Gorge in the dusk, rifles in hand, waiting for the unsuspecting cattlemen. I see him falling from a limestone pillar as Mingo Mick from down south fires that fateful shot not that long ago.

Many years after leaving school, my brother Tony met up with his old friend Jonathan, who was working as an attendant at Taronga Park Zoo in Sydney. They were now both in their twenties and had seen each other only once since Jonathan's departure from Adelaide.

They kept in loose touch after that. Jonathan was drinking heavily and moving around. Eventually he went back to South Australia to look for his parents, from whom he'd been taken as a child. He found some of his family around Yalata, Oak Valley and Maralinga, his ancestral country, added Kumintjara to his name and gave up drinking. After a while he began to paint. His work drew wide attention when he made a series of paintings on the atomic tests at Maralinga.

Jonathan Kumintjara started coming along to my shows when I visited Adelaide with the band. He also came to Melbourne quite often, spending time with the artist and collector Neil McLeod in Belgrave, at the foot of the Dandenong Ranges, and I got to see more of him. He didn't speak so posh now but he remained very soft-spoken and reserved. One night after a gig in Adelaide he told me he'd just been diagnosed with liver cancer. He looked fairly well, though he said he'd been having some pain. Not long after that he moved to Belgrave, where Neil looked after him.

Six weeks after his diagnosis he was admitted to the local hospital, and Tony and I drove up from the city to see him. He was very thin and barely lucid, drifting in and out of sleep, but he recognised us and chatted for a few minutes before closing his eyes again. We left to visit Neil up the road, returning in the afternoon. Jonathan was fast asleep, so we left a message with the nurse and headed back down to the city. By the time we arrived home there was a phone message from Neil saying Jonathan had died not long after we left. He was thirty-six years old.

Tony and I each have a painting of his that Neil passed on to us after his death. In his later work he'd developed a strong textural style using ochres mixed with a material called grog – fired clay that has been finely ground. They are paintings you long to touch.

Meanwhile Anzac Day ceremonies around the country get bigger by the year. After a period of decline in the seventies and eighties, as the diggers from World War I died, a new kind of nationalism took hold and the thinning ranks began to swell again. Now all ages march – children, grandchildren, great- and great-great-grand-children, nieces, nephews, friends, relations, acquaintances of any Australian who fought or is fighting in any war: World War II, Korea, Vietnam, Afghanistan, Iraq. Citizens with no personal links to soldiers leave their homes in darkness to join the throng at the dawn service, listen to the bugler play the Last Post, and remember those who fell for their country. They hear the words from the World War I poem 'For the Fallen' read aloud:

> They shall grow not old, as we that are left grow old;
> Age shall not weary them, nor the years condemn.
> At the going down of the sun and in the morning
> We will remember them.

Yes, remember them – remember Pemulwuy, Yagan, Dundalli. Remember Jandamarra. Remember Tunnerminnerwait and Maulboyheenner, resistance fighters deemed murderers, the first men publicly executed in Victoria, in 1842. At the going down of the sun and in the morning, remember them. Remember my friend Jonathan Kumintjara. Remember them all.

JUMP TO LOVE

You're on the edge now, leaning over
And down below you, the raging river
I can feel you tremble
Yes, I know you're scared
It'll be alright now – jump to love!

Don't hold back now
Inside you're crying
Let it go now and you'll be flying
And wherever you may land
I'll be there to break your fall
Come on, now – jump to love!
Take a chance – jump to love!

Get Bucked

In Edgar Allan Poe's short story 'The Tell-Tale Heart', a man kills his elderly neighbour and disposes of the body underneath the floorboards. When the police arrive to make enquiries – someone heard a shriek in the night – he's confident of his alibi. There's no blood and no evidence of the killing. He tells the police the old man has gone to stay in the country. The shriek was his own, caused by a bad dream.

But during the course of the conversation he begins to hear the beat of the old man's heart, 'a low dull, quick sound – such a sound as a watch makes when enveloped in cotton'. The insistent beat steadily increases in volume, though the police don't seem to notice. Our anti-hero begins to rave, getting louder and louder in an attempt to block the sound. Eventually he unravels completely and confesses his crime, crying out, 'I admit the deed! – tear up the planks! – here, here! – it is the beating of his hideous heart.'

In the early nineties, I wrote a song called 'Beat Of Your Heart', a love song with a nod to Poe in the second verse, which was covered by Christine Anu on her first album. I met Christine when she was with Bangarra Dance Company, before she became what's known in showbiz as a 'triple threat' – dancer, singer, actor. Wearing a scaly silver dress she sang a memorable version of 'My Island Home' at the closing ceremony of the 2000 Olympics, the year her second album came out. She'd done a lot of the writing and recording for that album in London the previous year. I was passing through on tour while she was there and had a couple of days off, so she asked me to help her with some tunes she'd started.

At the end of one of our sessions she said, 'I wouldn't mind another song like "Beat Of Your Heart".' So I walked back to my hotel in Hammersmith a mile or so away, pondering. Van Halen's 'Jump' came floating out into the street from a radio in a fruit and vegetable shop. Back in my room I played 'Beat Of Your Heart' a few times on acoustic guitar, gradually shifting chords and changing the tune.

Buck Owens – one of the great innovators and business minds of American music; inventor of the Bakersfield sound, distinguished by a driving bass and high ringing guitars; one of the first artists to retain ownership of his recordings and publishing; buyer and manager of a string of radio stations; writer of 'Act Naturally', recorded by The Beatles – once said about songwriting: 'I found a sound that people liked, that radio liked . . . I found this basic concept and all I did was change the lyrics and the melody a little bit . . . changed the song and the chord progression a little bit and I sold it to them over and over again.'

Now, when Buck talks it's worth listening.

Sitting in my dreary hotel room, I 'bucked' 'Beat Of Your Heart' into 'Jump To Love' in the space of an hour or two and took it to Christine the next morning. A week later she recorded it with an insistent dance beat that her producer 'borrowed' from a Kylie Minogue record.

'Jump To Love' works fine without the four-on-the-floor kick-drum and bass. And I've found a key to sing it in that suits my voice. So I carry it with me. It's a good working song and suits most occasions. My approach is more like the Aztec Camera version of 'Jump'.

As for 'Beat Of Your Heart' and its Gothic pretensions, it's no longer in the kit. It lies neglected and mouldering under the floorboards and I can't hear it any more.

JUST ABOUT TO BREAK

Handle me with care
I'm the answer to your prayer
I come from the great nowhere
Step back! Give me some air
I'm just about to break
I'm just about to break
I'm just about to break

I've been dreaming some
I'm a sleeping time bomb
When I wake it won't take long
I'll hit from here to kingdom come
I'm just about to break
I'm just about to break
I'm just about to break

They're gonna want to analyse me
Canonise or demonise me
Buy the rights and serialise me
Moralise and sermonise against me
I'm just about to break
I'm just about to break
I'm just about to break

I'm gonna rock your head
Start a burning in your bed
I'm making gold from lead
Multiplying fish and bread
I'm just about to break
I'm just about to break
I'm just about to break

My philosophy's eclectic
Things round here, they're gonna get hectic
There's no defence 'cause I got no tactics
I sing the body electric!
I'm just about to break
I'm just about to break
I'm just about to break

The thunderstorm is just above
Every soul one day must cry enough
I'm heaven sent to spill my stuff
My heart, my heart is full of love
I'm just about to break
I'm just about to break
I'm just about to break

Legion

I was living in God's own country, the United States of America, when Counting Crows were about to release their first album in the early nineties. The singer had a bit of a Van Morrison thing going on, though he did more interviews than Van, and a buzz was starting to build around the band. A friend of mine worked for their management company. 'They're just about to break,' she confided to me over margaritas and chicken mole in a Santa Monica eatery.

After being nothing more than a title for six or seven years – like a drought-resistant seed lying in the ground, biding its time and waiting for rain – 'Just About To Break' finally sprouted in 2000. There must have been something in the air – millennium weather, maybe. The clock ticked past midnight at the start of that year without the world coming to an end. And on the next New Year's Eve too, which according to the Ones Who Knew, was the real beginning of the millennium. It must have been very frustrating for those true believers, who knew they were right, that nobody was listening.

To have the knowledge and be scorned by fools. That must really stick in the craw. To be the chosen one and yet have those not worthy stand in your way. To hold the keys to right thinking and right living, yet be surrounded by armies of wickedness. It's enough to make you want to go out and make a bomb. Derail a train. Fly a plane into a building. Or give the order for a pre-emptive war.

Six years after 'Just About To Break', along came 'God Told Me To'. That old voice in the head said, Write this down! It was the same guy again (it's usually a he but sometimes a she). He's been coming around for centuries – Savonarola, Joan of Arc, Torquemada, Ned Kelly, David Koresh, Mohammed Atta, George Bush Jr. He won't be going away anytime soon. His name is legion.

> I sing the body electric;
> The armies of those I love engirth me and I engirth them;
> They will not let me off till I go with them, respond to them,
> And discorrupt them, and charge them full with the charge
>   of the Soul.
>
> Walt Whitman, from 'I Sing the Body Electric'

KING OF FOOLS

I'm the king, I'm the king of fools
The king kong king of fools

Now a fool always has a song
He sings it feeling proud
And before too long there's a crowd
And a fool finds himself alone
With grinning faces all around
Watch him dance 'til he falls down

I'm the king, I'm the king of fools
The king kong king of fools

Now a fool falls into a trance
He cannot help himself
He's a walking, talking someone else
And a fool buys another round
To keep out of the rain
Makes a promise to himself, 'Never again'

I'm the king, I'm the king of fools
The king kong king of fools

Nightclubbin'

Which clubs are fictitious?
Inferno
Heaven
Nightmoves
Mad
Fever

Fiasco
Secrets
Rumours
Breezes
Shenanigans
Carnage
Persuasions
Illusions
Spit
Amnesia
Envy
Pulse
Blackout
Mist
Paradox

(Answer at back of book)

Advice To Young Singer-Songwriters

Pay attention
Trust your instincts
Never sign anything without a lawyer
Play to the people listening, not the people talking
It doesn't always sound as bad out the front as you think it does
Remember that you employ the record company/manager/booking
    agent, not the other way around
You don't have to wear the funny hat the photographer has brought
    to the shoot
Thank the road crew – they start work before you and finish later
Try not to sleep with someone in your band
Sleep with whoever the fuck you want to, take what you want from
    old songwriters, and leave the rest

LATELY

Lately I must have changed
All day long I'm dreaming
Lately I lose my way
When I'm running some small errand
Maybe I'm lucky some people are kind
Lately you've been on my mind

It's funny what gets disregarded
Right before your eyes
It's funny – everybody else can see it
And you're the last to realise
A secret spell has caught me in the sweetest bind
Lately you've been on my mind

I had almost forgotten
The way it used to feel
From a sleep I've woken
Now the dream is real

Lately I don't take for granted
Every moment passing by
Lately I'm trapped in wonder
When you move I'm mesmerised
You have blessed me, you've made me shine
Lately you've been on my mind

Secret Spell

My sister Mary Jo teaches music during the week and plays keyboards for Latin bands around Melbourne on the weekends. That

takes stamina. The dancing doesn't start 'til midnight usually. She's got a strong left hand – you need that to lock in with the bass – and knows a lot of chords: inverted, augmented, diminished, suspended, sevenths, ninths, elevenths, thirteenths, and so on. She can hold her own in the more jazzy ensembles.

Many years ago, for my birthday, she gave me the *Frank Sinatra Songbook*. She said she bought it for me so she could borrow it herself. I considered it part of my education. Mary Jo was born fourteen months behind me, but ever since she turned thirteen she's been older; I'm still trying to catch up.

The songbook had a lot of chords I'd never played before. Fortunately there were little diagrams to show you where to put your fingers. I spent days slowly working my way through the lovely chords of 'All The Way' and trying to sing it at the same time. I never got it going very smoothly and my brain hurt after a while. But after a little lay-off, I picked up the guitar and out came 'Lately', a different kind of song for me, the kind you need to wear a suit to sing.

Any new musical object in your life can give you a song. I bought a Dobro in the late nineties, made of pressed tin. It has a clanky, old-timey sound. I brought it home, tuned it to an open D and out came 'I Wasted Time'. (Thank you, new guitar, you're not a waste of time.)

After visits from Nephew Dan, I often find a guitar in a different tuning lying around the house. Once he had my guitar tuned down two tones for some effect he was trying out on a recording. I picked it up to play and was delivered into a woozy, fag-end-of-the-night world. I felt like I'd taken a Mandrax. Out fell a woozy, fag-end-of-the-night song called 'One More Tune'.

Sometimes you need something new to come along to break you out of your old patterns and habits, something to tug you out of your rut and drag you through another door. A secret spell to help you see things fresh again.

LEAPS AND BOUNDS
(written with Chris Langman)

I'm high on the hill,
Looking over the bridge
To the MCG
And way up on high
The clock on the silo
Says eleven degrees
I remember, I remember
I'm breathing today
The month of May
All the burning leaves
I'm not hearing a sound
My feet don't even
Touch the ground
I remember, I remember
I go leaps and bounds
Down past the river
And across the playing fields
The fields all empty
Only for the burning leaves
I remember, I remember
I go leaps and bounds
I remember everything

1109 Hoddle

Your arrival from the provinces in the city.
Misted-over windowpanes of streetcars . . .
Your dread when you entered a place too expensive . . .

The house you approached trembling,
The apartment that dazzled you –
Look, on this spot the cranes clear the rubble.

Czesław Miłosz, from 'Youth'

I moved to Melbourne in 1977, the year Elvis died. I'd been putting words to music for a little while and had a dozen or so songs in my pocket. A friend of mine introduced me to some ex-Adelaide guys in a band – John, Chris, Tony – who had a share house in East Melbourne. They'd achieved some notoriety at home under the name Spare Change, then moved east seeking a bigger audience.

The house was a large, two-storey terrace on Hoddle Street, just around the corner from the MCG, with a front porch and balcony balustraded with wrought iron. The number of the house was 1109, the same number as the house in Luis Buñuel's film *The Discreet Charm of the Bourgeoisie*, a synchronicity which pleased the denizens within.

People came and went. It was a full house when I lobbed so I slept on John's floor on a thin single mattress. John, Chris and Tony had met in London and Amsterdam in the early seventies and were up to date with contemporary trends, well versed in popular culture, breaking bands out of the UK, the New York scene, French cinema, et cetera. Watching shows or movies on TV, they could say the lines before they came out of characters' mouths. I felt like a country bumpkin around them so I didn't say much and kept my ears open.

John, the singer, worked in a record store and had a turntable in his room with a huge collection of records. It was there I first heard Tom Petty, Television, Talking Heads, Jonathan Richman and The Modern Lovers, The Ramones, Elvis Costello, The Sex Pistols, and The Clash. He played me old records by The Velvet Underground, The Flying Burrito Brothers, The Stooges, The Beatles, and The Beach Boys, all of them revelations.

Marquee Moon, Television's first album, which had just come out, was the bible. Spare Change, now Parachute, practised 'Venus' for days in the music/TV/lounge room downstairs, Chris and Bob, the guitarists, reconstructing Tom Verlaine and Richard Lloyd's majestic, mathematical, interlocking guitar parts. On a trip back to Adelaide I took a cassette with *Marquee Moon* on one side and *Paris 1919* on the other, playing it in every house I visited, like Moses descending from the mountain top with tablets of stone.

Soon I moved into a closet room behind the stairwell – just enough space for a mattress, rucksack of clothes, books, a little tape player and a cache of cassettes. Chris and I sat around for hours, days, playing guitars – either two acoustics or Chris would plug his Stratocaster, which he played left-handed, into a small amp. He had a high-ringing mercury tone and could play like Robbie Robertson from The Band. I played him my new songs as they kept coming and we made up tunes together, mainly about girls we knew or wanted to know. 'The Hounds Of Juliet' was one.

Juliet came by the house quite often. She was a curly-haired, voluptuous, almond-eyed beauty with dangerous ways. Later on, the filmmaker Paul Cox would make a film based on her called *My First Wife*. Chris and I also started an exuberant song about nothing in particular called 'Leaps And Bounds', but didn't finish it.

Melbourne was jumping in the late seventies. Still is. There were a lot of small venues in the inner city – pubs mainly – which put on live music most nights of the week. Hearts and Martinis in Carlton, The Tiger Lounge in Richmond, the Station Hotel in Prahran, The Crystal Ballroom in St Kilda, and, just over the road from us, the Kingston Hotel. We could walk there.

The venue in the Kingston was in the basement. You walked downstairs into a dim square cavern. On weekends it was crowded, and especially packed when The Sports or Jo Jo Zep and The Falcons played. The Sports did a knockout version of The Searchers' 'When You Walk In The Room', and a song called 'White Honey' by a British singer, Graham Parker, I was just beginning to hear about. They were writing their own tunes as well – songs like 'Twist Senorita' and 'Boys (What Did The Detectives Say?)'

Their singer, Steve Cummings, had dark good looks but was pretty awkward onstage. He just stood there, spitting the songs out, looking very uncomfortable and hanging onto the mic stand for dear life. If he can do it so can I, I thought to myself.

The Crystal Ballroom was a big punk scene. The Boys Next Door, later to become The Birthday Party, were regulars there, fronted by Nick Cave. Also The Teenage Radio Stars – who mutated into The Models – and Jab, La Femme, The News, and early minimalists and electronic pioneers Essendon Airport, who onstage looked like scientists in a lab.

Whereas Sydney bands, as exemplified by Radio Birdman, seemed under the spell of the heavy Detroit sound of The Stooges and MC5, many Melbourne bands had more arty pretensions. Over in Carlton, young lords walked the earth – brainy, serious music architects, Martin Armiger and Eric Gradman, with their bands Bleeding Hearts and Man and Machine. I wormed my way to the front of smoky, sweaty crowds to watch them, agog at the angular, aggressive, bass-heavy noise pumping through big W-bin speakers.

And in winter, on the way home from those gigs in Carlton, Richmond, St Kilda, we'd scavenge bits of wood from building sites for the fireplace of the high-ceilinged, draughty front room of number 1109. And settle in for the late-night old movies on Channel Nine that ran 'til dawn, punctuated by Delmonti menswear ads for suits that 'Look good, feel good, are good!' If the movies didn't hook us we'd pull out the guitars and play 'til the firewood ran out, 'til we'd squeezed every last drop from the cask of wine or drunk every last can from the slab.

Eventually Chris helped me organise a gig at the Kingston Hotel. I remember the titles of some of the songs from that time, though I can't play them any more – 'She's The One', 'Habit Of Love', 'Recognition', 'Faster Than Light Our Love'. Chris knew Red Symons, the flamboyant guitar player from Skyhooks, just about the biggest band in the country at the time, and roped him in. Huck Treloar from Bleeding Hearts, who'd just broken up, played drums.

Rick Grossman from Man and Machine, who went on to play with The Divinyls and Hoodoo Gurus, had moved into the house by this time and was enlisted on bass. I had to rub my eyes at being onstage with these heroes.

That was a one-off lineup. Everybody had other fish to fry, but I managed to get a band together soon afterwards which included a waxing and waning horn section (some days we had two horn players, other times five), and the gaunt Prince of Carlton, Martin Armiger. We called ourselves The High Rise Bombers, after a newspaper head-line about people throwing stuff from the top storey of Housing Commission flats.

Martin wrote songs and so did a couple of others in the band. Most of mine were mid-tempoish. We got ourselves a residency in a beer garden at the back of Café Paradiso in Carlton on Sunday afternoons. We also played at hotels and universities. In those days the student councils of campuses like Melbourne, Monash, RMIT and Swinburne had decent budgets to pay bands and stage concerts. These were often at lunchtime, when most students were around. And in the suburbs, big beer barns booked bands five or six nights a week – the Sentimental Bloke, the Ferntree Gully, the Southside Six, and a host of others. We didn't draw big crowds but we must have drawn just enough to get rebooked at a hundred and fifty dollars a gig. If you got two or three of those a week and threw in a city show and a campus lunchtime, you could scrape by.

The High Rise Bombers lasted nine months only – too many chiefs – but, strangely, seemed to get more famous once we'd broken up. My main memory of being in the band is people in the crowd yelling, 'Play faster!'

I formed a band called The Dots after that, minus the horn sec-tion, and we did the beer-barn, campus and inner-city rounds for a few years, once in a while venturing to Sydney, Adelaide and even as far as Brisbane. The Dots were mainly distinguished by a succession of guitar players called Chris who kept leaving the band. Music writers described us as New Wave.

BUM 1700

Peter, Paul and Mary

ALBUM 1700
PETER, PAUL AND MARY

Allan's

1: I DIG ROCK AND ROLL MUSIC (Stookey-Mason-Dixon)
2: IF I HAD WINGS (Yarrow-Yardley)
3: I'M IN LOVE WITH A BIG BLUE FROG (Braunstein)
4: WHATSHERNAME (Stookey-Dixon-Kniss)
5: BOB DYLAN'S DREAM (Bob Dylan)
6: THE SONG IS LOVE
(Dixon-Kniss-Stookey-Yarrow)

Produc

Albert B. G

ST

MANUFACTURED IN AUSTRALIA BY A R

SCREAMING

JO JO ZEP AND TH

'HIT AND RUN (Camilleri-Burstin-F
Mushroom) 4.36
*DON'T WANNA COME DOWN (Camil
(Antipodes/Mushroom) 3.28
: *KATSCHARA (Camilleri-Burstin-Faehse)
(Mushroom) 4.13
4: *ONLY THE LONELY HEARTED (P. Kelly) (Mu
(Mushroom)
5: YOU MADE A FOOL OUT OF ME (M. Jupp)
(*Aust. Comps.)

979 Mushroom
Records, Australia

AUSTRALIAN
RECORDING

Pr
En
Re
Recorded
Remixe

JENNY MO
SHIVER

AUSTRALIAN
RECORDING

1. SAVED ME (J. Morris) (3.46)
2. BAG LADY (J. Morris) (3.11)
3. SHE HAS TO BE LOVED (J. Morris/A. Farriss) (4.0
4. CONSCIENCE (J. Morris/A. Farriss) (2.32)
5. STREET OF LOVE (P. Kelly) (3.03)

Produced by Andrew Farriss. Engineered by Alan Wright.
All Jenny Morris compositions published by MMA Music.
All Andrew Farriss compositions published by Tol Muziek.
Paul Kelly compositions published by Mushroom Music.
Manufactured and Distributed by
WEA Records Pty. Limited

M
Reco

ⓟ 1

ALL RIGHTS OF THE MANUFACTURER AND OF THE OWNER OF THE RECORDED WORK RESERVED. UNAUTHORISED PUBLIC PERFORMANCE, BROADCASTING, LEASING AND COPYING OF THIS RECORD PROHIBITED. WEA RECO

D RESERVED MADE IN AUSTRALIA BY FESTIVA

Beggar On The Street
Of Love **Peter, Paul and
Mary's 'Big Blue Frog'**,
written by (Braunstein),
and some (P. Kelly) credits

Big Fine Girl Catherine Kelly

Careless With members of the Tuvan throat singers
ensemble Shu-De, on the WOMADelaide train trip, 1996

Down To My Soul Rembrandt's *A Woman in Bed*, c.1645

Forty Miles To Saturday Night Robert Lougheed's
Ten Miles to Saturday Night, 1978

Forty-Eight Angels **Fra Angelico's** fresco *The Annunciation*, 1438–45

From Little Things
Big Things Grow
Prime Minister Gough
Whitlam pours dirt into
the hands of Vincent
Lingiari, to ceremonially
hand over leasehold
title of Daguragu to
the Gurindji people,
26 August 1975

Gathering Storm Hobbema's *The Avenue at Middelharnis*, 1689

Ercole Filippini Baritono

I Close My Eyes
And Think Of You
(opposite) Count Ercole
Tonti-Filippini in
costume for *Rigoletto*;
(above) John and
Jo Kelly; (left)
Nonna Nance, the
Contessa Filippini

If I Could Start Today Again **Norwood Redlegs** ruckman **'Big Bill'** Wedding soars in the 1961 **SANFL** Grand Final at Adelaide Oval

Leaps And Bounds
The High Rise
Bombers, live at
Café Paradiso in
Carlton, c.1978

No You Brian Wilson and The Beach Boys;
Johnny Cash and June Carter

(The Ballad Of) Queenie And Rover The final
resting places of Queenie McKenzie and Rover
Thomas, in a bush cemetery in the East Kimberley

Winter Coat
Sinatra – the
bobbysoxer,
and the eternally
middle-aged
crooner from
the Capitol years

Chris, my original co-conspirator, left early in the piece. He'd started working as a casual driver for Crawford Productions, makers of TV dramas, and soon became an assistant director and then director. He helped out his housemates by giving us occasional jobs as extras on set. The inmates of 1109 blended in with various crowds on late-seventies soaps: *Skyways*, *Cop Shop* and *The Sullivans*.

One day in autumn, after a cheque from Crawfords came through, I walked the three kilometres to the Black Mask bookshop in South Yarra. They had a beautiful, three-volume, annotated edition of Shakespeare's *Complete Works* that I'd had my eye on for a while. Each volume was illustrated and bound in maroon cloth and all three nestled in a sturdy box with a portrait of Will on the front. It cost thirty-four dollars, a princely sum at the time. I wanted it badly and had put it on lay-by some time before with a five-dollar deposit. Now, the proceeds of my cashed cheque in hand, it was mine at last.

I toted my twenty-pound treasure back home on the bus, along Punt Road, up the hill and down across the river, where Punt changes its name to Hoddle, past the silos and the playing fields and the eastern edge of the MCG. I leaned my head out the window to breathe in the smell of burning leaves in the parks, then pulled it back in to plunge deep into the fresh, sweet-smelling pages of *Volume III: Tragedies and Romances*.

Back at 1109 I had another monumental book set, which I was working my way through like a caterpillar munching a giant leaf: *Remembrance of Things Past*, Marcel Proust's seven-volume meditation on memory, desire and time. In between gigs and occasional work as an extra, I spent large chunks of my twenty-fourth year lying on my bed with Marcel, his beloved Albertine, his barons, snobs and duchesses as they loved and schemed and grew old in late-nineteenth- and early-twentieth-century France. I put the book down when Juliet came to bed.

Around that time, Juliet brought her friend Hilary along to a gig of mine with The Dots at the Kingston Hotel. I asked Juliet a few questions about her and not long after that we split up. Hilary and I started seeing each other and eventually moved in together, into a second-storey flat near the top of Punt Road hill. Slept on a futon on the floor. From our lounge-room window we could see the monumental circumference and light towers of the MCG.

In 1980 our son Declan was born. A year later I was playing through old tapes I'd made with Chris and came across a rough recording of 'Leaps And Bounds' – the two of us hacking our way through some chords and singing a mixture of gibberish and rhyme. I wrote a set of words, based on the original rhymes but still about nothing in particular, and took them down the hill to Chris.

I didn't record the song 'til years later. It was waiting for the right band. Steve Connolly wrote the riff and we did a film clip on top of the Punt Road silos. We shot it in midsummer, with the temperature in the low thirties, dressed up for an eleven-degree autumn day in long pants, shirts and jackets. That's show business.

The song became pretty popular but I got sick of playing it after a while and had to give it a long rest. Now it's back in the squad, though not a regular selection in the team. It gets a run from time to time, usually on big occasions – Commonwealth Games ceremonies, footy shows and the like. That's the song the producers always ask for. It's a proven performer, comes into its own around finals time. Not bad for a song about nothing.

Chris stayed in TV and made some movies as well. He directed Kylie Minogue in one of her early lead roles, in *The Henderson Kids*, and later her first video clip, for 'The Locomotion'. He works in America most of the time but we get together once in a while, swap music and try to remember stuff. He likes to fool around on the pedal steel.

I still have *The Complete Works* and *Remembrance of Things Past* (or, to translate the title literally, *In Search of Lost Time*). I also have those old companions the King James Bible, *The Louvin Brothers* box set and the *Frank Sinatra Songbook*. So I'm all set for Armageddon. Every now and then I go back to the first few pages of *Remembrance*, to the sound of the swinging gate and the madeleine cake dipped in tea, and dream of shutting out the world and rereading it all the way to the end. But like Marcel, I know I'll never, ever have the time again.

NIG

THR

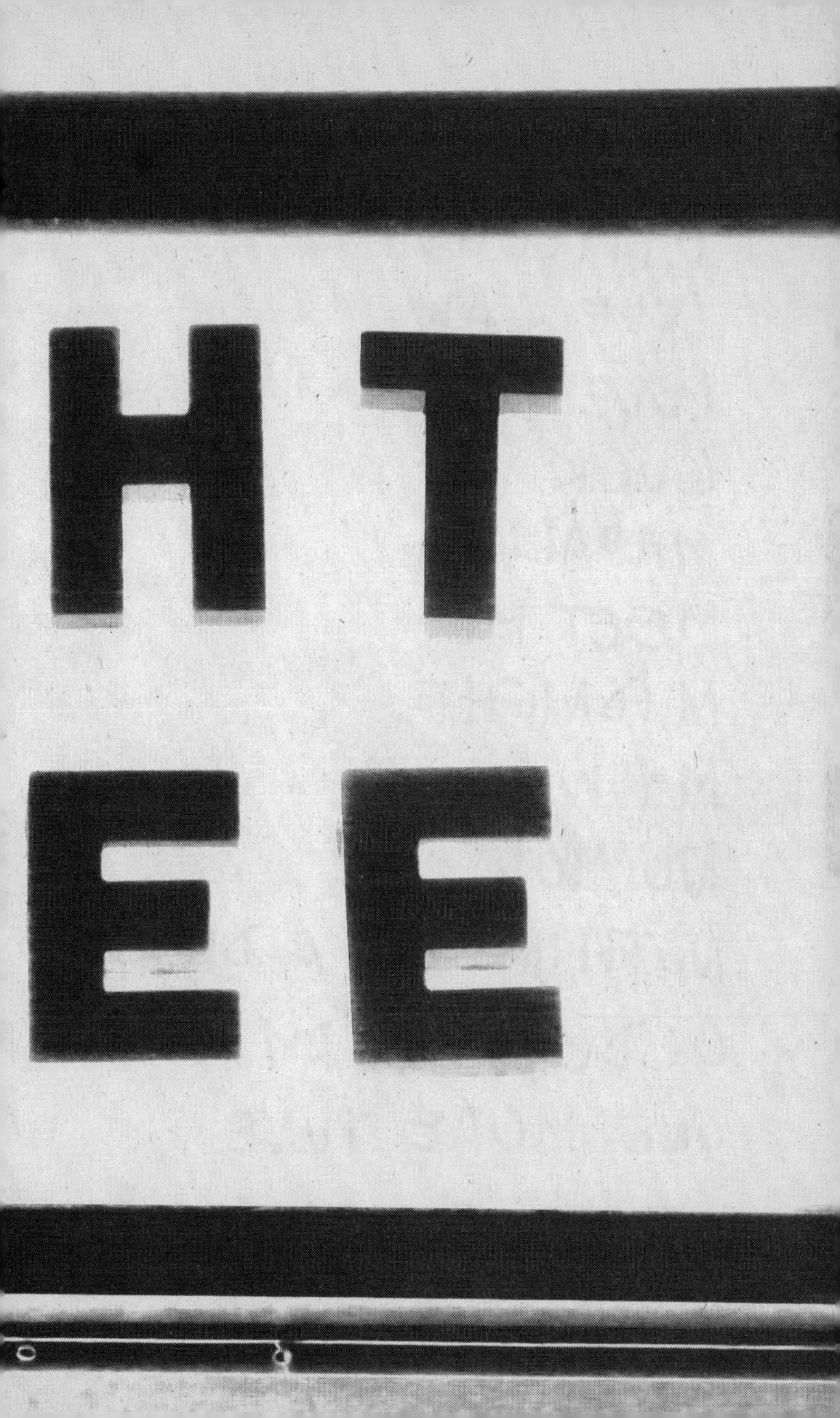
HT
EE

LITTLE BOY
LOVE LAW
LOVE NEVER
LUCK
MARALINGA
MEET ME
MIDNIGHT
MY WAY
NO YOU
NOTHING BUT A DREAM
OLDEST STORY
ONE MORE TUNE
OTHER PEOPLE'S

OUR SUNSHINE
PLEASE MYSELF
PRETTY
QUEENIE
RALLY ROUND
RANDWICK
SAT SUN
SHANE WARNE
SMOKE
SOMEBODY'S FORGETTIN
SOMEWHERE
SOUTH O GERMANY

LITTLE BOY, DON'T LOSE YOUR BALLS

Little boy, you look so clear around the eyes
And what they've got in store for you, you may not realise
So be careful when you hear the voices call
Watch out, little boy, don't lose your balls

'Cause you never know the rules until you play
First they stroke you, then they screw you, try to take your
    balls away
And once they're gone they're way beyond recall
Watch out, little boy, don't lose your balls

Balls run wild
Balls may get way out of line
You may not even know you've left your balls way behind

You know money only buys you what you want
And you can't buy your balls back like you buy a pair
    of pants
And once they're gone you've really got fuck all
Watch out, little boy, don't lose your balls

Money Is External

The Go-Betweens' Grant McLennan was a good postcard writer. Once every two or three years I'd get one from him. They came from all over – Sweden, California, Cairns – sometimes just a line or two. On one he sent a fragment of a poem by American John Berryman. It was called 'The Ball Poem' and described a boy who loses his ball when it falls into the harbour. Grant, in cramped, curly black script, prefaced the lines with 'Take this with you; pin it above the headboard. Good luck, knock 'em dead and all the other showbiz stuff as well. America calls!' The quote read:

> Now he senses first responsibility
> In a world of possessions. People will take balls,
> Balls will be lost always, little boy,
> And no-one buys a ball back. Money is external.

John Berryman killed himself with a shotgun in 1972, thirty-four years before Grant's untimely death. I guess that takes balls.

And I guess you never know what's in store.

The Bell And The Ball

See the ball just clearing the pack in a game of Australian Rules, hitting the ground and lurching towards goal. Sixty thousand people hold their breath as they follow its sick, confused path. Or see it, rounder now, in the air half a second after the basketballer has released it from outside the circle. The bell has rung and the ball is arcing in slow motion towards the net. It hits the rim and bounces straight up before coming down again. Slim matter wrapped around nothing, it is now beyond the players, transfixing the crowd and holding within its airy darkness the fate of the game.

Some sports without balls are compelling – boxing, for instance, the 1500 metre swim, the 5000 metre run, and those sports that get interesting every four years at the Olympics: weightlifting, diving, Greco-Roman wrestling and such – but in the general run of life, I lean towards the battle between man and moving spherical object (with the exception of golf).

If I go for a run I'm bored as soon as I start, but give me a ball to chase, swat, kick, catch or hurl and I'll run all day. Running hurts after a while but when you're chasing a ball you feel no pain. The ball is a thing of enchantment, caster of spells. It can mesmerise an entire stadium, cure what aches, and turn ponderous age into enthusiastic youth. Can turn into a lethal weapon when a fast bowler charges in on a bouncy wicket, or a plaything in the hands of a child.

I suspect that when a small child first encounters a ball they think it's alive. It moves across the floor with a life of its own. When you knock a toy or drop a book it falls and stops. You knock a ball and it runs away from you. With its unique properties the ball seems to straddle the division between living and non-living things. Not alive but not exactly lifeless either, the ball is in a separate world, in the shape of a world. Supernatural. To aficionados, great sportspeople are masters of the occult. We call Shane Warne, Roger Federer, Peter Daicos and Michael Jordan wizards.

Children make their first tentative efforts to come to grips with a ball's weirdness and discover it's not always controllable. It comes through the air to them and spills out of their hands. Slowly, over time, they start to gain some control. Some of us never leave that dance.

LOVE IS THE LAW

Though I speak in tongues of angels
And in many tongues of men
Though prophecy may sing through me
Without love I'm nothing
Though I understand all mysteries
And can see the story's end
Though my faith can move mountains
Without love I'm nothing

Love is the law, the law is love
Love is the law, the law is love

You may give away your riches
Do good deeds in the sight of men
You may be strong against temptation
But without love you're nothing
Without love you're just useless
Without love you're living in hell
Without love you're so hollow
An empty horn, a clanging bell

Love is the law, the law is love
Love is the law, the law is love

Love can suffer hardship
Love is tough and kind
Love is never envious
Or puffed up with pride
Love is always truthful
Love is never stale
Love is always hopeful
And never dreams that it can fail

Love is the law, the law is love
Love is the law, the law is love

Nothing

Sometime late in 1999, when I was doing nothing much, I was asked
to take part in an outdoor concert to open the 2000 Adelaide Festival
of Arts. Warumpi Band, pioneers of Aboriginal rock music, and Vika
and Linda had already been booked. The proposed venue was Elder
Park, a large swathe of grass sloping gently down to the River Torrens.
The organisers had big plans. The festival ran in March and they were
inviting parents of babies born that year to parade their newborns at
the end of the show. All parents wishing to do so were to register their
children, sending a photo and information – time and date of birth,
name, sex and other details – to be displayed on screens either side of
the stage. They wanted an anthem to close the night while the parade
was taking place – a song that involved the other performers on the
bill taking turns to sing and joining together in a big chorus.

'We want a song to celebrate the hope and sense of renewal that
comes with the new millennium. A song of optimism and inclu-
siveness . . .' There was more in the letter but I'd got the picture
already – Michael Jackson, Sting, we're all in this, in the one world
we have, moving forward together, blah.

I said yes before I could think about it too much. I thought it
would be a challenge and fun to write something large and choral.
I'm not usually a writer of anthems. Most of my songs have particular
people doing particular things. 'Leaps And Bounds' was probably the
closest I'd written to an anthem and that was about nothing much,
more just a feeling of free-floating joy. So maybe that was it. Maybe
it should be about nothing. An anthem needs to resound and something can only resound when it's hollow. Maybe an anthem, like a
football, had to be mainly nothingness.

Okay, so nobody's kissing under the pines, nobody's making a compilation tape, nobody's buying a round or running an errand, catching a bus or undoing a dress. No specifics, please. Off you go.

But – surprise – nothing happened. After all, how do you make something out of nothing unless you're God? And nothing happened the next week either. Nor the week after. The weeks became months and the deadline got closer. 'We hope you can send us the song, soon,' came the letter from Adelaide. The last stuttering days of the millennium drew to a close. Omens and portents were everywhere for those who had eyes to see. All the computers were going to fail. There would be massive pile-ups as traffic lights across the Western world stalled. Water would stop running from the taps and aeroplanes were sure to drop from the sky.

We were booked to do a New Year's Eve show in Sydney's Darling Harbour. For months bands had been quoting double, sometimes quadruple, for playing that night. It wasn't just New Year's Eve, it was New Millennium's Eve. *It won't come round again for another thousand years, so you'd better get in while you can.* Some bands did okay, some ended up scrambling at the last minute, some promoters overreached and got crispy. I was happy with our tidy sum and looking forward to being in Sydney for the big party. I'd already made sure there were a few extra tins of baked beans in the pantry, and just to be sure, filled up the bath with water before we left.

In Sydney every available patch of ground with a view of the harbour thronged with people, some of whom had camped out to get their spot. There were concerts going on all over, and lots of bands on the bill in our neck of the water. We played three songs soon after dusk on a warm night to a large crowd sitting on the grass. We'd just started and then we were finished. On a per song basis it was the most I'd ever been paid. Afterwards I went with Kaarin and the children back to the hotel – which cost a thousand a night, allegedly, but we weren't footing the bill – to watch the millennium roll out across the world on TV. We didn't make it past Adelaide, our eyelids were so heavy. When we cleaned our teeth water ran out of the taps.

The next morning from our window we could see planes miraculously flying in the sky. I lay on the bed while the others took their time in the bathroom. There was a bible in the bedside draw (thank you, Gideons), which I flicked through idly. We flew home that day. As well as my luggage I carried an invisible load – a four-word alliterative chorus and a first verse that rhymed.

anthem n. ME *antefne* f. OE *antefn* f. ML *antifona, antiphona* f. Gr *antiphōna* f. *antiphōnos*, sounding back f. *anti-*, over, against + *phōnē*, voice: *[see phono.]* **1** a religious song sung antiphonally (the anthem being sung by the choristers alternately, one half-choir answering the other). **2** a religious choral song usually based on words from the Bible. **3** a song of praise or devotion, as to a nation, college, etc.

Ten weeks later, with the song completed and partly rehearsed, I landed in Adelaide with the band on a hot late-summer's day. The Warumpi Band – straight out of the Central Desert and Arnhem Land – were at the airport. I handed out lyric sheets and we talked over the arrangement for the night's finale.

The sound check was shaky, as expected, with everyone working out their cues and phrasing, and settling on the harmonies for the choruses. But by the end I felt reasonably confident we could make it work.

Later in the evening Warumpi's lead singer George slayed the crowd with his skinny, shimmy, shaky moves and high throaty singing. They were always a tough act to follow. We did our best, doing our thing. It was nice to know we had them and Vika and Linda up our sleeve for our last song.

We'd arranged the song with a mind to The Chemical Brothers' 'Let Forever Be', featuring Noel Gallagher – nicking the drum part which they'd nicked from The Beatles' 'Tomorrow Never Knows'. Steve 'Stretch' Teakle from the Warumpis played a stuttering accordion line that sounded like a bush sequencer. We singers took turns, sharing verses, joining in choruses, Vika and Linda twirling their arms and fingers as rose petals fluttered down from the sky. I thought I was in a Bollywood movie. Meanwhile babies were promenaded on the shoulders and in the arms of proud parents, snaking down from the high ground to the stage and looping back again, the babies' images large on the big screens.

It was all a wonderful piece of nothing.

> Though I speak with the tongues of men and of angels, and have not charity, I am become as sounding brass, or a tinkling cymbal. And though I have the gift of prophecy, and understand all mysteries, and all knowledge; and though I have all faith, so that I could remove mountains, and have not charity, I am nothing.
>
> From St Paul's first letter
> to the Corinthians

LOVE NEVER RUNS ON TIME

I pulled out of the suburbs by sunset
Rain was falling, it looked like it would for a while
I had a radio, a six-pack and some cigarettes
The radio died after the first hundred miles
I sang all the way to the border and guess who starred
   in every rhyme
Ah, you know and I know that love never runs on time

I followed that old river 'til the morning
I stopped, I don't remember the name of the town
But the colour of the coffee was a warning
It was the colour of the river but not nearly as brown
The waitress poured me another, man, she was looking fine
You know and I know that love never runs on time

You're lost in the traffic
I've been asking around but you haven't been seen
I never thought we were perfect
Oh, but darling – what we could have been!

The rain came and went all the next day
I pulled over sometime for a sleep on the side
Then I gunned her back out on the highway
Hit a big pothole – the radio came alive!
I never heard a love song yet that I could call yours and mine
'Cause you know and I know that love never runs on time

The Biggest Little Thing

Happiness on tour is often just being able to tick off a list of little things. You've managed to get your washing done. You had time to eat a decent meal between the sound check and show and digest it so you could sing properly. The internet works at the hotel. You're reading a good book. You found fresh fruit in the morning. You got some exercise, maybe a swim or a walk, or you did your prison routine – push-ups, dips, squats, sit-ups – in your room. Better still, there was a gym at the hotel. You said no to another round of whisky the night before so you don't have a hangover. And so on.

There is the big happiness, of course, the long blurt onstage where you push sound out through muscle, sinew and bone into the air for two hours. Where you *do your work*. And the tools you've brought with you are in order. And you've done the job well. And afterwards your shirt is wet and you've got a little buzz on and beer never tasted so good – not since the night before. But around this good big thing (and it's not always good), you try to maintain those little things as well, reasonably consistently, despite long drives or airport delays or frustrating sound checks. If you can do that, you tend to stay in shape mentally and physically.

The biggest little thing for a coffee snob – and I'm one – is a decent brew in the morning. If you're staying in a capital city and you're near the barista belt or the latte zone, you'll have your favourite places, cafés with sturdy old Italian espresso machines and people who know how to work them. It gets tougher when you're in smaller towns or other countries.

In France, Spain and Italy it's hard to go too wrong – café crème, café con leche, caffè latte – but the UK and Ireland aren't so easy. One of the first things I do in London after landing is to go to Bar Italia in Soho. No matter where we're staying, I try to include a trip there sometime during the day, to get my hit and say hello to Rocky Marciano postered in his prime on the wall. And there's a place in Dublin, south of Temple Bar, called the Bald Barista which I make a beeline for whenever I'm in town. It's run by a New Zealander. The fact that these are the only places I can name is in itself a sad story.

America is sadder still. When I first toured there in the late eighties, before the 'coffee revolution', you'd drive miles to a place you'd heard had an espresso machine. Once there, you'd ask the bemused staff for a cappuccino without the froth and watch as they murdered the milk.

Seattle prided itself on being a coffee town. Still does. We stood at the coffee carts downtown cupping our hands around cardboard cups in the drizzling rain. Four Melbourne rock mafiosi dressed mainly in black. 'You guys in a band? I love your accents!' We smiled politely and bit our metaphorical tongues, slurping the hot wet flavoured liquid and dreaming of Carlton, Fitzroy and St Kilda.

It was from Seattle that Starbucks came, spreading like a virus across America. A mass delusion seized the nation. Americans from Maine to California, from Oregon to Tennessee, woke up one year ablaze with the conviction that they had discovered good coffee. And it was good, they were told, because there was so much choice. Walk into Starbucks anywhere, Main Street, USA, and you can take your pick of Caffè Americano, Caffè Latte, Caffè Mocha, White Chocolate Mocha, Espresso Macchiato, Espresso Con Panna, Caramel Macchiato, Iced Caramel Macchiato, Frappé, Frappuccino and more. And more is good.

Boutique chains, oxymoronically, sprouted like weeds in Starbucks' wake. You can get coffee now in any flavour you want – cinnamon, hazelnut, vanilla, apricot, pecan, amaretto, butterscotch, candy apple, macadamia nut. If you think of it, it can be done – black-forest-flavoured coffee, no problem. Crème brûlée, English toffee, chocolate raspberry. Absolutely, one hundred percent, no limit.

You do your best. You adjust. You bypass the tall Caffè Latte option, which is the smallest size on offer, ask for the smallest cup they have with an extra shot, and tell them to fill it only halfway up with milk. If you're lucky or especially vigilant, this may actually happen.

There's always someone in the band who couldn't care less about coffee, who mocks the pretentious affliction of the majority. It's true, some coffee snobs give the rest of us a bad name – those, for instance, who kick up a fuss in a Gundagai truck stop or complain one too many times in the van. I like to think of myself as a realist. I'm just quietly trying to get the best cup of coffee I can in this big old world. I usually pack a small stove-top espresso maker and a packet of Lavazza in the tour suitcase. It comes in handy when you stay in places with a hotplate. No need for questing in the morning. Even in no-frills motel rooms there are sometimes ways to make espresso coffee, but on that I'll say no more. Otherwise I'd have to kill you.

I will say this, though. When you're a month or so into an American tour and you pull into a Midwestern city at ten in the morning and there's a Starbucks on the corner opposite the hotel and you're inordinately pleased to see it, that's when you know it's time to go home.

LUCK

Well it hasn't changed yet
Each time I wake in a sweat
And the sun has slipped out of the sky
As I get to my feet and struggle to dress
All my fingers are thumbs, there's a fog in my brain
Only one thing is clear – I'm late for my train
And I know all at once that it's goodbye, my one
I'll be here when you're gone

Then I stumble outside
Try to flag down a ride
But the taxis just pass me by
So I run down the street, jump on a slow bus
When I get to the station the train is still there
I can't find my ticket, everybody just stares
And I'm turning to stone
As the train starts to groan
I just can't get on

I can see tomorrow
Long black train I follow
When it's all there in your eyes
And it's all no big surprise
Well it's goodbye my one
I'll be here when you're gone
I just can't get on

Yeah it's goodbye my one
I'll be here when you're gone
I just can't get on
'Cause I'm turning to stone
As the train starts to groan
I just can't get on

Reasons To Wear Black

Roy Orbison
Johnny Cash
According to Pablo Neruda, it's the garb for poets
It doesn't show the dirt and goes with any colour
You can wear the wedding suit to the funeral
Suits brown eyes
Looks particularly good with a gold guitar

MARALINGA (RAINY LAND)

This is a rainy land
This is a rainy land
No thunder in our sky, no trees stretching high
But this is a rainy land

My name is Yami Lester
I hear, I talk, I touch, but I am blind
My story comes from darkness
Listen to my story now unwind

This is a rainy land

First we heard two big bangs
We thought it was the great snake digging holes
Then we saw the big cloud
Then the big black mist began to roll

This is a rainy land

A strangeness on our skin
A soreness in our eyes like weeping fire
A pox upon our skin
A boulder on our backs all our lives

This is a rainy land
This is a rainy land
No thunder in our sky
No trees stretching high
But this is a rainy land

My name is Edie Millipuddy
They captured me and roughly washed me down

Then my child stopped kicking
And then they took away my man to town
They said, 'Do you speak English?'
He said, 'I know that Jesus loves me, I know
Because the Bible tells me so
I know that Jesus loves me, I know
Because the Bible tells me so'

This is a rainy land
This is a rainy land
No thunder in our sky
No trees stretching high
But this is a rainy land

Newspaper Song

We have made a successful start. When the nuclear tests
are completed, as they soon will be, we shall be in the same
position as the United States or Soviet Russia. We shall have
made and tested the massive weapons. It will be possible
then to discuss on equal terms.

> Harold Macmillan, UK Prime Minister

I am like the king of a rainy land,
Wealthy but powerless, both young and very old,
Who contemns the fawning manners of his tutors
And is bored with his dogs and other animals.

> Charles Baudelaire, from 'Les Fleurs Du Mal'

When Britain used Australian soil and Australian people to conduct
nuclear testing during the 1950s and '60s, our Prime Minister Robert
Menzies, a confirmed Anglophile, gave the Brits his government's

complete support. In 1956 and '57 a series of nuclear bombs were dropped in South Australia's desert country. The site they chose, Maralinga, was part of the restricted area the British had claimed a decade before for the Woomera rocket tests. It was supposed to be unoccupied land, but for thousands of years it had been home to the Pitjantjatjara and Yankunytjatjara people.

Security at the test sites was nonchalant and many Australian servicemen were exposed to radiation. The testing-range boundaries weren't properly monitored and people were allowed to walk in and out as they pleased. Plane patrols were sent out before a blast to make sure the area was clear, but the locals hid from them. Warning signs were put up in English, which they could not read.

Yami Lester, a Yankunytjatjara spokesperson and negotiator, wrote in the prologue to his autobiography:

> When I was a young boy living in the desert, the ground shook and a black mist came up from the south and covered our camp. The older people said they'd never seen anything like it before, and in the months that followed many people were sick and many died. I don't like to think about it now, but one of those people was my uncle, and he was very sick before he died.
>
> People had sore eyes too. I was one of those people, and later on I lost my sight and my life was changed forever. If I had my eyes, I would probably still be a stockman. Because I haven't, I became a stirrer.

Like many Australians, I didn't know of these events until almost thirty years later when Judge Jim McClelland was appointed to conduct a royal commission into what happened. McClelland went to England, where he interviewed the commanders in charge of Operation Buffalo, as the initial major tests were codenamed. Air Vice Marshal Menaul said, 'We got on very well with the Aborigines. We gave them beads. We gave them mirrors.' McClelland also went out to the lands north of the bomb sites, where many survivors were living, and asked more questions. I read about all this in an article written by Bob Ellis for the now defunct *National Times* in May 1985.

Yami Lester's haunting story and calm demeanour made a strong impression on the commission and its entourage. Ellis wrote:

The evidence that day . . . grew in the mind like science fiction. 'First there were the two big bangs. We thought it was the Great Water Snake, loudly digging holes, as was his custom. We wore no clothes in that old time. And then the Poilu, the Black Mist, rolling, oily, sticky, like black frost came. Very wide it was, low on the ground . . .'

Amidst the dust, heat and the remorseless flies, more gruelling testimony, some of it told in secret session, was recorded.

Jim, under a blue plastic shelter, heard the worst story of all – of Edie Millipuddy camping with her husband on the bomb crater itself, being captured by men in white uniforms, forcibly and obscenely washed down, miscarrying twice and losing her husband, who to prove to the soldiers he knew English, sang 'Jesus loves me, this I know, for the Bible tells me so.' And how the soldiers shot their beloved, irradiated hunting dogs.

The royal commission's report recommended a major cleanup of the lands and compensation for the traditional owners. The Australian government, with the eventual aid of the reluctant British, funded the cleanup, which took ten years and involved the removal and burial(!) of plutonium-poisoned soil. In 1994 the Maralinga Tjarutja people received 13.5 million dollars in compensation. After 2000 some people moved back to their lands. Many of them are suffering the consequences of dispossession, dislocation and long-term diseases, including cancers, skin and eye problems. The Australian Nuclear Veterans Association continues to fight for justice for individual servicemen, who claim they were exposed deliberately as well as negligently to radiation. There are fewer and fewer of them alive each year.

I first met Yami Lester in a Chinese restaurant in Alice Springs in the early 1990s and have had the good fortune to encounter him many times since, at barbecues, festivals and outstations. He has a big open face and a head of vigorous white hair. You can hear his voice from a long way off; it's not loud but distinctive, with a sweet gravelly cut, made for banter. He usually asks me to sing something for him. I'd sing for him 'til the end of time. He has walked through raining fire and come through with dignity and humour intact. To be with him and within the beam of his smile is to be blessed.

That first meeting was arranged by mutual acquaintances, people working for the Central Lands Council, which Yami sat on. I'd written and recorded 'Maralinga' a couple of years before. Not long after reading Ellis's article, I'd picked up the guitar and started fooling round with a melody based on a D-minor chord. It had a similar kind of drone to Neil Young's 'Running Dry'.

Charles Baudelaire's 'rainy land' poem about boredom had been in the air for a hundred and thirty years, doing its multiplying work, infiltrating the soil of his successors, Verlaine, Rimbaud and others. It had been in my head for ten, biding its time unseen, waiting for an agent to react with, waiting to mean the kind of rain Charles couldn't have dreamed of in a thousand years.

Plutonium lasts a lot longer than that. And plutonium doesn't get bored.

MEET ME IN THE MIDDLE OF THE AIR

I am your true shepherd
I will lead you there
Beside still waters
Come and meet me in the middle of the air
I will meet you in the middle of the air

I will lay you down
In pastures green and fair
Every soul shall be restored
I will meet them in the middle of the air
Come and meet me in the middle of the air

Through the lonesome valley
My rod and staff you'll bear
Fear not death's dark shadow
Come and meet me in the middle of the air
I will meet you in the middle of the air

With oil I shall anoint you
A table shall I prepare
Your cup will runneth over
Come and meet me in the middle of the air
I will meet you in the middle of the air

In my house you'll dwell forever
You shall not want for care
Surely goodness and mercy will follow you
Come and meet me in the middle of the air
I will meet you in the middle of the air

Qi

I played Scrabble with my mother in her final days and, surprisingly, almost won. Normally it was a doddle for her to beat me – I could count on one hand the number of times I'd toppled her in thirty years – but on this occasion she was labouring and not on her game. I got away to an early lead and she seemed unable to concentrate.

'Would you like to leave this for another day?' I asked.

'No,' she wheezed, 'I'm all right.'

I pulled steadily away. She was taking longer than normal between moves and muttering occasionally to herself in frustration. She didn't like losing. With only a few letters left I was fifty points ahead and home and hosed. It was then she calmly played the word 'qi', with the Q landing on a triple going both ways. Q is worth ten. Thirty times two – sixty points.

'What's "qi"?' I asked.

'It means "the life force",' she said.

'I thought you spelled that c-h-i.'

'Yes, that's the more well-known spelling. But q-i is acceptable too. It's in the new edition of the Scrabble dictionary.'

I knew it wouldn't be worth challenging her. When it came to fiendish two-letter words, she was an authority. She never played them without backup. She would nod towards the dictionary on the shelf. 'Check it if you want.' Who could forget 'zo', otherwise known as 'dzo', from a long-ago Christmas, meaning a cross-breed of a cow and a yak? (Z being also worth ten.) Or the legendary 'xu', a sub-unit of Vietnamese currency.

'Sub-unit?'

'Yes, a hundred xu make a dong, you nong!'

Such knowledge always allowed her to keep her edge.

I flailed around with my remaining letters P, H, F (three, four, four) and some others, but I was now well and truly phfucked, stuck with them as my mother got rid of her tiles on her next turn.

Defeated by a 76-year-old woman's life force, I packed up the letters and board ruefully. She gave me a small apologetic smile. A week later she was dead.

The day before the Scrabble game, Martin and I had moved Mum out of her unit in a retirement village south of Brisbane and into a single room with an ensuite bathroom at Marycrest Hostel, the aged-care facility that her mother had lived in happily for seven years. Marycrest, a Catholic institution founded by the Sisters of Charity, had a nursing home on the top floor. The sicker you got, the higher you went; just that little bit closer to heaven.

Mum's unit at the retirement village was at the end of two rows of six, facing each other. The paved path to the car park went straight up the middle. It was a bright sunny blue-sky day the day we came for her. Martin and I flanked her, supporting an arm each as we made our slow walk along the path. One by one her neighbours popped out of their houses and onto their doorsteps – like cuckoo clocks – to wave and say goodbye.

Two days after Mum arrived at Marycrest she had to be taken to hospital. Her liver was failing, and a few days later the family scrambled from far and near to be at her bedside. John, who was living in America, jumped on a plane and made it with a night to spare.

Uncle Peter and Aunt Coralie had come up to Brisbane too. We all stood and sat around Mum's bed, holding hands and listening to her jagged, rattly breathing. Dying is an effort. There were long gaps between each breath. She couldn't speak but we were sure she could hear us. We spoke to her from time to time, thanked her and told her we loved her. After a few hours we all got hungry, so one of us did a takeaway food run. Since she'd always loved getting us together for a meal, we thought she wouldn't mind us eating around her death bed. When the priest arrived to give her extreme unction – the last blessing – he looked a little disconcerted to see us all tucking into greasy hamburgers and chips.

The minutes ticked on slowly. The gaps between the breaths got longer and longer. There would be the terrible pause – 'Is this it?' – and then the stubborn body would shudder into action again. This went on for a long time. Then came the last pause, the one that never ended. I think of it now and imagine I heard a very soft click, like the sound of somebody walking out of a room and turning off the light.

The hospital staff were kind, giving us all the time and space we needed. None of us were in a great rush to do anything. We stretched our legs, stood up, sat down, just wanting to be around her for a while. Some of us talked. Someone called the people at the funeral home and those who wanted to stay on were delegated to deal with them. The rest of us, after our last goodbye – a kiss on the cooling head – went out to an Irish bar down the road and knocked back a couple of thick black Guinnesses in her honour.

I felt extraordinarily privileged and amazingly high.

It was a high that lasted for days. Adrenalin kept it going as the funeral arrangements kicked in. Mum had a far reach and knew a lot of people, so there was much to organise. My siblings and I met each morning, like a war cabinet, to discuss plans. Our emergency government quickly swore in its ministers, starting with the Minister for Communications (getting the word out to everyone who should know), then a Minister for Transport and Housing (picking up the old relations as they flew in and organising beds for them). The Ministers for Literature and the Arts (eulogies, music, program notes and printing) followed, then the most important ministers of all, the Ministers for Primary and Secondary Production (the shopping and prepping and cooking of food for the hordes). Some portfolios were shared, and it wasn't always entirely clear who was minister for what, but things got done, one by one. Everybody had their lists.

In the evenings we caught up with each other, and with cousins and uncles and aunts as the clan gathered; we ate and told stories, drank wine and whisky, laughed and wept, and every now and then pulled out the guitars.

One of the big debates in Cabinet was the matter of the coffin – open or closed. We all remembered Dad's open coffin at home more than thirty years before. Times had changed since then. The funeral director pursed his lips when it was proposed.

'It's not really done these days, you know. People aren't used to it. Some may find it a bit confronting.'

But John, who'd spent most of his adult life in the States, where 'death is euphemised all the time', was adamant. We came to a compromise with the undertakers. Lid off in the church before the service, so anybody who wanted to could pay their respects. Lid on once proceedings commenced.

Mum had a large proud nose. The Kelly nose, some call it, though she was born a Filippini. I have two vivid memories of the day of her funeral. The first is of Sister Anne – the Loreto nun, now the head of the family, the one to whom Mum had passed on the 'worry baton' – taking down the large portrait of Pope John Paul, whom she and Mum didn't agree with, from the church wall. The second is of being able to see from the front pew, while waiting for everyone to assemble before the mass, the tip of Mum's nose just poking up above the rim of the coffin, as if to say, 'What's going on?'

She never did like missing out on a family get-together.

Four years after Mum's death, the Melbourne filmmaker Alkinos Tsilimidos called me. I'd already worked with Al, writing the music for his two previous films, *Everynight . . . Everynight* and *Silent Partner*. *Everynight* was shot in black and white and set in the notorious high-security H-Division of Pentridge Prison. The script was based on an inmate's true-life account of relentless beatings and mind games inflicted by sadistic warders. *Silent Partner* is the tale of two not-so-smart alcoholic battlers who go into debt to buy a grey-hound. The shit hits the fan when their creditor instructs them to dope the dog, which then inconveniently dies.

Alkinos is a serious guy. Both films were pretty gruelling for audiences. Neither one tore up the box office. 'What have you got for me this time?' I asked when he called. 'Please tell me it's a romantic comedy.'

Alas, no. But *Tom White,* based on a script by playwright Daniel Keene, is a strong film with a *tour de force* performance by Colin Friels as a middle-class, middle-aged man who loses his job, walks out on his wife and children and joins the homeless. As he falls further and further from respectability he becomes entangled with various characters on the margins, each with their own particular trouble and grace.

When Al approached me the film was close to a final edit. He'd arranged the opening scenes as a kind of overture, short episodic glimpses of all the characters to come, and he wanted a song to somehow encompass the sorrow, dignity and yearning of the world; to have the effect of a balm. (Here we go, I thought to myself, another fucking anthem.) He had a temp track already laid over the scenes: it was Gary Jules' beautiful reworking of the Tears For Fears song 'Mad World'. And it worked perfectly.

The temp track is often the film composer's scourge. The film-maker has put bits of music and songs across various scenes as a rough guide to the score, but he can get very attached to these pieces, which won't be used because of the cost, or because they've already been used in other movies. And nothing the composer does works quite as well as the temp.

Alkinos said he didn't want to use the Gary Jules song. 'I want something new, something original. I know you'll come up with something great.'

Gee, thanks, Al. Perhaps the cost of using 'Mad World', which had been a hit song twice, was way over his budget and he was helping me save face. I didn't ask. If he was speaking truthfully, I appreciated his confidence; if not, I appreciated his tact. Either way, I took him at his word.

Coming up with a song was a daunting task. If you ever watch *Tom White* at home, try turning the sound down at the start and playing 'Mad World' instead and you'll see what I mean. I was in a tight spot, and as desperate men have done down the ages, I turned to the Bible, specifically to King David, who as a child slew the giant Goliath with a slingshot, and as a man sent his loyal servant into the hottest part of the battle to be slain so he could have his wife. As well as fighting mighty battles, governing his kingdom and taking women to his bed, he composed many songs. The lyrics have come down to us in the form of psalms (the word 'psalm' being derived from the Greek *psalmos*, meaning 'sung to a plucked instrument'), but unfortunately the melodies are lost. Psalm 23, attributed to David, is often recited or sung at funerals, having being set to music many times.

I seem to remember so much more of events surrounding the birth of a song than of the birth itself, the moment or moments when words and melody fuse. They say this happens to mothers, too – Nature's way of making them willing to go through the forgotten pain again. Pain is not something I associate with songwriting. When it's happening it's the opposite of pain – a flowing rather than a forcing – but the analogy to childbirth is apt. In both situations the deliverer is in an altered state; a different brew of chemicals is stewing the brain. Something is happening to you.

Whatever happened, 'Meet Me In The Middle Of The Air' wasn't there one day and was the next. Or maybe it was there all along. Psalm 23 has been around for three thousand years or thereabouts. And the only line in the song not from the psalm – the title itself – has been floating around for more than a hundred years in blues, gospel and spirituals.

When my plucking was done, Linda Bull came around and sang it in the back shed. We played it to Al and he was happy. Whew!

I put music to the rest of the film, minimally in the end, at Al's request. The year it came out, 2004, it was nominated for a swag of awards – nine in total, including best director, best film, best actor, best screenplay. It wasn't nominated for best music score but I was asked to sing 'Meet Me' at the Australian Film Industry awards.

That year wasn't brimming with memorable Australian films. 'We're in the doldrums!' drummed the media. There was a lot of comment on the thinness of the field. Two films dominated the nominations, *Tom White* and *Somersault,* a young woman's coming-of-age story. The word was that Colin Friels was a shoo-in for best actor. Colin and his wife Judy Davis are rarely seen at awards nights and industry dinners, preferring to keep themselves to themselves, but after some heavy pressure Colin decided to turn up. He wanted to support Al and so caught the plane down from Sydney in the afternoon.

I sang my song early on in the proceedings at Melbourne's old Princess Theatre then took my seat in the *Tom White* camp, spread over several rows. The mood was optimistic. Across the aisle from us were the *Somersault* posse, some of whom I'd worked with a few years previously on *Lantana.*

Somersault had thirteen nominations and jumped out of the blocks – best costume design first up. Fair enough. It's hard to compete in costume design with a movie about homeless people. Then came best production design and best editing. Oh well. Best music score – we were never in that one anyway. Best cinematography. Hmmm. *Somersault* was shot in the mountains and the snow. Cameras love mountains. Some shifting in the seats. We're sure to pick up something. Best supporting actress, best supporting actor – *Somersault.* Bugger. Best screenplay – *Somersault.* Geez, thought we were a chance there.

I was sitting behind Al and Colin and most of the others up for awards. Shoulders began to slump a little. Hands ran through hair. Al had said to me beforehand, 'I don't care about any of the awards except best actor. Colin deserves best actor. If we only get that award I'll be happy.'

Best direction – *Somersault*. Ouch. Best actress – *Somersault*. Shit! This is getting hard to take. Best actor, surely this is it. No, Sam Worthingon from *Somersault*. Jesus! Sam's a good actor but he wasn't the lead in that film. I was right behind Alkinos and could see the slope of his shoulders. They were as expressive as any face. Then the *coup de grâce*. Best film – *Somersault*.

The *Tom White* contingent sat shell-shocked. Faces were strained, gaunt. Ghastly smiles looked about to crack. Across the aisle there was celebration and hugging and pats on the back. Some of us wandered over to say hello and congratulate the winners, who had the grace to be a little embarrassed. I could tell Al was feeling awful and somehow responsible, like the captain of a sporting team that has just been routed. He felt particularly bad that he'd talked Colin, against his better judgement, into attending the slaughter.

I've been to quite a few awards nights, mostly music ones. Generally it's nice to be nominated, and it's extra nice if you win something but if you don't it's no big deal. But this was something different. This was death by a thousand cuts. *Somersault* walked away with thirteen wins from thirteen nominations, an AFI record. *Tom White* took nothing.

Afterwards we all went to a place where there was finger food and plenty of free booze. We put our arms around each other. We said life goes on. We drank more than we should have. It was just like a funeral.

The Lord is my shepherd; I shall not want.
He maketh me to lie down in green pastures: he leadeth me
    beside the still waters.
He restoreth my soul: he leadeth me into the paths of
    righteousness for his name's sake.
Yea, though I walk through the valley of the shadow of death,
    I will fear no evil: for thou art with me: thy rod and thy staff
    they comfort me.

Thou preparest a table for me in the presence of mine enemies:
　　thou anointest my head with oil; my cup runneth over.
Surely goodness and mercy shall follow me all the days of my life:
　　and I will dwell in the house of the LORD for ever.

Psalm 23

MIDNIGHT RAIN

Something woke me up
Must have been the rain
And for no good reason here you are
Inside my head again
I know I won't go back to sleep now
I'm in a mood
Must be the midnight rain, the midnight rain

So I get up and I wander around
In my dressing-gown
Put the kettle on, some music too
But not too loud 'cause the neighbours complain
So I keep it soft and low, just above the sound
Of the midnight rain, the midnight rain

Yeah, you told me so
I didn't want to know
You sure told me so
Don't you let a good thing go

What coast are you on? What country?
Is it raining there? Is it morning or midnight?
Are you walking barefoot or have you got your shoes on?
Is there somebody there with you?
Are you talking soft and low underneath the sound
Of the midnight rain, the midnight rain?

I just want you to know wherever you are
Wherever you go
I hope you're under a lucky star
Wherever you are
By the way, have you still got that stupid car?

A Minute To Midnight

Once, at the bottom of a southern land, there was a city famous for its rain. It spread itself west and south around a large bay and eastwards to wooded fertile ranges and green valleys. The weather usually came from the west, off the Southern Ocean. Its winters were cold, its skies often grey, and many were the days of drizzle and rain.

The inhabitants of the large warm surf-beach city 900 kilometres to the north wrinkled their noses at the thought of going there. If they had to visit for work or to see family they packed umbrellas, raincoats and thick jumpers. Rarely would they bother with swimming costumes.

Children in the grey city lay at night in their beds listening to the rain drumming on the roof. They felt safe and snug tucked up underneath their blankets, and usually drifted off to sleep before the rain stopped. Often they would wake in the morning to the sound of rain still pattering. They would lie in their beds for as long as possible, all toasty, listening to the creak of the water pipes as their teenage sister took her twenty-minute shower, dreading the moment when their feet would have to touch the cold floor.

After school or during the holidays they would play in thick-grassed parks that sometimes displayed a yellowish tinge right at the end of summer, but never for long. On winter Saturday mornings the boys would come home from football matches covered in mud and throw their soggy clothes straight into the washing machine.

The city had a saying: If you don't like the weather just wait a minute. A songwriter from across the sea, living in the city, wrote a song called 'Four Seasons In One Day'. Spring brought wind and sunshine and skies that would bucket rain, especially for the opening of festivals or big race meetings.

All throughout the leafy eastern suburbs during summer, sprinklers played freely on the lawns. Hydrangeas, roses, lilies, and all manner of thirsty flowers bloomed in verdant gardens. On weekends husbands luxuriously washed their cars, idly chatting to the neighbours, streaming hose in hand, as water cascaded carelessly to the street.

All that was a long time ago.

Once there was a mighty river system flowing down one side of a continent, across four states, emptying its load into the Southern Ocean. Great stands of red gums flourished along its courses and all kinds of birds – waders, ducks, swans – and fish feasted in its broad wetlands and teeming mouth.

The river was long. The river was large. The river had been there forever. Men planted all manner of crops in the surrounding dry land and opened up thousands and thousands of acres to cattle and sheep. There was nothing that couldn't be done. The government subsidised the thirstiest crops of all – cotton and rice – and big irrigation projects mantled the country, sucking water in pipes from the river all the way down.

The dry land got drier. People argued and fought for their share of the water. 'Water is life!' they cried. 'Water is a right!' The poor river gasped and gurgled its way through the seasons and barely made it to the sea. The once fertile lakes and wetlands around the river mouth grew saltier by the year. Saltier than the sea. Too salty for fish. The birds no longer came, because there was nothing for them to eat.

Clouds came to the cities east and west of the river mouth and to the country all around. Clouds built up and darkened and tried to cry but couldn't. A few pitiful drops fell and left no trace and the clouds moved on.

Once there was a rainy land. Once there was a Coorong. Once there was a film called *Storm Boy* where a young boy roamed the wilderness with wild things. It was made in 1976 when the Coorong was alive. Watch it and weep.

MY WAY IS TO YOU

Tall trees are trembling
Dark clouds are bearing down
God's tiny creatures are all
Going crazy on the ground
My way is to you
My way is to you

Your gates were guarded
I had to swing around
All your dogs are silent now
I can hear the softest sound
My way is to you
My way is to you

Many times I've stumbled
Many times I've fallen down
But always I've had
The dream of your dear ground
My way is to you
My way is to you

The Worrier Of Bath

22 June 2003

Dear J,

I've just arrived in the West Country of England where tomorrow I'll start mixing twenty-four songs, recorded with the new band in Melbourne late May/early June. The studio I'm working in is what they call a residential studio, where you live in and have your meals cooked for you. They used to be very common in the UK but as the studio business struggles more and more each passing year – due to falling CD sales, tighter record budgets and the proliferation of home studios – they are becoming increasingly rare.

This particular complex, Real World, was set up by Peter Gabriel and records all kinds of music, including many WOMAD artists, Peter being one of the festival's founders. We're nestled at the edge of a village amidst dairy farms, crops of peas, strawberries, clover and canola, in a lovely green valley near the ancient Roman town of Bath. Lots of walking paths and old stone walls and winding, hedge-hugged lanes.

I'm working with Tchad Blake, a producer/engineer who's worked with Neil Finn and Crowded House. Also Los Lobos, Tom Waits, Ron Sexsmith, Pearl Jam, Randy Newman, Peter Gabriel, and the great Nusrat Fateh Ali Khan. Tchad's records have a warm sound, never too pristine, and he's not afraid to leave a little messiness in. I'd sought him out five years ago, at the time of *Words and Music*, but our schedules didn't coincide. This time the cards fell the right way and he came to Melbourne for three weeks to record the songs, on the understanding that I would come here to mix, where he's been doing most of his recent work.

Everyone in the band (Peter and Dan Luscombe, Bill McDonald and Dan Kelly) was excited about working with him, the Luscombe brothers, to Tchad's surprise, being able to quote chapter and verse from various obscure recordings he's done. He had a good rapport with us, and his astute judgement and relaxed manner helped us get the best from ourselves. One of the hardest parts of recording is knowing when you've got a good take, when to push on and strive for better, when to have a break. Sometimes the early takes, though they may be a little ragged, are better than the later ones when everyone's thinking too much about what they're doing. Other times the song gets better the more it's played. It's hard to tell, so it's good that there's someone we trust at the helm – not out in the room playing – who can sense the moment and say 'That's the one!' Often you're so caught up in your own performance that you don't see the bigger picture.

This record is the first one with this particular combination of musicians. We've been together about a year. Peter on drums is the only member remaining from the previous lineup. His younger (by seventeen years) brother Dan is Dan Kelly's age and they mix in the same band circles in Melbourne. Dan L (Danel, rhymes with *panel*) plays guitar, slide guitar and keyboards. Having studied formally, he is more of a schooled musician than Dan K (Dank, rhymes with *rank*) and has a lovely touch. Dank is more shambolic and nutty. The interplay between the two of them is the defining sound of the band. They seem to have a knack for finding unusual and complementary guitar parts that are not overly structured.

Bill on bass completes the lineup. I worked with him on Vika and Linda's *Two Wings* a few years back, and I love his sound and the parts he comes up with. He's the only one of us not related to anyone else in the band. Bill's about my and Pete's age. We like having younger people to play with. Sometimes they look a little shabby at rehearsal after a huge night, but running a band is a bit like running a football team: it's good to renew and refresh from time to time, to blend youth and experience. Generally you're well served by hanging onto a couple of old-stagers who can hold the back line together as the forward line fizzes all over the place.

I had a few already-written songs in my back pocket, and some ideas Dank and I had started, when we all first assembled last August for weekly jam sessions. We recorded the jams on my trusty old cassette recorder. Similar in many ways to the Professor Ratbaggy process but with more song-y results: verses, choruses and bridges, less minimalist. A dweeby little Casio keyboard line over a simple drumbeat Peter brought in turned into 'Beautiful Feeling'. A guitar riff of Danel's became a surf instrumental. And so on.

We stepped up the frequency of rehearsals towards the end of the year, and then again this year from March until we went into the studio. In between times I would go for long walks around the neighbourhood, trying to pound lyrics for the group tunes into my brain. Bit by bit the songs built up.

24 June

Slept fitfully last night after the first day. Unwound after the studio with Kathleen Battle's *Grace* and started *Soul Mountain* by Gao Xingjian. We want to get two mixes a day but we struggled yesterday with the first song, 'Won't You Come Around?' By the end of the day Tchad seemed to have lost his way with it and even seemed a little rattled, which is unusual. But he took a rough mix home and this morning, after a sleep, he came in and undid some of his later moves, which had made the vocals and guitar riffs sound too effected. And pronto, we were ready to print. The song had sounded fine to me around three o'clock yesterday.

I remember playing tennis with my brother John in Manhattan many years ago. It was too cold to go outside but after ringing around we found an indoor court. Walking onto it we noticed it wasn't very level. There seemed to be a few minor undulations. No problem, we thought, let's get into it. But the longer the game went on, the more pronounced those undulations became, until we felt we were playing over ditches and ridges.

A similar thing happens in mixing and recording. Listening to a song over and over again, you start to hear all its flaws – a lumpy bit of time, a line you could have sung better. The small imperfections grow larger and larger. What once sounded fresh and exciting now sounds either a mess or banal. You feel embarrassed that you're spending so much time and money on it and in bad cases you go home at night feeling like you've spent all day polishing a turd.

I've learnt over the years to stay away as much as possible from the mixes and let the engineer do his thing. There's a little room here next to the mixing room where I think I'll be spending most of my time. The room of refuge. I can hear Tchad working on the song faintly through the door. He and I usually have a discussion about the general direction before he starts and then I hold any comments until he feels he's getting close.

I've become more relaxed about making records as I've got older. I used to listen closely to every little thing and worry about it. My earlier records sound over-tidy to my ears now. During the recording of this one, Dank reminded me of my younger self, worrying about things he hadn't played quite right and wanting to redo parts to make them better. Tchad had a great Voltaire quote for us: 'Better is the enemy of good.' It was a way of encouraging us not to always fix up 'mistakes', or the things we hadn't meant to play. Often the thing you thought you hadn't done quite right in the moment makes perfect sense after a few listens. That's the value of having an outside pair of ears, someone who's never heard the song and doesn't have a fixed notion of how it should be played.

Another quote Tchad was fond of: 'Ugliness is superior to beauty because it lasts.' Fair enough, but 'Jesu, Joy Of Man's Desiring' seems to have done pretty well so far.

It's a strange, flat limbo time right now. Getting those twenty-four songs down in one long blurt has predictably left me empty and flat. I can't imagine ever writing a song again and I'm heartily sick of myself. It will be very easy to get depressed these two weeks, just hanging around like a fifth wheel, never being quite able to shake off that moaning, tiresome voice through the door as Tchad does his microscopic work. And worse, because the record company wants to hold the release until early next year, it will be seven long months until the album comes out. Now, *that's* depressing.

But I had a good long ramble through the meadows this morning – a sweet mild English summer's day – past sleek, contented Jersey cows. Then swung around through the village and picked up two bottles of French wine to have with dinner tonight, a dinner that will be cooked by hands other than mine and brought to me to be eaten al fresco on the long wooden table in the company of various affable Brits, two Americans and an Irishman. So who am I to complain?

27 June

I sleep with earplugs in when I sleep. Trains hurtle past my window. Woke this morning at five-fifteen with the first train, earlier than I wanted, but it was my first uninterrupted sleep since arriving and for that I was grateful. Lay in bed for an hour and a half trying to go back to sleep, but couldn't – so got up finally and went for a run in the countryside on a grey morning. Hard work, up and down hills, but good to get great gulpfuls of fresh air into the lungs, pain and pleasure at the same time. Back in my room I stretched for a while on the floor to Mozart's Clarinet Concerto. The second movement is so aching and beautiful it always gives me chills. In my travelling CD pouch I have mainly classical, Indian, African and Brazilian music, anything but the Western rock-pop such as I make.

After a big country fry-up breakfast of scrambled eggs, bacon, baked beans, mushrooms, wheat toast and coffee (the full English), I listened to the mixes so far – seven down, seventeen to go – on the ghetto blaster in my room, then went to work just across the path.

29 June

We're in the groove now. Every day is much the same. I wake around six, six-thirty and read *Soul Mountain* for a while, which is turning out to be a kind of Chinese *Dharma Bums*. I get up around seven-thirty/eight and go for a run or do some exercises, shower, then go to breakfast in the dining room downstairs around nine-thirty. Usually there are one or two others there at that time leafing through the papers. Afterwards I go back upstairs, listen to the mixes from the day before and worry, before walking over to the studio at ten-thirty.

Lately I've been worrying about the bass – is it too loud or too boomy in some songs? I can't make up my mind on 'My Way Is To You'. I don't entirely trust the ghetto blaster in my room. It sounds different to the studio speakers, of course, so I fret over whether we've got the balance right. Should I have turned the harmonies up more? Is the guitar too loud in the verse? Should I put Dank's amateur fiddle part on 'To Be Good Takes A Long Time' up the front, loud, ugly and proud, or swamp it with effects and bury it in the general murk? The drums sound too boisterous in 'Your Loving Is On My Mind'. And so on. We're mixing pretty quickly, two or three songs a day now, and Tchad likes to keep rough edges. And he's stubborn in his own way. He'll adjust things if you insist but he has a way of making you feel like he's the adventurer and you're being timid when he does. I know I always do this towards the end of a record – obsess over things I probably couldn't care less about in a few months' time. It's because each day we're making decisions that can't be changed. I tell myself, Relax, it's just odd pop music from a little country – not the Sistine Chapel.

We work 'til lunch; that is, Tchad works, sculpting, colouring, balancing. I drift in and out from the room of refuge, where I write or play guitar, or from my other favourite spot – a wooden bench facing the garden just outside the studio, where I read when it's sunny. Every now and then I watch some of Wimbledon live on the big telly in the lounge; it gets more interesting by the day. After lunch we go through 'til seven, when everyone comes together at dinner.

There are three other studios here besides ours, and two of them are in use at the moment. In one, Kevin Killen, a New York-based Irish engineer with whom I've run once so far, is remixing *So*, Peter Gabriel's huge hit record, in surround sound for DVD. Kevin worked on the original recording seventeen years ago. In the big studio an American female songwriter is recording with Robbie Williams' producer, Guy, and various musicians.

In good weather we all sit outside at the long wooden table. The conversation is often gossip about other engineers, producers and artists. Kevin has worked quite a lot with Elvis Costello and has some interesting stories. Elvis has a very loud voice – he destroys microphones – and when he worked with The Brodsky Quartet on *The Juliet Letters* they had to build him a little glass booth to sing in because he was drowning out the musicians. He's also been known to fall into utter despair on listening back to his vocals, and to suggest that other singers come in and take his place. When I hear that, my heart melts for the kindred soul of a fellow worrier.

Guy, who writes as well as produces Robbie's songs, knows such things as 'the average BPM [beats per minute] on American commercial radio is much slower than in the UK', which I guess is important to know in his line of business.

The last couple of days, we've finished a mix not long before dinner, and while the assistant backs up, Tchad and I sit on the wooden bench with a glass of wine in the sun, like two old men on the plaza with nothing better to do than watch the girls go by. After dinner we work for a short time, 'til nine or ten. I wander back to my room while it's still light to watch an hour of Wimbledon highlights on BBC Two. Perfect. Read for a bit then fall asleep if I'm lucky.

30 June

We're over halfway through now. Yesterday was our first day off. I went to Bath with two friends, Bleddyn and Jude, who drove up from London and picked me up. Wandering around the old town, I was pleased to see stone angels climbing the facade of the soaring fifteenth-century abbey in the main square, 'Forty-Eight Angels' being the last song we mixed on Saturday night. Inside we marvelled at the workmanship of the high ribbed arches and stained-glass windows depicting the life of Christ. Somewhere an invisible organist was pumping out Bach on the huge pipe organ. There was a list of names on the wall near the altar of all the abbots, abbesses, priors and rectors of Bath since 670 AD. It was striking how suddenly the names changed after 1066 from Old English – Aelfwig, Wulfwold, Bernguidis, etc. – to the Johns, Williams and Benedicts more familiar to our present-day tongue.

Outside we walked past a busker singing 'That's Entertainment' by The Jam, followed by another playing 'The Carnival Is Over' on recorder – a couple of big tunes. Maybe we should have used recorder on one of the tracks. Twenty-four songs and not one of them has recorder. Or wind instruments of any kind. Just guitars and keyboards. The record all sounds the same! *Stop thinking about the record, it's a day off.*

On to the Roman baths then, where I stood looking down at the green pool fed by the ancient springs and made myself dream of caesars and centurions and kings and queens and the ceaseless, 2000-year parade of bathers. Afterwards we had pints and fish and chips in a beer garden by the river, then walked for miles along the embankment as the legions, fishermen, river-walkers and boats of old thronged in my head.

3 July, 7.40 a.m.

I was up late last night listening to mixes, fooling around with possible running orders and fretting. Woke too early this morning and started worrying again about little things that can't be changed. The keyboard line on 'You Broke A Beautiful Thing' sounds too happy for the song. My falsetto on 'My Way Is To You' is never gonna get anywhere close to Curtis's. I've been chasing the bass for days and telling Tchad to turn my vocals down, and now I think they're too low on some songs. I know I'm being ridiculous but I can't stop picking at the same sore – playing a mix repeatedly and willing it to be different. So much for my resolution not to obsess over details.

We've mixed the twenty-one songs I've decided on for the record, which is to be a double album. There are three more to go, which will be bonus tracks, but before we tackle them we're going to review, starting this morning, all the mixes we've done and redo anything we feel we haven't nailed. We can recall most of the mixes fairly quickly because the moves are in the computer and we have notes. We have two days to do all that and then on Saturday we'll assemble the lot and attempt a sequence. That'll be tricky. I'm thinking of dividing the twenty-one songs into two distinct groups. Having a Saturday-night side and a Sunday-morning side. And maybe calling it *Ways and Means*.

5 July

Things went well yesterday and today. We turned down the bass on a few songs that were bugging me, and Tchad fixed a couple of others that were bugging him. So I've calmed down a little inside. We knocked off the three extra tracks. I started to get excited as we trawled through the songs in the computer, playing snatches to hear how they compared with one another. So many! They're all out of my hands now. Apart from the little tweaks in mastering, I can't change them any more. I say to myself I've done my best. Nothing to do now but sit tight and wait until they go out into the world and make their way.

So good luck, little seeds. May you not fall on stony ground. May you flourish and be sturdy. Fare ye well, travellers. May the winds be fair and the going steady. May the doors of strangers open at your knock.

(See back of book for 'The Mystical Art Of Track Listing')

NO YOU

I woke up with all my clothes on
Cigarette smoke in my hair
Unglued my eyes and saw a dirty room
Spilling ashtray by my bed
Empty bottle on the chair
No one else was there

I was ready in two minutes flat
Just washed my face and combed my hair
I had an eight-twenty-five train to catch
I was out of there
Flying through the front door
Then I hit the air!
No you! No you! No you! No you!
No you, no you, no you!

I was sucked into the subway
Like an ant into a hole
I stood in the crowded carriage
Shoulder to shoulder
The wheels began to roll
A tattoo in my soul

I do not lack good companions
They pick me up when I'm feeling down
We go to the track on Saturdays
Spread our money round
I go up and down
And every single sound says
No you! No you! No you! No you!
No you, no you, no you!

Club Illusions

'I Walk The Line' by Johnny Cash is one of the weirdest songs around. On first hearing, it's a straight country and western song with a simple sturdy tune and a no-frills arrangement, espousing tried and true values, speaking of the ties that bind, and pledging undying fidelity between man and wife. Rock-solid, square and wholesome. Johnny has to go away sometimes for work and finds himself alone when each day is through. No other arms are going to snare him, though, because he keeps his eyes wide open all the time.

But at the end of each verse the key changes. The band steps up a fourth, Johnny hums a note and then sings the next verse in a new key. This is not unusual, especially in country music, where the key often steps up to create interest. Its use has become so stock-standard that it's called the truck-driver's key change, and in many cases only serves to unintentionally highlight the banality of the song, the gear shift sounding obvious and clunky.

This is not the case with 'I Walk The Line', though there *is* something clunky about the song – a clunkiness with a purpose. Johnny's brief humming before each verse sounds like he's establishing his note before he sets off in the new key. It's the musical equivalent of someone clearing their throat before making a speech. It creates an uneasy effect, undermining the pledges made in the lyrics, as if Johnny's been out playing around and is rehearsing what he's going to say to his wife June when he gets home. The song never settles. By the end of it Johnny's back in the key he started with, but he's singing the same words an octave down, reminiscent of the way people, when they're nervous, start speaking at too high a pitch, catch themselves and then begin again lower down. Johnny is so low by the end of the song he's sounding a little forced. Where to go from here? He sounded more convincing first up.

I imagine June at the front door tapping the palm of her hand with a rolling pin as the Man in Black creeps in, stammering his lines. She's looking hard at him through narrowed eyes, saying, 'Yeah, yeah, sure, Johnny, sure.'

(I've made the all too common assumption here that the narrator of the song is the same person as the writer. I of all people should know better. I could go to songwriter Siberia for this. But I just can't shake that rolling pin out of my head.)

Great Key Changes is one of the topics of discussion that come up in the band Tarago every once in a while, along with such other perennials as Great Opening Lines to Songs, The Best Male High Singers, Names for Nightclubs, The Use of Milk in a Bolognaise Sauce. Topics to make the miles go by. When you're talking inspired modulations – and high singers, for that matter – you can't leave The Beach Boys out. 'God Only Knows', 'Don't Worry, Baby' (that song again), where the second half of the verse effortlessly swings up a tone to the chorus, and 'Good Vibrations', where the key changes not just for the start of the chorus but twice during it as well.

A key change, or modulation, often occurs in the middle eight of a song, a term deriving from the early pop tradition of having a contrasting section of eight bars – a change-up from the verse and chorus melodies. People often use 'middle eight' and 'bridge' interchangeably, and a middle eight nowadays can be any number of bars. 'Things We Said Today' by The Beatles is a fine example of the perfect eight-bar (no more, no less) bridge. Most of the song is in G minor, setting up a mood of future nostalgia. (I wonder if the Germans have a word for that.) The narrator is looking forward to the time when he and his beloved will remember the things they did today. When the song hits the big bright G-major middle eight, it roars into the present like an aeroplane taking off. Then, as nonchalantly as you like, it glides chromatically back to the *Zukunftigevergangenheit*. It thrills me every time.

If there were a PhD in songwriting and a university department of which I were the dean, the first book I would have on the curriculum is The Beatles' Complete Songbook. They wrote just about every kind of song and were constantly experimental, even in simplicity. 'And I Love Her' has a sweet melody and predictable chords, but just when you're being lulled along pleasantly the solo kicks off a semitone higher than the preceding verse.

The semitone clash is the most discordant interval in Western music. Try going to a piano and hitting a white note and the adjacent black note at the same time. It's the horror-movie suspense sound, makes your body feel uneasy. Paradoxically the closest key to the one you're in is the 'wrongest' if you play them together. When a guitar player goes to hit a big note with the band and misses by one fret the cacophony is dire. Some guitarists I know wake up with the night sweats every now and then thinking about it. So when George Harrison hits the first note of his 'And I Love Her' solo loud and proud it's a bold move. The rest of the band are right there with him, though, and it makes your head go *zing* when you hear it, like you've just popped a sherbet in your mouth. The Fab Four don't bother turning back. In their new clothes that say 'We know how to make a stir', they stroll right on to the end of the song, topping it off with a triumphant D-major chord instead of the expected D minor – another semitone surprise. (Not that The Beatles invented this trick, ending a piece in a minor key with a major chord. The *tierce de Picardie*, along with every other modulation, has been around in classical music for hundreds of years.)

Marvin Gaye was quite fond of the upward semitone shift. Not only does he use the same trick as The Beatles, shifting up for the sax solo in 'Mercy Mercy Me (The Ecology)', but he casually slips in a matching interval lift during the intro, before he comes in singing. The music sounds like you've just arrived at a party – a party for the end of the world – and Marvin's little key change has the same effect as your host greeting you at the door with a glass of champagne to get your buzz on right away.

In 'Harlem', Bill Withers doesn't bother with a chord progression at all during the verses and choruses. But no less than five times in two minutes he shifts up a semitone in the breaks as Saturday night in Harlem heats up. He takes us right on through to Sunday morning, where the hustling's still going on, and leaves us simmering on the street listening to a crooked preacher. We've been up all night, our clothes are sticky, and we don't know what we're going to do next.

Ash Naylor, who's played guitar with me in recent times, is one of those guys, like Steve Connolly, who can remember stacks of songs complete with chords and words. He has a particular fondness for British pop, especially The Small Faces, Squeeze, and The Kinks, and can play David Bowie songs for hours. We badger him backstage to play the big singalong songs as a warm-up before we go on. In amazement I watch his hands move all around the fret-board as he and the rest of us belt out 'Tin Soldier', 'Up The Junction' or 'Days' at the tops of our voices. Songs with shifting chords and keys seem to get us all buzzing, ready to go out onstage and serve it up. If he's in the mood, Ash might pull out 'Kooks' or 'Space Oddity'. Just what the fuck key is 'Space Oddity' in anyway? Sort of C, I suppose, but it keeps wanting to tug away from home base as Major Tom in his tin can drifts further into space. During the instrumental, the music breaks loose at last into a higher key to tell us he's gone – the major's in E major now, two whole tones above C. That's where he's drifting as the song fades out. He won't be coming back.

Driving home from country gigs, the Tarago becomes Club Illusions. People from the audience we've just played to may kick on at a local disco after the show – they often ask us to go with them – but we have to get back to the hotel an hour or two away. So we make our own disco in the van. There's music and alcohol and chat and it's crowded, usually shoulder to shoulder. On the way down to sound check in the afternoons the Tarago is more like a public library, but at night, post-show, the transformation is complete.

Greg Weaver, our non-drinking sound man, is at the wheel. In the olden days a couple of us would perhaps be carrying a few CDs. CDs themselves were once novel, at the end of the prehistoric era when cars only had cassette players. But now most of us carry iPods. If we have four or five drives in a row radiating out from a central hub – say Brisbane, coming in each night from Toowoomba, Ipswich, the Gold Coast, the Sunshine Coast – we take turns playing DJ. There's left-over beer from the rider, maybe a bottle of wine. A couple of us have made a little vodka-mix traveller. The anointed DJ sits up the front with his iPod hooked up to the stereo. Generally they're given a free run, but as at any nightclub, after a few drinks people start calling out requests.

Maybe we've been kicking the key changes around again.

'You've gotta have some Gurus on there. "Bittersweet". It's classic.'

'"Oliver's Army"!'

'"Coffee And TV"!'

'"Back On The Chain Gang"!'

'Settle, bro dudes. Yes, yes, got 'em all, but first, how about "Son Of A Preacher Man"? Now, *that's* a key change.'

'You wouldn't have "Something In The Air" by Thunderclap Newman, would you? Remember that nutty piano bit in the middle? Just how many keys does that song work through anyway?'

'I dunno. But who can name another song by Thunderclap Newman?'

Silence for a second. Then: '"How To Make Gravy".'

'Ha, ha, very funny.'

It's not always jolly in the van going home, though. Maybe it's been a shitty gig. The sound was horrible and no matter what the monitor guy did he couldn't fix it. You came off stage with your head clanging. Or you misread the crowd and lost them and could never quite get them back. Maybe you'd started a song off on your own, sung a whole verse with the capo a semitone out on the wrong fret, and when the band joined in it was as wrong as could be. Or your voice was struggling all night. Maybe it was a good gig but you and the others are all tired towards the end of a long week. You've been away from home a while now and missing your family.

Whatever the reason, it's quiet in Club Illusions on the way home. Nobody feels like talking. You're leaning your head on the window, looking at the white lines rushing by, listening to the swish of the tyres. After a while, Bill, who doesn't have an iPod, reaches into his bag and pulls out a CD, leans forward, slides it into the stereo and dials up a track. You hear a door being shut, then an engine starting up and a car pulling away. Now German voices speaking through a vocoder – *vocodersprechweise* – followed by synthesisers. It's 'Autobahn' by Kraftwerk. A soft 'All right!' can be heard from the back of the bus. And a few seconds later, 'Turn it up.'

For the next twenty-two minutes we ride with those *seriousfriendly* Germans as they carry us through faraway shifting landscapes. No-one says a word but you can feel the mood lifting slowly, like morning fog off a country highway. It's night-time outside the van but inside glorious scenes are constantly coming into view. The song changes key up and down and all around. At times the music makes you imagine cresting a hill and seeing sunlight breaking over the ridge. You glide along in the same gear for miles, then suddenly sweep around a bend to a fresh vista. Perhaps a still, silver lake. Or a dark forest of birch. Or a distant new city glowing like a mirage.

Somehow Bill's timed it perfectly. Did he plan this? The Tarago pulls into the hotel car park just as the song ends. The pictures fall away. The door slides open and a couple of empty bottles fall out, clinking on the concrete. My good companions and I stretch and sigh as one, thank Bill, pour ourselves out of the van, mumble our goodnights and stumble into the lobby, then up to our lonely beds.

NOTHING BUT A DREAM

High on a hill, deep in a forest
At the end of a lonely road
Inside a house of New Zealand timber
Lives a young queen all on her own
She took me in and did her healing
And said, 'You can stay if you know when to go
But don't take too much when you start your stealing
Just a little's enough – you're the one who should know'

You will fall, you will fall
Nothing but a dream, nothing as it seems
You will fall, you will fall
Nothing as it seems, nothing but a dream

She sat me down at her dark piano
And said, 'Can you play me that old Spanish song?
I know a verse and all of the chorus
But there's just one chord I keep getting wrong'
She threw down three coins and said, 'There's a purpose
In all that we do, every fall of a leaf
Now drink from this cup, I made you a potion
And lay yourself down and get you some sleep'

You will fall, you will fall
Nothing but a dream, nothing as it seems
You will fall, you will fall
Nothing as it seems, nothing but a dream

I woke to the sound of somebody strumming
She held in her hands a parlour guitar
She said, 'If you like this song that I'm strumming
Take it with you, it's only a prayer'

You will fall, you will fall
Nothing but a dream, nothing as it seems
You will fall, you will fall
Nothing as it seems, nothing but a dream

All Heaven Breaks Loose

Carl Wilson
Ira Louvin
Skip James
Curtis Mayfield
John Jacob Miles
Jimmy Scott
Jordan Ireland
Rev. Claude Jeter
Sam Cooke
James Mercer
Aaron Neville
Ross Wilson
Art Garfunkel
Smokey Robinson
Antony
Glenn Richards
Barry Gibb
Jim James
Al Green
Bon Iver
Carter Stanley
Jackie Wilson
Roy Orbison
Thom Yorke
Richard Manuel
R.H. Harris

(THE) OLDEST STORY IN THE BOOK

Tom and Harry were the best of friends
They called themselves The Dharma Bums
Lit out from their home and kin
With a mandolin and a pair of thumbs
Worked side by side all that summer
Picking those grapes from the vine
Read by one light, took turns to cook
The oldest story in the book

Enter Richard and his sister June
Just before the season's end
Richard's guitar knows a whole lotta tunes
Harry starts a-picking on the mandolin
Down by the dam in the moonlight
They play 'til their fingers are sore
When June kisses Tom, Harry doesn't know where to look
The oldest story in the book

The band pull into town in the afternoon
They've got a hit song on the radio
Richard calls up his sister June
And says, 'We're playing tonight, do you want to come along
    to the show?'
June scrapes the money together for a babysitter
Tom's working late, she's glad she's on her own
Especially when Harry sings that song about the girl
By the lake and how the moonlight looked
The oldest story in the book

Puppets And Puzzles

I was driving back from Ballarat once and noticed a billboard by the freeway. It was an ad for an all-woman gym, Fernwood, with the slogan in large letters: NO TOMS, NO HARRYS AND DEFINITELY NO DICKS. I thought to myself, smiling, it would be good to write a Tom, Dick and Harry song sometime, and stored the thought away.

Over the next couple of years I'd occasionally try to slip the three-some into a melody I was fooling with, but they never stayed long. I was also carrying around a title, 'The Oldest Story In The Book', to which I was attempting to fit a melody. I had a couple of different tunes where the title was working well as the last line of a series of verses – a kind of punchline – but I couldn't nail the scenes leading up to it. There always seemed to be one too many guys.

I was pleasantly playing with what I thought were two separate puzzles when, blow me down, Tom and Harry jumped into one of the 'Book' melodies. Of course! Why hadn't I thought of splitting up the three musketeers before? Clumped together they'd been a dead weight. Breaking them up made each of them mobile. With Tom and Harry I had the start of an on-the-road buddy movie – two young men hitchhiking into the great yonder with a head full of Kerouac. Then along came Dick and June in the next verse and things started to brew. With a woman in the picture I had the set-up for a love triangle, and with the extra man, a buddy triangle. Intersecting triangles. It's also possible that Dick's gay – the song doesn't say either way – so there may be a third triangle in there as well.

Singing this song is like visiting old friends. It can be good or strange and sad. I feel a little sorry for the four of them, trapped in an eternal loop. They lie still and lifeless, like puppets abandoned in a cupboard, until I bring them to life every once in a while. And then they have to go through their motions. Again and again Tom gets the girl, Harry gets the song, and Dick rolls along in a rock'n'roll band.

I wonder sometimes what would happen to them if they got to live their lives outside the song. Would June and Tom get through their tough times? Would Harry get over June? And June, Harry? Would the band stay together and have another hit? Would Tom and Harry's friendship survive? I strum the strings that make them dance and bathe them all in love. But though I set them going I can never set them free.

Writing a song is much like solving a puzzle. There's the overall puzzle of trying to get words to match the sounds you made when you came up with the melody, words to make some kind of sense. There are sometimes more specific puzzles too. They may take the form of restrictions. David Byrne from Talking Heads supposedly made it a rule never to use the word 'baby' in a song unless he was singing about an actual baby. Or they may take the form of a challenge. A friend of Lou Reed's once said to him, 'I bet you can't write a song called "I Love You".' So he went and did just that. It's on his first solo album and it's a beauty. In 'The Foggy Fields Of France' I set myself the task of making each verse correspond to a specific colour.

Anglo-Saxon poetry from the sixth to the tenth century has a rich tradition of riddle poetry, which sets a puzzle for the reader. Here's one:

> I am a wonderful help to women
> The hope of something to come. I harm
> No citizen except my slayer.
> Rooted I stand on a high bed.
> I am shaggy below. Sometimes the beautiful
> Peasant's daughter, an eager-armed,
> Proud woman grabs my body
> Rushes my red skin, holds me hard,
> Claims my head. The curly haired
> Woman who catches me fast will feel
> Our meeting. Her eye will be wet.

(Answer at back of book)

Sometimes after finishing a song you get the feeling of having solved a puzzle you weren't aware of. It's only by a kind of reverse engineering that you arrive at the hidden plan, the challenge that was set. In the case of 'The Oldest Story', I imagine sitting around a back room somewhere with a gang of wisecracking songwriters, passing the guitar around. There are pints of Guinness on the table and a bottle of whisky. Maybe some Norwegian backpackers are there too, some curly-headed Irish girls, and possibly a drunk blonde holding tabs of ecstasy. All right, yes, we're in the upstairs room of Whelan's in Dublin.

'Okay,' says one of the hipsters, 'I bet you can't write a song with "June" and "moon" in it that's a buddy song, a love song, a song about being in a band *and* a song about songwriting. See if you can throw in the title of a novel as well, and three guys called Tom, Dick and Harry. Oh yeah, and how about a yodel too?'

Well, fuck you, I will.

ONE MORE TUNE

Night is turning into morning
This shindig's winding down
The cops have been and the cops have gone
Somebody didn't like our sound
Now all this fuss has come down to just us
Singing soft inside a room
Won't you stay now?
Let's play one more tune

Martin's sleeping, we won't wake him
Nothing could do now
He and Ruby've sure had some doozies
But never such a row
Blame it on the bottle
Or blame it on the moon
Oh come on, stay with me
And play with me one more tune

Close we huddle to keep warm
So frail our candle, so strong the storm

I can't do this on my own
Make the sounds that make me swoon
Please stay a while
Make me smile with one more tune
Every cup, every glass is empty
If you go now it'll be too soon
Won't you stay here
And play one more tune?
Come on, won't you stay
And slay me with one more tune

Flow

'Writing's easy,' claimed Red Smith, the famed American baseball writer. 'You just sit at a typewriter and open a vein.'

If only. It's a good quote to pull out when some dullard says Americans lack irony. I like it, too, because as well as saying one thing and meaning another it can be read as meaning exactly what it says. For some people writing *is* easy. Perhaps it was for Red. Perhaps he really did come back from the baseball game with an evening deadline for the morning paper, sit at the typewriter with his notes and just let the words flow. Recovering may have been the problem.

Some writers indeed write in torrents, or appear to. Walt Whitman with his endless, fertile lists. The big nineteenth-century novelists – Dickens, Dostoevsky, Balzac, Henry James, Sir Walter Scott, Emile Zola – it seems they never put down their pens. You can feel their ferocious engines, their eternal, infernal thrum. With Henry James the flow's like lava. Once it gathers around you there's no getting out.

Other writers ooze more lightly. Reading Haruki Murakami is like having him chat to you in a bar. There seems to be nothing between his thinking and his writing. The topic wanders. Dreams, banalities, heart confessions, odd speculations and stories make the night go by. The thirteenth-century Persian poet Rumi, from the day he encountered his True Friend, became a vessel through which poured a never-ending stream of verse, song, stories, jokes, riddles, advice, parables and praise. He left behind thousands upon thousands of odes and quatrains, collected into monumental books.

My true friend John K, another sportswriter, is also someone for whom writing is like breathing. His professional output is dwarfed by the pages and pages of letters he's written to me and others over close to forty years. Dense packets of paper, verging on parcels, covered with close-written longhand at first, then tight typescript. In the late eighties came fax machines. 'They were invented for us,' we exclaimed across thousands of kilometres. 'Now we can write to each other in real time.' At home I would hear the beep and then the whirring of the fax machine and rush to load more paper. At hotels on tour I would get a call from reception saying 'A 27-page fax has arrived for you, sir. I'm afraid that will cost twenty-seven dollars, at a dollar a page.' I didn't mind. The pages were pure gold.

On Australia Day 1993, updates of the last three hours of the fourth Australia v West Indies test match, which Australia lost excruciatingly by one run, came to me in fifteen-minute instalments at my apartment in the Highland Gardens Hotel in Hollywood. Towards the end the score came every minute or two. And cricket was a sport in which John at that time had little interest. No greater love hath a man.

On 14 March of that same year, sitting on a ferry between Vancouver and Victoria, BC, Canada, on my way to a gig, I read a blow-by-blow account over fifteen faxed pages of Australian Prime Minister Paul Keating's surprise victory the previous night in the 'true believers' election. John being a member of the Labor Party, his delight danced off every page as he paraphrased Keating's ebullient speech for me. I wanted to jump up from my seat and shout to the quiet passengers on the deck and the seagulls wheeling around us, call out across the water to Joni Mitchell in her big house on the promontory, 'LABOR WON! LABOR WON!'

In the late nineties came the internet and email. (Well, a long time before then, but as anyone who's seen my mobile phone knows, I'm what marketing people call a late adopter. Never having typed a word in my life, I was the second-last of my family to get online, and am famous for the remark 'What do I need the internet for? If I want to look something up I can just go to the library.') Once I made the big leap, I could follow the sports results and news from home for myself, but John's writing never stopped. I'd read him on my laptop at the back of the tour bus, and still do, with a picture in my mind of him sitting at his desk tapping away, bottle and glass of wine by his elbow. Mini-novels on the life of a pennant squash player, or living with a stepchild; theses on the philosophy of Neil Craig, coach of the Crows; forensic accounts of the workings and backroom deals of South Australian state politics; diaries of trips to Africa, England, France; a dozen pages on preparations for a dinner party and how to cook a rabbit; arguments with friends; sagas of his father's stroke and slow recovery, the faltering comeback to speech, dogged son by his side filling in the words; his father's eventual death; his blind mother's slow dying . . . All this a mere fraction of the whole. I have boxes stacked with folders of his letters, faxes and emails going back thirty-five years. John doesn't think first then write second. For him, writing is his way of thinking. He told me once, 'I just sit down and turn on the tap.'

This kind of flow is beyond me. I'm in awe of it. John knows I will never match his volume and doesn't mind. I write back to him when I can, much shorter letters. Any prose muscles I've developed started from this. My writing has always seemed a thin thing. At school my lowest marks were for English as I struggled to meet the required word length. My secret scribblings as a teenager tended towards brevity. Not long after leaving school I fell for *The Narrow Road to the Deep North, and Other Travel Sketches* by the seventeenth-century Japanese poet Basho, and imagined myself as a writer of seventeen-syllable haikus. It's not surprising that I drifted into songwriting, a short form. The first song I wrote that I can remember had four lines and one rhyme.

> It's the riding of trains that takes you
> It's the running around that breaks you
> It's the going down that wakes you
> It's the falling apart that makes you

Over three decades I've averaged around twelve songs a year. There have been a couple of fallow years and the odd bumper crop, but generally I've written between ten and fifteen. And by writing I mean finishing off, finishing something that was started several days, several months or several years before.

People often talk about songwriting as a craft. It's never felt that way to me. When you craft something you know what you're doing.

It's something you can do daily, like making shoes. I would call most musicians I know craftsmen because they play their instruments all the time. If they're not gigging, they're practising. They have a high level of skill, years of built-up muscle memory, whereas the tips of my fingers often get sore when I take up my guitar after a break. I don't play the piano much. I have no feeling of mastery over what I do.

If you've written three or four hundred songs you get called prolific. But a dozen songs a year is not a lot. There's always plenty to do arising out of those come-along-once-in-a-while songs – recording, touring (mostly travelling and waiting), the daily email and phone chatter of business. But the real juice is fleeting, whether it's the great oceanic feeling onstage and in rehearsal, or the tingling rush taking you over as the song or the start of a song falls out.

It means that a lot of the time a songwriter like me feels useless, which creates a constant, free-floating anxiety, occasionally relieved by finishing a song. I think of the Brill Building songwriters like Carole King and Gerry Goffin, Doc Pomus and Mort Shuman, turning up to work each day, nine to five, in 1950s and '60s New York, pumping out hits for others – 'Up On The Roof', 'Will You Love Me Tomorrow', 'Suspicion', 'Little Sister' and countless others. I say to myself I should set up an office and lock myself in there 'til sundown every day, write a few songs a week, get a flow going; learn some cool Brazilian chords, expand my range, figure out how to use GarageBand, commit to memory old songs I like and new songs I hear, so as to build up a bigger database in my head that I can access every time I pick up the guitar.

But I don't. Or I haven't yet and it's hard to teach an old dog new tricks. My memory doesn't retain things very well. Mostly I just scratch along, following a random scent here, poking my nose in there, lose interest after a while then wander off to have a little lie-down in the shade and think about what food will be in my bowl later in the day.

Somehow the songs turn up, one by one. Or so far they have. I never know where the next one's coming from. There may never be a next one. I take comfort from the words of Thomas Mann: 'A writer is somebody for whom writing is more difficult than it is for other people.' I wake up every morning and hope there's still one more tune ambling towards me down the road.

OTHER PEOPLE'S HOUSES

His mother always let him stay up late on Fridays. They would lie in her room together watching TV. Sometimes she fell asleep before he did and he'd be watching a talk show – one person talking, then another, then all this laughter coming from nowhere. Next thing he knew she would be shaking him gently. *Wake up, little one, wake up.* Saturday morning. So he'd get up, dress himself, put his shoes on and leave the house without breakfast. Breakfast always came later, in other people's houses.

They had to catch two buses to reach their destination and the trip seemed to take forever unless he fell asleep along the way. When they got off at their stop they were in a bigger, brighter neighbourhood. The houses were a long way back from the street and some of them were hidden from view by big hedges. Looking down the street was like looking through the wrong end of a telescope. His mother guided him through this country. She knew exactly where to go. She carried in her bag a big, heavy ring full of keys – all keys to other people's houses.

She would turn one of the keys in the lock. Some of the doors needed two keys. Then, presto! – they were in. The houses had so many things in them yet still so much space. He liked to rub his feet quickly on the thick pile then touch a doorknob with one finger and give himself a small electric shock. In the first house they always went straight to the refrigerator. There were things in there he couldn't imagine anyone ever eating – strange-looking pastes in jars and horrible concoctions in plastic. His mother would fix him up with a jam sandwich and a glass of milk, then set to work cleaning other people's houses.

And so they would go all day long from one house to another, his mother scrubbing, mopping, vacuuming, cleaning, washing the dishes, leaving him to his own devices. Often, if no-one was home, she would play music on the stereo. There was one record she always put on and sang along to. It had two men and two women on the cover and they all looked sort of blonde except one of the women had dark hair. The stereo flickered like the controls of a spaceship. Other houses were full of books and sometimes he was allowed to take one of the books down from the shelves and open it up. There were books on war and cricket and movie stars. He was very careful with the books. He was very careful with everything in other people's houses.

Many of the houses had other children in them. They would rush right past him into the yard. He'd follow them out back where the backyard was as big as the house, sometimes even bigger. He'd play with them for a while then sit on the steps watching them. He felt slower than the others. There was a girl about his age who lived in a house they went to every second Saturday. Her name was Stephanie. She used to take him everywhere with her, wherever she went, all around the house, even into her room. He'd never see his mother until it was time to leave. One Saturday his mother told him that Stephanie and her family had moved away. Just like that. He still thinks of her now, thirty years later, moving, laughing, sitting down to dinner, making conversation, making love in other people's houses.

A Tiny Broken Heart

He was just a little farm lad so busy at play
In his little play house down by the gate
He stopped to watch a truck that was parking next door
At the home of his tiny playmate

Then he saw his Daddy watching too
As the man swiftly walked to the cottage door
He knew they were strangers that came from the town
Men he had never seen before

They soon were at their work and he heard his Daddy say
Our neighbors are moving today
Oh no, he cried, dear God don't let it be
They can't take my sweetheart away

I know Dad that you don't understand
How a heart so young can conceive a plan
I'm only seven now but it's just like you said
Dad, someday I'll be a man . . .

                                        The Louvin Brothers

OUR SUNSHINE

(written with Michael Thomas)

There came a man on a stolen horse
And he rode right onto the page
Burning bright but not for long
Lit up with a holy rage
No turning back for the child of grace
With the blood red on his hand
Never known to hurt a woman
He never robbed an honest man
His mother held in jail, his daddy dead
And daily rising the price upon his head

Our sunshine, our sunshine
Through fire and flood, through tears and blood
Through dust and mud still riding on

Forever trapped in a suit of steel
With the hotel burning behind
Betrayed by his companion
And the train waiting down the line
Forever tall on a bareback horse
Getting through by the skin of his teeth
It's one more for the ladies
Now one more for the police
Riding all night hungry, tired and cold
Into the misty morning
He'll never grow old

Our sunshine, our sunshine
Through fire and flood, through tears and blood
Through dust and mud still riding on

As he stood before the judge's chair
He said, 'I'm free and easy – I'll see you there!'

Our sunshine, our sunshine
Through fire and flood, through tears and blood
Through dust and mud still riding on

Such Is Life

The *Age* newspaper in Melbourne once asked me to interview Nick Cave. I'd met him a few times but didn't know him well. I rang him up in São Paulo and we spoke for about forty-five minutes. I'd never conducted an interview before, but though I had nothing to compare it to, it seemed to go well. Nick's not the tongue-tied type. He talked about how much he missed Australia, its trees and light and smell. We also spoke about the humour in his work, which is often overlooked – not so much now as it was then, in the early nineties.

I had been looking through *King Ink*, his first collection of lyrics, and noticed a song called 'God's Hotel'. As far as I knew, it hadn't appeared on any of his records. Towards the end of our chat I asked him about it. 'It's just a blues,' he said. 'You can use the words if you want.'

Not long after that, Yahoo Serious was making his second movie. His first, *Young Einstein*, had been a great success. He wanted a big, all-inclusive, unifying song to open with – one of those anthems again – and he wanted me to record it with Yothu Yindi, with whom I'd recently co-written 'Treaty'. I thought immediately of Nick's lyrics. Perfect, I thought, taking Nick at his word, and made up a tune to them over the chords to 'Bittersweet' by The Hoodoo Gurus, who've written an anthem or two in their time. Then I got together with Yothu Yindi, bashed out a demo in a rehearsal room and sent it off to Yahoo.

The first line of the song is 'Everybody has a room in God's Hotel.' And the first line of every verse ends with 'God's Hotel'. And in my version the first line is repeated three times each verse. Though I'd used only five verses out of Nick's original twelve, there were still a lot of 'God's Hotel's in the song. Too many for Yahoo, who said, 'All that God stuff will turn people off. We can't have that at the start of the movie. They might walk out.'

That was that, then. Fair enough. These are ungodly times. But waste not, want not. I'm told Slim Dusty used to call any tracks left over from making a record 'offcuts'. Every time he made a new record he'd throw in an offcut or two from the previous one. So I took Nick's and my Godsome offcut to America a year or two later, recorded it with some funky guys and released it in 1994.

There's a long tradition in songwriting of the collaborators not working face to face. Gilbert and Sullivan famously didn't like each other that much but had huge success with their operettas in the nineteenth century. Gilbert came up with the story and the words and sent them to Sullivan, who wrote the tunes. They came together for rehearsals with the cast, both fiercely protecting their turf.

These days, with mp3s whizzing around the world on emails, it's very common for songs to be written by people who never see each other. Most of my co-writes, though, except for those with the dead – Carver, St Paul, King David and so on – have usually been with people sitting in the same room with me. Most times there's food and a bottle of wine involved. With the Bull sisters we always start with lunch.

Co-writes can happen by accident. 'What's that?' I might say to Nephew Dan as he sits on the sofa doodling on his guitar. 'Oh, it's nothing really.' An hour or two later we're on the way to *something*. Or I've come late to rehearsal and the band is jamming when I walk in. I start singing over the top and off we go. But a lot of co-writing is pre-arranged.

The main job of music publishers is to pitch songs to recording artists, and to the directors and music supervisors of films, TV shows and ads. But as well as working existing songs, they try to generate new ones. So how do they get proactive? Most writing is a lonely, obscure business. A publisher can't really go round to one of his writers' houses and say, 'How's it going? Need a hand?' Or ring up every few weeks and say, 'Have you written a song yet?' But they can feel they're doing something when they put two writers together. 'Yes, so-and-so's with so-and-so this week,' they say knowingly down the phone to so-and-so. 'They're writing together!'

Some publishers go a step further, making their song-generation more tangible by running workshops. Mushroom Music, for a number of years now, has held songwriting camps at the Mt Macedon country mansion of company head Michael Gudinski. They usually run for a week or ten days in late spring. His house of many rooms is an hour's drive from Melbourne. People can commute or stay the night, work for several days or just one. You get rostered with one person in the morning and another in the afternoon. The grounds around the house are extensive, with lawns and gardens, and it's very pleasant working outside in nice weather. A sound engineer is on hand, with a compact recording set-up in one of the rooms to make demos of the songs hot off the press. And all the meals are cooked for you.

It's a sweet arrangement but it doesn't mean the songs will be any good. Writing a song with someone you know well is a hit-and-miss affair, writing with a stranger even more so. Songwriting is a form of play, and true play is aimless. But it's hard not to feel the pressure to come up with something in that kind of situation. Some dodgy cobblings can result. When you're struggling, the minutes slow down in the drowsy sunshine, you both wish you were somewhere else, and it seems forever until lunch.

So what happens? How does it actually work, writing with someone else? Sometimes one party has a song started and the other helps them to finish it off. I've written a few times with country singer Troy Cassar-Daley, and usually he has the song well on the way – a title, an idea, some lyrics, chords and a melody – when we meet. He's the one who's pregnant and I act as the midwife. It's harder when you start from scratch. You might play little bits on guitar or piano to each other, until one of you says, 'I like that.' And then you take another step, hoping it will lead to the next. It can be painful, torturous, embarrassing if no spark is struck. You're both trying to be respectful to each other but nothing good is happening.

Working with singers who don't play an instrument, you get to talking until you hit upon a phrase or idea that might be a song. You play a couple of chords, hum a phrase, and they pick it up and start developing the melody. You scramble to find the chords that fit. Then you both start filling in the words. Sitting around the kitchen table with Vika Bull, talking about a wealthy persistent suitor who wouldn't take no for an answer, turned into 'Thanks I'll Think It Over'. Monique Brumby telling me about childhood summers on her grandmother's block in country Tasmania became a song called 'Melting'.

Overall, I'm sure the songwriting camps work out well for Mushroom, despite the many misfires. Good songs get written as well as dreck, and in the end it's only the good songs that matter. Connections get made that lead to long-term collaborations. Maybe you've spent a day or two making squibs and little failures, then you go home to find something has shifted inside you, something suddenly unlocked, and out comes a song that knocks you sideways. And that's all a writer ever wants – to be taken by surprise.

The year of my first visit to the Mount Macedon song factory, I'd recently read two books about Ned Kelly. *Ned Kelly: A Short Life*, written by historian Ian Jones, is a detailed, heavily researched account. *Our Sunshine*, by novelist Robert Drewe, seems to draw inspiration from Michael Ondaatje's *The Collected Works of Billy the Kid*. Both portraits are very sympathetic.

Not all views of Ned are as partisan. Alongside those who claim him as a fighter against injustice, a visionary and a brave hero, there are others who say he was nothing but a thief, a ratbag and a callous murderer.

Ned down the years seems to burn with righteous rage. He claimed that he and his family were unfairly targeted by the police in and around the town of Greta in north-eastern Victoria. Ned was involved in cattle rustling and didn't always own the horses he rode, or care who did, but it seems he was often charged for crimes he didn't commit. In Ned's view this was symptomatic of the oppression of the poor selectors (small land-renters, usually Irish Catholic) by the squatters (large landowners, usually English Protestant). He was in and out of prison.

When his mother Ellen, still nursing a baby, was put in jail and charged with attempted murder for attacking a policeman, events inexorable as a Greek tragedy were set in motion. The policeman had come to her home looking for Ned, and according to Ellen had made a pass at his younger sister.

At Stringybark Creek, Ned and his brother Dan ambushed a heavily armed police party looking for them and in the ensuing fracas three policemen were killed. There was no turning back after that. The Kelly Gang – Ned, Dan, Joe Byrne and Steve Hart – became the talk of Victoria and New South Wales, hiding out in the country they knew so well and staging daring bank robberies with a keen sense of theatre. They dressed up as policemen, took hostages for whom they bought drinks, burned mortgage deeds, and entertained the locals with displays of stunt horsemanship.

Ned wrote long raving letters to the newspapers, justifying his actions as those of an Irishman of 'true blood, bone and beauty' suffering tyranny and condemnation under the 'saxon yoke'. In the famous, incendiary Jerilderie Letter he railed against the 'big, ugly, fat-necked, wombat-headed, big-bellied, magpie-legged, narrow-hipped, splay-footed sons of Irish bailiffs or English landlords . . . better known as officers of Justice or Victorian Police', and threatened those who might be thinking of assisting the authorities.

I shall be compelled to make an example of some of them . . . by the light that shines pegged on an ant-bed with their bellies opened their fat taken out rendered and poured down their throats boiling hot will be cool to what pleasure I will give some of them and any person aiding . . . the Police in any way whatever . . . or those who would be so depraved as to take blood money will be outlawed and declared unfit to be allowed human burial and their property either consumed or confiscated and them theirs and all belonging to them exterminated off the face of the earth . . . I am a widows son outlawed and my orders <u>must be</u> obeyed.

Ned's language in the Jerilderie Letter wouldn't have been out of place on Nick Cave's album *Murder Ballads*, and obviously influenced the tone of Peter Carey's novel *True History of the Kelly Gang*, narrated entirely in Ned's voice.

But Carey's novel was as yet unwritten as I drove up to the Macedon mansion one fine morning to meet Michael Thomas of Weddings, Parties, Anything for the first session of the day. Mick was the right person for the song I had in mind. We'd played and sung together often and shared an interest in folk music and Australian history. I had the beginnings of a melody, a few lines and, most importantly, a title – 'Our Sunshine'. Our Sunshine, according to Robert Drewe, was what Ned's father called him as a boy. Mick and I knocked off the song by lunch.

The Ned Kelly outbreak came to a head in 1880. Aided by many sympathisers, Ned had been leading the police a merry dance. The colonial authorities, spurred on by the newspapers, organised a big push. Hundreds of policemen were loaded onto a train from Melbourne heading north to Kelly country. Ned found out about this and ordered the train tracks pulled up just outside the town of Glenrowan, intending to cause a derailment. Then he and his gang took over Anne Jones's inn and waited. And while they waited they drank and revelled the night away with their seventy hostages, one of whom managed to escape and raise the alarm.

The large contingent of police laid siege to the inn in the early morning. Eventually Ned emerged clad in heavy armour made from old plough parts. Reports describe an eerie apparition in the swirling mist. His head and torso were well covered but the weight of the armour slowed his movements down. He exchanged fire with the police, who shot him repeatedly in his unprotected legs until he collapsed. The hotel was then set alight to flush out the rest of the gang, but by that time they were already dead from gunshot wounds.

Ned was taken down to Melbourne and tried by judge Redmond Barry, an old adversary, who sentenced him to death. Replying to the judge's customary words 'May God have mercy on your soul,' he said, 'I will see you there when I go.' Ned waited for his execution inside the thick bluestone walls of Melbourne Gaol just yards away from his mother, who was still serving her sentence.

Many years after recording 'God's Hotel' I finally heard Nick's version, set to his own music. It's a live performance on radio and Nick and the band sound gloriously drunk. They stagger their way rambunctiously through eight verses. In the second verse Nick sings:

> Everybody got wings
> Everybody got wings
> Everybody got wings in God's Hotel
> You'll never see a sign on the barroom wall saying:
>> 'At no time may both feet leave the floor!'

Ned's feet left the floor on 11 November 1880. As the hangman put the noose around his neck Ned's reported to have said, 'Such is life.' Judge Barry died twelve days later from unforeseen complications arising from a carbuncle.

PLEASE MYSELF

If you won't be letting me please you, baby
Guess I gotta please myself
If you won't be letting me please you, baby
Guess I gotta please myself

Girl, your head's so hard I don't know what to do
Girl, your head's so hard I don't know what to do
If you won't be letting me please you, baby
Guess I gotta please myself

Stones in my passway, I'm pushing to get through
Stones in my passway, I'm trying to get through
If you won't be letting me please you, baby
Guess I gotta please myself

I've been so hard so long, you're breaking me in two
I've been so hard so long, you're breaking me in two
If you won't be letting me please you, baby
Guess I gotta please myself
Guess I gotta please myself

Fiddlin'

'Pictures Of Lily' – The Who
'I Touch Myself' – The Divinyls
'She Bop' – Cyndi Lauper
'Pump It Up' – Elvis Costello
'Dancing With Myself' – Billy Idol
'Dancing On The Ceiling' – Frank Sinatra
'Touch Of My Hand' – Britney Spears

'Rosie' – Jackson Browne
'I Concentrate On You' – Cole Porter
'Whip It' – Devo

Every songwriter worth their salt has probably had a crack at a masturbation song at some stage. For help with the second verse, thanks to Robert Johnson, who also sang, 'Squeeze my lemon, baby, 'til the juice runs down my leg.'

PRETTY PLACE

Take me to the pretty place where once we used to run all day
From silver dawn to golden setting sun
Take me where the water flows and bumps along on pebbled stones
And sweetly sings its never-ending song
We're going to the pretty place, going to the pretty place

Take me where the fishes swim and shimmer in and out of vision
Underneath the hanging willow tree
Do you remember Charlie Boots? He broke the rope
Back on the slope we laughed so hard I thought I'd have to pee
We're going to the pretty place, the pretty place

In my mind it's shining bright
I've had enough of all this stuff
Now I'm going to the pretty place

I know our pretty place has gone, it's been so long
And everything and everyone I know is moving on
But though my eyes are growing dim, still I can see the fishes swim
And I can hear that never-ending song
I'm going to the pretty place, going to the pretty place

In my mind I see the light
I've never been so ready
Now I'm going to the pretty place

What's Bad For Children

Threats or promises that aren't kept
Put-downs

Too much choice
No chores
High self-esteem
Conditional love

What's Good For Children

Places to run
Boredom
Music
Uncles and aunts and cousins
Other children
Other languages
Limits

What To Teach Children

Good manners
How to use both sides of the brain
How to use both sides of the body
The value of money
Curiosity
Argument with respect
The difference between Frank Sinatra's Columbia and Capitol
    years (or the difference between a raven and a crow, or
    between reverse and orthodox in-swing)
How to leave you

(THE BALLAD OF) QUEENIE AND ROVER

Queenie was born on the banks of the great Ord River,
    1930 maybe
Her mother was black, her daddy white
Papa was a fine horse-breaker
Mama sang the songs of the old law-makers
She used to hide young Queenie in the bush
And rub black charcoal over her hair and her face
Every time the police came round
Looking for any blonde-haired brown-skinned children
To round 'em all up, take 'em on downtown

Shine on, shine on, immortal one
Shine on, shine on, immortal one

Rover was born in the desert
He lived out there 'til his mother died
Then he moved around a lot from place to place
Bedford Downs, Bow River, Lissadell, Wyndham
Building fences, working as a stockman
Then he had a series of dreams
He started painting what he'd heard and he'd seen
Rainbow Serpent, Krill Krill, Cyclone Tracy
The killing fields
Everything that lives and breathes

Ride on, ride on immortal one
Ride on, ride on immortal one
Your story will always run

When Rover and Queenie were young
They met out on Old Texas Downs station
She worked as a cook there, for a long, long time

When she first saw him she said, 'Hey cowboy!'
Later on she said, 'Nice boy, good worker, top rider, lucky one
   that one'
One day a mean horse ripped the scalp from his head
She stitched him up with a boiled needle and thread
Good as any doctor
They were friends ever after
She said, 'I wanna paint'
He said, 'I'll teach ya'
They died within months of each other

Ride on, ride on immortal ones
Shine on, shine on immortal ones
Ride on, ride on, immortal ones
Shine on shine on immortal ones
Your story will always run, forever run
Forever young, forever young

Immortal Ones: The Road From Kununurra To Derby, 2007

Kununurra and Warmun, 6 August
In a small bush cemetery just off the Great Northern Highway in the East Kimberley lie two giants of Australian art – Queenie McKenzie and Rover Thomas, who died several months apart in 1998. Queenie's grave is a simple white wooden cross on which her name is handwritten. Rover's, fifteen metres away, is more substantial, with a headstone and a plaque piled with plastic flowers.

In the distance is a low red mountain range. Queenie and Rover, who both started painting late in life, made extraordinary pictures just up the road at the community of Warmun, also known as Turkey Creek. Their paintings now fetch prices in the hundreds of thousands of dollars, and Warmun, a tiny dot on the map on a lonely outback highway, is the centre of a thriving art movement and home to a number of artists whose work is eagerly sought by collectors all over the world.

I am standing there on the dusty pink-red ground with my manager Bill Cullen. We are on our way to meet the rest of the band in Derby for the first show of a seven-week national tour.

I became aware of Queenie and Rover in the mid-nineties. I already had some knowledge of the modern Aboriginal art movement that began in Papunya, west of Alice Springs, in the seventies and soon flowered all over the country. When I first saw Rover Thomas's paintings I was struck by their mystery and severity. There was nothing decorative, ornate or fussy about them. And no dots except sometimes as a border. The colours were dark earth tones – he was unafraid of black – the paintings uncompromising, monumental, brooding.

Not long afterwards I saw some of Queenie's paintings. You could tell they were from the same area but Queenie's, although employing a similar minimalist style of broad flat colour planes, seemed softer, more welcoming. She used striking pinks and purples.

Over the years, I heard and read stories about them. Queenie was born on a cattle station on the banks of the Ord River, and was strikingly blond as a child and relatively light-skinned. Her mother would blacken her face with charcoal and hide her in the bush whenever white officialdom came calling, for fear Queenie would be taken away.

As a young woman, she was employed as a cook on Texas Downs station when Rover came to work there as a stockman. Not long after they met she saved his life. A horse kicked him in the head and Queenie stitched up his flapping scalp with camp cotton, which she'd first sterilised. So competent was her surgery that when the doctor finally arrived he pronounced there was nothing more he needed to do. From then on Queenie and Rover were lifelong friends.

Rover started painting after a female relative who had recently died came to him in a series of dreams, and took him flying to various places that she told him to paint. His first paintings were on board for ceremonial purposes. Later, on canvas, he depicted sites of massacres as well as interpretations of Cyclone Tracy, which he believed to be a manifestation of the Rainbow Serpent. Rover, by example, started Queenie painting. 'If he can do that so can I,' she said.

We are here, Bill and I, because after carrying the idea and the title around for years, I eventually wrote a song called 'The Ballad Of Queenie And Rover', recorded it with the band last year and included it on our new album, *Stolen Apples*. We sent some copies up to the art centre a couple of months ago and have been invited to visit. Warmun is only 670 kilometres from Derby, where I'll meet the band tomorrow – a mere run to the shop in these parts.

At seven-thirty this morning, Bill and I landed in Kununurra via Darwin and went straight to visit Kevin Kelly (no relation) and his family, who run Red Rock Gallery, an exhibition space for local artists. Kevin is the executor of Queenie's and Rover's estates and has helped with sourcing and arranging permission for images we plan to project on-screen during the show.

They serve us coffee and melon, and, having never met before, we ease our way into conversation. Their youngest daughter is named Queenie after her godmother. Rover lived with them for two years. There is much to talk about but our visit was always going to be way too short as they have a show that needs to travel to Darwin that day and we're expected at Warmun before lunch. Kevin tells us, among other things, how sorrowful Queenie was after Rover's death, how she pined for him right up until her own a few months later. After three-quarters of an hour that goes too quickly we say our reluctant farewells and walk out into the warm sunny day.

It's a two-hour drive to Turkey Creek/Warmun. We head west-ish for a while, towards Wyndham, then turn south. Not long after that the country begins to look like paintings. I get that same jolt of recognition I had years ago driving from Hermannsburg to Alice Springs through Arrente country and thinking, Oh, Albert Namatjira

wasn't making this up. Those colours in his pictures aren't expression-
istic, they're photo-real. Queenie and Rover and the Warmun painters
seem more abstract on the surface than the Arrente watercolourists,
but the shapes and colours in their work correspond to the landscape
we're travelling through – scattered reddish ranges, small clumps of
rounded hills, pinkish earth, purple shadows. Their paintings are all
about Country.

It's weird passing signs to places I've read about, seen as titles
of artworks, and listed in song but have never been to – Lissadell,
Bedford Downs, Bow River, Texas Downs. Places where mythical
beings lived, travelled and died. It reminds me of my first trip to
America, where everything seemed deeply familiar though I was seeing it for the first time.

We arrive at Turkey Creek around eleven, drive through the 'suburbs'
of Warmun – Top Camp, Bottom Camp, Middle Camp, Garden –
and cross the creek to Other Side, where the art gallery is situated on a
ridge. There we are met by Roger, Jackey, Anna and Ned, who run the
gallery. It is cheque day for the artists, so people come and go and sit
for a while before heading back home for the ritual payday-afternoon
card game.

Our visit unfolds informally, the conversation casual as we sit on
plastic chairs under the awning of the old shed. A light wind is blowing from the east. We meet artists, senior law men and women, quiet
people who've seen thousands of strangers like us breeze in and out
within an hour or two. Some of the younger ones are more chatty.
Rover's daughter, Jane Yalunga, is there preparing some canvases. A
couple of men on the CDEP program (Community Development
Employment Projects) swing by to say hello and get an autograph,
before going back to work.

Sadie Carrington, a young girlish grandmother who's just back
from heart treatment in a Perth hospital, discusses with us the relative
merits of the Dockers and the Crows before requesting a photo in

front of one of her paintings. There are strips of pink in it that remind me of Queenie's strange pinks. When I ask her how she makes that colour she shows us the tubs of ochre that most of the painters use. Red, brown, yellow, orange and white ochre are all found locally. The pink that stops my heart comes from simply mixing red and white.

Roger takes us on a tour of the new art centre building, which is to be opened in three weeks' time. A large boab tree stands sentinel before it. It's an airy, light-filled structure of wood and corrugated iron, freshly carpeted, and the artists, Roger tells us, are keen to cover the pristine walls. He takes us next to the Turkey Creek road-house, where the petrol bowsers are all painted in distinctive Warmun designs. Inside the store, by the cash register, a Rover mural sleeps under perspex, partially obscured by postcard racks, knick-knacks and Aboriginal tourist craft.

We circle back to the arts centre again, where Patrick Mung Mung and his wife Betty Carrington, Sadie's mother, have just arrived to say hello. Both ex-drinkers and major painters, they have taken a break from the rehab classes they've been running over the past couple of weeks. At home I have a print of one of Betty's paintings. It's of the Bungle Bungles (Purnululu), not far from here. In it, concentric lines, cones and cylinders coloured in delicate gradations create wonderful depth. The hills appear to be bound and floating at the same time.

Bill is itching to buy a picture so we go to the storeroom, where the artwork on the floor and walls makes your head swim. The influence of Rover and Queenie and the other early Warmun painters is visible everywhere you look, underneath the many and varied elaborations. Certain paintings exude real power, others come across as merely formulaic, and some that hardly catch you on first glance hold you longer with a second and third look.

Bill points to a small-to-medium, simple-looking painting of vertical spearhead strokes and asks, 'How much is that?'

'Eighteen thousand dollars,' says Roger. The painting's by Lena Nyadbi, who doesn't paint very much and whose work the international collectors are standing in line for. Bill gulps and shifts his gaze elsewhere, though his eyes keep flicking back. He eventually buys a painting more moderately priced.

It's time now to say our goodbyes, as we still have many miles to travel. We wheel around slowly in the dirt and head back over the creek, past the shacks of Warmun. A card game has started on the ground under the shade of a tree, and fifty-dollar notes are flying across the blankets.

We drive four hours to Fitzroy Crossing on a single-lane bitumen highway, passing the turnoff to Wave Hill, where Vincent Lingiari and the Gurindji stockmen walked off Lord Vestey's cattle station forty years ago. Paintings dance in my head as the country outside the car slowly changes. We're heading towards Jandamarra country.

Fitzroy Crossing, 6 August
I'm looking forward to seeing June Oscar again, who first showed me around here fifteen years ago. We've kept in touch since. She visits Melbourne from time to time as part of a cultural exchange, teaching Bunuba language and culture to primary-school students.

The last couple of hours to Fitzroy Crossing are tough driving into the setting sun. It's a long straight road most of the time. Bill's at the wheel. Every now and then we slow down for crows feasting on road kill. One of them, gorged with roo, rises too slowly and hits our windscreen hard, chipping it, then amazingly flies lazily off. (We imagine him waking up in the morning, shrugging his feathers and saying, 'Geez, my left wing feels a bit sore today.')

Around dusk a bullock looms suddenly out of nowhere in the middle of the road, but our brakes are just up to it. We arrive weary and hungry, and after a feed at the Fitzroy Lodge on the bank of the mighty, ever-changing Fitzroy River, turn in.

Fitzroy Crossing/Derby, 7 August
June Oscar and several other Aboriginal women from the town visit me at breakfast. They were at a meeting out bush last night and are on their way to another meeting next door in one of the lodge's function

rooms. It's a busy time for them right now. The women of Fitzroy Crossing are fighting to impose a total ban on takeaway alcohol sales. Naturally there is a fair bit of resistance. Most of the population of the town and the surrounding area are black, and there are many social problems associated with heavy drinking.

The determination of June and the others is obvious as we chat. These women are heroes to me. They carry appalling burdens with grace and pride. 'Sing that "Little Things" song for us in Derby. That's our song,' says one of the older ones with a big smile as we farewell each other.

After an uneventful three-hour drive across the plains, Bill and I reach the King Sound Resort in Derby about two o'clock. The word 'resort' is perhaps used a touch loosely around these parts. This is mudflat and mangrove country. There are no picturesque beaches, no gentle waves lapping at the hotel perimeter, and no holidayers lounging by the pool with umbrellas in their drinks. Here the housemaids call you 'darls'. The rooms are fine, though, and the pool looks just big enough to get wet in.

The rest of the band soon arrive, along with Katy Steele from Little Birdy. She'll be doing all the WA dates with us. We head down to the civic centre, a large, open-sided shed with a corrugated-iron roof, where the crew are setting up. We have four of our own crew, supplemented with four from WA who travel with the PA rig and lights. A touring party of sixteen, spread among four vehicles – a truck and three Kia Carnivals – we will be driving all the way down the coast doing gigs. Broome, Karratha, Carnarvon, Geraldton make up the first week.

Patrick Davies, an Indigenous health worker and songwriter from Fitzroy Crossing, is also on the bill tonight, so we have a lot to get through before showtime – sound checks for three acts as well as running our whole set (close to two hours) in order to go through the lights and projection cues. Our plan is to perform *Stolen Apples* from first to last note, then swing into a mix of old songs for the second half of the show. Shannon, the lighting director, test-runs the projection of the images – mainly paintings – on the screen behind the band.

We work steadily through the warm afternoon, playing every song, some more than once, in order to get the visuals right. This is unusual territory for us. Generally our shows are more freewheeling. We always start with a set list but quite often it goes out the window, and our crew are used to winging it with the changes. But since this show is more structured we use up all the available time nailing little details down. Eventually, around six, we call it quits. The whole thing's still feeling pretty loose but that's to be expected. Hopefully it will tighten up as we head further down the road.

After a feed and change of clothes at the hotel, I head back to the civic centre around seven to see Patrick Davies play. With him is Steve Pigram, who along with six of his brothers sang on the recording of 'The Ballad Of Queenie And Rover' nine months ago on a visit to Melbourne. Colin Pigram, who works as a mechanic in Derby, is around as well. The Pigram Brothers will be playing with us tomorrow night in Broome. They are musical royalty up this way.

Patrick has just started and is sounding strong. Steve's earthy voice harmonises with him as his guitar and ukulele filigree around the tunes. There are a few of his countrymen here tonight and he goes over well. Katy plays solo next and sings a mix of Little Birdy songs, new ones and a brave cover of 'Do Right Woman', first recorded by Aretha Franklin. Katy makes it her own and the crowd are right into her. This is going to work well, I think to myself.

The band have gathered by now – Peter, Bill, Dan, Ash and newbie Cameron Bruce. We're all a bit toey, but feeling good because we know we've done the necessary work in rehearsal over the previous few weeks. We warm up singing some of our big harmony songs ('Song From The Sixteenth Floor', 'God Told Me To'), then Ash picks up the guitar and takes us through 'Itchycoo Park' and 'Lazy Sunday Afternoon' at full volume. Now we're set. Peter mixes up six Brother Petes – last tour's favourite pre-show nip; three parts vodka, one part Lift or lemonade – for the quick ritual clink and knockback.

Before we know it the lights have dimmed and we're walking

slowly onstage. 'Feelings Of Grief', the first song, is a slow-building lament – a tough opening for band and audience. 'God Told Me To' keeps things serious and intense but the band's beginning to open its shoulders. By the third song, 'Stolen Apples', we're starting to smile and the feeling in the crowd is good. People are dancing up the front. Others sit outside at long tables with a good view of the band. I can see Steve Hawke out there. He's easy to spot, sporting a big bush-ranger beard and nodding his head to the music.

We get to our ninth song, 'The Ballad Of Queenie And Rover'. Steve and Colin Pigram slide onstage to a mic and sing the parts they sang on the record. During the instrumental section I look around to the screen behind us, where large images of Queenie's and Rover's paintings slowly dissolve into each other. The crowd is swaying. I'm thinking, Good, good, sweet . . . we have a show. (Only thirty-four and a half more shows, seven weeks and around fifteen thousand kilo-metres to go.)

I look around again as the song comes to an end and a big photo-graph of Rover in a white cowboy hat materialises. He's looking off to one side. 'That way,' he could be saying. 'You go that way.'

RALLY ROUND THE DRUM

(written with Archie Roach)

Like my brother before me
I'm a tent-boxing man
Like our daddy before us
Travelling all around Gippsland
I woke up one cold morning
Many miles from Fitzroy
And slowly it came dawning
By Billy Leach I was employed

Rally round the drum, boys
Rally round the drum
Every day, every night, boys
Rally round the drum

Hoisting tent pole and tarpaulin
Billy says, 'Now beat the drum'
Rings out across the showgrounds
And all the people come
Then Billy starts a-calling
'Step right up, step right up, one and all
Is there anybody game here
To take on Kid Snowball?'

Rally round the drum, boys
Rally round the drum
Every day, every night, boys
Rally round the drum

Sometimes I fight a gee-man
Yeah we put on a show
Sometimes I fight a hard man

Who wants to lay me low
Sometimes I get tired
But I don't ever grouse
I've got to keep on fighting
Five dollars every house

Rally round the drum, boys
Rally round the drum
Every day, every night, boys
Rally round the drum

Like my daddy before me
I set 'em up and knock 'em down
Like my brother before me
I'm weaving in your town

Yeah, rally round the drum, boys
Rally round the drum
Got to keep on fighting
Rally round the drum

I Can't Go On, I'll Go On

In 1991 I was booked to play with The Messengers at the Melbourne Concert Hall, now called Hamer Hall. It was our first time there as the headline and a step up for us, playing on a stage usually graced by orchestras and operas. We wanted to make it a special show and were casting around for a suitable opening act. Steve Connolly called and said, 'I've just seen the most amazing singer on TV. We should get him.'

The program Steve had caught by chance was *Blackout*, an Indigenous arts show. The singer was Archie Roach and the song was 'They Took The Children Away', his story – and the story of generations of Aboriginal people – of being taken from his family as a child. We tracked Archie down and booked him.

I met him for the first time in the dark wings of the Concert Hall, just minutes before he was due to go on. He walked onstage and sang for twenty-five minutes, closing with 'They Took The Children Away'. As I watched from the side all the hairs on my body stood up. I could feel the same thing happening out in the hall. The writer Martin Flanagan, who was there that night, describes what it was like in the audience:

> When he finished his performance there was no sound in that vast auditorium, no sound at all. He thought he had failed . . . He started to walk from the stage and the applause began running after him . . . this man who had done something magical, raising the darkness of the past, telling it in truth, but with a largeness that excluded no-one . . . and the applause was building and building like the crest of a wave but when the wave broke and the applause which was supposed to sweep him up crashed on to an empty stage he was gone.

We walked onstage minutes later. I don't remember a thing about our performance. By the time we'd finished, Archie had gone again.

Steve and I got in touch with him shortly afterwards. He'd only played two songs – long ones – at the Concert Hall but said he had others. We went to his house in Reservoir, in the northern suburbs of Melbourne, where he lived with his wife Ruby Hunter, their children and two foster children. Over the course of several visits, song after song rolled out from him as we sat around their kitchen table, drinking tea, eating sandwiches and yarning.

Archie was from Framlingham, an Aboriginal mission just outside Warrnambool in western Victoria. He was born in 1956, the year after me. I grew up with my seven brothers and sisters, but at the age of three Archie was taken away from his parents, who he never saw again, and sent to live in foster homes.

He was tracked down in his teens by his older sister Myrtle, who wrote him a letter telling him about his family. She and another sister had been taken on the same day as him, and their mother had recently died.

For a long time after that, he says, he was hurt, angry and disillusioned. He drifted around as a young man, fought in the boxing tents, played guitar and started drinking hard. At the People's Palace in Adelaide, a dosshouse run by the Salvation Army, he met Ruby, a small, cheeky woman from the Riverland. She was musical too and they began to knock about together. Everywhere they went they drank.

Sitting at the kitchen table, Steve and I and Archie and Ruby sang songs back and forth. George Jones, Sam Cooke, Ted Hawkins. We sang our own as well. Ruby had a few songs but Archie had a whole swag. Ruby would prompt him, reminding him of ones he'd forgotten. They kept on coming.

'Play that "Charcoal Lane" song,' said Ruby a month or so into our sessions, and the hairs stood up on my neck again as he took his guitar and sang about their drinking days in the back lanes of Fitzroy, before he and Ruby got sober – a song, I thought to myself at the time, Richard Thompson would kill for.

Later that year, Steve and I went with Archie into a home studio owned by Greg Ham from Men at Work and recorded ten songs, including one written by Ruby called 'Down City Streets'. Steve played most of the guitar and we both sang harmonies. We invited a few musicians in to help here and there, but were mindful not to clutter up the songs. The singing and the stories were the main thing. Archie's voice, full of sweetness, longing and pain, was in the tradition of great soul singing.

The album, *Charcoal Lane*, came out in 1992 and stirred people all over the country. For many, Archie's songs were like reportage from a hitherto hidden world – stories from the shadows, from the margins, from the dispossessed. This was before the *Bringing Them Home* report detailing the breakup of Aboriginal families, before the term 'stolen generations' became widely used. 'I didn't know this kind of thing was going on in this country!' was a common response.

Sometime after the record came out, Archie and I were on tour together. One night in Perth, sitting around in the hotel room after a show, he started talking about his days as a tent boxer. From the 1930s through to the 1970s these travelling shows were a big part of Australian country life. Troupes of young trained boxers, usually employed and looked after by a larger-than-life showman/entrepreneur, would go from town to town and take on local challengers.

Billy Leach operated a troupe in Victoria. Archie fought for him when he was young, as had his father and brother. Archie's dad fought under the name Snowball, so when Archie joined up, Billy dubbed him Kid Snowball. They would arrive in a town and set up their tent on a fairground or oval, along with other travelling sideshows. Billy would bang on a 44-gallon drum to announce the commencement of each show and spruik his boxers over the megaphone, encouraging the crowd to have a go and win a prize by lasting three rounds in the ring with a pro. Sometimes, if things were slow, he'd plant one of his boxers in the crowd as a sham challenger, to gee up the audience and get them to come forward.

Billy was well known in the pubs of Fitzroy, a fertile recruiting ground for him. He'd front up to the bar, buy a few rounds, and by the end of the night have a couple more boxers on the string. Most of them were Aboriginal. Often in the tents they would be fighting men much bigger than them – raw-boned, strapping country lads fuelled on beer and rum, egged on by their mates, lumbering around the ring trying to land a knockout blow. Goodnight if one caught you. The boxers had to keep their wits about them, duck and weave out of the way of the hefty whirling arms, avoid the low blows and ignore the taunts of the crowd.

Due to changing entertainment fashions, and public-health and safety concerns, the boxing tents were all but closed down by the mid-seventies. 'But it wasn't a bad life,' said Archie, cradling his guitar in the hotel room. 'There were good days. The money was okay. Old Billy, he'd beat on that drum and call on everybody to rally round, rally round.'

We pulled out some pens and paper and went to work.

Archie had been playing music for quite a number of years before we met, performing in folk clubs and at country music festivals. Writing songs was a way out of alcohol dependence. He and Ruby were well known in the Koori community and looked after other people's children as well as their own. Their house was a haven to many. But after *Charcoal Lane* came out they were buffeted by a whole different degree of fame.

Travelling with Archie as he sang and spoke his pain at gigs, on radio stations, TV and for the press, I could see the toll on him of a thousand little cuts. 'You got me into this,' he'd say to me. 'I don't know whether to kiss you or punch you.' On the one hand he was glad to have the chance to tell his Dickensian story and the wider story of the stolen generations. And proud to be still standing. But the telling was raw for him each time. He's had things taken away he'll never get back. And everywhere he went it seemed everyone wanted another little piece of him.

The glare of the spotlight dimmed eventually, but it's the way of show business for the spotlight to come back around every so often, each time with a different focus. Ruby made her first solo record in 1994, another in 2000, and in 2004 she took centre stage in *Ruby's Story*, a series of acclaimed performances with Paul Grabowsky's Art Orchestra describing her life in song. Like Archie she was taken from her family; she left the Murray River where she was born but returned there many years later with Archie and their family. They both wrote songs for *Ruby's Story*, which continued to be staged in subsequent years, and found a way to manage the rhythms of fame, to take care of their own, and support each other's work, never leaving each other's side.

On 17 February 2010 Ruby died suddenly at home of a heart attack, while playing with her grandchildren. She was only fifty-four – too young to die. The causes of many Indigenous deaths are listed as cancer, stroke, heart attack, diabetes, suicide and car crashes, but behind all these is a deeper stress, the load of more than two hundred years of mayhem.

Everything we do is political. No-one bears that out better than Archie and Ruby. All their songs are love songs – to country and clan – and at the same time they cry out for a better world. Ruby and Archie carried those songs, the stories of the men, women, children, sisters, brothers, mothers and fathers of Aboriginal Australia. They told terrible truths but refused to despair. Two days after he buried his true love and life companion, Archie somehow found the strength to walk onstage at the Port Fairy Folk Festival, open his mouth and sing. Although many of the stolen children never came back, although many of the children of the stolen have never known the way, he keeps singing them home.

They Took The Children Away

This story's right, this story's true
I would not tell lies to you
Like the promises they did not keep
And how they fenced us in like sheep
Said to us, 'Come take our hand'
Set us up on mission land
They taught us to read, to write and pray
Then they took the children away
Took the children away
The children away
Snatched from their mother's breast
Said this is for the best
Took them away

The welfare man, the policeman
Said, 'You've got to understand
'Cause we'll give to them what you can't give
And teach them how to really live
Teach them how to live,' they said
Humiliated them instead
And they taught them that and taught them this
And others taught them prejudice
Oh, they took the children away
Oh the children away
Breaking their mother's heart
Tearing us all apart
Took them away

One dark day on Framlingham
Came and did not give a damn
My mother cried, 'Go get their dad!'
He came running, fighting mad
Mother's tears were falling down
And my dad shaped up and stood his ground
He said, 'You touch my kids, you fight me!'
Then they took us from our family
Took us away
Yeah took us away
Grabbed from our mother's breast
Said this is for the best
Took us away

Told us what to do and say
Taught us all these are white man's ways
But then they split us up again
Gave us gifts to ease the pain
Sent us off to foster homes
And as we grew up we felt alone

'Cause we were acting white and feeling black
One sweet day all the children came back
Yeah, the children came back
Yeah, the children came back
Back where their hearts grow strong
Back where they all belong
The children came back

Yeah, the children came back
Oh, the children came back
Back where they understand
Back to their mother's land
The children came back
Back to their mother
Back to their father
Back to their sister
Back to their brother
Back to their people
Back to their land
All the children came back
All the children came back
Yeah, the children came back
Yes, I came back

Archie Roach

RANDWICK BELLS

Randwick bells are ringing
Must be Saturday
I woke late in the middle of the day
Must be Saturday

Put a blanket on the window
And come on back to bed
We got nowhere to be and no place to go
So come on back to bed

We're gonna rise up singing
We're gonna rise up singing

Randwick bells are ringing
Through the empty rooms
The bells are ringing high and wide
For the bride and groom

Put a blanket on the window
Cover it up, cover it up
It's much too bright in here
Stop walking around with just that towel on
Come on back to bed
Make me smile
We're gonna rise up singing
We're gonna rise up singing

Randwick bells are ringing
Randwick bells are ringing
C'mon baby, let's cook something up
C'mon baby, let's fix something up

Campanology

She lived in a share house in Glebe and played bass in an all-girl trio. There's something about a good-looking woman playing a Fender bass that can't be denied. She was a Saturday-night and a Sunday-morning kind of girl and she liked to come and visit me by the sea. She didn't mind dirty dishes and a pallet on the floor. The church bells rang through the windows every weekend and they were always out of tune. She gave up heroin and she gave up me.

SATURDAY NIGHT AND SUNDAY MORNING

She's a screamer but no-one knows
Just me, the neighbours and her old boyfriends, I suppose
When I take her to see the folks they eat from her hand
On the way home I'm driving
I have to stop the car or crash it right there
She's my sticky treat, she's my bag o' sweets
She's my medicine
Oh, she's Saturday night and Sunday morning

Like Princess Grace in *Rear Window*
She's a volcano under snow
Sometimes our action's all slo-mo in holy candlelight
I give her all my devotion
But sometimes she can't wait to be mashing on me
She's country soul, she's jelly roll
She's mountain high, she's valley low
Oh, she's Saturday night and Sunday morning

She's heroin, she's crystal methedrine
She's mountain high, she's valley low
She's my sticky treat, she's my medicine
She's my medicine, she's my murder scene
She's Saturday night and Sunday morning

I Thought I Heard Buddy Bolden Say

Grant me chastity and continence, but not yet.

St Augustine

When Buddy Bolden was coming through slaughter early in the twentieth century, playing trumpet in New Orleans, Saturday-night music and Sunday-morning music were supposed to be two different things. Jazz belonged to the Devil, gospel to the Lord. Buddy heard voices in his head and started mixing them up. This was long before Ray Charles, who came along in 1954 and put Saturday-night lyrics – 'I got a woman way across town, she's good to me' – to a Sunday-morning song, 'Jesus Is All The World To Me'. So much for the Devil having the best tunes. The hipsters were electrified, the hymn-singers scandalised. Later on somebody called Ray's update soul.

Not long after that, gospel's biggest star, Sam Cooke, left his God-fearing group The Soul Stirrers and crossed over to pop music. There was wailing and gnashing of teeth, rending of garments and burning of records at this defection to Mammon. Sweet Sam sailed on with 'You Send Me' and a string of Saturday-night hits, including one called 'Another Saturday Night'.

But pop music couldn't hold him either. Sam kept on pushing. He stood front and centre in the civil rights movement, studied 'Blowing In The Wind' and wrote 'A Change Is Gonna Come'. He had big plans, until Saturday night caught up with him in his prime and laid him dead from gunshot wounds in a Los Angeles motel. A woman cried *Rape!* and ran into the night, Sam went after her and got into a fight. Oh, Sam, Sam, what a shame.

Curtis Mayfield carried on the torch, singing for freedom, God and women, eventually spawning his spiritual son, Prince, the Priest of Porno, later known as He Who Shall Not Be Named (or glimpsed, just like Yahweh), who explicitly put the sex back into godliness, and the holy spirit and dove back into sex, taking us back to The Song of Solomon, back to the sacred body and the ceremony of skin, way before the long, long shadow of St Augustine – who decreed that the physical and the spiritual were separate states, that the mind was one thing, the body another – darkened the face of the earth.

It was the sons and daughters of St Augustine who founded America with their Manifest Destiny, with their unbending belief in the higher impulses versus the lower, and with God on their side to civilise the savage. And thereby laid down the roiling infection deep in the soil of the American character, the potent brew that travels up the root to the trunk, bursting to get out.

So fissured men walked and continue to walk the American earth – sinner/preachers Jimmy Swaggart and co., Jerry Lee Lewis, Little Richard, Al Green, Martin Luther King, Bill Clinton. Heaven and hell contending inside them, the redemption dove sitting on one shoulder, the damnation vulture on the other.

Pops Staples walked the earth righteously until the angels came to carry him away in 2000. In my mind I see him ascending into the air, strumming his tremolo guitar. The group he started with his children sang the gospel tune 'Ain't That Good News' (which sounded a lot like 'I Got A Woman') early on, before they, like Sam, crossed over to the pop charts. His daughter Mavis, no matter what she sang, was always sanctifying, always moaning for God. She still is. Aretha Franklin, too, who at Barack Obama's inauguration in January 2009, swaddled in a big thick coat, sang 'My Country, 'Tis Of Thee', and left a gap you could drive a truck through between the first and second syllables of *count—ry*.

Which brings us all the way back to Buddy. Who couldn't contain the gap in his head, who broke down in 1907 with a fissure inside that couldn't be fixed, who was declared deranged and taken to an asylum on the edge of town from which he never returned. His Saturday nights and Sunday mornings from then on were pretty much the shuffling same.

SHANE WARNE

(sung to the tune of 'London Is The Place For Me' by Lord Kitchener)

Shane Warne – well known to history
Shane Warne – bowler of mystery
Whenever he walked up to the wicket
A change came over the game of cricket
He had the leg spin, flipper and googly

He came on the scene in 1992
Those Indian batsmen showed him a thing or two
'This fellow,' some said, 'he don't stand a chance!'
But soon he began to make the ball dance
In Sri Lanka he first showed his colours true

In Manchester, England, 1993
He bowled what they call the ball of the century
Mike Gatting looked up, struck as dumb as a post
And walked from the crease like he'd just seen a ghost
Shane Warne's first Ashes delivery

From that time on he played with the batsman's mind
From Brisbane to Durban he had them in such a bind
To go forward or back, to play or abstain
Intensely the pressure built up in the brain
And always the chirping from behind

Mr Warne on his phone sent a lot of texts
'Cause he liked to have quite a lot of sex
He took a prohibited pill to lose his love handles
Said, 'Mum gave it to me!' – what a terrible scandal!
We wondered, 'What will Warney do next?'

Shane Warne – truly a sporting magician

Always played like a man on a mission
Each time he came in to bat or to bowl
He believed in his powers to take control
Even when he was not in the peak of condition

Shane Warne bowled with his friend Glenn McGrath
In Sydney they took their last hurrah
Now Ponting and Taylor, Steve Waugh all agree
To have two such men they were lucky indeed
Shane Warne and his good friend Glenn McGrath

What Keeps Our Stout Hearts Pressing On

No ball bowled is as difficult as one which leaves the bat
and goes towards the slips. The really good leg break beats
them all.

Sir Donald Bradman
(bowled by a leg break in his last innings)

I never planned to write three cricket songs. As I lay on the floor in
1968 with the lights out, a thirteen-year-old trumpet player listening
to *The Lonely Bull* by Herb Alpert and The Tijuana Brass and imagining a life in show business – the roar of the crowd, the silhouette
in the spotlight, the sighing of the women in the front row – three
oddball odes to the 'gentlemanly game' weren't part of the fantasy.
As the years went by and I became a writer who sensed there was
nothing that couldn't be turned into a song, I may have thought, One
maybe. Two perhaps. But three? That seems excessive, even a touch
obsessive. People start to ask questions.

'Okay, you're obviously a huge sports fan. Would you describe
yourself as a cricket tragic?'

'Well . . . er . . . I've written around three hundred songs . . .

um . . . nearly all of them are love songs, you know, fiction, but er, yeah, I like test cricket, but not all cricket. Three songs out of three hundred, that's like one percent, isn't it? Is that such a big deal?'

If the cap fits . . .

It's true that visitors on certain summer days have commented on the droning of three radios and a TV in different parts of the house, all tuned to the test cricket commentary so I can hear the action wherever I am and get to the TV in time for the replay if a wicket falls.

And it's true that the band and I went onstage twenty minutes late at Wrest Point Casino in Hobart in 2005, despite all being in readiness for the show to begin, because we couldn't tear ourselves away from the radio broadcast of the final overs of Australia's run chase against England – a chase that fell agonisingly short and in so doing set up the losing of the Ashes.

True, too, that my crooked boxer's nose is not the result of a left cross or a straight jab but a missed hook shot in the nets at school cricket practice.

'Deflected septum,' said the doctor and straightened it, but come football season it deflected again in the middle of a crunching tackle. 'Bring him back to me when he's finished playing sport,' said the doctor to my mother the second time. 'You're breathing okay, aren't you, son?'

I never went back.

Like Samuel Beckett, I always read the back of the newspaper first – the sports pages. What's good for Sam's good for me. It was in the back pages that I first read about Shane Warne, a pudgy leg spinner from Victoria, supposedly a bit of a lad, who'd been picked to play for Australia against India after only a handful of games at state level.

I was intrigued. He didn't look like a sportsman, but cricket is a broad church and part of its charm has long rested in its accommodation of the non-athletic – players like the pear-shaped Colin Cowdrey, casually catching the ball at first slip and slipping it into his pocket; or Pakistan's tanker, Inzamam-ul-Haq, jogging down the pitch for a single, uninterested in the second run, to the frustration of his partner.

The modern era, with its increased demands of 'professionalism', may be threatening this particular species with extinction, but the leg spinner, by virtue of his rarity, is still allowed a little more latitude in terms of personality and physique. Leg-spin bowling is fiendishly difficult to control, harder than all other types of bowling – pace, swing, seam, off spin – and is only attempted over the long term by the foolhardy, stubborn and quixotic. Consequently, when one breaks through to the national level he is usually a different cut of man.

I was perhaps more interested than most at first in Shane Warne, being a leg spinner myself. Richie Benaud, all-rounder and Australian captain in the early sixties, had inspired me as a young boy to take up the dark art, and despite many frustrations I toiled willingly through high-school summers, in the nets and on game days, seeking to deceive. I could spin big, had good loop, and bowled a sometimes handy wrong 'un, but alas, I lacked control. Fast bowlers can get away with a few loose deliveries, but when a slow bowler strays it's feasting time for batsmen. The worthy leg spinner, though, operates on a different kind of maths. Our few glories always outweigh our many humiliations. This is what keeps our stout hearts pressing on.

I was in Sydney at the time of Shane's first test against India and went to the SCG to see him play. He was bowling to some of the best players of spin in the world and they handled him easily. I thought he looked all right, though. Thankfully the selectors thought so too, and when he nabbed a few crucial wickets later that year in a surprise touring victory over Sri Lanka – also good players of spin, especially at home – he was up and running. A little confidence goes a long way.

What was extraordinary about him was that, as well as being able to make the ball loop, drift, dip, grip, spit and spin in befuddling ways, he could land it nearly every time exactly where he wanted to. Leg spinners weren't supposed to be able to do that, the mechanics of their wrist action usually causing them to stray more than other bowlers. But Warne's accuracy was uncanny and allowed him to build up pressure. By placing the ball time and time again in the same spot he could, through little variations – big turn, small turn, straight on – bring the batsman undone. And more often than not the undoing was mental.

A shudder went through the England team's dressing room in 1993 – a shudder that lasted the whole series – when Warne's first ball in test cricket on English soil bowled their best batsman, Mike Gatting, neck and crop. I've watched this ball many times on replay – thanks, YouTube – and still it astounds. It starts straight, then drifts weirdly in the air to land at a place on the pitch where it seems it can do no harm. Gatting appears to have it covered. But once it hits the pitch it spits and turns viciously, past his dangling bat, and strikes like a cobra the top of off stump. Gatting has no idea what's happened. He has to ask the umpire – the legendary Dickie Bird, a name worthy of an old-time fiddle player – if he's out or not. He seems completely spooked, looking behind him disbelievingly a couple of times as he walks off.

That was the end of England that year right then and there.

Great leg spinners when they do come along tend to make their mark. Four of Australia's top fifteen bowlers of all time are leggies – Grimmett, O'Reilly, Benaud, Warne – a proportion far greater than their ratio in the ranks. What added to Warne's impact was the dearth of leg spin worldwide before his arrival. The seventies and eighties were dominated by fast bowlers as the West Indians set the template and reigned supreme.

So Warne, bottle-blond, pie-eating, fag in hand – the Mozart man/child of cricket, the larrikin of loop – shuffled onstage with a script no soap writer could top and an audience hungry for a performer who was freakish and ordinary at the same time. He's just like us, he's a dag, he does stupid things, he can't keep his pecker in his pants, but even when the shit's raining down on him he turns up to play body and soul.

I had never thought to write a song about him. I never think to write a song *about* anything. I loved to watch him bowl, loved the way he ambled in so casually before he ripped his shoulder round and sent the ball fizzing; even when nothing much was happening it felt like something was about to. But the way he reacted after almost every ball, as if he'd nearly got the batsman out whether they'd played him comfortably or not, tended to grate after a while. And taking money from an Indian bookmaker, who told him there were no strings attached, seemed not only greedy but unbelievably dumb. Dumber still was his taking a diuretic pill containing a prohibited drug to lose weight, which led to him being banned from cricket for a year. And it looked pretty lame when he brought his mother into it, saying she'd given him the pill.

So, like many Australians, I had mixed feelings about him. As I watched him play his final test match in 2007 at the SCG, the scene of his first, a song was the furthest thing from my mind.

A test match goes for five days, seven hours a day. I could happily watch every ball if left to my own devices, but it was early January, summer holidays, with the children and Sian and I going back and forth to the beach, friends dropping by. The telly was on, but often with the sound down. I'd check in on it every once in a while to get an update on the score. England was going down the gurgler again.

Declan had brought over a CD of calypso music recorded in London during the fifties, a collection called *London is the Place for Me*. I found myself humming the title song, by Lord Kitchener – a lilting, infectious tune – around the house for days. From one second to the next a couple of fresh lines jumped into my head, with the two syllables of 'Shane Warne' replacing 'Lon-don'. Oh, no! I thought. Do I really want to chase this down? But I couldn't stop myself, and the song wrote itself in a couple of hours.

Over the next few days we gave it the house test. Maddy and Memphis liked the tune and made up keyboard and guitar parts to play with me. Sian pulled out her clarinet and adapted the horn lines from the original recording. We played it to visitors and got a laugh every time. There was no turning back now. The melody seemed to fit the subject, and the song itself sat in the long tradition of calypso cricket songs – a genre in its own right.

Not long after that, back home in Melbourne, Sian and I recorded the song with cricket fan Ray Pereira on congas. We put on Hawaiian shirts, had a friend film us, and uploaded the song on YouTube. As a courtesy we also sent a copy to the office of Shane Warne Enterprises.

Shane and I had met a few times when I played at a couple of his Boxing Day charity breakfasts. He was friendly and genuine, very likable. He invited me to visit the Australian cricket team's dressing room and we exchanged phone numbers. We sent each other a couple of texts – Happy New Year, stuff like that. I didn't visit the dressing room. Why would you? It's like going to visit someone at work. I didn't get any more texts from him after I sent the song, though his PA rang up and said Shane says thanks but he's not too sure about it.

I've never been sure about it either. Sometimes I like it, sometimes I think it's totally naff. The song it's based on has this beautiful loose, greasy feel that I just can't touch. Once in a while it's fun to sing, to teach the audience the clarinet riff and get them to sing it when it comes around after the verse. It's a little jazzy and involved, so a mob of people trying to whistle the tune sounds like a cacophonous aviary. I like that.

Anyway, the song's out there now and, good or not, I have to live with it. It comes into its own at certain times, like one of those special-job tools in the toolkit. You're glad to find it there amidst the clutter, under everything else at the bottom of the bag; glad you brought it along.

Eleven Calypso Cricket Songs

'Victory Calypso (Cricket Lovely Cricket)' – Lord Beginner
'The Cricket Song' – Lord Kitchener
'Two Great Bowlers' – Sugar Aloes
'Gavaskar Calypso' – Lord Relator
'Sir Garfield Sobers' – The Mighty Sparrow
'Rally Round The West Indies' – Charles Roots, featuring
   David Rudder
'Chinese Cricket Match' – Dictator
'Stroke It' – Red Plastic Bag
'West Indian Cricket' – Joker
'Lara Again' – Alston Becket Cyrus
'Calypso Cricket' – Chalkdust

SMOKE UNDER THE BRIDGE

All day long I've been walking
And mostly to myself I've been talking
The lonesome night is too quickly falling
In this unfriendly town
It's cold when the sun goes down
So I'll head for the river and look for smoke under the bridge
I'll keep on moving 'til I find smoke under the bridge
A little shelter, a friendly fire under the bridge

Once I had a place I could call my own
Now wherever I lay my head is home
Ran into some trouble back on down the road
They didn't like the look of me
Someone swung a hook at me
I'll keep my eyes open for smoke under the bridge
Keep on hoping for smoke under the bridge
A warm fire, some company under the bridge

I'll keep on looking for smoke under the bridge
Keep on walking to smoke under the bridge
A little shelter, a friendly fire,
Some ragged company under the bridge
I'll keep on walking
I gotta keep walking
Gotta keep walking

That Kind Of Day

Banjo Clarke, elder of the Gunditjmara people of western Victoria,
law man, philosopher, guru, died in March 2000. I sang at his funeral,

although I'd never met him. Many others sang and spoke too, at the request of his family or because they wanted to pay their respects. The Uncle Banjo of Archie Roach's song 'Weeping In The Forest' was widely loved, an inspiration to songwriters Neil Murray, Shane Howard and Andy Albert, and mentor to many young people from all over the world. The door of his house at Framlingham – on the old mission Archie was snatched from as a child – was always open to travellers and those seeking guidance, respite, knowledge, or just a yarn.

Two thousand people or more assembled for the service, spilling out of a large marquee on a field not far from his home. Songs were interspersed with speeches and readings. Banjo had joined the Baha'i faith later in his life, feeling that its Unity of Mankind philosophy dovetailed with his spiritual beliefs. He'd been working on a book before he died and a couple of people read excerpts.

Two phrases from one reading flew like arrows into my brain from the speaker's mouth, the first being 'the pretty place', which was the name Banjo gave to a particular spot on the river he used to visit as a child – a place to play and fish and dream. The second came from his description of his travels as a young man, going up and down the country looking for work, often hitchhiking or walking. He would always head towards the river when he first arrived in a strange town and look for 'smoke under the bridge'. It could be dangerous, as an Aboriginal man, getting caught alone on the streets after dark. Smoke curling from under a bridge signalled refuge and the warmth of kindred souls around a campfire.

Later during the service a young man spoke about his connection with Banjo, who'd told him to 'close your eyes and think of me' whenever he needed him, no matter how far away he might be. The young man almost drowned years later off the coast off America, and believed he'd only been saved after summoning Banjo's spirit, who told him not to panic, that he was going to be okay.

It was that kind of day.

Afterwards, after the sandwiches and drinks, the conversations with strangers and catch-ups with old friends, Neil Murray offered me a lift back to Melbourne, a three- to four-hour drive. Neil, co-founder of the pioneering Warumpi Band, also grew up in the Western District, north of Banjo's country, around Lake Bolac – once full of eels but nothing but dirt now. Neil and another local, Shane Howard, wrote a song with Banjo called 'The River Knows', which describes the journey of the eels from the lake to the sea. Shane had sung it that afternoon. Back when they were thick in the water, the eels used to go right through Banjo's pretty place, heading downstream, thirsting for saltwater.

I'm a big admirer of Neil's. I like his dour, dig-down manner and his shy humour. He has a complicated life with ex-wives and children and thousands of miles between. He wrote 'My Island Home', 'Fitzroy Crossing' and many other classic songs. His novel, *Sing for Me, Countryman*, is a vivid, straight-talking document from the front lines of black and white relations. 'Windy Mick And The Falcon', one of his many memorable poems – a laconic tall tale of escape, return and a car that flies – is a sheer joy.

We spoke of pretty places and haunted country, one-man tribes, smoke under bridges, gigs done and gigs to come as we drove through rolling hills in the gathering dusk. About halfway home his phone rang. It was a long-distance call from the desert west of Alice Springs. After what seemed to me a cryptic conversation he put the phone down and said, 'I've just become a grandfather. My daughter's just had a baby. My first grandchild.'

It was dark when we pulled into Melbourne. A warm night. We stopped at a hotel near the Vic Market to wet the baby's head by remote, and raise a glass to Banjo. It's hard to tell with Neil, but he seemed pretty chuffed. Apprehensive too, I imagined. He seemed to be staring down the years, from the womb to the tomb.

I left him there in a cloud of smoke and a drinkers' din. Caught a cab across town to my house near the sea, with three phrases dancing in my head I couldn't wait to write down.

It was that kind of day.

SOMEBODY'S FORGETTING SOMEBODY
(SOMEBODY'S LETTING SOMEBODY DOWN)

Are you lonesome tonight?
Are you feeling like me?
I'll bet you're dancing tonight
Running around so carelessly
Somebody's forgetting somebody
Somebody's letting somebody down

The door to my heart
Your kiss is the key
The keys to the car
Now they're useless to me
Somebody's forgetting somebody
Somebody's letting somebody down

And every time I hear those bells
I think I'm done for
And every time they cast their spell
I think I'm done for
Nowhere to run for
Somebody's forgetting somebody
Somebody's letting somebody down

Et Tu, Paulus?

When our mother was still alive my siblings and I, scattered around
Australia and overseas, would speak to her in Queensland every week
or two by phone. We got a lot of news about each other this way, with
Mum the central hub, receiving and sending information along the
spokes of her children. The information disseminated wasn't always

reliable, our mother being a great believer in never letting the facts get in the way of a good story. And as she got older she sometimes got things muddled up.

'The record company want me to release a collection of my most popular songs,' I told her one Sunday in 1996. 'I've been putting it off for a while but I think it's the right time to do it now. I have a new song out for Christmas, just the cherry to top it off.'

'Oh, that's a good idea, darling. Can I give you some suggestions?'

'Well, sure, but most of the songs are decided already. Two per album is my rule of thumb, and generally they're the singles. There's room for only twenty altogether. Which ones did you have in mind?'

'I'll send you a list.'

A letter arrived the following week, with her list filling a couple of sheets of paper front and back in her loopy handwriting. Sixty-one songs.

'Once I started I couldn't stop,' she said the next Sunday.

'Mum tells me she's helping you select your Greatest Hits,' said Mary Jo when she dropped in later that week.

'Yeah, more like the Complete Collected Works.'

Top of the maternal list was 'Somebody's Forgetting Somebody'.

'That song's my favourite,' Mum said.

'Why's that? What do you like about it?'

'I don't know. Maybe it's because it's one of your early ones. It's a nice tune.'

'I'm sorry, Mum, but I don't think it's going to make the cut. I've chosen three songs from that record already, songs that we did film clips for and that got lots of airplay.'

'That's okay, darling. I can still play it anytime I want.'

Three years later, Martin phoned me. 'The doctor's rung again,' he said. 'You know we've been trying to get her to quit driving for a while. Softly, softly, gentle hints and so on. Well, she's getting pretty dangerous out there. Her eyesight and concentration, reaction time, they're all getting worse. He says we've got to get the keys off her or else he'll have to report her to the police.'

I knew what he meant. The last time I'd visited her we decided to go to a movie and she insisted on driving. Halfway down the freeway she started spacing out and saying disconnected things. She'd gotten confused with her insulin dose and given herself too much. I had to make her pull over so I could take the wheel and bring her back home.

'It's hard for her,' Martin continued. 'She doesn't want to give up her independence, I can understand that. But she doesn't have a choice now. The kids and I will be able to drive her around. And there's a bus from her place to town and back. She thinks it's just Anne and me with a bee in our bonnets so she's going to try and get sympathy from you younger ones. I need you to back us up. Next time you talk to her, will you bring it up with her, please? If we all work on her she'll get the message.'

There was no need to bring it up. The first thing she said in our next phone call was 'Oh, Anne and Martin are making such a fuss about my driving. They want me to give up the keys to the car. Can you believe it?'

'Well, you know, Mum, I have to agree with them. Remember trying to go to the movies last time? I'm really sorry, but what if somebody got killed?'

There was a sharp intake of breath at her end of the line. A breath with no words but a breath that said, as clear as a tolling bell, *Et tu, Paulus?*

Three days later, one of the strapping grandchildren came and took the yellow Pulsar away.

SOMEWHERE IN THE CITY

She's somewhere in the city and the clock has just struck nine
This great big city and I can't get her off my mind
I called her today but alas she never got back to me
Maybe I said something wrong
Or something's wrong with her message machine

She's somewhere in the city with a glass of wine in her hands
This great big city with a lowdown sorry man
It's tearing me up bit by bit the way she runs hot and cold
I so love her face but I sure worry about her soul

She's somewhere in the city, somewhere in the city

She's somewhere in the city but she might as well be
    somewhere on Mars
This great big city with its nightlife, restaurants and bars
So many places in the city for someone to have a good time
On a night like this I feel like committing a crime

She's somewhere in the city, somewhere in the city
Somewhere in the city, somewhere in the city

Nine Simple Tips On How To Write The Perfect, Less-Than-Three-Minute Pop Song

1 If you don't have a copy of 'Summer In The City' by The Lovin' Spoonful, call a friend and find one. Or download it from iTunes for $1.69. If you download it for free somewhere else I won't tell anyone.

2 Imagine it hasn't been written. Now . . .

3 Start with two ominous organ notes followed by a loud drum crash. Repeat three times. Take seven seconds to do this.

4 Come in singing over a rock band playing urgent, descending chords. Use six lines to describe the claustrophobic feeling of a hot day in a big city. Paint both the macro picture – 'doesn't seem to be a shadow in the city' – and the micro picture – 'back of my neck getting dirty and gritty'. Towards the end of the verse, ratchet up the tension with a key change, concentrating everything down to one vivid image of danger and release – 'hotter than a match head'. Do all this in fifteen seconds.

5 Modulate again only six seconds after the last modulation, using open breezy chords to set up the relief of the chorus, which heralds a change of scene, a sense of escape, and the myriad possibilities of a warm summer night. Change keys again halfway through the chorus for a little philosophising. Keep this two-part chorus to seventeen seconds in total.

(So far you've used up only thirty-nine seconds and you have all the ingredients in place. Good.)

6 Sing a second verse over those pressing, clangy chords again. Reiteration with variation. Lyrically leave the day behind now and stay with the brewing night. The city's cooled down but the hunt for lovin's stepped up. Cool cats are prowling. Continue the quirky imagery – 'wheezing like a bus stop' – and repeat the double-barrelled chorus.

7 Now break the song down to a guitar riff with organ, throw in a sample of car horns over the top, followed by what sounds like a jackhammer, then have the whole thing fall away to a solo piano playing those thrilling, descending verse chords again. Ensure this *musique concrète* mini-symphony goes for no more than nineteen seconds.

8 Repeat first verse and chorus, fulfilling the rule of threes, then break it down again to guitar and organ, leaving a one-bar hole where

nothing happens save for a long thin organ note that stretches out to snap back to the driving piano riff. Have the drums and the guitars crash in again over the piano to drive it home. Give the drummer his head and start fading at two and a half minutes. Fade quickly so it's all over by two-minutes forty.

9 Send it to radio late spring.

SOUTH OF GERMANY

Many lives I could have lived, many trails taken
It always seems that way at twenty-three
You walk into a room sometime and then a window opens
My life changed forever in the south of Germany

A morning train I had to catch, I just lay there sleeping
There was nothing in that town to hold me
By the time the clock had done another day of creeping
My life had changed forever in the south of Germany

Oh I'm so sorry that today I have to go away

Seven children have I raised, I love some more than others
The hardest thing to do is set them free
So I learned my lesson hard seven times all over
My life changed forever in the south of Germany

I never was the kind of girl for acting sentimental
I never called our meeting destiny
I just call it good luck to meet a man so gentle
My life changed forever in the south of Germany

Oh I'm so sorry that today I have to go away

Sometimes when I wake at night I'm dreaming of another
Then I turn and touch him next to me
And I know where I belong; still I sometimes wonder
My life changed forever in the south of Germany

Oh I'm so sorry that today I have to go away

Puff!

My dad's younger sister Judy was a fun-loving woman, according to reports, who studied nursing after she left school. She and a friend went travelling in Europe not long after World War II ended. On their way to France through Germany they looked up some old family friends in a small town south of Frankfurt, planning to stay one night with them before catching the train to Paris the next morning. But they slept in, missed the train and had to rebook for the following day.

The elderly couple they were staying with, looking for something diverting for their guests to do, rang around their friends. There was a dance on at the nearby US army barracks, and young women were in short supply. So that night two soldiers came around to pick up the young Australians. One of the soldiers was named Bob and I came to know him many years later as Uncle Bob, or, as we used to say as kids, Uncle Barb Wire, because we thought it was hilarious the way he said his name.

The sparks flew immediately between Bob and Judy, and after a speedy courtship they were married. They lived in Germany for a year then went to live in the States. They moved around a lot with Bob's various army postings – New York, Oklahoma, California, Kansas – eventually ending up in Los Alamos, New Mexico, Bob's home state. Along the way they had eight children and that's how I came to have a bunch of American cousins.

We didn't see much of them growing up, as they only made two trips out with the whole family. Air travel wasn't cheap in the sixties, and still isn't for a party of ten. They fascinated us, though, talking like they'd walked straight out of our TV. And I like to think we amazed them too: 'You play football without padding? You eat shark?' And that was just the stuff we didn't make up.

Most of the cousins had left home by the time I visited the family house in 1987. Bob by then worked as a physicist at the Los Alamos National Laboratory, helping to develop nuclear weapons, and naturally believed strongly in nuclear deterrence against the Soviet Union.

He was a sharp debater and you had to have your wits about you to take him on. My wits tend to stray.

I stayed a couple of days. They took me on a drive to show me the sights – the adobe towns of Taos and Santa Fe, the old governor's palace – and filled me in on the Spanish and Native American history of the area. On the morning I left, Judy served me tamales, which I'd never had before. They were delicious – exotic, warm and comforting.

That was the last time I saw her. She died nine months later from a heart attack.

The story of how Bob and Judy got together was a famous one in our family. 'If she hadn't slept in they would never have met,' we were told in tones of wonder. I'd imagine my eight cousins – *puff!* – all disappeared in an instant. You think about a story like this long enough and you start to float away. You could go back and forth all day arguing over what has the greatest effect on destiny – chance or character. The story of Judy and Bob seems to hold both in perfect balance. Sure, they met by accident but she had a reputation as a party girl and it wasn't that unusual for her to sleep in.

Writing depends on accidents. And a certain kind of character too – a character with ice in his veins, an attender of accidents, a ghoul on the scene, someone who makes up stuff about people he hardly knows, who murders for a rhyme, exterminates a child without a qualm, lopping one from eight to make seven – *puff!* – so that everything fits just so.

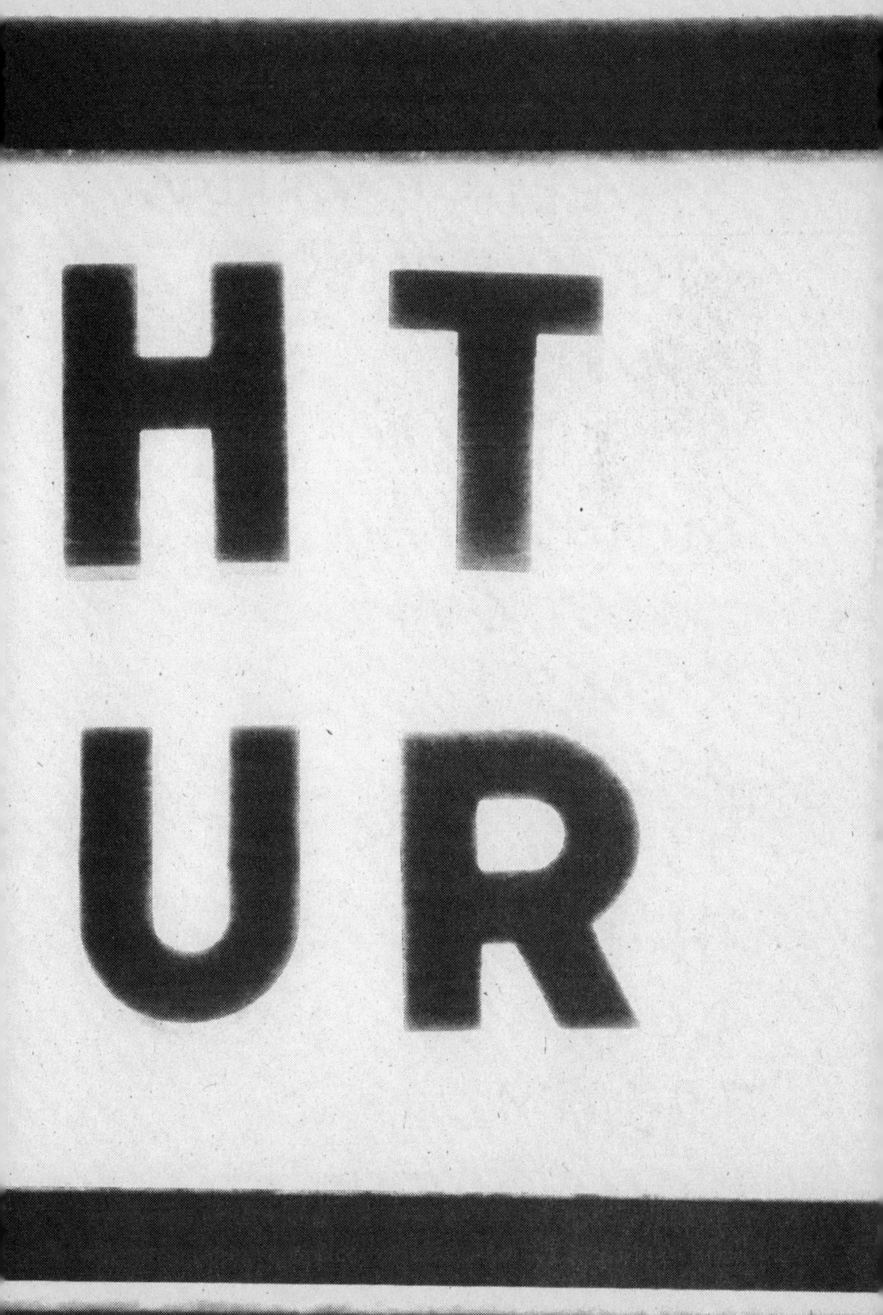
HT
UR

STREET OF SORROWS
STOLEN APPLES
STORIES
STUPID SONG
SUMMER RAIN
SWEET GUY
SYDNEY
ASLEEP
THIS LAND
THOUGHTS
DOOR
TREATY
UNTIL DEATH

MA
WIN A COAT
COME AROUND
WOULD YOU
BEAUTIFUL THING
SHOES
YOU CAN'T TAKE IT
LITTLE SISTER
YOUNG LOVERS
39
YOUR LOVIN
ZOE

STANDING ON THE STREET
OF EARLY SORROWS

It was just a quarter mile
To your house in Kensington
It was always 95 degrees (Hey Julie)

Walking to the swimming pool
February back to school
All that summer you were cool (Hey Julie)

I'm standing on the street of early sorrows

You never know just what you've lost
Until it's yours and then it's dust
But you remain and never rust (Hey Julie)

I'm standing on the street of early sorrows

She Was Just Seventeen

Goodbye, dear Pocahontas! Goodbye P.T. Barnum! Goodbye, Street Of Early Sorrows and may I never set eyes on
you again!

> Henry Miller's adieu to Brooklyn
> before leaving for Paris

Julie Thompson lived a few streets away. She had long, long hair and
soulful dark eyes. The two of us spent a lot of time in her room,
where nothing much happened. She'd be well over fifty now, wherever
she is, but she's always seventeen in this song.

STOLEN APPLES

Stolen apples taste the sweetest
See them hanging in the pale moonlight
You won't feel those cuts and grazes
As you reach out for your prize in the night
And pluck it down and take that very first bite

'Don't tell anyone our secrets'
Said the farmer to his darling wife
'There are some here in the district
Not so happy with their lot in this mean, old life.
Now, sweetheart, won't you pass me the paring knife'

Stolen apples, plucked down in their prime
Stolen apples, hanging heavy on my mind

Eve called Adam in the garden
'Hey Ad, come over here and look at these, won't you try some?'
'Oh, no,' said Adam. 'That's forbidden!'
'Come on now baby,' said Eve, 'what could be wrong with
   just one little one?'
So Adam bit and cried out, 'That's the bomb! That's the bomb!'

Stolen apples taste the sweetest
Stolen apples taste the sweetest

Fourteen Apples

Once upon a time, back in the days Homer sang, everything was
going along hunky-dory, sweet as apple pie, at the wedding of Peleus
and Thetis, until a gatecrasher turned up and upset the applecart.

Eris, the goddess of discord, angry at being uninvited, decided to make mischief by throwing a golden apple into the centre of the banqueting crowd.

Inscribed on the apple were the words 'To the fairest'. Three goddesses claimed it – Hera, Athena and Aphrodite – and turned to Zeus to settle the dispute. Zeus, knowing a wormy apple when he saw it, delegated the judging to Paris, a good-looking Troy boy, the apple of his mother's eye, no doubt, but perhaps an apple or two short of a box.

The three goddesses bribed Paris in turn. Hera offered him power, Athena wisdom, and Aphrodite the love of the most beautiful (mortal) woman in the world. Paris – natch – declared Aphrodite the winner, and sure as apples falling from a tree hit the ground, trouble soon followed.

After the wedding, Paris went home and hatched a plan, with Aphrodite's help, to sail to Sparta and steal their married queen Helen, the most beautiful woman in the world.

'Don't do it,' said his sister Cassandra.

'She'll be apples,' Paris replied and went ahead with his plan, successfully nabbing a willing (by some accounts) Helen and bringing her back to Troy.

His stolen apple may have tasted sweet for a while, but not for long. He woke up one morning to find a thousand bristling ships on the shore of his city, bent on bloody retribution.

You know the rest – the siege of Troy, the wooden horse and all that. Wily wandering Odysseus, stiff-necked Agamemnon, brooding Achilles. For the Greeks, one bad apple threatened to spoil the whole batch until Achilles threw off his sulk. Comparing Achilles, the great warrior, to Paris is a bit like comparing apples to oranges, but somehow Paris managed to kill Achilles by spearing him in the heel, though Paris didn't last too long after that. He and his city were soon destroyed.

All this happened a long time ago, one of the oldest stories in the book. People were talking about it well before they'd heard of Adam tasting Eve's apple. And if I made any of this up, well then, God didn't make little green apples and it don't rain in Indianapolis in the summertime.

STORIES OF ME

Ever since you said goodbye
I've had a reputation
I'm not drinking on the sly
I'm the star attraction
Every morning I wake up
Fill my cup and listen bitterly
To stories of me

They say a man is going round
He looks a lot like me
They say that man is going down
It's looking pretty likely
Every morning he wakes up
Fills his cup and listens shamefully
To stories of me

Everybody come on down
Set 'em up and pass 'em round
We're all here for a drowning

I was down at Baker's Hall
I heard somebody talking
That's the last thing I recall
Then my mind went walking
I woke up with a heavy head
On a hard bed trying to believe
These stories of me

Yeah I woke up in a stranger's bed
Wondering about the things she said to me
These stories of me

Sing To The Shy Goths

The same people you misuse on your way up
You might meet up on your way down
                    Allen Toussaint, 'On Your Way Down'

Music promoter and record-company honcho Michael Gudinski rang me up late in 2008. 'How do you think Leonard Cohen would go here? We've been offered the tour but he's asking a lot of money. And of course it's in US dollars. We'd have to do big places.'

'If I were you I'd do it. It'll be huge,' I replied.

His next question was, 'Would you do the support?'

'Well, you know I don't often do supports these days,' I said, playing it cool, 'but I'll have a think about it.' Meanwhile my heart pumped a little faster. *Songs of Love and Hate* and *Songs From a Room* are imprinted on my soul.

A few days later, despite the falling Australian dollar and the GFC, Michael decided to take the plunge. That's what I like about him. He sniffs the wind and takes a chance. I stepped back and let him and my agent do a little dance, and after a couple of turns on the floor I got the gig.

Being the opening act can be sweet. Your price is set, your set is short, and you don't have the responsibility of filling the venue. You strut and fret your half-hour or forty minutes upon the stage and fire your best shots. Sometimes you get over, sometimes you don't, but either way you finish work early. You're free to stick around and watch the main act or head out into the night.

It's not always easy, though. Supporting American bands in the eighties, here and overseas, was often challenging. Many appeared to follow a philosophy best summed up as: 'We hold this truth to be self-evident – that all have the unalienable right to pursue and flaunt success. When you're on top, show it.' This flaunting was usually enforced by martinet road crews who wouldn't move their masters' gear one inch to accommodate ours, who taped up most of the lighting board, and who set sound limits for us so far below those of the main act that when they came on they sonically blew us away.

And more often than not the headliner would meander their way through sound check in the afternoons, doodling, jamming, fussing, stopping, starting, stopping, then starting again as we waited – eating up time all the way to the opening of the doors so that we couldn't make a noise and had to scramble to set up as the crowd came in.

Not all were like that, of course. There were those who kept Allen Toussaint's warning from 'On Your Way Down' in mind and treated their openers with respect. But this didn't always mean your troubles were over. Midnight Oil or Cold Chisel or The Angels might have done you the honour of selecting you to play before them, their crew might have even pushed amps back a few feet to give you some room, you might have got a brief sound check, but their audiences were a whole other class of beast. 'OILS! OILS! OILS!' or 'CHISEL! CHISEL! CHISEL!' the whole room would chant, psyching you to crack and flee the stage so their heroes could take over. Up the front at Angels gigs, scary-looking young men with shaved heads and missing teeth would needle you relentlessly during each song, intoning in low voices, just audible, 'Fuck off, fuck off, fuck off . . .'

Some of the longest half-hours of my life have been spent onstage as a support act. Not long after *Post* came out in 1985, I toured under a double bill of Australian Crawl and The Motels, both of whom were high on the charts. I was performing with Steve Connolly and Michael Barclay, who'd made the record with me. The songs were pretty downbeat, but with the two of them singing high harmonies and Michael banging a tambourine, things had been going okay on the east coast. My name was on the poster and there'd been some good reviews.

The final show was in Perth at the Entertainment Centre, the largest venue I'd played to that point. I couldn't afford to fly Michael and Steve over so elected to play solo. I noticed when I arrived in town that my name wasn't on the posters. At the gig I waited side of stage listening to the excited buzz of seven thousand people. When the lights went down hundreds of teenagers ran to the front squealing, only for their faces to fall as one when I walked on. The next excruciating twenty minutes felt like twenty hours as I strummed my down-and-out, bottom-looking-up, bus-riding ballads to a disgruntled and uninterested audience. I couldn't get off stage quick enough.

I found out the next day, though, that at least one out of the seven thousand liked it. Fortunately for me he wrote for the newspaper.

In 1995 I toured Europe and the UK, opening up for Joe Jackson and his band. They found a bunk for me on their bus and made me welcome. It was my first time in continental Europe. We played in France, Spain, Germany, Italy and England, often travelling overnight after gigs. I would wake up in the morning in a city I'd never seen before, put on my knapsack, find a map and tramp all day – visiting museums, churches, galleries, the old parts of towns and the banks of rivers.

In Munich in early spring, I came across a large park called English Garden. It was the first warm sunny day of the season. Families and lovers gambolled and canoodled on vast swathes of soft green grass threaded by trickling streams. Frisbees flew, boys tossed balls, dogs frisked and snouted and sniffed. Groups of happy people sat at long wooden tables drinking beer from large glass mugs that sparkled golden in the sun. I felt as though I'd wandered into heaven. It was the first time I truly understood the intensity of the Northern Hemisphere seasons. It seemed the whole world was springing back to life after the cold dead clutch of winter.

My little show was working well with Joe's audiences. He was playing to around 1500–2000 a night in seated theatres. They paid attention and responded warmly. I'd learnt French at school and picked up some Spanish over the years, so I was able to work out things to say between songs in the language of the audience. The local promoters and stage managers helped me with pronunciation and idiom.

Joe being popular in Germany, we did a lot of shows there. His bass player, Graham, with whom I got friendly, had studied German at school. I had a German grammar book so we did a bus class every day, and my onstage script grew each night. I met a woman in Hamburg who showed me round and helped me translate 'Summer Rain' into German. The next show I sang it as my closing song. It brought the house down.

Then we got to Italy. They do things differently there.

I was brimming with confidence when I walked onstage in Roma. Why, I was quarter Italian. The crowd were very noisy as they came in. They'll settle in a minute, I thought, and announced myself, 'Buona sera. Mi chiamo Paul Kelly. Vengo di Australia.' No response. No-one turned a head. Okay, start singing then. 'Stories Of Me', a nice loosener. As I sang the noise got louder. It was a sit-down theatre. In every other European country I'd played, the audience had been mostly seated and ready, while those who came in late took their seats quietly. But here people were calling to each other across the rows. I couldn't be sure what they were saying, despite five years of high-school Latin, but in my head the translation went something like this:

HELLO, HELLO, WHERE ARE YOU SITTING? I'M SITTING OVER HERE. HOW'VE YOU BEEN? GOOD, THAT'S GOOD. I'VE BEEN FINE. HEY, THERE'S GIUSEPPE. HI, GIUSEPPE. WE'RE OVER HERE. CIAO! CIAO! KISS, KISS. I'VE GOT A BIG SANDWICH HERE. DO YOU WANT SOME? IT'S HUGE. IT'S PLENTY. HERE, TAKE SOME. NO? PASS IT TO CARLA. CARLA, BELLA! KISS, KISS. CIAO! YOU DIDN'T TELL ME YOU WERE COMING. OH, IS THIS YOUR SEAT? I THOUGHT IT WAS MY SEAT. FINISH THE SANDWICH. NO, NO, IT'S TOO MUCH FOR ME. I CAN SEE VITTORIO OVER THERE. I'M GOING TO SAY HELLO. HEY VITTORIO, WOULD YOU BELIEVE IT, I WAS IN THE WRONG SEAT. BUT IT TURNS OUT IT WAS CARLA'S SEAT. CRAZY, HUH?

CIAO. KISS, KISS. I ALMOST DIDN'T MAKE IT, THE TRAINS
ARE ALL FUCKED UP. HEY, WHAT'S IN YOUR SANDWICH?
OH, GRAZIE, GRAZIE . . .

And so on, getting louder all the while as I sang gamely on. I
could see the big clock by the monitor desk. I swear it wasn't moving. But everybody out front was. They all seemed to be friends who
hadn't seen each other in a long, long time. I dropped a song and
finished early, cutting my losses. My 'arrivederci' was swallowed up
by the hubbub. As I slunk off stage a couple of shy, smiling Goths up
the front clapped.

I wonder if they wrote for the paper.

Many people assume that because you're the opening act for someone you'll get to spend time with them. This is not always the case.
I toured with Tracy Chapman for two weeks all around Australia
and we never met. Prince, supposedly, won't let anybody outside of
his own posse look at him. The word from the local crew was 'You
may glance at His Purpleness but not look directly at him.' You
don't always know if the things you hear are true or not. I've always
thought it would be fun to support Prince just to test this out. He's
pretty short, though. It might be hard to get a bead on him through
a phalanx of burly bouncers.

Bob Dylan's a pretty short guy too, but mooches around backstage
without too much fuss, friendly and quiet. I did four shows with him
in 2001. We swapped gifts after the last show in Sydney. I gave him
Peter Carey's *True History of the Kelly Gang* and he gave me a big brass
belt buckle – western-style, embossed with the words THE STATE OF
TEXAS 1836, which I like to wear once in a while.

The shows with Leonard Cohen in the summer of 2009 went like a
dream. There were ten in all, half outdoors at wineries and half in big
entertainment centres in the cities. Dan Kelly played guitar and sang

with me as we performed our sets of thirty to forty-five minutes. All throughout, the crowds gave us a big lift.

Watching Leonard go about his work was like attending a master class for two and a half weeks. At the age of seventy-four, at an age when some performers are merely phoning it in, he attended every sound check, which lasted usually between an hour and ninety minutes, and then backed it up each night with an intense three-hour show.

His drummer, Rafael Gayol, whom I knew from The Bo Deans – they'd supported me in Australia seventeen years before – said they'd rehearsed the show for eleven weeks before the start of the tour, which had been going a year.

'What was the main thing that changed over the eleven weeks?' I asked him.

'The sound,' he said. 'Leonard is very particular about making sure the instruments don't get in the way of the voice. We pride ourselves on being the quietest ten-piece band in the world.'

The diligence of the long rehearsals and sound checks had paid obvious dividends. The sound was immaculate. There was no distortion, no blending of instruments, no smearing or low-end boom. No 'rock' elements, in other words, no 'grunt'. But rather than coming over as too pristine, the space so carved allowed Leonard's deep bass/baritone voice full play – every detail of its grain, every crack in it, could be heard.

This attention to detail was evident in all aspects of the concert, from the serious, dark-suited be-hatted appearance of the band – who looked like they'd walked off a Sicilian movie set – their flawless yet passionate musicianship, the creamy harmonies and moves of The Webb Sisters and Sharon Robinson singing back-ups, to the choreographed camera shots on the big screens with plenty of close-ups of Leonard, which created intimacy night after night to crowds of up to ten thousand people.

Leonard's performance was studied, gestural. A kind of holy vaudeville. He knelt. He bowed. He doffed his hat in thanks. When a band member was soloing he stood still, facing them, hat held to his chest, like a penitent receiving absolution. I saw the show half a dozen times and though he sang pretty much the same songs in the same order each night, saying the same things between them and making the same jokes, there was nothing rote or jaded about the performance.

The devotion coming at him from the audience, the release of the pent-up hunger created by his songs over the years in his absence, were matched, and more, by his devotion in turn to them. He served his audience sacramentally, giving proper weight to his words and actions as he offered up his song-prayers, everything in due order like the Stations of the Cross. You know he meant it when he said, 'Thank you for keeping my songs alive.' He was paying everyone back with full honour and respect.

I watched him and thought, That's a way to be, that's a way to act, there's a road to travel. To walk with gravity and lightness, to be serious but not take yourself seriously, to pay attention, to know that ye shall reap what ye sow.

One evening in the Hunter Valley, as I was halfway through singing 'Everything's Turning To White', a flock of seven snowy egrets flew across the sky above the huge crowd, large birds radiant in the setting sun as they carefully stroked their way back to their nesting grounds.

Golden days.

You never know what's around the corner, though. As Leonard himself says, 'The older I get, the surer I am I'm not running the show.'

The wheel keeps turning. I opened once for Ani DiFranco in Madrid. The venue was a noisy rock club filled mostly with loud-talking ex-pat Americans. It was one of those nights when you're singing and thinking to yourself, What the fuck am I doing here? Who talked me into this? One of those nights when you have to square your shoulders, take a deep breath and say to yourself, Sing to the people listening. They're out there. They just don't make as much noise as the people talking.

Sing to the shy Goths.

STUPID SONG

She's a melody; when she goes by she disturbs my soul
She's a melody and she's playing me with cool control
I try to keep a quiet heart but all in vain
I'm falling, falling in a trance again

She's a stupid song that once it's heard never goes away
She's a stupid song, sorely nagging me night and day
And just when I think she's gone, well! here she comes again
She's running around my brain

I will carve her name upon the air, not in wood or stone
I will carve her name and tell the world the beauty I've known
And when we both are dead and gone
The melody will carry on, yes, only the notes remain

From Sonnet 81

Your monument shall be my gentle verse,
Which eyes not yet created shall o'er-read;
And tongues to be, your being shall rehearse,
When all the breathers of this world are dead;
You still shall live, such virtue hath my pen,
Where breath most breathes, even in the mouths of men.

William Shakespeare

SUMMER RAIN

She comes and goes like summer rain
I wait all day for summer rain
And when she comes, I smile again
She cools my brain like summer rain

She'll change your plans like summer rain
I raise my arms to summer rain
I lift my head and taste again
The sweet, sweet drops of summer rain

She's warm, she's fresh like summer rain
She comes in a rush like summer rain
And when she comes, she makes a change
I wait all day for summer rain

Belgian Radio

On tour with Joe Jackson in France and Spain – both Romance-language countries – I worked hard at understanding people, on radio, on TV, on the street, in cafés and bars. Though I could compose sentences, order in restaurants and speak onstage, I had trouble understanding anyone who spoke back to me at normal speed. I couldn't parse the torrent. Despite knowing much of the vocab and grammar, I found it hard to tune into the music of speech and was constantly asking people to slow down – *Pardon? Plus lentement, s'il vous plaît. Despacio, por favor.*

When I first heard German being spoken, though, for an instant I thought I was hearing English. The rhythm, cadence and sounds were similar, and in that split-second I had the illusion I was back among speakers of my own tongue. A fissure opened up and through it I imagined I could see and hear fourteen hundred years into the past, when the Angles and the Saxons sailed west from Europe to a small green land, speaking the forthright language that became the basis of English. Then the fissure closed abruptly and all I could hear was Babel again.

The fissure kept opening up briefly all the time we were there. *Guten Tag.* Good day. *Gute Nacht.* Goodnight. Understanding German seemed so tantalisingly close each time, before the shutters closed again. When my friend Maria sat down with me to translate 'Summer Rain', the first line looked and sounded eerily the same as the English: *Sie kommt und geht wie Sommerregen.* Likewise, 'She's warm, she's fresh like summer rain' became *Sie ist warm, sie ist frisch wie Sommerregen.*

And so on throughout the song. 'And when' – *Und wenn*; 'my arms' – *meine Arme*; 'I wait' – *Ich warte* . . . With the phrasing and sound matching the original so closely, the German was fairly easy to remember.

Later on, buoyed by my success, I had a go at translating it into French. It didn't overlay as closely as the German but the song, with its slow waltz time, short phrases and long gaps, allowed the extra syllables to be sung reasonably elegantly. *J'attends toujours la pluie d'été* – 'I wait all day for summer rain.'

To my mind, what also made the song easy to translate was the lack of cultural content requiring explanation – there were no place names, no Australian or English idioms, no historical or local references. Unlike some of my other songs, 'Summer Rain', I believed, was detached from time and place.

But a year later I was back touring in Europe again. On a Belgian radio station I pulled out my supposedly borderless song. '*Elle vient, elle part comme la pluie d'été,*' I sang, hoping the listeners would understand my 'orrible French. The interviewer understood every word but something else was puzzling him. After I'd finished he asked earnestly, 'Why is the woman like summer rain?'

'Well, you know, he's longing for her like in summer you long for rain.'

'But why would anybody long for rain in summer?'

'Well, er, um . . . you see, back home, the long hot summer days, the thunderclouds building up, everyone hot and sweltering, waiting for the sweet relief of the cool change, you know?'

He looked blankly at me and returned doggedly to his question. 'But who wants rain in summer? We get enough rain in winter. We don't want the summer rain. We want the sunshine.'

I realised then that no matter where I go, no matter what I sing, my songs will always smell of home. My birds will always fly north in winter. And what a foreign audience may lose in nuance they gain in mystery. You always take the weather with you.

Good Smells

Bakeries at dawn

Onions frying

Stolen lemons

Old books

A new Sherrin

Burning leaves

Streets after summer rain

Children after a bath

Jasmine at night

Coffee in the morning

Her neck

SWEET GUY

In the morning we trash the bed
You bring me coffee from the kitchen
Then we start up again and the coffee goes cold
I wake up drinking from your lips
Kisses warm and tender
And I'd give up the world just to see you smile

One thing I will never understand
(It's become my problem)
And it's something that's right out of my hands
(My hands are clean)
What makes such a sweet guy turn so mean?

I went to town with a moody man,
A handsome Dr Jekyll
He was right by my side turning into Mr Hyde
I ran for cover but I ran too slow
I was stitched by strangers
And they shook their heads that someone could do the
     things you did

One thing I will never understand
(It's become my problem)
And it's something that's right out of my hands
(My hands are clean)
What makes such a sweet guy turn so mean?

I must be mad, I must be crazy,
Everyone tells me so
All of my life I've seen it coming,
Now I'm facing the wall, waiting for the blow

In the morning you kiss my head
You say it was somebody else, you weren't feeling yourself
Now you're down on your knees
Begging me, 'Baby, baby, baby, forgive me please!'
I wake up aching from your touch
I wake up sore and tender
Then I look in your eyes, the way you smile
And I'm hypnotised

One thing I will never understand
(It's become my problem)
And it's something that's right out of my hands
(My hands are clean)
What makes such a sweet guy turn so mean?

Cross-Singing

The first music I sang was folk music. I wandered through a world of wonders, slayings and apparitions. All sorts of odd characters sang in voices distinctly their own, but often from fantastical points of view. Dock Boggs in one song shifted between a dying man, pleading with death personified, to Death himself, replying, 'I hold the keys to heaven and hell!' Dick Justice sang from inside the head of a little bird that had witnessed a murder. Twentieth-century singers sang as doomed eighteenth-century ship captains, nineteenth-century outlaws, ghosts, or moles in the ground. Women sang as men, young people as old, and vice versa. Any event or subject could become a song – floods, drownings, fires, Spanish leather, drinking gourds, catfish, jail, whisky, poisonings, press gangs, train wrecks, boll weevils, mean bosses, tall tales . . .

The lyrics of rock and pop music, a more self-expressive form where the song and singer are more closely allied, seemed quite limited to me in comparison. The country of Pop was where I took up residence, but like an immigrant I always held onto those first songs, the dark, unruly hymns of home.

When I wrote 'Sweet Guy', the first song I'd written from a woman's point of view, I was hesitant to sing it myself. I was in a rock band with four other guys. I tried to pass it off to women singers I knew, but no-one bit. Then I took it into rehearsal and the boys, themselves called The Coloured Girls, jumped on it right away.

'Don't give *this* one away,' said Jon, 'we can do it.'

'Yeah,' chipped in Steve. 'Joan Baez sang "The Night They Drove Old Dixie Down", didn't she? What's to stop you cross-singing?'

I'd sung 'Single Girl, Married Girl' by The Carter Family, and always sang along to 'To Sir With Love' and 'Dancing Queen', big favourites at our late-night singalongs, but 'Sweet Guy' somehow felt different. I had less distance from it, having written it, but paradoxically felt I had less right to sing it – as if I had to be more 'honest' singing my own songs.

'If you wrote it you can sing it,' pressed the gang. 'You have more right than anybody.'

We were playing bigger rooms by this time. Our songs were on the radio. We drove into country towns and big crowds would show up to see us play. We unveiled 'Sweet Guy' for the first time at a Leagues Club on the central coast of New South Wales. Steve had written a killer guitar riff to kick things off. The song felt odd coming out of my mouth, but Michael's harmony sounded sweet, the dancers stayed on the dance floor and the drinkers kept drinking.

It didn't take long to get used to. After a couple of gigs, singing 'Sweet Guy' felt perfectly normal. The record company liked it and said, 'Let's put it out as a single. We'll do a video.' The recording sounded good but the video was another story. It looked like an ad. Film clips *are* ads, I know, but this one looked like an ad for coffee or sheets. Claudia Castle, the director, had worked with us on a couple of videos previously – 'Darling It Hurts', 'To Her Door' – that had turned out really well. We'd talked this one through and made a plan, thought we were on the same wavelength, but when I saw the rough cut my heart sank. And there wasn't much I could do to change it. Sometimes that's just the way it goes.

The film clip had cost too much to bury, so out it went. Radio got on board and people started singing along at gigs. Eight hundred or a thousand jam-packed people would sing at the tops of their voices, 'What makes such a sweet guy turn so mean?!'

Round the same time, Melbourne band Hunters and Collectors were peaking in the pubs, gathering an army. Their audience was mainly young men, hungry for devotion. Hunnas had a big, fat industrial bass sound, an anthemic horn section, and their singlet-clad singer Mark Seymour, as fit as a trout, held nothing back. One of their big songs was 'Say Goodbye', in which a guy who's been away too long comes home to a tongue-lashing from his girlfriend. I went to see them play at The Venue, a club by the sea in St Kilda, where fifteen hundred blokes in the audience bellowed the song's punchline in unison: 'You don't make me feel like I'm a woman any more!!'

What was going on in Australian pubs in the late eighties?

Singing 'Sweet Guy' shifted something in me. This is fun, I thought. I might not know what it's like to be a woman but I know what they say. Women talk to me as much as men do. Maybe more. All I have to do is write it down. A couple more songs in women's voices followed pretty quickly – 'South Of Germany', 'Everything's Turning To White' – both of which appeared on the same album as 'Sweet Guy'. I was up and flying. A shapeshifter. I could be anything I wanted in a song. Soon I was a ghost, a dog, an Aboriginal stockman, a nineteenth-century outback policeman.

Women began to sing my songs, and asked me to write songs for them. Over the years they added up, and eventually some bright spark at the record company came up with the idea of collecting a number of them on an album. As well as compiling existing songs, Eleanor, the bright spark, commissioned some new covers and called the record *The Women at the Well*.

Throughout 2001 tapes began arriving sporadically in my letter-box, each containing one song. They sounded both familiar and strange. Some were surprising, others were how I'd always imagined they'd be. Rebecca Barnard did some cross-singing herself, changing into a man for 'She's Rare'. 'Before Too Long' turned up with a soul groove and a new tune snarled by Chrissie Amphlett, bringing out the song's hidden menace. One of the last to come in was the murder ballad 'Everything's Turning To White', sung by Kasey Chambers. A body in a river. A wonder, a slaying, an apparition. She sang it slow and sparse, like a folk song. It sounded as old and as cold as the hills.

SYDNEY FROM A 747

Have you ever seen Sydney from a 747 at night?
Sydney shines such a beautiful light
And I can see Bondi through my window way off to the right
And the curling waves on a distant break
And the sleeping city just about to wake
Have you ever seen Sydney from a 747 at night?

Now the red roofs are catching the first rays of the morning sun
My eyes are full of sand from my midnight run
And the captain says 'Belt up now, we'll be touching down in ten'
So I press my seat and I straighten up
I fold my tray and I stash my cup
As the red roofs are catching the first rays of the morning sun

Have you ever fallen for a girl with different coloured eyes?
And sent her letters full of lies
Have you ever longed to see the sun fall where it used to rise?
And quit your job on the spot
Bought that ticket, yeah, spent the lot
Have you ever fallen for a girl with different coloured eyes?

Have you ever seen Sydney from a 747 at night?
Have you ever seen Sydney from a 747 at night?
Have you ever seen Sydney from a 747 at night?
Me I've never seen Dallas from a DC9

Twelve Texan Tunes

'Gimme A Ride To Heaven, Boy' – Terry Allen
'Me And Billy The Kid' – Joe Ely

'She Never Spoke Spanish To Me' – Butch Hancock
'All My Ex's Live In Texas' – George Strait
'Who Were You Thinking Of?' – Texas Tornados
'Anchorage' – Michelle Shocked
'Hello Walls' – Willie Nelson
'Randall Knife' – Guy Clark
'Have You Ever Seen A One-Eyed Woman Cry?' – Lightning
    Hopkins
'Dallas' – Jimmie Dale Gilmour with The Flatlanders
'Pancho And Lefty' – Townes Van Zandt
'My Wife Thinks You're Dead' – Junior Brown

Conjunto

There's something about Texas. I seem to have known of it for as long as I can remember. Without a moment's hesitation I can, if asked, sing the whole chorus of 'The Ballad Of Davy Crockett', a paean to the American frontier hero who was born on a mountain-top in Tennessee but famously died in Texas at the Battle of the Alamo in 1836. The song must have wormed its way into my brain at a tender age, via Walt Disney, I guess.

As young boys, my brothers and friends and I brought Davy to life countless times, taking turns to play him as he made his last stand, outnumbered by hordes of – who, exactly? Indians? Mexicans? We didn't care who they were. They were simply the bad guys.

Davy Crockett was a great role to play. It had all you needed – courage against the odds, bear-wrestling, a prolonged death scene with a big body count, and interesting headgear. One of the kids down the road had a fake coon-skin hat, but if he wasn't around we would improvise with rags. We also had a plastic knife and sword or two, toy guns, and long sticks to serve as rifles.

Texas seemed to be an exaggerated version of an America which already loomed large in our imaginations. It was the biggest state, with the tallest tales and the broadest accents. People said 'thang', not 'thing'. It had prairies, tumbleweeds, cowboys, coyotes, crazy road runners and gushing oil geysers. (Come to think of it, the Road Runner and Wile E. Coyote were probably from Arizona or Colorado, states wormed with canyons, where poor old Coyote perpetually met his *splat!* end. But it was all Texas to us.)

At the age of thirty-three I went there for the first time, played with the band in shimmering Dallas and steamy Houston. People all over were friendly and made us feel right at home. 'You Australians are like us,' they said. 'Y'all like the wide open spaces, y'all don't have airs and graces. Here, try some of this barbecue. Best barbecue you'll ever eat!'

And it was – beef brisket grilled on mesquite coals, falling-apart tender, with smoky barbecue sauce on white bread and sides of spicy pinto beans, coleslaw, jalapeños and crinkle-cut sweet/sour pickles. The lot washed down with Tecate beer. It was a revelation, as was the realisation that we were in border country. The bottom of Texas – miles and miles and miles of it – backed onto the Rio Grande. Hop over the river from El Paso and you were in Juarez, Mexico.

Border states always have a different feeling to those ensconced deep inside the mother country. More unhinged. Unruly. Far from the seat of government, they interpret the law a little more creatively. *We do things differently here.* Individualism and eccentricity are prized, culture improvised and mongrelised, especially when the border is porous.

Someone slipped me a tape one night over margaritas. On one side was Bob Wills and His Texas Playboys mixing up jazz, blues, country and polka, swinging hard as their bandleader called out asides and high cries of joy during songs. That was followed by the even nuttier Freddy Fender singing melodramatic country songs in Spanish over reggae beats.

The other side of the tape featured a band called The Flatlanders – a rare recording made in 1971 that had never been officially

released. Nearly every track had a singing saw on it. Their main vocal-
ist had a high, old-timey voice. One of the songs was a bittersweet ode
to Dallas, the first line of which was 'Have you ever seen Dallas from
a DC9 at night?'

There were three songwriters in the band, all from Lubbock,
Texas, Buddy Holly's home town. I found out more about these three
amigos – Jimmie Dale Gilmore, Butch Hancock and Joe Ely. They
sang each other's songs and those by other writers, many of whom
tended to congregate around Austin, a big music town with a vaguely
hippie reputation. The songs they wrote were often skewed and slyly
humorous. They seemed to have a fresh take on things, unbound
by the usual country music formulas. Joe sang a Terry Allen tune in
which a man driving late one night on the highway pulls over to pick
up Jesus Christ, hitchhiking to heaven. Jesus gets in, helps him drink
his beer, gives him some New Age advice then hijacks the car.

Joe himself spins an even taller yarn of being involved in a love
triangle with Billy the Kid. Joe visits Billy's girlfriend on the sly while
Billy's away robbing banks, and eventually frames him. The song ends
happily with Joe and the señorita lying around in Billy's old hotel
room. Joe's the one she always really loved. And who wouldn't fall for
a man who rhymes 'La Cucaracha' and 'chihuahua' without blinking?

Bart Bull, the tape-slipper, was a writer from Arizona, and boyfriend at the time of East Texas singer Michelle Shocked. Later on
they were living in LA around the same time I was there recording
with the band, and we saw more of each other. Bart made me tapes
of other stuff. He was friends with Jimmie and Butch and Joe, and
when they came to town for some shows he invited us all to dinner
on a night off.

I went over to Bart's mid-afternoon to get a lesson from him on
how to make gumbo, a creole dish from Louisiana, the state bordering Texas. 'It's all about the roux,' he told me. There was also much
deep-frying of chicken in a huge pot. My band and the others drifted
in later with beer and guitars. After dinner the guitars were passed
around and we took turns singing songs. Butch slayed us with 'She

Never Spoke Spanish To Me', later covered by Texas Tornados and featuring the lines:

> She said, 'If you're from Texas, son
> Where's your boots and where's your gun?'
> Well, I got guns that no one can see.

Whenever Texan songwriters get together, it seems a Guy Clark or a Townes Van Zandt song gets played at some stage during the night. Melancholy, death-a-meditating, hard-drinking Townes and master-builder Guy, best of friends, are the two pole stars in the Texas firmament. Guy wrote a beautiful father-and-son song by writing about his father's knife. Lone Star staters seem to find curly ways to say straight things. When Willie Nelson addresses a whole song to the walls, windows and ceilings of his house, you get a little shiver on your skin. It's just another 'my baby left me' song, but nobody ever said it quite like that before.

A few years after Bart's mighty gumbo, Jimmie and Butch came out to Australia and we met up again. They invited me to sing with them at their Melbourne show, which was recorded live. I sang harmonies on the Lucinda Williams song 'Howlin' At Midnight', and Jimmie sang my song 'Special Treatment', with me helping out on the chorus. Jimmie, of Cherokee ancestry, knows a thing or two about special treatment, and his sweet yearning voice was made for the song. The recording turned up on a Butch and Jimmie album, released in 1992 and called *Two Roads: Live in Australia*.

Now all I need to complete my Texas trinity and die happy is for Willie Nelson to cover 'Cities Of Texas' and George Jones to cover, well, anything. Time may be against me. But what else is new?

THEY THOUGHT I WAS ASLEEP

We were driving back from the country one night
Mum and dad up the front and the rest of us snug and tight
My kid brother grizzled for a little minute
'Til my big sister told him he'd better quit it or die
It had been a long day in the countryside
Playing with the cousins on my mother's side
The sound of the radio closed our eyes drifting across the seat
And then I fell asleep

I don't know what woke me up
Maybe a country song or a big truck passing by
I could hear mama and papa talking
Papa said something then mama began to cry
No more words then, just soft sobs and my head began to throb
I just lay there playing dog, breathing slow and deep
They thought I was asleep
They thought I was asleep

It seemed like forever 'til the sobbing stopped
Then they talked for a little but just too soft to hear
Daddy kept looking at the side of her face
One hand on the wheel and one hand stroking her hair
The headlights shining from the other way
Showed tears on the cheeks of daddy's face
I prayed for Jesus to send his grace
And all our souls to keep
Back then I believed
They thought I was asleep
The night was dark and deep
How I wish I was asleep

Heredity

I am the family face;
Flesh perishes, I live on,
Projecting trait and trace
Through time to times anon,
And leaping from place to place
Over oblivion.

The years-heired feature that can
In curve and voice and eye
Despise the human span,
Of durance – that is I;
The eternal thing in man,
That heeds no call to die.

Thomas Hardy

Doppelganger

Three months after I was born in Adelaide, my cousin Alexander McGregor was born in Sydney and immediately assigned to me. We've been stuck with each other ever since. I've tried to mislay him from time to time. Once, when we were both eleven, I gave him the slip in the basement of Myer in Adelaide. We'd had a fight so I abandoned him to the teeming throng of Christmas shoppers and caught the bus home alone. I don't remember the particulars of the argument but it probably had something to do with how hicksville Adelaide was compared to fabulous Sydney. This was an ongoing theme of his. I do remember thinking on the bus, See if you can find your way home in Hicksville now! Naturally he did, being self-reliant from a young age, and arrived not long after me, plotting revenge.

Alex and I are corresponding cousins. Coming from a large clan that produced children at a good steady Catholic rate, we both had matching cousins, sometimes two or three. I also had Geraldine in Gawler, with her seven siblings, only forty kilometres to the north. We often drove up there and back on Sundays to visit. But Geraldine lived in Girl World. (Or, to put it more accurately, I was in Boy World.) Alex, far away in New South Wales, seemed like a parallel version of me. We were both one of eight. He was taught by priests and I by the Christian Brothers. We both did well at school, liked reading and were keen on sport. Both of us were competitive, with a tendency towards anxiousness. The infrequency of our visits to each other built up a kind of longing for him on my part. I was curious to see what he would be like each time.

We would go to Sydney for the summer school holidays, or the McGregors would come to us. We'd load up the station wagon, suitcases on top, maybe eight of us in the car: Mum and Dad and a young one up front, three in the next row, grumbling and grousing over the position of elbows, legs and arses, and two littlies in the back tray – prime spot! – curled up with pillows and blankets and comics. The overflow, an older child with a young one, would catch the train. We'd drive up through the Riverland and then across the Hay plains, which seemed to go forever. Somewhere in the middle of that vast emptiness we'd stop and sort ourselves into three motel rooms, excited about little bars of soap in plastic wrapping and dinner in a restaurant.

Some years, instead of the whole family travelling, two or three corresponding cousins would be sent to their interstate counterparts. Alex and I, on meeting again, would quickly appraise each other then head out to the backyard. Most of our activities were sporting. I could generally beat him in cricket – he couldn't pick my wrong 'un – but in swimming and matters aquatic he reigned and still does reign supreme. Their house in Sydney's north was a short walk from the beach. I am eternally grateful to him for teaching me how to bodysurf.

As a young adult he moved away. He worked in the mines in Western Australia and wrote to me about that. Then three years travelling in South America. He wrote to me from there too – hair-raising tales of cocaine and Bolivian prisons. Alex was a great corresponding cousin. There were long letters and short aphoristic postcards. Later on, faxes and emails. Clippings of interesting articles and recommendations of books. And more postcards.

Alex came home from that first long trip to South America a different person. It wasn't his way to talk about it directly. With him you work for your information – a hint here, a cryptic clue there. But I sensed on his return that he'd been tempered and forged by experiences beyond my ken. Here I was, still mooching about on the dole, trying to make three guitar chords sound interesting, and there before me stood a man of the world. He'd seen things and knew things. He could speak fluent Spanish. I felt unformed next to him.

The German word *Doppelgänger* is a beautiful, spooky word. Made up of two words meaning 'the double who goes', it rolls off the tongue with a whiff of sinistry – Dr Jekyll and Mr Hyde, Narziss and Goldmund. I think of Alex as my doppelganger – the other me who moves through the world somewhere else. Nearly all our lives we've lived in different cities, and for long periods of time in different countries. Travelling for work, I would get to see him on a regular basis. He lived in Los Angeles for fourteen years, making a living as a freelance journalist, writing about books, film, culture and Mexico. The double who wrote.

Every time I went to America the arrival ritual was the same: get through Customs at LA airport, then head to Venice where Alex would take me, or me and the band, to his favourite burrito stand for tacos and Tecate beer. I might have a tape for him with bits and pieces of recent Australian music, or new songs I'd been working on. In exchange he'd give me some jarocho music from Veracruz maybe, or a collection of cumbia. If I was staying a few days we'd go out and meet some of his American friends and acquaintances. On first introduction, invariably they'd say 'Are you two brothers?'

Doppelgangers aside, coming from a large clan can give you a feeling of being interchangeable with others. Notions of individuality or specialness get rubbed away in the familial jostle. This can be good or bad, depending on your state of mind, either a relief or a constriction. You know you're always being monitored and looked out for, even from afar, and your actions will be called to account. You journey through this world bound to other beings made of similar you-stuff, fellow planets hurled into orbit from long-ago events, following different grooves but held together by a fixed attraction – an alliance you didn't choose. You might wobble from time to time, but there's a system in place to keep you roughly in check.

Two of my brothers and I are looking more and more like each other the older we get. The hair's receding, the cheeks are hollowing, the same dark eyes stare out from the same skull. I imagine us in our eighties, if we last that long, being like three gummy peas in a pod, indistinguishable to mildly curious grand-nieces and -nephews.

'Is that one Uncle Paul or Uncle Tony?'

'I don't know. It could be Uncle Martin.'

'Uncle Tony's face is a little pointier. Uncle Paul has a bump on his nose.'

'Didn't one of them used to be a singer?'

I first started playing 'They Thought I Was Asleep' on tour with The Stormwater Boys in 2005. Sara Storer was touring with us as the opening act. She would do a set of her own tunes and later in the night get up and sing the Slim Dusty song 'Hell Of A Party' with me.

One night over dinner she said, 'A lot of your songs have children in them. Or they're written to children. Or in the voice of children.' Once she'd pointed that out, I saw them everywhere. They're always sneaking in, jumping the fence, losing balls. Adults tell them stories, they wake up with fevers in the night, strangers come and take them away.

Mick the fiddle player puzzled over 'They Thought I Was

Asleep' like a tongue working a missing tooth. A couple of times he asked me, 'So what happened to that family? Did the parents break up? Did one of them have cancer or something? Did they stay together? Why was the mother crying?'

'I'm sorry, Mick,' I said, 'I honestly don't know.'

What I do know is what I remember. Coming home at night with the family after a long drive. Being all tangled up with my brothers and sisters in the back seat, falling asleep eventually, then waking up just as we arrived. There were many trips, not just one. I remember pretending to be asleep still so I could be carried inside and laid in bed by Dad, and not have to clean my teeth or get undressed. I remember all that, hearing the creak of the gate, feeling the little lift as we went up the step into the house, floating across the threshold and into the bedroom, keeping my eyes closed all the while as I was gently deposited on the bed and covered with a blanket. It was the best feeling in the world.

All that I remember, yes. The rest I made up.

THIS LAND IS MINE
(written with Kev Carmody)

FARMER

This land is mine
All the way to the old fence line
Every break of day
I'm working hard to make it pay

This land is mine
Yeah, I signed on the dotted line
Camp fires on the creek bank
Bank breathing down my neck

They won't take it away
They won't take it away from me

TRACKER

This land is me
Rock, water, animal, tree
They are my song
My being is here where I belong

This land owns me
From generations past to infinity
We're all but woman and man
You only fear what you don't understand

They won't take it away
They won't take it away from me

FARMER, TRACKER

They won't take it away
They won't take it away
They won't take it away from me

Tom And Jerry

> I hadn't gotten old enough yet to realize that living sends a person not into the future but back into the past, to childhood and before birth, finally, to commune with the dead. You get older, you puff on the stairs, you enter the body of your father. From there it's only a quick jump to your grandparents and then before you know it you're time-travelling. In this life we grow backwards. It's always the gray-haired tourists on Italian buses who can tell you something about the Etruscans.
>
> Jeffrey Eugenides, from *Middlesex*

Auntie Pat, eighty-two years old, and Auntie Gwen, mid-seventies but coy about her age, are sitting on high stools, holding court at the bar of Bentley's Hotel on a Sunday night in the South Australian town of Clare. They're on their third or fourth Jameson whiskey and don't look like slowing down. I'm feeling a bit weary and bleary but I don't want to go to bed yet in case I miss out on something.

It's been a long thirty-six hours since Saturday morning, when my family and I and two hundred others assembled in the Clare town hall to celebrate the coming of Jeremiah and Mary Kelly (née Baker) to South Australia from County Clare, Ireland, a hundred and fifty years ago. Nearly all of the throng, bar spouses, were directly descended from this original couple, who had four children – Honor, Patrick, Anne and James. Anne was childless but the others went forth and multiplied.

On our way into the hall, we'd all been given name tags, in one of three colours which represented the lines of these children. My children, my siblings, my first and second cousins wore green, representing the James line. I knew all the first cousins and many of the second. Things got pretty sketchy with the third, and with the second cousins once or twice removed, and so on. There were lots of people I'd never met who looked weirdly familiar. They had a certain stance, a certain shape of the brow, a darkness of eye or the smile of a long-ago aunt.

Proceedings began with a prayer, then sandwiches, followed by various presentations of family history – with PowerPoint and photos – by a representative of each clan. Many County Clare emigrants had taken up farmland to the north of Adelaide and then pushed further north from the town they named, falsely encouraged by several years of above-average rains. When we visited some of the old family places the next day, the house of Great-Grandfather James and his 'big fine girl' Catherine was a tumble of stones and a totter of walls. Other ruins dotted the dry lonely landscape.

James had got out of farming in his fifties and he and Catherine went back to Adelaide to live. He spent the next thirty-seven years retired, though active and always interested in politics. Their house became a gathering place for the clan, and his longevity, combined with his natural authority and public standing, inevitably turned him into the family patriarch. He spent much of his last years sitting on the verandah, terrorising his grandchildren with maths puzzles and writing letters to the newspapers. On the night he suffered a stroke and died his granddaughter Joan had brought him his glass of hot milk as usual. As she left the room he said, 'Men may come and men may go but I go on forever.'

One of the presentations at the reunion included an acknowledgement of the Ngadjuri people, traditional owners of the area. There's not much about them in the history books. Guns and germs mowed them down and their language is hardly spoken any more. Driving around the next day across wide open country, you could see they wouldn't have stood a chance. What did our ancestors have to do with this? What did they think? What did they choose not to see?

Saturday night ended in the pub. As the drink loosened everyone up, people began to move out of their original knots, from catching up with people they knew quite well to those they knew vaguely, followed by going up and shaking hands with complete strangers and tracing connections. A half-dozen people had come from Ireland for the occasion, relations on the Baker side – Monica, Sean, Michael and family. Mary Jo and I got talking with them and found we knew some of the same songs. 'Galway Bay' started up, then 'Arthur McBride', 'I'll Tell My Ma', 'Marie's Wedding', 'Slieve Gallion Brae'. By midnight the place was roaring.

The next morning began with mass in the old church at the Sevenhill winery. A few hands trembled, a few heads ached. The James line had been dubbed the musical line so we led the singing again from the choir loft. A barbecue lunch followed soon after, underneath the tall pines. In the afternoon everyone scattered in small convoys of cars to visit various ancestral sites, before assembling again for dinner and drinks at the pub.

Auntie Pat, sipping her Jameson, is telling a story about her father, Frank. I've heard the story before but lean in with the others. My doppelganger is there too.

'Francis, son of James, your grandfather, as a young man was riding north of Hornsdale to visit some cousins. It was a two-day journey, so he made camp along the way and slept under the stars. He woke in the night to discover a brown snake on his chest underneath his blanket, coiled and still. Now, brown snakes are deadly. He knew that if he tried to move it off him it would wake and strike. He also knew that the snake had snuck into that position to get warm. So very, very gently, moving ever so slowly, he lifted the blanket up and back onto his legs, until the snake was completely uncovered. Then he lay perfectly still, breathing slow and evenly, until the snake got cold after a while and slithered off. Now, what do you think of that? That was a man with his wits about him.'

'Oh yes, a very cool customer indeed,' we chime.

'Talk about sangfroid! More cold-blooded even than the snake.'

'Lucky for us, then. One false move and that little snake would have wiped out most of us here at the bar.'

It's closing time not long after that. Alex and I walk his mother, Gwen, and our Aunt Pat, to their motel room over the road. It's a cool, blustery night, rain showers coming and going. Not a night to be sleeping outdoors. The next day, driving back to Adelaide, I tell the story of their great-grandfather and the snake to my daughters, aged eleven and nine. Their eyes shine.

Two years later Nephew Dan and I are touring Ireland, and by good fortune we have a couple of days off between Galway and Cork. I have a few phone numbers of Kellys and Bakers in my pocket from the reunion. They live in and around the towns of Ennis and Ruan in County Clare.

'Meet me at the West County Hotel in Ennis,' says Frances O'Halloran, whose mother was a Kelly. 'It's on the road to Limerick. You can't miss it.'

We drive south from Galway along the coast, skirting the harsh limestone rock of the Burren, country of which Edmund Ludlow, one of Cromwell's generals, said, 'There's not enough water to drown a man, wood enough to hang one, nor earth enough to bury him.' After an invigorating bodysurf at Spanish Point, we head further south before cutting inland. Frances, farmer's wife, teacher, and mother of two boys, turns up at the hotel ten minutes after our arrival. She's a friendly, brisk, bright-eyed woman and, as we're soon to find out, the most knowledgeable cousin we meet concerning the family history.

Our first call is to two elderly Kelly sisters, Criona and Becky, both spinsters, who greet us in their small Ennis house like long-lost sons. They've only recently moved into town from the farm. There are five siblings in their family and only one married. This was not uncommon. Becky worked in Dublin for the civil service most of her life, and for years Criona and her brothers Tom and Jerry lived in the farmhouse together.

The sisters twitter like birds and fuss over us in great excitement. They ask us to sing them something so we drag our guitars from the car and play 'Don't Stand So Close To The Window', because it's a country waltz with nice harmonies. Halfway through I realise to my embarrassment that we're singing of lust and drinking and adultery to two elderly Catholic spinsters. However, they enjoy it very much and demand another, so I sing 'Carrickfergus', which I learnt many years ago from a Bryan Ferry record.

My questioning of them, and later of Frances, about their parents and their relationship with Jeremiah Kelly, our great-great-grandfather, results in confusing answers. They trace their ancestry back to a Jeremiah, of the same generation as our Jeremiah, but theirs seems to be a first cousin of ours. It's a Kelly tradition to name the first two sons Jeremiah and Thomas, so there are Toms and Jerrys everywhere in the family tree. My rough calculation has Criona and Becky as our fourth cousins once or twice removed. My brain hurts thinking about it. And starts to throb when I realise I'm only scratching around the branches of one out of a possible eight family trees, beginning with the generation of the Kelly 'founding couple' and branching through me and my siblings via my parents, their parents, their parents' parents, and their parents' parents' parents. And so on.

Feeling existentially nauseous, we go with Frances back to her place. There her Jeremiah looks sternly down at us from a picture on the wall. According to Frances he was fond of disowning children who married the wrong person. This adds weight to the theory, tentatively put forward later by the Baker sisters, that the reason our Jerry and Mary moved to an impossibly faraway country with four young children was because Mary was a tenant's daughter and not considered good enough for a Kelly. Nothing much is certain. Most is speculation.

Anyway, I like to think our great-great-great-grandparents married for love, not for land or status as many did in those times and these parts. Frances told us a chilling story of her grandfather, known as young Jerry, who courted the second-eldest sister of a high-born but financially strapped family. The family was keen on the marriage because the Kellys had money, but it was considered a shame for the eldest sister not to be married first so they swapped brides on him on his wedding day. The eldest sister hid under the wedding veil during the vows. Jerry went through with the consecrated marriage but was never happy about it, especially when the bride's younger sister and her parents moved in with them. It makes you shudder to think of it – the one he wanted being under the same roof but forbidden to him.

Not surprisingly he spent a lot of time at Murphy's pub in Ruan (still in business), and it was there one night he announced to the assembled company, come closing time, that he was going off to drown himself in the lake. His drinking companions thought it was just the grog skiting but his friend Paddy wasn't so sure, so he followed at a distance. Sure enough, Jerry turned off to the lake instead of for home and went straight into the water. By the time Paddy got to him he was drowning and would not allow himself to be saved. He had four children and one on the way.

Yes, the Kellys had money and land. Those who had land survived the famine, most everybody else did not. As happens in all calamities, some people made money from others' misfortunes. As we crisscross the district with Frances, we hear stories of the big Protestant houses offering food to starving Catholics on the condition that they convert, of 'soup schools', closed to Catholics, where a meal was provided each day, and of people changing their religion for material advantage and then at a later stage changing back again. Frances's voice holds a quiet anger relating these things and the past seems very close, singing strongly to us from the green fields and grey stone fences.

She takes us to a graveyard where Kelly gravestones and plaques are scattered throughout. Then to Ruan, to the church where Great-grandfather James was baptised, and to a family house that's been in continuous Kelly possession since the early 1800s. After this it's back to Frances's place, where we meet up again with the Baker sisters who came to the reunion, and more recently to our Galway show.

As far as I can ascertain, Marjorie and Monica Baker are our closest relations in the area. Their great-grandfather was Mary Baker's brother. I believe that makes them my third cousins once removed. My head's hurting again. Tag-teaming now with Frances, they take Dan and me out to the house a few kilometres away where Mary Baker, daughter of a tenant farmer, was born, which is also the house Marjorie and Monica grew up in, and where one of their brothers now lives. It's a small house and all ten of the Bakers grew up there, though some were gone by the time others were born. They top-and-tailed at night in their beds, which were folded up by day. During the reunion, I'd stood at the grave of Mary Kelly (née Baker) in the deserted Appila cemetery on a lonely, windswept South Australian plain – so far away from this, her place of birth, and in a vastly different landscape.

Now we are taken to Monica's place, where a feast is in preparation – wild salmon from the local Fergus River, barbecued spare ribs, creamy potato salad, fresh coleslaw, carrots and soda bread, followed by apple pie, cheesecake, tiramisu and jugs of cream, all washed down with mugs of milky tea. Members of the clan are gathered. They're farmers, teachers, butchers, IT workers.

Then it's off we go to the pub in Ennis for a trad music session. We sit in one corner drinking pints of Guinness. An informal band sits in another – banjo, tin whistle, flute, mandolin and guitar – playing a tune, resting and chatting a bit, then playing another, mostly instrumental, sometimes a song. Another Baker sister, Eileen, joins us. They are all friendly, hospitable women and after a while Monica, unbeknownst to me, inveigles the band to ask me to sing something. So it is that just before closing time I find myself singing a circle song, 'From Little Things Big Things Grow', as the musicians plunk along, followed by 'Our Sunshine', with Dan on harmonies and the tin whistle arabesqueing beautifully over the top.

That night, we sleep at Monica and her husband Mike's farmhouse, in the small bedrooms of their gone-away daughters, and wake up to a plate of soda bread, bacon, sausages and black pudding (vegaquarian Dan politely declines). Mike likes to talk about buying and selling, but unfortunately I'm not much help to him in the matter of the price of various breeds of Australian cattle.

Though Dan and I are humbled by the warm welcome given us, we can't help feeling self-conscious at times about our perceived status as faraway relations looking for their roots. Another elderly spinster aunt whom Frances had taken us to see the day before received us as neutrally and blandly as if she were looking at passing clouds.

Like clouds, we are there for less than twenty-four hours.

In the morning, before we leave, Monica and Frances take us for a walk in the woods by the ruins of a fifteenth-century castle. The woods border the lake where young Jerry drowned himself – a beautiful, peaceful, mysterious lake on this particular day, with a lone swan gliding slowly across it. I half expect one of the mythic heroes of old – perhaps Finn MacCool himself, strong-sinewed, sword in hand – to come striding along the shore.

Frances, never short of a yarn, tells us an ancient tale of Red Mary, who married soldiers to acquire land and then killed them in various ways. Some she threw from the top of her castle towers. She also had a special horse trained to gallop headlong to the Cliffs of Moher then come to a dead stop at the brink, thereby flinging the rider seven hundred feet down onto the rocks below. Once, she had a widow's house destroyed because it was in her way as she rode to Limerick. The widow put a curse on her and shortly afterwards Red Mary's lovely long red hair caught in a branch as she was riding and strangled her. ('File that story under "Bitches of the Seventeenth Century",' says Dan.)

Land and the getting and losing of it, long memories and old grudges are still a big theme around these parts, and the Kellys continue to be in the thick of it, a prolonged intra-family property dispute having just been unhappily settled. Frances, the day before, had snuck us up the driveway of the big house she lived in for twenty-five years. She's now unable to set foot in the place and has been pointedly uninvited to her relative's wedding in two weeks' time. The bride, a Dublin lawyer with 'airs and graces', is having the house restored for the ceremony. The painters were there when we arrived but we stayed hidden under the trees, and as Frances watched them she muttered darkly, 'They'll never have it ready in time.'

I'm sure she was casting a spell.

THOUGHTS IN THE MIDDLE OF THE NIGHT

All is dark but for the greenish glow
Of the bedside clock radio
It's 3 a.m. – here they come again
Just like they've done before
First there's one and then a couple more
Like little birds perching on a wire
And soon there's a gathering
A crooning restless choir
Of thoughts in the middle of the night

You toss and turn – 3.45
When little things magnify
Lists uncrossed, chances lost
A conversation gone awry
Now they're lining up – all these old mistakes
You're looking back at the sad parade
Warnings you chose not to hear
Calling now loud and clear
But too late! In the middle of the night

5 a.m. – you haven't solved a thing
You're right back where you started from
And they just won't go away
They have come to play
These thoughts – until the break of day!

Things That Go Bump

Two marriages
Two divorces
Three children to two mothers
One grandchild
Dying rivers
Sick friends
Lost friends
Gone parents
Old recordings
Young blues
Black dog
Red mist

TO HER DOOR

They got married early, never had no money
Then when he got laid off, they really hit the skids
He started up his drinking, then they started fighting
He took it pretty badly, she took both the kids
She said: 'I'm not standing by to watch you slowly die
So watch me walking out the door'
She said, 'Shove it, Jack, I'm walking out the fucking door'

She went to her brother's, got a little bar work
He went to the Buttery, stayed about a year
Then he wrote a letter, said I want to see you
She thought he sounded better, so she sent him up the fare
He was riding through the cane in the pouring rain
On Olympic to her door

He came in on a Sunday, every muscle aching
Walking in slow motion like he'd just been hit
Did they have a future? Would he know his children?
Could he make a picture and get them all to fit?
He was shaking in his seat, riding through the streets
In a Silver Top to her door

Agamemnon At The Wheel

Once, coming home from gigs interstate, I got into a Silver Top taxi
at Tullamarine Airport. It was back in the day when drivers had
names as well as numbers. My driver's name was Agamemnon.

'So you play guitar?' he said. 'You're a musician?'
'Yeah.'
'Your face looks familiar. Are you on TV?'

'Sometimes,' I said, 'but not that often.'

'Are you famous?'

'Well, I sing songs and make records.'

'Oh, yeah, I know who you are now. I like that song of yours "Out The Door".'

'Thanks.'

'Yeah, yeah, you got good songs. There's that other one you wrote too, I really like. What's it called now? It's on the tip of my tongue.'

'Er, "Dumb Things" maybe?'

'Nah, nah. Hold on, let me think now . . . "They Got Married Early", that's it! That's a good one too.'

'Thanks. Maybe take the ring road this time of day.'

'No worries. Some bad language in that song. My kids think it's funny. I gotta be careful when I play that song. But, you know, it's nothing they haven't heard before.'

'No, I guess not. Kids these days.'

'They hear much worse in the playground.'

'Yes, that's true. I see your name's Agamemnon.'

'You know that name?'

'Well, yes. That's a big name in history. King of the Greeks in the Trojan War. Proud man. And didn't his wife have him killed when he came home?'

'Yes, yes. That's true. But they weren't known as the Greeks until later. Homer had different names for them. You know your history.'

'Well, not as much as some. It's not a very common name these days, is it – Agamemnon?'

'Maybe three thousand years ago, ha. Not so much now. But it's still around. It's my uncle's name.'

'Did your parents actually call you Agamemnon as a child?'

'No, no. They called me Menio, or Maki, which means "little one". I didn't know my name was Agamemnon until I went to school.'

'And you went to school in Greece or here?'

'Here. But everyone called me Menio, the teachers too. It's easier to say. People here find Agamemnon a bit much.'

'No-one called you Aggy?'

'No. No Aggy.'

'That's good. You know how we always shorten names, put an "o" or a "y" on the end – Barnesy, Farno, Robbo, Micky. Imagine if someone had gone up to King Agamemnon and said "G'day, Aggy!" I reckon he would have cleaved them in two on the spot.'

'Ha, yes, no mucking around! I'm still called Maki by the family. Menio, Maki. So I'm a true Aussie.'

'I know a guy named Sophocles but everybody calls him Phil. And I have another friend, Demosthenes. He tells me he's named after a famous Greek orator. We call him Demos.'

'Kings Way or Canterbury Road?'

'Six of one, half a dozen of the other.'

'All right, we'll take Kings Way, my friend. For the ancient kings.'

'One of my daughters has an ancient name. Memphis. Most people think it's something to do with Elvis, but she's named after the old city of Egypt.'

'Yes, one of the first sites of civilisation. That's a good name. Strong name.'

'Like Agamemnon.'

'It used to embarrass me when I was younger but I'm proud of it now. Does Memphis like her name?'

'Well, she's only three, so she hasn't really expressed an opinion either way. It's just her name. But her grandfather wasn't too happy with it when we first told him. "Memphis!?" he said. "You might as well call her Wagga Wagga!" So I did. For the first year I called her Wagga Wagga. Now we generally call her Mem. Or Memmy.'

'Wagga Wagga. That's good. Well, I guess Memphis *is* a wog name, coming from the Mediterranean. *Mem*phis and Aga*mem*non. They're nearly the same.'

'So they are. Swing around the Junction Oval. Across Fitzroy Street, then right on Barclay.'

'Sure. Grandparents always have a lot to say. My wife is Australian and we called our first boy James. They weren't happy. "Why not

Dimitri?" they said. "You can call him Dimitri," I said, "but we're calling him James. I want him to have a nice easy Anglo name." They kicked up a fuss at first but they calmed down. Now they call him Dimitri and everyone else calls him Jimmy. Even *they* call him Jimmy sometimes.'

'You did well not giving in,' I said, and then told him how Memphis wasn't the only name to give us trouble. Her older sister was two weeks old before we named her. My mother was ringing every day saying, 'You have to give that little girl a name!' We were sick of telling people the possibilities as everyone felt they had to put their two bobs' worth in. They sat next to someone awful at school with that name, and so on.

'You'll be the first to know when we decide,' I told my mother.

'Oh, please tell me what you're thinking. I won't breathe a word,' she promised.

'Okay, well, we're thinking of calling her Dusty. After Dusty Springfield.'

'*Dusty!* You can't call a little girl Dusty! It's like calling her sooty. Or dirty!'

So we ended up calling her Madeleine. With Dusty as her second name.

'Sometimes you just have to give in to your parents,' said Agamemnon. 'It's not worth it.'

'That's true,' I replied. 'I tried pointing out that Sandy was a perfectly acceptable name but she wasn't having a bar of it. Here we are. The house with the white picket fence. Thank you very much.'

'Okay, there you go, right to your door, ha. In a Silver Top, yes. Very good. Before you go, did you write the words or the music first for that song?'

'"They Got Married Early"?'

'Yes.'

'The music. Usually it's the music. I wrote the tune on piano and it was seven years before I put proper words to it.'

'That's a long time.'

'Yes, well, Homer took his time too, I'd guess.'

'Who knows? Maybe there were lots of Homers. We don't know. But thank you, it's been a pleasure to chat with you.'

'And with you too. Thanks, Agamemnon. Keep the change.'

TREATY

(written with Mandawuy Yunupingu)

I heard it on the radio
I saw it on the television
Back in 1988
All those talking politicians

Words are easy, words are cheap
Much cheaper than our priceless land
And promises can disappear
Just like writing in the sand

Treaty, now
Treaty, yeah

This land was never given up
This land was never bought or sold
The planting of the Union Jack
Never changed our law at all

Now two rivers run their course
Separated for so long
I'm dreaming of a brighter day
When the waters will be one

Treaty, now
Treaty, yeah

Balance

I first met Mandawuy Yunupiṅu backstage at Chicago's Aragon Ballroom, where his band Yothu Yindi was on the bill before Midnight Oil. It was October 1988 and my band and I, also touring, and with a night off in the same city, had been invited along. A cold wind was blowing as we arrived at the theatre, a glorious old dame built in the twenties in the style of a Moorish castle. We were looking forward to seeing a Midnight Oil show without having to play before them.

I hadn't seen Yothu Yindi before but I knew a little about them. They were from East Arnhem Land and had just released their first album, *Homeland Movement*. They were already playing when we arrived and it took only one look to see they weren't experiencing the usual Midnight Oil Support Band Syndrome. Rock guitars and drums mixed with yidaki (didgeridoo) and bilma (clap sticks) as dancers in tribal dress and full body paint mimicked animals, and Mandawuy, with his wide proud face and bushy black hair barely tamed by a brightly patterned headband, sang driving anthems to culture and country in English and his own language. The crowd was agog.

Midnight Oil followed them and blitzed the grand old ballroom, of course. This was the time of their pomp, with lead singer Peter Garrett, tall, skinny and bald, whirling like a dervish as he spat out his manifestos, and Rob Hirst putting on his own show on drums at the back of the big-riffing band. They tore through 'US Forces', 'Short Memory', 'Power And The Passion', 'Beds Are Burning', and other big-chorus singalongs at full volume, leaving the audience ecstatic and exhausted.

We milled around afterwards in the band room, drinking their beer and catching up with news. Got introduced all around. John Trudell, a Native American singer-songwriter known as Graffiti Man, who'd played the opening set, was there. I knew Bart Willoughby, from No Fixed Address, who was playing drums with Yothu Yindi. Most of the others in the band were pretty shy but Mandawuy, with his big beaming smile, and I soon got to talking.

'I like your song "Under The Sun",' he said. 'The honey sun. That's my dreaming.'

It was the first of many encounters. Over the next decade we were to play with them often, at festivals and concerts all round Australia.

A couple of years after that chilly Chicago night, I got a phone call from Alan James, aka AJ, Yothu Yindi's manager. The band were getting ready to record their second album. Mandawuy had a batch of songs completed and wanted me to come up to Arnhem Land and work with him and the others on arrangements, and possibly some lyrics. The plan was to spend some time in and around the community of Yirrkala, Mandawuy's home on the Gove Peninsula, then move on to Darwin for rehearsals. The band wanted to stretch out musically and explore new rhythms for their songs. I suggested the percussionist Ray Pereira come up with me as well.

Though I hadn't visited yet, Yirrkala was known to me. In 1963 a group of Yolngu elders from there, including Mandawuy's father, had made a bark petition protesting against the takeover of their land by a French company that wanted to mine bauxite, the ore from which aluminium is made. The petition comprised two panels of bark and combined words in two languages – English and Gumatj – with ochre paintings describing the Yolngu's long-standing links to their country.

The petition meandered through parliament and various courts over the years as the mine, subsequently leased by Nabalco, and its accompanying town, Nhulunbuy, got up and going on Yolngu land. The claim was ultimately denied in 1971 but the case laid bare the legal fiction that the land had had no owners before the coming of the British. Clearly the land was not vacant, said the petition. We were always here.

That same year, 1971, Mandawuy's older brother, Galarrwuy Yunupingu, recorded a song with Ted Egan called 'Gurindji Blues', in support of the ongoing Gurindji strike and land claim a few hundred kilometres to the south. These two long protests from two distinct Aboriginal nations were the vanguard of the land rights movement and the fight, nationwide, for Indigenous justice. Twenty years later, when I arrived in Yirrkala, Galarrwuy was head of the Northern Lands Council, Mandawuy was principal of the local school, and the Yolngu were receiving mining royalties. Galarrwuy had the air of a feudal chief.

One of the first things Mandawuy said to me when Ray and I got off the plane in Nhulunbuy was, 'I want to write a song with you about the treaty.' He was referring to Prime Minister Bob Hawke's famous pledge, made at the Barunga Festival in 1988, to formulate a treaty between black and white Australia. It had received a lot of publicity at the time, many words had been written and many speeches made, but two and a half years on it seemed that Bob had bitten off more than he could chew and the debate had long slipped off the pages of newspapers. For a while the idea of the treaty had morphed into a pact of reconciliation – whatever that was – but even that trail had gone cold.

Although no national government had ever signed a treaty with Aboriginal Australia, a treaty was made in 1835 with the Kulin nation in Victoria, by a group of land developers called the Port Phillip Association. It came to be known as the Batman Treaty, after one of its members, John Batman – often considered the founder of Melbourne – and was understood by the association to be a purchase of the land on which Melbourne now stands. Who knows what was understood by the 'sellers'. Gifts were exchanged – tomahawks, blankets, knives, beads, scissors from the settler side; cloaks and weapons from the Indigenous side – deeds drawn up and signed and marked, and a yearly tribute pledged.

But the treaty was disallowed by the colonial government. A treaty acknowledged prior ownership and that opened up too big a can of worms. Heavens, they couldn't allow this kind of thing willy-nilly!

It would give people ideas. And in another example of our great forgetting, Batman's treaty and its implications slipped into disrepute. It's often regarded now as a curious historical footnote, but as Bain Attwood's book *Possession* shows, it's worth a closer look.

Mandawuy still believed in a treaty – an acknowledgement of Aboriginal sovereignty – and wanted to get people talking about it again. He made it clear that he'd chosen to work with me – a well-known whitefella – not only for my songwriting skills but in order to make a political statement. He reasoned that a black and a white writer together would have more impact than him alone.

He didn't state it as baldly as this – Mandawuy speaks in circles and images – but I knew I was dealing with a shrewd operator from a political family. Over the next fortnight I became acquainted with his concept of balance, a word he used all the time as he showed me his life and his world. Yolngu life was all about balance – the balance of the kinship system, and the division of every living thing into moieties, Dhuwa and Yirritja. The name Yothu Yindi was an expression of balance between mother and child. If the mother was Dhuwa the child was Yirritja, and vice versa. A Dhuwa woman could only marry a Yirritja man. So father and child were always the same skin.

Balance was also at the heart of black–white relations, between Yolngu and Balanda. To survive, the Yolngu had had no choice but to find balance with their invaders. As a young man, Mandawuy was sent south to study and became the first Aboriginal person from Arnhem Land to get a university degree. He came back to Yirrkala to teach, and developed a method of education which blended traditional skills, philosophy and language with reading, writing and arithmetic. The motto of his school was 'Two Ways'.

After a few days at Yirrkala, getting to know Mandawuy's family, visiting the school and the art centre and walking in the bush, we went down to camp at a place called Birany Birany, by the Gulf of Carpentaria. I waded in the warm water with Mandawuy as he speared fish I couldn't see. We put them straight on the coals and picked the flesh off the bone with our fingers as he talked about freshwater and saltwater, another big balancing idea. When freshwater meets saltwater, things happen.

On and off – at Mandawuy's house in Yirrkala, at Galarrwuy's big house by the sea, and around the campfire at Birany Birany – we worked on the already written songs. We drank a lot of beer. Witiyana, Milkayngu and Stu from Yothu Yindi were there, as well as two young men, Makuma and Gurrumul, who were being groomed to step into the band. Gurrumul, blind from birth, was a talented guitar and keyboard player with a beautiful high voice. Makuma was learning the yidaki from Milkayngu, an anointed master, who'd had it played into his back as a young child so he could absorb his culture's vast canon.

Yothu Yindi's first album was a collection of rock tracks and traditional songs, and while there was some yidaki on the rock songs there wasn't much blending of the two forms. The album as a whole was a balance of modern and traditional music, but the band were looking now to achieve that balance within each song. Ray helped pull the tracks out of their straight-ahead rock grooves into more fluid beats and Mandawuy began to sing sections in Gumatj, his first language, between the English verses.

When he and I got time on our own every now and then, we'd pick away at the treaty song. Nothing much was happening. I was finding it hard to grasp the idea of a treaty – how would it work, for instance? A treaty with one group called Aboriginal Australia? Or separate treaties with different language groups? Before the arrival of the British, Terra Australis was made up of around two hundred different nations. What were those nations now? So much had been broken and thrown around.

Even if I could get a working idea of the treaty in my head, I'd never been someone who wrote from an idea or a concept. I saw myself more in the tradition of Chekhov, who said, 'I don't have what you'd call a philosophy or coherent world view so I shall have to limit myself to describing how my heroes love, marry, give birth, die and speak.'

Mandawuy, on the other hand, had a very clear philosophy and world view, passed down to him by his ancestors and which he in turn would pass on to his descendants. He saw himself as a teacher and message bearer. To him the band was a school, both a place of learning for his own clan coming up – who would eventually replace him and the other founding members, and carry the band on over time – and an institution for teaching the rest of the world about Yolngu culture. This two-way education, within Arnhem Land and without, maintaining culture by showing it, would ensure that culture's survival.

I saw writing more as a way to find out things than teach them. Although I'd written what some people called 'message' songs – 'From Little Things Big Things Grow' and 'Bicentennial', for example – they hadn't been conceived that way. They'd begun with details, specific images – with a story, not a concept.

It seemed to me that Mandawuy and I were songwriters with completely opposed methods. He wrote from the top down, I from the bottom up. Could we meet somewhere in the middle? Could freshwater meet saltwater? White meet black? Politics meet art?

Apparently not. When we left Arnhem Land after a week to meet the whole band in a Darwin rehearsal studio, Mandawuy's swag of songs were in good shape, but all we had for the treaty song was a scrap of a verse and two chords. In my mind the attempt seemed doomed.

The week-long rehearsal of the other material went well in the Darwin heat. The songs were coming together. Everyone was excited about the interesting mix of influences, the new grooves. We felt we were making a new hybrid, creating true mongrel music. One song we loved playing sounded like Plastic Bertrand had been shipwrecked in the Gulf of Carpentaria, saved by the locals, and sent out five years later with a guitar slung over his shoulder.

On the last day of rehearsal we came back after a lunch break and the band started jamming a funky thing in E minor, the same key as Mandawuy's and my squib. I started singing the only four lines we had over it, and called for a change to our second chord, C, and back again. It sounded okay. I sang the same four lines again to fill out the verse and then, for want of a better idea, sang/yelled, 'Treaty, yeah! Treaty, now!' a couple of times as a kind of chorus.

'Hmmm,' we all said, 'maybe there's something there. It'd be good if we could come up with a proper chorus.' We played around with it some more but didn't get much further. We recorded what we had on the little beat-box in the middle of the room, went back to work on the other tunes, and pretty soon it was beer o'clock. That was a wrap for the week then, and the end of my and Ray's time up north. We flew home the next morning.

I wrote to Mandawuy a week later from Melbourne to sum up my thoughts on the fortnight we'd spent together, and to offer some arrangement suggestions. I also said that if he wanted to persevere, perhaps we could continue the treaty song by correspondence, but I didn't hear back from him for a while.

A few months later, Yothu Yindi came to Melbourne to record a single. Their record company (and mine), Mushroom, were taking things step by step. A song called 'Tribal Voice', which we'd worked on up north, seemed the likeliest contender. I'd been away on tour and when I got home there was a message on my machine to call AJ.

'The band recorded that treaty song as well as "Tribal Voice",' he told me when I rang, 'and Mushroom reckon it should be the single. The trouble is, the words aren't very clear. They want him to redo the vocal. I know why the words aren't clear. He's mumbling them because he doesn't have any proper lyrics. Can you get together with him and finish this thing off? The band's in Sydney this week. We'll fly you up.'

'What about the chorus? Did they write a chorus yet?'

'Yes, there's a chorus. It's "Treaty, yeah! Treaty, now!" That's the good bit.'

A few days later, Mandawuy and I sat on the balcony of a Glebe motel room and nutted out the rest of the words. There's nothing like a deadline. The chorus, I thought, was still just lying there, but

Mandaway said, 'It's working for me. Now let's go and play it to Peter Garrett.'

The Midnight Oil offices were just around the corner. We walked there with a guitar and the tape of the band recording. Savvy Mandawuy had a plan. 'I want input from Peter on this song. It will help if his name's on it.'

The most honourable Lord Peter was expecting us and graciously bade us be seated. Like a pair of petitioners humbly come to court, we played him the tape so he could hear how the final version would sound, then sang him the song with the new lyrics. Peter praised our work and suggested adding a bridge featuring counterpoint backing vocals – 'Promises! Priceless land!' Perfect! Cups of tea and smiles all round. Mandawuy had his imprimatur and Peter had a songwriting credit.

Mandawuy sang the new words in the studio the next day, and in May 1991 the song was released as a single. But not before AJ had haggled me down to a 17.5 percent cut of the publishing royalties. So many writers!

The vocals were clear, the music was rock-funk with a Yolngu breakdown section. And the chorus was still 'Treaty, yeah! Treaty, now!' It got good reviews and airplay on non-commercial radio and did quite well.

Enter three Melbourne DJs, Gavin Campbell, Paul Main and Robert Goodge, who had started doing remixes under the name Filthy Lucre. One day I got a call from Mushroom Records to come down to the office and hear what they'd done with 'Treaty'. Gavin and Rob sat at the round table in the boardroom looking slightly abashed as the remix played loudly on the huge sound system. They'd stripped and rebuilt the song, underpinned it with a shiny house groove, and tossed out most of the lyrics, retaining the 'tribal' elements – the Gumatj language singing, the yidaki and the bilma – and throwing in a sample: 'Clap your hands and dance!' They'd also put front and centre the chorus that wasn't a chorus. 'Treaty, yeah! Treaty, now!' was now the main hook of the song. It sounded great.

'You don't mind us taking out the lyrics?' said Gavin.

'Sounds like a hit to me.'

And it was, going to number eleven on the pop chart, the first record by an Aboriginal band to go so high, eventually kicking the album, *Tribal Voice*, even higher to number four. It made the Top Ten on the UK dance chart. All around the world the song pumped out across packed dance floors. You couldn't go into a club and not hear it. Everybody ran onto the floor when it came on. Their limbs flailed, their eyes glazed, their mouths sang along. 'Treaty, yeah! Treaty, now!'

The remix set the template for the Yothu Yindi sound, which some called tribal dance music. They had other tunes remixed – 'Gapu' became a chill groove, 'Djapana' got the disco treatment – and collaborated fruitfully with various DJs on following albums. The band continued to tour well into the next millennium, mostly overseas. As his brother Galarrwuy had been in 1978, Mandawuy was named Australian of the Year for 1992, just months before he was refused service at a bar in St Kilda because of the colour of his skin.

True to Mandawuy's vision, the band personnel turned over down the years as the young ones came up, though sometimes not in ways foreseen. Makuma's sister-in-law died in 2000 after he kicked her in the head. He was sent to prison for fifteen months. Milkayngu, an inspiration to yidaki players all over the world, took his own life in 2007, setting off a wave of copycat suicides in East Arnhem Land. And in 2008 another young member of the band inflicted multiple stab wounds on a 23-year-old woman. Believing that he'd killed her, he hanged himself.

Gurrumul left Yothu Yindi in the mid-nineties and started his own band on Elcho Island – Saltwater Band. They made three albums, and in 2007 he released his first solo album, *Gurrumul*. It's a collection of soft, acoustic, mainly Gumatj songs sung in his distinct high, keening voice. Its sadness and longing remind me of Portugese *fado* music. The album started off slowly then gathered word-of-mouth momentum. Professionals in the leafy suburbs began playing it at dinner parties, festival crowds fell under his spell, and the ripples continued around the world. In 2009 Gurrumul sang with Sting on a French TV show, and by the end of that year the album was on many countries' best-selling world music lists.

Mandawuy doesn't sing that much any more. But the band's legacy lives on, influencing new generations. The Yothu Yindi Foundation produces the Garma Festival each year, near the Arafura Sea, where clans from all over Arnhem Land gather to share song, dance and storytelling. The foundation has also set up the Wellbeing Project, which focuses on alcohol education and suicide prevention. Yolngu culture fights on against frightening odds. There is still no treaty.

A Yothu Yindi Playlist
'Mainstream'
'Yolngu Woman'
'Yolngu Boy'
'Matjala'
'Dharpa'
'Tribal Voice'
'Treaty' (Filthy Lucre Radio Remix)
'Gapu' (Tidal Mix)
'World Turning'
'Timeless Land'
'Djatpa'
'Matter Of Choice'
'Cora'
'Djapana' (Radio Mix)
'Ghost Spirits'

UNTIL DEATH DO THEM PART

We are gathered here today
To join a woman and a man
And to witness what they say
As before us they stand
In sickness and in health
Through the rich times and the poor
They are bound to be together
And to live under God's law

Until death do them part
Or the stars fall from the sky
Until death do them part
And it's time to say goodbye
What God has joined together
Let no one tear apart
For they are bound to love each other
Until death do them part

We are gathered here today
To join a husband and a wife
So I call on you to pray
For good luck in their life
Through thick and through thin
Through the good times and the bad
May they always be respectful
And make each other glad

Until death do them part
Or the stars fall from the sky
Until death do them part
And the rivers all run dry
What God has joined together

Let no one tear apart
For they are bound to love each other
Until death do them part

Mongrel Musical

For me the tragedy's most important act is the sixth;
The raising of the dead from the stage's battlegrounds,
The straightening of wigs and gowns,
Removing knives from stricken breasts,
Taking nooses from lifeless necks,
Lining up among the living
To face the audience.

The bows, both solo and ensemble –
The pale hand on the wounded heart,
The curtsies of the hapless suicide,
The bobbing of the chopped-off head.

The bows in pairs –
Rage extends its arm to meekness,
The victim's eyes smile at the torturer,
The rebel indulgently walks beside the tyrant.

Eternity trampled by the golden slipper's toe.
Redeeming values swept aside with the swish of
    a wide-brimmed hat.
The unrepentant urge to start all over tomorrow . . .

Wisława Szymborska, from 'Theatre Impressions'

I was out drinking at the Darwin Festival in 1990. A beer always
goes down well up there. The bar was in the open air, under the

stars, and the night was balmy, as usual. A man came up to me, introduced himself and talked with me for a while about music, theatre and football. His name was Steven Gration and he was the artistic director of the Corrugated Iron Youth Theatre Company.

'Have you ever written music for the theatre?' he asked.

'No,' I replied, 'but I like musicals.'

Nine months later Steve tracked me down. He was now the director of the Magpie Theatre Company in Adelaide and he had an idea for a show. He'd been collecting newspaper clippings of race-related incidents from around the state. An Aboriginal family had discovered their cat dead in a bag on the roof of their front porch one morning, not long after they'd moved to the town of Crystal Brook. A young Aboriginal man had received in his change a bicentenary ten-dollar note, one side of which depicted an Aboriginal man in ceremonial paint. A noose had been added around his neck.

Steve wanted to devise a play with music, set in a small country town where everyone knew each other, exploring the tensions and misunderstandings between white and black Australians. He already had a name for it – *Funerals and Circuses* – and was putting together a cast of Indigenous and non-Indigenous performers, including playwright Roger Bennett, a Murri man from Queensland now living in Alice Springs, who'd previously written the successful *Up the Ladder*, based on the life of his tent-boxing father Elley Bennett. I was asked to be the musical director.

Steve had experience in theatre sports, community theatre and group-devised pieces. His skill lay in working with inexperienced actors and developing plays not from a finished script but from improvisation around themes.

Roger welcomed this method of working where the line between actors and writer was blurred. He was also keen on breaking down the wall between cast and audience. *Up the Ladder* had a street-theatre feel to it. He liked things to be freewheeling, for the action to spill into the crowd.

Steve invited both of us to act in the play, as well as to help shape the script and music, and employed Kaarin as assistant director. Madeleine was two months old when we started rehearsal in January 1992. She spent most of her time in the rehearsal hall sleeping or being passed around from person to person. There was never any shortage of cradling arms.

There were twelve performers in the cast, who ended up playing sixteen characters. Not all of us were trained actors. Five were Indigenous, four from South Australia – of Pitjantjatjara, Narungga and Ngarrindjeri descent. Lily Sansbury, a Narungga dancer and singer, played the town preacher and traditional elder.

We had nine weeks of workshop/rehearsal. Steve started us off playing ball games and trust-building exercises, then followed with theatresport improvisations. In one of these, three players had certain information the fourth didn't – I recognised this years later as the basis for the TV show *Thank God You're Here*. They were scary and fun.

Soon we moved on to improvisations related to the characters and events Roger and Steve had sketched before rehearsal. We worked in groups exploring scenes, fleshing out the townspeople and coming up with their back stories. All the while, Roger took notes.

The play began with a wedding, so I wrote 'Until Death Do Them Part' for Lily to sing in the opening scene. Now all the others clamoured for a song, so I set myself the task of writing one for each character. The policeman's came next – 'They Don't Have To Do My Dirty Job'.

'Do you have my song yet?' the songless ones asked each morning. Sweet pressure. My songs often come to me via characters anyway, by hearing a particular voice or imagining people in particular situations and following them, so writing situational songs for theatre wasn't that different to what I do normally. One by one they came. When your petitioners are walking, talking and making up stuff all around you, you can't help but pick up a few leads. Generally the melodies I found were simple and within a small range, as not everybody was a confident singer. They could also easily be talked/sung if necessary. Again, this was a lot like many of the songs I write for myself.

At the end of each day's work we farewelled each other with 'Nukkanya', a compound Aboriginal/English phrase made up of *nukkan*, the Ngarrindjeri word for 'see', and 'you'. So *nukkanya* – see ya, see you later. 'Nukkanya' became a song, and eventually everybody got one.

Now we had a kind of mongrel musical – a musical containing rape, violence and suicide – that involved the audience throughout. In the first scene, they're enlisted as wedding guests, and at interval the foyer becomes the front bar of the town hotel and the site of a talent quest. The publican stops pulling beers, gets up on the bar and sings a funny, racist song exhorting the audience to sing along with him. (I'm reminded of this fifteen years later watching Sacha Baron Cohen's character Borat singing 'Throw The Jews Down The Well' in a country and western bar in America.) The talent quest is interrupted by a funeral procession filing through the bar and into the adjacent hall, which is the town set. An Aboriginal boy has been found dead in a dam under suspicious circumstances. The audience follows the procession and before they know it are into the second act.

I had the role of Tony, who runs the local garage, plays guitar and sings a little – he's the town observer, not on any particular side. This allowed me to accompany people during their songs. Sometimes I did so hidden behind a wall. The whole play required strict timing from everyone as they performed their multiple tasks on and off stage. It felt like being inside a giant clock, knowing that if you, a little cog, failed in some small task the gears would seize up. Do your job right with the others and you could feel the big engine humming.

Every night backstage I peeped through the little hole of my door at the front row of the audience. Every night they gasped and laughed. Most nights someone would be weeping. And every night I was amazed as the thuggish skinhead bouncer came offstage after assaulting a young girl, shucked his Klansman costume and played a tender, plaintive tune on the recorder to bring in the yellow morning.

The mongrel musical received great notices and standing ovations night after night. The season, part of the 1992 Adelaide Festival of Arts, was extended. And the following year we took it to Melbourne and Canberra. By now Kaarin and I were expecting our second child, due during the Melbourne run. She went into labour the afternoon of a show and I drove her to hospital, staying there 'til the last possible minute before returning to the theatre. I raced back again straight after the curtain came down.

'Good luck! *Nukkanya*, Dad!' the gang cried as I shed my costume and ran out of the theatre. I made it to the hospital just in time to see Memphis being born.

Kaarin and I gave her the second name Lillian, in honour of Lily Sansbury, of whom we were very fond. Lily loved kicking back on a Saturday night after the two shows, including a matinée, a rum and Coke in her hand, yarning and singing songs. 'How are my *kutjeri miminis* [beautiful girls]?' she'd say when we spoke on the phone over the following years. And she'd spoil the *kutjeri miminis* with sweets and little presents whenever she came to visit.

Roger went back to Alice Springs after the play and continued his work in drug and alcohol counselling. He'd been in and out of juvenile detention and prison for much of his life, could handle himself and was well respected. He was a gentle man with a hidden steel – a steel refined by years of suffering and anger. In 1997 he died of heart failure. Another big tree down. His heart gave up. He was forty-eight years old and looked sixty.

Lily married a Ngarrindjeri musician, Carroll Karpany, and I sang at their wedding. For many years they worked together with a troupe of performers, combining traditional and contemporary song and dance. Carroll played the didge. They performed at festivals, openings and Welcome to Countrys, as well as touring overseas; moved to Uluru for a while, then back to South Australia. Lily developed lupus, a nasty, chronic auto-immune disease, and became more and more ill, unable to perform. She died in 2002 and was buried in Point Pierce, her home country on the Yorke Peninsula in South Australia. At Carroll's request, I sang 'Nukkanya' at her funeral.

Nukkanya, Roger. *Nukkanya*, Lily. *Nukkanyas* both, sweet brother and sister.

WHEN I FIRST MET YOUR MA

When I first met your mother
I was playing in a bar
She walked in with my girlfriend
My foolish girlfriend brought her there
She looked so pretty and dangerous
As she brushed back her hair
And I was not the only one
Taking notice in that bar
When I first met your ma

When I first kissed your mother
I was single once again
We walked through Fitzroy Gardens
There she took my hand
We could not stop our kissing
Then she whispered in my ear
'I gotta be home soon, I gotta get home
So let's not go too far'
When I first kissed your ma

Love like a bird flies away
You'll find out the only way
Love like a bird flies away

When we first lay together
Inside her father's house
We tried so to be quiet
As we held each other close
Then her dad came pounding and kicked me out of there
I walked two miles in Melbourne rain
I could have walked ten more
When I first loved your ma

Love like a bird flies away
You'll find out the only way
Love like a bird flies away

God Only Knows

The great lyricists and songwriters of the golden age of American songwriting – Irving Berlin, Ira Gershwin, Cole Porter, Johnny Mercer, Lorenz Hart and others – nearly always wrote in exact rhyme. Many of the songs of the thirties, forties and fifties were written for musicals, and in musicals that was the unbreakable rule. As well as writing immortal, plain-speaking songs like 'Blue Moon', 'Love For Sale', 'Fools Rush In', 'Summertime', 'Night And Day', these inventive chaps pushed as far as they could against the tight bands of convention, rhyming 'laughable' with 'un-photographable', 'irreplaceable' with 'embraceable', 'antiseptic' with 'dyspeptic', and stacking their songs with fresh, internal rhymes: 'If I took even one sniff that would bore me terrifically too.'

Cole Porter, the terrific sniffer, was fond of raiding other languages, particularly French, to coin new rhymes – 'ennui' and 'spree', 'camembert' and 'Fred Astaire' – and he and the others often deliberately generated comedy from forcing rhymes to fit, Lorenz Hart, for example, yoking 'spoil' to 'goil' (girl) in 'Manhattan'. At times their efforts can seem contrived to modern ears. Not even Frank Sinatra can get away with 'When love congeals it soon reveals the faint aroma of performing seals.' One shouldn't quibble, though, with these masters. Between them they left an enduring body of vivid, playful and immensely satisfying songs that work like beautiful machines. The rules made them sing the way oyster grit makes a pearl.

America being America, of course, everything there has its opposite, and during this glittering golden age, right under its nose, another, grittier, earthen age was grinding along – dustbowl refugees heading west, sharecroppers and ex-cotton-pickers heading north, hillbillies heading to the coalmines, 'wetbacks' pouring across the border. Work songs, drink songs, courting songs, children's songs, church songs; songs for dancing, fucking and fighting; blues, hollers, stomps and moans. The singers of these weren't so concerned about diction or that fussy about rhymes. Down south, people spoke different anyway. So rhymes were different. 'Door' rhymed with 'go', 'sin' with 'friend', and 'man' with 'pain'.

Howlin' Wolf sang 'Who's Been Talking?', every line of each verse rhyming, though Broadway wouldn't have thought so.

> My baby caught the train, left me all alone
> My baby caught the train, left me all alone
> She knows I love her, she doin' me wrong
>
> My baby bought the ticket, long as her right arm
> My baby bought the ticket, long as her right arm
> She says she's gonna ride, long as I been from home
>
> Well goodbye baby, hate to see you go
> Well goodbye baby, hate to see you go
> You know I love you, I'm the causin' of it all

Uptown, of course, had been drinking from the well of blues, folk and country all along, but through the refining filter of jazz. Rock'n'roll drank huge gulps straight from the source. Chuck Berry – the Colossus of Missouri, the man who blended cinematic poetry with dance music while simultaneously inventing a new style of guitar playing, a man whose genius so permeates the culture that we don't see it any more; not a nice man, according to reports, who epitomises D.H. Lawrence's maxim 'Don't trust the artist, trust the tale' – throws everything in the pot in his sum-it-all-up song 'Rock And Roll Music', rhyming:

music / choose it

jazz / fast
melody / symphony
band / hurricane
jubilee / jamboree
wooden cup / all shook up
(and in a final exuberant spree) tango / mambo / congo / piano.

Exact rhyme was never the same after that. It still plays its part in pop music, but except in certain musical-theatre bastions it's no longer king, just one of many dukes. Fifties rock'n'roll was a major tributary feeding sixties pop, and rough rhyme rode with the current, spawning itself everywhere. Now no-one thinks twice about rhyming 'language' with 'sandwich'. Dylan did it first, then Men at Work, and it's still going round. Rough rhyme's informality suits songwriters looking for a greater naturalness of expression, enabling singers to sound more conversational. The listener's ear has the satisfaction of hearing – sometimes only sensing – a rhyme without getting snagged on it. The lyric gets loosened up, the story gains fluency.

This is perfect for hip-hop, with its musical speechifying and mass of rhymes of all kinds – internal, sprung, long, short, across the beat, on the beat. Hip-hop, like calypso, needs words to be malleable so that rhymes can be supple. (A nice rough rhyme – malleable/supple.) Rough rhymes give you a whole lot more options. So Sydney hip-hoppers The Herd, in 'We Can't Hear You', hardly raise a sweat rhyming 'hands up / stanza / answer / Pauline Hanson / mansion / imagine / handsome / Branson' in the space of a few lines. Out of those eight words, only two exactly match but they sound like they're all the same rhyme.

On the other hand, if you do want to snag the listener's attention, to create a certain effect – comedy or a dramatic punchline – then using rough rhymes widens your palette. Modern musical-theatre writers, freed from the icy clutch of exact rhyme, can come out swinging. Casey Bennetto, writer of *Keating! The Musical*, had audiences splitting their sides when he twinned 'jiggery-pokery' with 'piggery locally'. Meanwhile his comrade-in-arms Eddie Perfect spews out a fountain of funny, fresh rhymes in *Shane Warne The Musical,* including the memorable couplet from 'bunny' Daryll Cullinan: 'I'm the least, he's the mostest / He's fighting fit while I've got myxomatosis.'

But it's the humble, almost hidden rhymes I like the mostest, the ones that don't draw attention to themselves. The ones that lurk in a song like a pattern of pebbles under flowing water, that help carry the listener along as the story unfolds. Simple little hardy, hardly rhyming rhymes like hair/bar, again/hand, ear/far, house/close, there/more, that burble away beneath the surface, a secret music, there but not.

You could write a book about all the different types of rhymes and the ways to use them. People have. You can split – and split again – exact and rough rhymes into multiple categories: masculine, feminine, dactylic, syllabic, oblique, slanted, imperfect, half-rhyme, semi-rhyme, rhymes of assonance and rhymes of consonance. You could write a rhyming dictionary and make yourself and the world a set of guidelines and rules.

When genius is at work, though, why worry about rules? In 'God Only Knows' each line of each verse ends with the same word. So 'you' rhymes with 'you', 'it' with 'it', 'me' with 'me'. You can't get more exact than that. Do the rhyme Nazis allow this? And do they approve of singing the word 'God' twenty-two times in a three-minute pop song?

When you use the word 'genius' in relation to The Beach Boys, everyone assumes you're talking about Brian Wilson. But Brian didn't write the lyrics, Tony Asher did, including most of the lyrics on *Pet Sounds*. (Now, that's something to tell the grandkids.) If you listen closely to what Tony's doing in 'God Only Knows', you'll notice it's the second-last word of each line – 'love' with 'above', 'doubt' with 'about' and so on – that's doing the work. The rhyme is tucked in. This is well allowed. The golden age used this trick quite often. You can hear it on 'Bewitched, Bothered And Bewildered', or 'Taking A Chance On Love', where lines end with 'again' over and over again.

There's plenty more in 'God Only Knows' to talk about – the friendship of 'above' and 'about'; the internal rough rhyme of 'nothing' and 'living', giving sweet breath to the third verse; and, for such an unabashed statement of love, the beautiful uncertainty of the first line, 'I may not always love you', which Brian was initially reluctant to sing because he thought it was too negative.

'Trust me,' I imagine Mr Asher saying to his sulky partner.

As Bacharach / David, Morrissey / Marr, Goffin / King, Rodgers / Hammerstein and countless others prove, genius often hunts in pairs.

WINTER COAT

We were lovers once long ago
Walking through cold city streets
Like lovers do
Stopped inside a market
Kissed behind a stall
Someone said you'd better move on
If you're not buying at all
Then I saw the winter coat hanging on the rack
I thought about that winter coat
Hanging on my back
So you helped me try it on
It was just my size
Then you bought that coat for me
After haggling over the price

Now when it's chilly
Up in these cold, cold hills
I just put on my winter coat
My winter coat
Keeps me warm

Years have come along
Years have gone
Some friends have risen
Some have moved on
And my old winter coat still
Hangs by my front door
Holding all the stories
I don't remember anymore

And when it gets freezing
Up in these cold, cold hills

I just put on my winter coat
My winter coat
Keeps me warm
My winter coat
My winter coat

I Love My Leather Jacket

I wear my leather jacket like a great big hug
Radiating charm – a living cloak of luck
It's the only concrete link with an absent friend
It's a symbol I can wear till we meet again
Or it's a weight around my neck while the owner's free
Both protector and reminder of mortality
It's a curse – I cannot shirk responsibilities
From the teacher to the pupil it's a gift to me
So I love my leather jacket and I wear it all the time
I love my leather jacket

The Chills

In The Wee Small Hours

From Mascot Airport in Sydney to the city usually takes half an hour by car. Sometimes more. Frank Sinatra did it in twelve minutes. According to Michael Chugg, aka Chuggy, the Australian promoter who toured Frank in the nineties, the singer was met as he came off the plane by two federal police and taken to a waiting limo, which then cruised through synchronised traffic lights all the way to his hotel without stopping. I've heard that visiting American presidents can have this kind of thing arranged. The Queen too. And the Pope. But an entertainer? Who describes himself as a 'saloon singer'?

I'm agog, backstage at a festival with Chuggy, talking about Frank. 'Well, you know what they say,' he says. 'It's Frank's world. We just live in it.'

Frank truly created a world. Down and out in the early fifties, after a dizzying rise and fall in the forties, he teamed up with young arranger Nelson Riddle and Capitol Records to make, over the rest of the decade, a string of albums brilliant in conception and execution.

Long-playing records were just coming into their own as a way of selling music. The first albums were, as the word suggests, collections of singles. Frank and Nelson were the first to think of them differently. They sensed the possibility of making an album a considered and coherent statement, by conceiving a theme and then seeking the songs to fit. Frank didn't write songs himself but knew where to find them. He took old songs which, in the novelty-seeking musical climate of the time, were considered passé, and with the help of Nelson's fresh and bold arrangements made them new again. And in so doing established a large part of what is considered to be the canon of American popular music. The golden age, just when people thought it was gone, now had its king.

That's how golden ages work. They never actually exist at the time. They get invented later. Frank and Nelson were inventors, like Bill Monroe, founding a new kingdom on a mythical past. And through that vanished/present world walked a new man – tough, tender, bruised, knowing. A traveller reporting back from love's far shores of ecstasy and heartbreak. Swaggering on one record, staggering on the next.

The night of the day Frank died, 14 May 1998, I waited 'til the children were asleep, poured myself a whisky, shut the door to the back room, put *In the Wee Small Hours* on nice and loud on the stereo, lay down on the couch and turned out the lights.

The first 12-inch LP Frank and Nelson made – they'd made two 10-inch records of eight songs each the year before – *In the Wee Small Hours* was a chance to really dwell on a theme. They carefully chose sixteen songs. Half of them are under three minutes. None go over four. Every single song deals with the aftermath of a love affair. One sad song ends and another one begins. Then another and another. There's no letting the listener off the hook, no mid- or up-tempo songs to balance the mood or provide a contrast. 'We're serious here,' Frank and Nelson seem to be saying to us. 'Can you go the journey?'

Frank's swinging records – *Songs for Swinging Lovers*, *Come Fly With Me*, *Sinatra at The Sands*, and so on – are great to put on in company. People sing along, start talking differently, snap their fingers, feel like changing their clothes or mixing a martini. But you have to play *In the Wee Small Hours* alone, or with somebody in your arms. Put it on as background in a crowded room and it all sounds the same. Someone will inevitably say, 'Turn that sad sack off. He's bringing everybody down.'

It's a record that requires concentration in order to mine its deep lode of riches, and each time I come back to it over the years I'm struck by the concentration brought to bear on its making. You can feel the fierceness of its aesthetic, the uncompromising realisation of a vision. The record has a low, subdued pulse. Every song sounds slowed down. Frank and Nelson take standards and melt them in their glowing crucible to forge new shapes, taking the rhythm out of Duke Ellington's 'Mood Indigo' and ruthlessly chopping verses in other songs to raise the intensity. In 'What Is This Thing Called Love?', written by Cole Porter, who was no slouch with a lyric, two-thirds of the words are tossed out. Who needs verses? Nelson's opening clarinet figure says it all, before Frank steps in to say it all again in one chorus. That's all they need. By reducing the song they enlarge it beyond measure.

Anyone who's serious about singing popular music gets around at some stage to studying Frank. Listen closely and you hear all the things people talk about – the timing, the detail in each word, the long breath, the tone like a horn, the little slurs up and down to the note, and so on. Other singers have all this too. Many got it from Frank, true, but others had it before him, Billie Holiday, for example, Louis Armstrong. What's so special about Frank? You can talk about the perfect balance he has between talking a song and singing it. 'The microphone is my instrument,' he said. But that came from Bing Crosby. Before Bing realised the possibilities of the microphone – how you could use it to create a mood of intimacy, a warm conversational tone – most popular singers were belters, like Al Jolson. Bing changed all that. And Frank studied Bing.

So what *is* so special about Frank? What's the X-thing? Sex? The bobby-soxers heard that, sure. Frank put the *ba-da-bing* into Bing and we've been hearing it ever since. But sex symbols come and go. Frank has remained. There must be something else.

I remember my shock the first time I saw a photo of Frank as a young man. My image of him up to that point was of someone eternally middle-aged – someone who made music for grownups. That whippet-thin, high-cheekboned, wavy-haired, handsome boy-next-door in the photo – that was Frank? The same person as the round-faced, sinister-looking balding man who made lame jokes and crooned with his drinking cronies in Las Vegas casinos? It seemed unbelievable to me. I was young myself when I received this shock, and over the years since then, like everybody, I've had plenty more of the natural shocks flesh is heir to.

The gap between youth and old age, that big sea we cross, is the story of our life, and all our other stories – of love, work, power, family, health – fit within it. We all make our adjustments to that slow-unfolding car crash as best we can. If you look at photos of a person over the course of their life you can see their different stages, sense the transitions. But when you examine photos of Frank Sinatra, one of the most photographed humans on the planet, there seems to be a gap in the record. One minute he's young, the next middle-aged. It's weird.

Did no-one take photos of him during those few years in the late forties when he bottomed out? Well, of course they must have, but in my imagination there's a short crucial period they missed. It could have been just a few weeks or months, maybe around the time of which Sammy Davis Jr said, 'Frank was walking down Broadway with no hat on and his collar up, and not a soul was paying attention to him. This was the man who, only a few years before, had tied up traffic all over Times Square. Now the same man was walking down the same street, and nobody gave a damn.'

Not long after that his own publicist said, 'Frank is through. A year from now you won't hear anything about him. He'll be dead professionally . . . The public . . . doesn't like him anymore.'

He was thirty-four years old.

The story's been told endlessly. Everybody loves a comeback yarn. Frank, dropped by Columbia Records, going through the wringer with Ava Gardner, deserted by his fans, the younger stars shooting past him, begs and pleads his way into an acting role in *From Here to Eternity*, meets Nelson Riddle and has the brainwave, survives a long count on the canvas and comes up swinging. And stays swinging into the sixties and seventies and beyond. Along the way he flounders here and there, snarls at rock'n'roll, gets stood up by the Kennedys because of his mob connections, gets fed up and retires for a minute, gets into punch-ups with reporters and cameramen, and travels with a large collection of toupees and assistants, including a dedicated toupee minder. He loses his hair but never loses the crown again.

Music writers like to say that *In the Wee Small Hours* derives its intensity from his breakup with Ava. Breaking up with Ava would be tough, no doubt. The publicity machine had him supposedly breaking down in the studio after he sang 'When Your Lover Has Gone'. All this may be true but his singing goes deeper and further than that. It's more than despair at the end of an affair. Just as his appearance in photos suddenly changed, so too had his voice. Bono, who writes beautifully about Frank, describes his voice as 'a knotted fist'. Someone else said the violin had turned into a viola. Others speak of aging wine. The voice is now more knowing. It knows loss. Not just the loss of the love of one woman but the loss of status, the loss of reputation, the loss of fame, and most important of all, the loss of the opportunity to make art. It's as if he stared at the possibility, however briefly, of his music being taken away from him and the shock turned him old overnight.

He came back from that dark night down at the crossroads like Robert Johnson, needy and dangerous, armed with a whole new power.

So you lie in the dark on the night of his death, listening to Frank singing 'Glad To Be Unhappy' and 'I'll Never Be The Same' and all the songs between, and you enter a wondrous church of conjuration. Frank is praying to his icons. He summons up his pictures of worship, and like the old-time fasting saints, surrenders to ecstatic visions. In 'Deep In A Dream' the walls of his room fall away and the smoke from his cigarette becomes a staircase for his lover to descend on. Even when his cigarette burns him he feels no physical pain, such is his trancelike state. 'Deep In A Dream' is followed by 'I See Your Face Before Me'. And further along, in another hallucinatory song, his beloved dances on the ceiling as he lies in bed.

You lie in the dark as Frank sings of loss and try to pay attention to all the little exquisite details – the way the rhythm section drops out temporarily in the title song, leaving us with floating strings before the voice comes back in; Frank's playing with the melody in 'Mood Indigo', his eleven 'no's when he restates the opening lines, the burbling, muted trumpet breaking loose from the horn section before rejoining – but after a while you find yourself drifting off and thinking about your own life and all its losses, how life over time is simply a series of losses: loss of parents, of friends, of love, of possibilities; loss of innocence and your children's innocence.

The knowledge that you'll never be able to sing like Frank is another kind of loss. You'll never even get close, and Frank will never sing 'Winter Coat', the song you wrote to conjure him. It was always a long shot, getting longer by the day, but now that tiny daydream is forever snuffed.

Loss's sphere grows wider now, and included in it is all possibility. You reflect on all you've missed – how much of your life you've forgotten, how much has streamed by you, how paltry the haul in your little net. There are the books you haven't read, the ones you've read but don't recall, the history you don't know, the languages you haven't learnt, the music you've haven't heard, the songs you haven't written, the things you wish you'd asked your parents, the hugeness of the world, the tiny fraction of it you've gleaned, its sadness and suffering and deterioration, the friendships you didn't have with people you admired, that beautiful stranger you saw in the street the other day who you'll never know.

Still you lie in the dark. Frank has sung every permutation of unrequited love. He's covered the classic kiss-off – 'Can't We Be Friends?' He's said he'll wait around 'til she breaks up with the new guy. He's looked ahead and seen himself growing old alone. He's sung about the pleasures of melancholy. The entire record, in fact, luxuriates in its sadness. It dawns on you that there's one permutation he's avoided. Not one song expresses anger. Deep hurt, yes, but not the rage that hurt can engender. There's resignation, yearning, and a glimmer of hope. Every song is bathed in love.

'This love of mine goes on and on' is the very last line you hear as the album ends. The torch will never go out. You get up off the couch, refreshed by tears, thankful for Frank, and drain the last dreg of whisky, forty-eight minutes older and glad somehow to be sad.

WON'T YOU COME AROUND?

Well, I know it's getting kinda late
I guess I should turn out the light and bide my time
Tomorrow eight o'clock, you said, would be just fine
But tomorrow's so far away
And only you can make this brain shut down
Oh, won't you come around?

Now, I think I'm getting much too fond
I know you've got a lot of stuff going on
You've got your rules and you need your beauty sleep as well
But time moves like glue
And in my head it's you I'm always talking to
I've been found! Oh, won't you come around
With your long hair down?
Won't you come around?

Well, I don't want to move too fast
I'm hoping this is gonna last – the way you smile
When you catch me coming makes me ten foot high
No, I don't want to rush you now
But maybe tonight you can break your rule somehow
Oh, won't you come around
With your long hair down?
Won't you come around?
And shut my thinking down?
Oh, won't you come around?

Numbers
Tour diary, USA, March–May 2002

The band and crew:
Spencer Jones – guitar
Steve Hadley – bass
Bruce Haymes – keyboards
Peter Luscombe – drums
Dave Alpress – tour manager, sound
Marcus Bennet – stage
Ben Lyons – lights

Somewhere south of Portland, Oregon, 18 March
Forty-something hours since we left home and we're still travelling to the first show. The flight from Melbourne was fine. I slept a fair bit on the plane, started Tim Winton's *Dirt Music* and watched a couple of movies. Strangely, when we arrived at LA airport there was no mention of the Wayne Carey/Kelli Stevens scandal in the sports section of *USA Today.*

We hung around for a while waiting for our tour bus, which then dropped me and the band in Venice while the crew did some running around with Floyd, our driver, picking up gear and organising a cell (mobile) phone. Alex took us out for the ritual welcome-to-America burrito and beer. Then back on the bus for the 28-hour trip to Seattle. It's been nothing but truck-stops ever since – strange neon outposts by the interstate in the middle of nowhere, where burly men wolf down pork chops and pancakes and eggs and we feel like we're from Mars.

I finished the remaining 380 pages of *Dirt Music* in one gulp. Couldn't stop turning them – perhaps it was something to do with my wired, limbo-like state. I love the vividness of his writing, his fresh language, but I'm not so sure about the ending. I finally fell asleep in the bunk, woke up and wandered out to the front lounge to see mountains covered in snow. Today's paper says the maximum temperature in Calgary, where we'll be next week, is minus 7°C, minimum minus 14°C. Two hours to Seattle and a hotel room for the night. First show tomorrow.

Seattle, 21 March
Yesterday was the spring equinox – all over the world the night was as long as the day. Peter and I decided to go for a run, despite the non-spring-like temperatures, as part of our keep-fit program. (America's huge servings, the large amounts of beer at our workplaces, and the time we spend cooped up in confined spaces demand vigilance.) Just after we'd done our Rocky impersonations, running the streets in beanies and gloves, down came the snow, barely perceptible at first, then slowly, slowly building to big thick sleepy flakes drifting by the hotel window.

Last night a hundred and ninety-nine people stood shoulder to shoulder listening to us in a funky little rock club. They hung on every word. It was good to be onstage again and my voice felt fresh and strong. Jars of chat and whisky after the show with a writer and his wife, who'd driven up from Portland, as well as only four hours' sleep, left me a little fuzzy this morning and afternoon as I ground through phone interviews with journalists and radio stations further east.

Tonight's a night off. We're going to see *Gosford Park*. These couple of days in Seattle are a nice breather before our long march. Tomorrow, Canada!

East of Vancouver, 24 March
We're crossing the Rocky Mountains on our way to Calgary – snow, fir trees, frozen lakes and rivers, thrusting peaks, elks and yaks and eagles. Picture-postcard scenery outside the bus window all day, which I lift my eyes to every once in a while from my big American novel, *The Corrections*. I'm chewing through it, savouring its chunkiness and sting.

We left Vancouver around midnight after playing to five hundred and forty pretty excited people. We had strange yips early. I fluffed lyrics. The band made a few mistakes. 'I'd Rather Go Blind' was a complete train wreck. Spencer had a loud buzz in his guitar we could never get rid of. The pretendies were rampant. Still, the crowd was with us. 'Winter Coat' sounded good just with piano – the audience was quiet enough – but when I started to play 'If I Could Start Today Again' my guitar, capoed up high, was out of tune and Spencer's buzz was horrendous. The murmur in the room began to rise. I pulled out of the song halfway through the second verse, called the rest of the band back onstage, played the opening, crunching chords of 'Pouring Petrol', and from that point we just kept the pedal to the metal. Our encore was short because the club was turning the room over to the Saturday-night DJs, but we left that crowd roaring.

Vancouver yesterday was beautiful in the sunshine. I walked up to Stanley Park, bordering a vast, ship-studded bay backdropped by white-capped peaks. (Another picture postcard.) You feel like an alien, dropping into a city you're going to leave the next day. Everywhere the locals are doing the things they do on a Saturday afternoon – walking, jogging, rollerblading, holding hands, pushing children on swings, eating hotdogs and gossiping. You're there but you're not, like the man who fell to earth, sensing detachedly the happiness, the energy being released by emerging spring.

I met my niece Miranda and her boyfriend Seth at the teahouse near the park entrance. They'd driven up from Portland on their spring break and hooked up with us in Seattle and Victoria (just like Grateful Dead fans following the band around). Seth studies massage, drives a small truck for two with a guitar, a mattress and camping equipment in the back, and a sticker on the bumper that says 'Acupuncture Works'. He talks about music and books and recites Walt Whitman's *Leaves of Grass* softly into Miranda's ear on the ferry from Victoria to Vancouver. What's not to love? We walked and walked and talked and walked around the park, my legs aching happily by the time I got to sound check.

Three out of three good shows this week, which is good for morale.

We're like a little band of guerillas on a campaign – we kill, we conquer, we claim territory. Notice the murderous and acquisitive nature of the language used to describe performance – *we slayed them tonight, we knocked 'em dead, we got 'em*. It's important to stay focused, to keep well and not fall apart physically or mentally. It's a long lonely road ahead; we're travelling without wives, partners, girlfriends or children, and we have to look after each other. Outside the window, the countryside's flattened out. A heroin landscape: blank, all-covering white as far as the eye can see. We'll be rolling into Calgary soon, and hotel rooms, a night off – the Academy Awards on TV and emails (I hope) from the ones I love.

West of Winnipeg, 27 March
It's a long way from Alberta to Minnesota (2000 kilometres). We blew a tyre an hour ago and ever since we've been creeping along at 15 k's an hour. We're on the endless white plains where Canada goes forever. Finished *The Corrections* this morning. It's a beauty. The funniness builds and builds. I started slowing down towards the end, reluctant to finish. Saul Bellow's *The Adventures of Augie March*, published in 1953, is next on my list (530 pages, thirty fewer than *The Corrections*). Ploughing my way through the great American novels.

Our bus is long and blue. It has the usual front and back lounges, with the sleeping quarters between them. The usual DVD/stereo player, fridge, and bench space for toaster, kettle and microwave. The usual small cubicle toilet and washbasin off the front lounge. Only pissing allowed. Anything else must be quelled. Unquelling is for truck-stops, hotels and venues. You learn to get your timing right most of the time.

Passing towards the back of the bus, you open a door and enter the eternal dark catacombs. The doors to this area are always kept shut. Each sleeping pod has a curtain and a reading light. That's where we recharge. Everyone treads softly in there because at any time, day or night, someone could be hooked up to oblivion. The last couple of nights we've spent on the bus, and tonight as well. (We usually get a hotel every three nights for proper R&R.) I seem to wake up quite often but the drone of the bus soon sends me back to sleep. It's weird sleeping so close to seven other people. You get up in the night for a piss and you're inside a fug of animal warmth, deep breathing, little catch-in-the-throat sounds. It's like being back in the Stone Age, sleeping with the pack in the cave, as we hurtle through the dawning twenty-first century.

Our bus has a few foibles. Maybe because it's a low-budget model. There are draughts from the windows, and even with the heating on you can feel them licking in from the chilly outside. The satellite TV in the front lounge keeps cutting in an out, and no-one's figured out yet how to get the set in the back lounge to work – which I don't mind. Other buses we've been on have had a cache of videos for getting through the long miles, but this bus has none. Last week the generator was playing up for a day or so. The reading lights didn't work – disaster! – and so the catacombs were like a mine, with all of us using little truck-stop-purchased torches. Floyd seems to be fiddling under the bus every couple of days, muttering and mending things. He's complaining today about his dashboard lights not working properly.

The tyre's fixed now. We're in the middle of freezing fucking nowhere, a few hours west of Winnipeg, where Neil Young comes from. Sometime tonight we'll drive through Fargo. We've all started talking like Frances McDormand in that film. When we get off the bus in Minneapolis, tomorrow morning at a guess, we'll lurch around on land – as we did in Seattle, as we did in Calgary at the end of the other marathon drives – like sailors after a long voyage at sea.

Minneapolis, Good Friday
Today I rose in a Holiday Inn and sent a letter to my girl
And stole a Gideon's bible and stashed it on the bus
And walked for miles in Minneapolis, fair spring rising,
Nine degrees Celsius and sunny, perfect for perambulation.
South first I went along sidewalks edged with dirty snow,

Up Hennepin then west to Lake Calhoun.
Saw birds walk on rigid water and a beach butted up against
   breaking ice.
Felt the cool wind on me and still the lake never stirred;
An impossible pale blue sky in the south, the colour so stretched I
   thought it might snap.
Swung east into the student district, hungry as a bear
Stopped for spaghetti and wine and cheap coffee
And browsed a while in a Borders bookshop.
Thumbed through a copy of the Koran
And thought about Mohammed, the businessman, and Jesus, son of
   a carpenter
Both saying the same thing – *Take care of each other*.
Thought about Walt Whitman, American prophet, that great lister
   and tramper of cities,
And Bob Dylan, who followed him singing, who came
   out of Minnesota, further north,
And landed here in 1960 soundin' like Woody Guthrie,
And who stayed awhile and played the coffee shops before moving
   on to New York City
Onwards I tramped, Walt's hum rising in me now,
Through Black and Hispanic neighbourhoods –
Suddenly the only pale face was mine,
Hip-hop and Mexican rancheros blaring out of the low riders –
Past the moneychangers and taquerias, clubs and clothes stores,
Young men clustered on the corners.
I swung around, back towards downtown, keen to make the river
   by dusk
The sky darkening, soft spring rain swirling,
Down Cedar Avenue, cemetery on the right, pushing north
Bare winter trees filigreed against grey clouds.
Finally, footsore on a footbridge, I stood above the great Mississippi
Where the twin cities meet, and watched her icy flow.
Miles and miles this river goes,

From Lake Leech in the north, all the way to the Gulf of Mexico.
Turned my back on the river then, hotel-bound as sky turned dark
   and lights grew bright,
Chanting all these things to remember, to remember
To sing my day to her
And make a song for her.

Cleveland, 1 April
Aretha Franklin's hometown. We played just now in a little club to
forty-five people on a cold Monday night. A nutty trainspotter crowd
calling out for obscure songs. We pulled out 'Maralinga', Charlie
Owen', 'Shoes Under The Bed', 'You Can't Take It With You'. The guy
who called for 'Gutless Wonder' all night went home disappointed
(but not too disappointed). I don't remember the words to that song
and I don't have a lyric book with me. But our repertoire's building.

We were good tonight. And Saturday night in Chicago. (Two
hundred and twenty people.) I'm proud of us. We're like no other
band in the world.

We drove overnight from the Windy City. I walked a couple of
hours by Lake Eyrie, then stopped in a diner for Polish sausage, sauer-
kraut and mashed potatoes with gravy. A lot of lakes round these
parts. And I'm a walking fool. Nailed the third and final verse of a
new song in my head. We had the chance for a long sound check and
worked on it for a while. It's called 'Won't You Come Around'. The
song's narrator is a little impatient. The band like it and we're closing
in on an arrangement.

Tonight we're driving to Detroit. We're playing live on the radio
in the morning. Better try to get some sleep. No hotel 'til Toronto.

Boston, 7 April
Boston is cold and sunny and appears to be full of beautiful girls.
Peter and I ran along the river before sound check. We played at a
rock club called The Paradise – dark and cavernous inside – to four
hundred people. 'Won't You Come Around?' had its first run. It seems

like a goer, sort of country-stomp Stones/Small Faces. There were quite a few Australians there – students mainly, I'd say. One woman was weeping for a long time up the front.

Some things I know about Philadelphia
It's the first capital of the United States
They wrote the American constitution here, and the bill of rights
There's a famous bell with a crack in it under glass
They named a bridge after a poet
That poet, Walt Whitman, tramped these streets and slept in now-
    vanished woods
A hundred and twenty years later, Rocky ran these streets
George Washington defeated the British on the Delaware River
The Ojays, The Spinners, and Harold Melvin and The Bluenotes
    made sweet soul music here
Springsteen wrote a song about it which won an Oscar
The name means 'brotherly love' in Greek

Philadelphia, 9 April
Tough show last night at a little club called The Tin Angel. I've played there before, solo and as a duo but never with the band. A few years ago, Spencer and I drove down from New York to do it on our own. No crew. I broke a string halfway through the set and asked if anyone in the audience could change it while I swapped guitars. A scraggy-haired lanky guy came up and did so in no time by the side of the stage. When I looked for him afterwards to say thank you he was gone.

'Gee, that guy looked a lot like Tim Rogers,' I said to Spencer.

'It *was* Tim Rogers,' said Spence.

You Am I were playing at the club next door and he'd slipped in early to see a bit of us before their show. We went over afterwards and had many drinks at the bar with them before they poured themselves into a tour bus. And that's how I met Tim Rogers.

Last night, though, the stage was too small to fit all of us, so we decided to go semi-acoustic. Steve (bass) had the night off, and Pete played shakers and tambourine instead of using the kit. These adjustments made the show a little shaky. On top of that the PA was buzzing and crackling and going up and down in level. We battled through. Evidently it wasn't as bad out front as it seemed onstage. (First rule of show business.) The audience demanded us back twice and we finished the second encore with Bruce playing lovely delicate piano on 'From St Kilda To Kings Cross' – like we were playing it for the first time – which salvaged the whole show for me.

New York, 10 April
The bus is crawling into Manhattan from the Bronx. Our arrival here marks the halfway point of the tour, which is something I always look forward to – the hinge that swings us towards home. It's a psychological lift. (Just like when you're swimming laps.) And each day the ratio of days to go to days gone gets smaller and smaller.

We drove overnight from Massachusetts to a university radio station this morning, set up and played live on air for an hour, as well as answering some questions. With a bit of luck we'll have time to check in before sound check. Then drinks with the record company before the show.

The New York skyline has just come into view. It's a beautiful sunny day but no twin towers thrusting into the blue – an eerie sight. I remember the first time I saw this mythical city from afar, driving in from New Jersey, and how my stomach flip-flopped in awe.

Camp Hill, Pennsylvania, 12 April
The New York show was triumphant – fourteen people short of a full house, close to four hundred. We were up for it, to quote Spencer. Afterwards, many drinks in the bar with lots of friendly faces. We all know people who live there. I met Artie, the restaurant owner from *The Sopranos* (real name Johnny). Pete's a friend of his wife, and when he went to visit them in Brooklyn yesterday, Pete was proud to report, Artie cooked him hamburgers!

The next day was an early start for me – a day of meetings. All the people we work with in the States – record company, publicists and booking agency – are based in and around New York, so I did my round of go-sees. Since I had time between appointments in Brooklyn Heights, Staten Island and Manhattan, I chose to walk most of the day, the weather being cool and sunny.

Heading towards the Staten Island ferry after crossing Brooklyn Bridge took me right past where the World Trade Center used to be. It's a huge area of absence, a couple of large city blocks, like teeth ripped out of a mouth – fenced off so you can't see in from the street. I noticed a group of people looking into the hole from a platform, but there was a queue which I didn't bother to join. No matter what you talk about with anyone in New York, it isn't long before *that* day comes up. Everyone who was here has been seared by the event, and they're still fingering the scar. The record company guys talked about being on the ferry with the rescue workers and firemen, a lot of whom lived on Staten Island and who would go to and from work silent, red-eyed and exhausted, caked in grime and dust, pouring Visine in their eyes.

My last stop of the day was the ritual visit to Strand Books, where I found an obscure volume on Shakespeare. Then the night off (hooray!) – a Harp lager and a Jameson with a friend in an Irish bar on 25th Street; pork and beans and rice in a Brazilian place with another friend later on. And this morning, huevos rancheros around the corner from the hotel. It's hard to get bad food in New York City. Or much sleep. When we got on the bus at ten this morning we all crawled straight into our pods.

Now we're in the parking lot of a mall by a nondescript highway, where tonight's club is, waiting for sound check. It's a grey day and this is nowhere. Or anywhere. We're heading into some back country for a while.

The back lounge, 14 April
All night long I rolled in my bunk as we wound our way through the Allegheny Mountains, part of the great Appalachian Ranges, a fertile musical area, home of hillbilly music, where song collectors went combing earlier this century and were amazed to find intact ancient

forms that had long since disappeared from the British Isles – songs such as 'Oh Death', 'Man Of Constant Sorrow', and others that I fell for when I first started singing and playing guitar.

Last night in Arlington was packed – a little bar that held two hundred and thirty people. They had to turn some away, and the unlucky ones stood in the street with their ear to the window, smiling and waving whenever they caught my eye. The bar being close to Washington DC, some people from the Australian embassy showed up and gave us a slab of VB. And my sister-in-law Liv and her husband Bob, who live close by, visited the bus afterwards with a bag of chocolate-chip cookies she'd just baked. Delicious. We ate them for late-night supper on the bus, washed down with the embassy beer – a weird combination, true, but sometimes you're just thirsty and hungry, and things always taste better spiced with the kindness of strangers.

Somewhere, 14 April still
You notice here how often speech is a kind of spinning out, a way of passing the time. An exchange of information or feeling is not necessarily its main purpose. Americans can be uncomfortable with silence. They like to riff, to fill the air with sound. Irish speech has that quality too. It finds long playful ways to say short things ('God and Jesus and Mary be with you' for 'Good morning', for instance). This is also one of the main characteristics of African-American speech.

Is this an intrinsic African trait, or is it something that happened when slaves came to America? They arrived with nothing. They owned nothing – not soil, not possessions, not even their own bodies. Their languages were banned, so they made up a new one, loosely based on English but unintelligible to their owners. This and their music were their own – their delight, their plaything, their recreation. The place where they could get away from the shit raining down.

African-American innovation, the heartbeat of jazz, is a strong yeast in the cultural bread America sells to the world. Wave after wave of styles in popular music and dance have come from it. Experimentation and playfulness are its core ingredients, the flip side being a tendency towards self-indulgence and showing off. Black music has always had a very competitive streak. The tradition in jazz and hip-hop of 'cutting' – exhausting your competitor with the fertility and endless variations of your solos or rhymes – can get tedious for outsiders. Hip-hop, like soccer, is made for travel anywhere. The tools are portable and versatile. Gospel's travelled a long way too, since it escaped from church. Now pop music worldwide abounds with singers 'flowering' – singing ten notes where one would do – gospel's testifying tradition gone viral.

Two speeches a couple of weeks ago at the Oscars represented the best and worse of American cadence. Sidney Poitier, accepting his lifetime achievement award, made ringing oratory, speaking of those whose shoulders he stood on 'to see where I wanted to go'. His speech, which should be studied by all aspiring speechmakers, blended the personal and the universal, the humble and the grand, using all the rhetoric, repetition and passion of old-style preaching. But the passion was corralled. He delivered his words with restraint, and the feeling, by being tightly controlled, was conveyed with great force. Halle Berry, on the other hand – overcome by being the first black woman to win best actress – let the tide of her emotion carry her way over the top, leaving a lot of her audience behind, despite the important things she was trying to say. She's not the first American actor to do this. If only she'd taken a few deep breaths.

Charleston, West Virginia, 15 April

The weather's warm everywhere we go now – we're stepping off the bus in T-shirts. It *feels* like the south. The heat's tropical, and snow-covered Canada is a fast-receding dream. People talk differently, their vowels more drawn out, their manner more friendly. For the first time in a month, a taxi driver actually filled in the receipt for the fare, rather than handing over a blank one. A crucial Civil War battle was fought here almost one and a half centuries ago, but all seemed quiet in the town when we pulled in on Sunday afternoon.

We came to play at the Mountain Stage Theatre, as part of a weekly live-to-air concert on National Public Radio, syndicated across the country. We were one of five acts on the bill, each playing twenty minutes. There was a house band also, and an MC filling in during changeovers. The whole show was two hours long and taped for broadcast – with no stops – in front of an audience of around four hundred.

We were fourth on the program, among highly regarded company. Bill Kirchen and his band were first. Bill, whom I knew as part of Nick Lowe's band when I toured with them in England eight years ago, is a dazzling rockabilly/country-swing guitar player and singer. He was followed by The Bottle Rockets, a rambunctious rocking roots band from Missouri, who played with panache despite colds and dodgy leads, then a Portuguese traditional *fado* singer, Mariza, with her band. Renowned jazz guitarist John Scofield closed the show.

The *fado* group were amazing – full of drama and verve. Nobody told us we had to follow the *fado*, I thought to myself, watching from the side of the stage. Mariza, a tall, elegant, striking-looking woman with short, bleach-blond hair in tight ripples on her head, wore a lacy flamenco-style dress that billowed from the waist down. She prowled the stage singing with great power, going from a whisper to a siren with easy control, accompanied by three dark-countenanced, dark-haired, dark-clad musicians on chairs. She spoke to the audience in a singsong, childlike voice – 'Do you like wine? I like wine too. Let's share the wine' – wrung emotion from every line, and swept grandly from the stage as the audience cheered.

There was a three-minute changeover – like pit-stop mechanics at a Formula One race, the house technicians swarmed the stage – as the MC bantered and gave the crowd a little history of us. He was well briefed, well prepared, the whole show a slick operation. A hundred and ninety seconds after Mariza's sweeping exit, we walked blinking into the light.

Although I hadn't been that keyed up before we went on – no more than usual – as soon as we started playing, the nerves kicked in big time. It may have been to do with the skill level of the other artists on display before us, but that doesn't usually bother me. It was probably more the shock of being on a big stage. We'd been on small stages for a while, where we were used to hearing each other play tight and close. Now the sound was so much more separated and clinical. The other band members seemed miles away. And live radio is the scariest medium of them all, scarier than live TV. If you fuck up on TV, people can see how you deal with it, it can become part of the performance; a fuck-up on radio's just a fuck-up. Moreover, playing only a few songs is different to a proper gig, where if there's some kind of train wreck you just have a laugh and bash out the next tune. One train wreck in this situation and you've wrecked a large part of the show. A voice was running through my head as I sang, saying, Don't forget the words, don't forget the words, and I was thinking of what I was going to say in between songs. You shouldn't be doing this when you're trying to put something over to an audience. I bet Mariza wasn't, but you never know. I could tell the rest of the band was feeling the pressure too. The songs were racing a little.

I have no memory of the audience response to our midnight rain, deep dirty places of shame, recipes for gravy, kisses by train stations, and lowdown sorry men. We escaped without major catastrophe, and backstage people were slapping our backs and shaking our hands. But Americans often do that.

Talking to the band afterwards confirmed my inklings. They'd all been freaking out too. Spencer said he'd been feeling like selling his guitar and slitting his wrists as he watched Bill Kirchen and The Bottle Rockets before we went on. Then Pete said, 'You know, whenever I feel like that, watching some band that's technically way better than us, I just tell myself, So what, we've got the best songs, and that's the thing that counts.'

Every band needs a Pete.

We watched side of stage for a while, greatly relieved, as John Scofield and his band did their jazz-fusion thing. I was trying to enjoy it. I have a record of his from a few years back that I like, but when he announced the next tune as 'hip-hop jazz' and the drummer started rapping badly, that was enough for us. One sideways look between us, involving ten eyebrows, and off we shuffled discreetly, one by one, eschewing the all-in 'We Are The World'-style jam at the end.

But I remembered to thank the house crew before we left. (Second rule of show business.)

The bus has been making a funny noise and smell for the last minute or so. We're stopping to check it out. There goes dinner in Pittsburgh.

Back in the hotel restaurant we sent a bottle of Australian wine – it's everywhere here now, usually with a picture of a marsupial on the label; they call it 'critter wine' – to the *fado* band and they came over to drink a toast. Then we headed off to a bar called The Empty Glass where Bill Kirchen was due to play later.

Every now and then something extraordinary happens in America that couldn't happen anywhere else and reminds me why I love this country so. There was a band playing when we walked into The Empty Glass – a black singer, a black drummer who also sang lead, a black percussionist, two white guitar players and a white bass player. One of the guitar players was from the Mountain Stage house band, released from his mild duties comping in the background behind the MC and now playing swinging, funky, loud guitar.

They performed a Louis Jordan-style song followed by an exquisite country-gospel tune with harmonies, and then an old number, 'Rabbit In A Log', that I knew as a bluegrass standard. But done in this instance as a combination of R&B and vaudeville, complete with dog barks and the singer and drummer bantering back and forth. A mini-history of American music in the space of three songs. You don't often see this kind of stew in Australia, this easy melding, melting and sampling of regional styles. The music – country, R&B, blues, soul, funk, swing – has made its way around the world to underpin most Western pop music, but at heart it's deeply local. It's borrowed music for us; sure, we can study it and study hard, get good at it, but it doesn't live inside our skin the way it does with those gentlemen onstage last night. Our strength lies in bastardising it, mutating it into something else. But America is the source, the well we draw from.

Then Bill Kirchen and his band got up – a classic trio, bass, drums and guitar, with Bill playing bravura licks around his vocals. Hillbilly, rockabilly – the kind of country-creole they were serving up, is essentially simple music, but people make a big mistake when they say 'Oh, that's easy.' You hear it quite often from jazzers, pop bands and classically trained musicians. They think it's a snap to play something in a country or old R&B style. They have no idea how far away, how outside the music they are. I could have listened to that drummer lay it down all night – inventive, disciplined, soulful.

Other people sat in with Bill and his group after a while. The guitar player from the previous band, who up to this point had been leaning against the wall in the shadows, peeled off a couple of blistering solos. (I saw three astonishing guitar players last night – all local guys. In America, anywhere you turn there's always someone who can play the shit out of the guitar.)

Eventually we got coaxed up – minus Bruce, who was out roaming somewhere – and mashed our way through 'Love Letter' and 'Deeper Water' (circle songs with minimal changes, good for jams), with Bill filigreeing over the top.

On our way back to the hotel in a taxi, the night sky was alive and crackling with a spectacular electrical storm – jagged, retina-branding lightning and hair-raising thunder. We seem to have skipped spring and gone straight from winter to summer. The storm flared through the gap in the bedroom curtains, lighting up Bruce, my roommate, sleeping four feet away.

What I know about Pittsburgh
It's Andy Warhol's hometown
Steel largely built it
America's first professional songwriter, Stephen Foster, lived
    downtown
It's where Heinz Baked Beans started
Peter Luscombe went to school here for two years (His dad worked
    for Heinz)

Pittsburgh Symphony Orchestra rocks! (Saw them two months ago in Melbourne)

17 April

Wednesday. We're loitering outside Louisville, hometown of Cassius Clay/Muhammad Ali, also known as the Louisville Lip, and probably the most famous man in the world. The bus is parked at a truck-stop, after we drove overnight from Pittsburgh, and I've just had my five-dollar shower (you buy a ticket and they call your name). So that's a small victory already today. We're due at a radio station at two-thirty, and an in-store at four-thirty, before sound check and a show tonight. This is a busy week – five gigs in five nights and quite a few miles between them, as well as promo and press, which seems to have picked up some since our manager, Rob Barnham, knocked a few heads (in the nicest possible way) at the record company last week in New York.

We arrived in Pittsburgh Monday night, in time for dinner after all, as Floyd managed to get the bus going again pretty quickly. Stayed in a rundown hotel near the university, walked into the student neighbourhood with Peter and Steve and found an alehouse/restaurant. All the waitresses were wearing tight, breast-moulding tops. Good grief! I downed three pints of porter (dreaming of Coopers Ale) and ate a bowl of alligator stew before returning to the hotel to write and send emails.

In strange cities I always try to find the water, my purpose both practical and philosophical. Locating the lake, river or sea is a way to orient yourself and set the mind dreaming. On Tuesday afternoon I rambled to the Allegheny River, which is draped with many steel bridges. (This is a steel town, let's make everything out of steel, let's cover the river with steel!) Over the other side stood the Andy Warhol Museum. Spencer was there when I arrived. He'd been there for a couple of hours already. Warhol is one of his idols, so he was in heaven.

It was good to see the diversity of Warhol's art and obsessions in one place, his fine-art training and technical skill evident throughout.

People often assume that what he did was easy. (The dimwitted response to modern art: 'Oh, anyone could have done that.' And the obvious riposte: 'Well, why didn't you?') Warhol was also a ferocious and eclectic collector, and the tiny fraction of his collection that was on display was fascinating – Edward S. Curtis photos from the turn of the last century, Navajo rugs, art deco furniture, household artifacts. There were some beautiful prints by Warhol based on Native American designs and many other surprises and delights throughout the seven floors of the museum. None of my favourites were on postcards in the shop downstairs but I did come away with a rather spiffy Elvis tie.

I was a little late for sound check and the band was jamming something slow and funky when I walked in. I got up and started singing over the top: 'I got a heavy thing for you, sure got a heavy thing,' making up some words about waking every day with a heavy thing, walking around all the time with a heavy thing, just can't seem to lose this heavy thing, and so on. It sounded good so I grabbed the beatbox from the bus and recorded it on cassette. Could be something.

The gig was hard work. About a hundred people in a club that could have held six hundred. This had the effect of making the audience more inhibited than usual. They were into it, I think, but restrained. We got there eventually and coaxed them onto the dance floor towards the end.

After the show a guy came backstage with a book called *Honeymooners: A Cautionary Tale*, recently published by Pittsburg writer Chuck Kinder, a good friend of Raymond Carver. Evidently the book has caused a bit of a stir in literary circles, being a thinly disguised *roman-à-clef* with the main character based on Carver and chronicling wild years of carousing in San Francisco and Montana. Richard Ford and Jay McInerney are among the writers touting the book on the cover. Chuck couldn't come to the show because he was doing a reading but there was a note from him saying how much he liked the song 'Everything's Turning To White', and how much Ray would have liked it if he'd heard it.

Chuck in turn has been fictionalised in a movie. He worked on this book for years and years, wrote three thousand (!) pages while teaching writing at Pittsburgh University. One of his students later wrote a novel based on him – a dissolute writer working on an endless novel – which was made into a movie. The movie's called *Wonder Boys* and stars Michael Douglas as the Chuck character. Bob Dylan won an Oscar last year for the song 'Things Have Changed' from the movie.

Connections loop and span and loop again, like steel across the Allegheny. More weirdness and wonder to follow down the road. Of that we can be sure.

Concerning Kentucky
Home of bluegrass music (mythical) and bourbon whisky (fact)
Is prone to tornadoes
Hosts a big horserace once a year
Lost the Civil War
Bears dogwood trees that bloom in pink and white
Never saw us before

18 April
I went to the radio station on my own to do an interview and play a couple of songs. It was just as well I took my guitar as the DJ hadn't received a copy of the CD yet from the record label. A journalist from the local paper, a big fan, had come in, and afterwards he drove me to the in-store. He told me he'd tried to set up a phone interview with me but it had fallen through. Strike two against the label. So I interviewed him, asking questions about Louisville. He filled me in on some of the neighbourhoods, the local music scene – stoner, jamming-type bands are pretty big here – and the build-up to Kentucky Derby day, which is coming soon. The whole town's in a bit of a tizz.

The in-store was a total waste of time. I'll never get that hour and a half back again. There had been some miscommunication between the label and the store, so they hadn't known we were coming until two days ago. Strike three. Because the store hadn't had time to set things up and advertise, no-one was there except the journalist and a friend and a few shoppers. Spencer and I played for twenty minutes and then packed up and waited for a taxi to the sound check.

Following the afternoon's exercise in futility, it was appropriate that the club we were playing in was called Rudyard Kipling, after the man who wrote 'If you can meet with Triumph and Disaster and treat those two impostors just the same . . .'

On the way there, the oppressive muggy weather broke and lovely warm rain bathed the streets and blooming dogwood trees. I asked the taxi driver about the trees and she said that the cross of Jesus was made from dogwood, and that if you look closely at the flower you can see the shape of the cross traced in red on the petal, from the blood of Jesus Christ, our Saviour, Himself. (Oh yes, we're in the south now.) She was also quite excited because she thought when we spoke we sounded like The Beatles.

Freedy Johnston, the American singer-songwriter who's opening up for us on this leg of the tour, arrived towards the end of our sound check. He's on his own, following us around in his car, sometimes driving very long distances to get to the venues. He's a likable but nervy character who had trouble with our crowds on his first few shows. He hates people talking while he's playing – who doesn't? – but seems to forget that there are people listening as well. He harangued the audience in Boston, told them they were rude, and did the same in New York, even though he had obvious support from most of the crowd, at least until he put them offside. I made a bet with the band that he wouldn't last the week.

In Arlington he walked on to a talky crowd, said he was Dave Matthews, played all covers – Beatles, Hollies, Gordon Lightfoot – and walked off halfway through his last song. By now we were beginning to think it was part of his act. Afterwards, over a couple of beers on the bus, I suggested to Freedy we work out a song to sing together on the remaining shows. We settled on 'Don't Worry, Baby'.

He'd driven eight hours to get to Louisville and we ran the

song in the afternoon. He had his best gig yet. A small but packed room – around a hundred and thirty people – and they hung on every note of his songs. The same for us. And when he came back on late in our set for 'Don't Worry, Baby' it brought the house down, even though we bungled it a little. (What *is* that chord at the end of the chorus?)

Floyd, our Afro-American bus driver, is from Oklahoma, as country as a chicken coop, as they say in these parts. It took us a while to understand each other, so thickly southern is his accent and so alien ours to him. He's the best driver we've had – smooth, dependable, likable – and thought it was hilarious when we started singing 'So fresh and so clean . . .' and 'I'm sorry, Miss Jackson, I am for REEAALL' (from songs by Atlanta hip-hop group Outkast) as we drove into Atlanta. 'Where y'all know that from?' he asked, as if we were from another planet. (We are.)

When he's hanging out on the bus, while we sound-check or do a show, he likes to watch basketball and wrestling, or the black entertainment channel – nonstop music videos which are pretty close to soft porn most of the time. He drops in and listens to our set sometimes. 'Love Letter', 'Gravy' and 'Ma' are his favourites. He's getting teased at the moment because he went and got one of his eyebrows pierced on a day off. Too long on the road with a rock'n'roll band.

Poor Freedy was late for the show in Atlanta. It's a nine-hour drive normally – he doesn't drive overnight like us – and he struck a detour which delayed him further. Pete and Steve and Bruce went on early and played some dubby instrumentals to cover for him until he got there. He joined us in our set again for 'Don't Worry, Baby', which went off without a hitch.

We're getting quite fond of Freedy. You never quite know what to expect with him. I explained to the Louisville audience the Australian tendency to call people by shortened versions of their surnames. 'He may be Freedy to you,' I said, 'but he's Johnno to us.' Last night Pete dubbed him The Johnster. He looked truly nonplussed but wanted to laugh, I think. You could see him thinking, Okay, I'm supposed to be having fun. Have fun with these guys.

I was so tired onstage last night, mentally and physically. The others were too. Sometimes we're all in the same state, as if we're just one group mind. Perhaps it's just week five on the bus. I fell asleep in the pod with the headphones on, listening to the last four songs of Richard Strauss.

Georgia
Peaches and swamps
James Brown, Outkast, Babyface, REM
Gone With the Wind
Midnight in the Garden of Good and Evil
Flannery O'Connor
Coca-Cola
Rainy night in ⁓

20 April
Didgeridoos and djembes in the main street of Asheville, a hippie hilltop town in North Carolina. Lots of students and bookshops. The one I wandered into had a whole section on shamanism and a young bluegrass band playing in the café. Two other shows were on in town as well as us – The Wailers (remnants of Bob Marley's band) at a club around the corner, and Ween, who drew a large crowd at the civic centre. We saw some of Ween's nutty, entertaining show before we had to go to our gig. There was a strong smell of pot in the air.

We began around eleven. Only about fifty people were there – I knew it would be tough drawing crowds this week – but most of them, it seemed, were rabid fans. We had a really good sound onstage, which made the show enjoyable. I'm finding new things in my voice – new resonances, more suppleness. Gigging is good for it. The Freedster had trouble with the talkers but he hung around for his song with us again. I had a nice chat afterwards to a British couple – the woman a fine-looking sixty-year-old with a cigarette in one hand and a beer in the other – who'd driven two hours from Knoxville, Tennessee to see us.

Today we're in Birmingham, Alabama. Not far south of here, in the town of Montgomery, in 1955 – the year I was born – a middle-aged black woman by the name of Rosa Parks refused to give up her seat on the bus to a white person. This was against the law at the time. She said she was tired and her feet were aching after a long day's work. Her subsequent arrest led to a boycott of the buses, organised by Martin Luther King, and kick-started the civil rights movement. From little things . . .

Driving to Denver, 24 April
Good show in Austin last night. We needed it after a quiet Monday night in Dallas and the thin crowds of the week before. It was a full house (a hundred and thirty) in a small place called the Cactus Café, with the audience seated at tables and chairs. FreeJo, as we dubbed Freedy on his last night, had parted from us somewhat wistfully over margaritas in a Mexican disco bar in Birmingham two nights previously – contract fulfilled; I lost the bet – and there being no support act, we were required to do two sets.

It was a nice change breaking up the show this way and we did a killer quiet first set – 'Smoke Under The Bridge', 'Would You Be My Friend' getting rare outings – followed up with the two-three punch of the second act and encore.

Austin is a simpatico kind of town with a strong music scene. A lot of good songwriters and singers of tall tales round these parts. We drank Mexican beer in between sets and on the patio at the back of the café after the show, enjoying the balmy night as people dropped by to pay their respects and have things signed. Then we filed onto the bus to drive the nine hundred miles to Denver, Colorado. Right now it's two in the afternoon the next day and we're *still* in Texas. Outside the bus window it's flat, flat, flat, scrubby and dry. Cattle country. We're on the great Texas plains just north of Amarillo, not far from

Lubbock, the town where the well-hung (so I've heard – or is it just another Texas tall story?) Buddy Holly grew up.

Although I'm dreaming hard of home, I know a part of me will miss the Bus Life – its simplicity, its reductionism. In the same way that a junkie's life becomes a pared-down purity, the day's only necessity being to score enough to keep you going until the next score, so all our hours drive towards one thing – the next show. As with the junkie, it's the rush we do it for, the moment of transcendence where nothing else matters. Or, more accurately, where everything matters. To get to these brief oasis hours we slog through the desert of time, disciplined, focused, monastic. The muddy, muddled outside world – the world of family and friends, of loved ones, of bill paying, shopping, local politics, house running, notices from school, making the lunches, the whole *bummph* of life – is far away and dim, muted behind the glass. All we have to do is eat, sleep, ride, maintain our health, do our job, keep our spirits up and our clothes clean.

26 April

I had lunch in Denver with my cousin Frank and his wife Julie, who'd driven in from Boulder. Afterwards I walked around downtown for a while. This is where Neal Cassady – hero of Kerouac's *On the Road* and Tom Wolfe's *Electric Kool-Aid Acid Test*, the living embodiment of the Beats, man of nonstop motion – grew up. The city is all clean and new and shiny now, and the old buildings on Larimer Street – the poolhalls, warehouses and flophouses that Jack visited with Neal – have been converted into arcades, wild-west theme shops and glossy restaurants. Every fucking city . . .

The gig was good – a hundred and twenty people in a small theatre with a dance floor. There was a nest of Australians there with a large flag (groan), but they behaved themselves pretty well and I was touched despite myself when, just after we'd finished – lights up, second encore done and we hadn't played 'Leaps And Bounds', which they'd called for all night – they sang it a cappella all the way through.

Then onto the bus and six hundred miles to Salt Lake City. Red wine and hip-hop in the back lounge.

Things to do in Salt Lake City
Um . . .
Er . . . hmmm . . .
Let me see now . . .
Ahh, mm . . .
We–ll . . .
Maybe . . . ?
Umm . . .
You could . . .
The temple?
Yeah?

Things to do in Salt Lake City after one a.m.
. . . ?
. . . ?
. . . ?
. . . ?
. . . ?

Los Angeles, 1 May
The end of the line at last – back where we started from, after rolling into LA Monday morning, all the way down to the sea. We're staying right on the boardwalk at the Cadillac Hotel. From my room I can see mountains in one direction, and in the other, below us, the sandy expanse and dark blue water of Venice Beach. Looking west in brilliant sunshine across the mighty Pacific, I squint and try to imagine home, way out beyond the waves, beyond the light, Melbourne sleeping in the misty autumn night.

Sunday's show at a smoky cellar bar in San Francisco was packed. The sweat poured off us. We rehydrated afterwards with whisky and Guinness. Richard Flanagan, who's doing a reading tour for his latest novel, *Gould's Book of Fish*, helped us out before we poured ourselves onto the bus.

Spencer and I did an in-store Monday afternoon, which turned out quite well despite the PA breaking down. We invited the audience to come forward and sit on the floor and played to them campfire-style. The final show at The Troubadour was a hit with the crowd, and of course with us, except for one pain-in-the-arse noisy drunk who ruined a couple of the quiet songs. In Australia somebody would have decked him; here they are a little more polite.

Today I stepped into Cousin Alex's big black full-length wetsuit and went swimming in the chilly Pacific Ocean. There was no-one else in the water and hardly anyone on the beach. I dived under waves and lazily caught a couple. I did some breaststroke, some freestyle, lay on my back under the brilliant sun, imagining life as a dolphin. I looked back at America. Twelve and a half thousand miles we'd come. Twenty-nine shows in forty-three days, with a rough average of two hundred people a gig, making a total of six thousand. You could say it works out at around two miles per person. This arithmetic conjures the bizarre image of us travelling all around America, stopping every two miles and playing to one person, before moving on to the next.

My brain's gone a little loopy. Like the Allegheny River. I've been too long away from love.

WOULD YOU BE MY FRIEND?

If I fell into confusion
Got scared but couldn't say
If I lost my rhyme and reason
And threw away the gift of grace
Would you be my friend?

If they said I don't deserve you
That my credit was no good
If they told you I'm not worthy of your love
And you should cut me like you cut dead wood
Would you be my friend?

And if you heard that I was on the town
Pissing loudly on your name
Would you find me, would you face me down?
Though your ears burned with shame
Would you be my friend?

And if I said I wished I'd never been born
And my mouth could only curse
If I'd passed the point of no return
Like a poor, puking child in church
Would you be my friend?
My only friend

Things You Can't Buy

Good weather
Good parents
True friends
Green lights all the way from St Kilda Junction
    to Clifton Hill
A good night's sleep
Eight goals by Jeff Farmer in one half of footy
Sex with laughter
Sex with tears

YOU BROKE A BEAUTIFUL THING

Like a child acting so carelessly
You destroyed something you just didn't see
I'm not angry
How could I be angry with a child?

You broke a beautiful thing
And it won't ever mend

Thoughtless child
All wrapped up in the shape of a man
I tried so hard to get you to understand
I'm so sorry
Why am I always the one saying sorry
Like a mother does for a child?

You broke a beautiful thing
And it won't ever mend
I'll never have the pieces again

I hate the way I keep losing things
And I hate the way when I lose something
I never seem to find it again

You broke a beautiful thing
It won't ever mend
I'll never have the pieces again

Days Of 1903

I never found them again – the things so quickly lost . . .
the poetic eyes, the pale face . . . in the dusk of the street . . .
I never found them again – the things acquired quite by chance,
that I gave up so lightly;
and that later in agony I wanted.
The poetic eyes, the pale face,
those lips, I never found again.

C. P. Cavafy

In Dreams

I don't dream very much. That is to say, I don't often remember my dreams. When I do remember them they're usually quite mundane, not different in any way to normal life. I was eating lunch. Or I walked up to the milk bar on the corner. Every now and then I get a little déjà vu: I'm putting on my shoes and I think to myself, Did I dream last night I was putting on my shoes just like this, first the left foot and then the right? There are no long dream sequences written in italics in these pages. They make my eyes glaze. However, I do appreciate it when authors put their dreams in italics so you know to skip them straight away.

Very occasionally I have dreams about music. They're usually performance-anxiety dreams. You're supposed to be onstage in a couple of minutes but you can't find the stage. You're walking down corridors that lead to locked doors. It's like the scene from *Spinal Tap* where they can't find the stage, but less funny. You know the audience is ready and waiting for you, getting impatient, the rest of the band too. Now you're running down corridors that all look the same, trying doors that all look the same, and none of them will open. You wake up suddenly in a cold sweat.

This actually happened to me once, at the ARIA awards, when I took a wrong turn from a dressing room deep in the bowels of the theatre and couldn't find the stage. They'd called my name several times before I got there.

Nearly every musician I know has these kinds of dreams. Usually they're recurring. Peter Luscombe finds himself onstage just about to count the first song in and realises he can't find his drumsticks. The pouch where he keeps his spares is empty. Another variation has me telling him to hurry up and start the song and him looking around to see that all the drums are still in their cases.

Sian dreams she's the star of a recital about to play Brahms' Clarinet Quintet to a full concert hall and she's only just noticed the reed for her mouthpiece is broken. The audience and her fellow players are waiting, but her clarinet's completely unplayable. Dan Kelly has some doozies. For some reason things are never straightforward for Dan – in life or dreams. In one he's playing keyboards for Dire Straits, forty metres above the rest of the band, looking down on their tiny heads.

I seem to remember having dreams of indescribable beauty maybe once or twice. I'm with the band playing amazing, out-of-this-world music. It's a new song, it must be the best song I've ever written, it modulates in ways the world's never heard before, each instrument singing gloriously yet still serving the whole sound, intertwining in diverse and melodious ways Bach never thought of. The lyrics, when they come in, are simple, perfect, mysterious. The whole thing goes on and on, endlessly inventive. I'm coming to the surface slowly, about to wake up, thinking to myself, I must remember this! I must remember this! I want to reach out for a pen and paper or the little tape recorder – where *is* that little tape recorder? – but how could one person sing such a cathedral and I'm so drowsy, so drowsy, and the music's so lovely and I don't want to break this spell and I'm coming to the top now and the light's leaking through the bedroom window and if only I could get this down but the strains are starting to fade – Adieu! the fancy cannot cheat so well as she is fam'd to do, deceiving elf – and the music's going now, getting fainter, it's going.

I lie there still, not moving a muscle, not daring to move lest I shake it loose altogether, but it doesn't matter what I do, I can't hold it, I know I can't hold it, it's going, going, gone, over St Kilda Road and up Carlisle, now 'tis buried deep in the next suburb. Fled is that music: Do I wake or sleep?

So you lie there bereft, hoping beyond hope it will come back again, but whatever it was – something so vivid a minute ago – has disappeared like water in the desert.

Some dreams *do* cross to the other side, somehow find their way from shadowland to day. Junior Brown plays an instrument – a Telecaster welded to a lap steel – he dreamed in a dream and then went out and made himself. Many writers claim inspiration from dreams. The riff for '(I Can't Get No) Satisfaction' supposedly came to Keith Richards fully formed one night. Townes Van Zandt walked into Guy Clark's kitchen one morning after sleeping over and said he'd just written a new song. 'When? How?' said Guy and his wife. 'You went to sleep before us and you've only just got up. We never heard anything.'

'I dreamt it, the whole thing,' said Townes, and then sat down and played them 'If I Needed You'.

Texas tall stories aside, the closest I've got to dreaming a song was waking up in the middle of the night with the chorus lyrics and melody of 'You Broke A Beautiful Thing' sweetly formed in my head. I knew straightaway it was a song for Renée Geyer. I got up and wrote the verses and bridge before the sun came up. The first time I played it to her she said, 'It's a country song. I don't sing country songs.'

'Not really, Renée,' I said. 'It's a soul song, a country/soul song.'

'Sounds like a *country* song to me.'

I knew from experience that Renée can sometimes be persuaded.

'Think of it as a Dan Penn/Spooner Oldham song. Imagine it as "Dark End Of The Street" or "I'm Your Puppet".'

'All right,' she said dubiously. 'No harm trying, I suppose.'

Try it she did. Just as she did with 'Difficult Woman'. She took it out of my hands and Renée-ified it. It sounds like a soul song now.

YOU CAN PUT YOUR SHOES UNDER MY BED

It's a pretty pass
How you always seem to land on your feet
A little undone
Anybody else by now would be cold meat
Whenever you fall
You can put your shoes under my bed

Anytime, anytime you're passing by this way
Remember you will always have a place to stay
Whenever you call
You can put your shoes under my bed

Trip the light
And who of us can tell what's real and what's fantastic
Bring on the night
No one else could have such grace and be so spastic
Let heaven fall
You can put your shoes under my bed

Pick The Odd One Out

'Johnny Walker's Shoes' – The Pigram Brothers
'(The Angels Wanna Wear My) Red Shoes' – Elvis Costello
'Walk A Mile In My Shoes' – Joe South
'Diamonds On The Soles Of Her Shoes' – Paul Simon
'Italian Shoes' – Mink DeVille
'Purple Sneakers' – You Am I
'Dirty Boots' – Sonic Youth
'Boots Of Spanish Leather' – Bob Dylan
'These Boots Are Made For Walkin'' – Nancy Sinatra

'Bootylicious' – Destiny's Child
'Old Brown Shoe' – The Beatles
'Hole In My Shoe' – Traffic
'Good Old Shoe' – Willie Nelson

(Answer at back of book)

It's A Bitch To Pitch

Every once in a while when you're writing a song a rhyme pops into your head that makes you think, Well, if I leave that in no-one's ever going to cover this. No-one but me would want to sing that line. You get a lot of bad or boring rhymes pass through your mind while you're writing and you do your best to weed them out, but sometimes an awkward one muscles its way in, hunkers down under the song-skin and won't be removed for love or money.

'Keep On Coming Back For More', which I wrote under the influence of 'The Seed (2.0)' by The Roots, is a chance to be covered by a female soul singer – it has the melody, the groove, the sentiment – except for one line in the last verse that goes 'Like a sick dog, licking at his spew, I keep on turning back to you.' I just know the publishing company would pitch that song with trepidation, carrying it gingerly to a singer like a dog walker carrying their barker's egg in a plastic bag. I've thought to myself I should clean that line up, find another rhyme, but so far it's resisted my desultory efforts. The image expresses the central idea of the song perfectly. It has an ugly force, and the virtue of being a rhyme, to my knowledge, not often coined before. Still, if Amy Winehouse were considering recording it and wanted a line change, I'm sure I could come up with something else. Then again, Amy's just the kind of woman who could pull off a line like that.

I had a meeting with a music publisher once in Nashville who thought 'You Can Put Your Shoes Under My Bed' had 'real potential' to be pitched to country singers. 'You'll have to change that line about the spastic, though,' he said. I agreed.

That was twenty-two years ago. The line's still there. It may be defective but it's where it belongs and it has all my love.

YOU CAN'T TAKE IT WITH YOU

You might have a happy family, nice house, fine car
You might be successful in real estate
You could even be a football star
You might have a prime-time TV show seen in every home and bar
But you can't take it with you

You might own a great big factory, oil wells on sacred land
You might be in line for promotion, with a foolproof retirement plan
You might have your money in copper, textiles or imports from Japan
But you can't take it with you

You can't take it with you though you might pile it up high
It's so much easier for a camel to pass through a needle's eye

You might have a body of fine proportion and a hungry mind
A handsome face and a flashing wit, lips that kiss and eyes that shine
There might be a queue all around the block
Long before your starting time
But you can't take it with you

You might have a great reputation so carefully made
And a set of high ideals, polished up and so well displayed
You might have a burning love inside, so refined, such a special grade
But you can't take it with you

My Left Foot

I've been playing Australian Rules football for fifty years. I'm still working on my left foot, which forever needs improvement. My fingers have been broken a couple of times, so, needing them for work, I haven't played competitively since 1988. On Sundays and Wednesdays, when I'm in Melbourne, I do circle work in the park with a loose coalition of men and a few children. This anarcho-syndicalist collective has been going for close to twenty years. Not all those who started it are still alive. I hope it's still going when all the founders are dead.

We have no leader, no official status, no president, treasurer or secretary. We are builders, taxi drivers, comedians, opera singers, rock'n'rollers, writers, teachers, anaesthetists, IT people, public servants and surveyors, all of whom love footy. Someone buys a new ball once in a while, then collects the money. We run, kick, carry, bounce, lead, mark, handball, call and banter for an hour or so, until we stagger to a stop. There are no teams. We do not tackle or compete, though once in a while a few fellas fly for a mark, or someone tries to sell a dummy.

All we're trying to do is execute simple things perfectly: to drop the ball sweetly on the boot and watch it lob with pretty spin into the hands or chest of the leading man without him having to check his step; to be on the receiving end for the same result, running flat out for twenty or thirty metres to take the ball in outstretched hands and deliver a precise handpass to your mate who, timing his intersecting run to the dot, now demands the ball; to be cogs in a smooth machine, stringing a sequence of possessions together that feels like poetry, looping the leather round the oval without touching the grass, once, twice, three times – never too long before the inevitable error, but no matter, pick it up and start again.

Round and round we go in pure, purposeless pleasure, one ball and twenty-odd men at physical prayer in their outdoor church, making the thing that none of us can make on our own.

Being a travelling salesman I'm away for sometimes months at a time, but the ragtag park crew, some of whom I only know by first name or nickname, will always be there, more or less, when I return. I wake up in a motel room in Cairns, say, on a Sunday in July, and think of my fellow parishioners three thousand kilometres south, at their morning service, receiving their chilly communion. Later, after sound check perhaps, when the heat of the day has dimmed a little, I take my scuffed old Sherrin out of the suitcase and seek a sports ground, any piece of flat grass. If I can't get one of the band to come with me, I run a few laps bouncing the ball and kicking it to myself.

These days I bounce mostly with my left hand. The art of kicking is all about getting the drop of the ball right. My right hand does this instinctively. There's hardly any gap between where I let go of the ball and where it hits the boot. Not so on the left. I have to think about it more, guiding the ball down. The drop always seems longer. And the longer the drop, the greater the margin for error. I'm running around an oval in Cairns trying not to think about how I release the ball from my left hand. When it goes well I'm not thinking about anything. My left foot will never quite catch up to my right, but lately I've noticed some improvement. One day they'll both be completely still.

YOUR LITTLE SISTER IS A BIG GIRL NOW

She was always bugging us
Every day on the way home
Riding on the back of the bus
Every time we tried to kiss
She was there right beside us
Putting on a funny face
Your little sister's a big girl now

It seemed to happen in a dream
Like the corn at summer's end
She was standing fully grown
Peaches hanging on the tree
I shook some loose, she bit too quick
All the juice came running down
Your little sister's a big girl now

We were married in the spring
Little sister carried fresh flowers
My best friend held the ring
Later at the reception
I saw them dancing in a corner
She was kissing him slow and long
Your little sister's a big girl now
Your little sister's a big girl now
Such a big girl now

Young Love

'The Girl Across The Street (Just Turned 18)' – Jo Jo Zep
   and The Falcons
'Young Girl' – Gary Puckett and The Union Gap
'Young Blood' – The Coasters
'Younger Girl' – The Lovin' Spoonful
'Good Morning, Little Schoolgirl' – Mississippi Fred McDowell
'Little Sister' – Elvis Presley
'Are You Old Enough?' – Dragon
'Don't Stand So Close To Me' – The Police
'Sick Again' – Led Zeppelin
'So Young' – Jo Jo Zep and The Falcons

It's Not The What, It's The How

They say the human mind has a tendency to make patterns. To seek cause and effect, to find meaning in coincidence. We're supposed to be hardwired to do this. The theory goes that being able to read signs effectively – the lion's footprints to the waterhole, for example – had an evolutionary advantage, but at some point in our history the interpretation of signs took off, giving rise to schizophrenia and religion. Examine the gizzards of this bird and it will tell us whether to go to war tomorrow or next month. Sacrifice this young virgin at full moon and the crops will be plentiful. Say a prayer to Jesus and your mother's cancer will be cured. Early human existence was precarious, and belief in gods and rules may have been an aid to survival. Belief helped tribes to bond and organise; provided hope, will and comfort, so perhaps believers did better than nonbelievers, especially if the latter were shunned. Religion got us through and now we're stuck with it.

The little tribe that is a band on tour develops it own codes, rules and rituals, quite removed from rationality. A drink made up one night by the drummer, improvising with vodka and a can of Lift and thrown back by all of us before a killer show, now becomes necessary every night. We have to drink it just before we go on, clinking glasses and looking each other in the eyes, or else we'll put the mozz on the gig.

Those who join a band on the road, a band that's been together a long time, often have trouble understanding the conversation at first. You may be a wife or a friend, someone from the record company or management office, but you can't help feeling like Mr Jones in 'Ballad Of A Thin Man'. Everyone seems to be speaking in code, a whole different lingo. There are made-up words, funny voices, in-jokes, running gags, things that are funny only because they've been said a thousand times before, cryptic associations and silly games. You wonder if you've joined a cult.

After a few days, you start to feel like you're becoming one of them. You're all driving together down the Queensland coast from Townsville to Rockhampton, say. You stop at a roadside diner, and as you're mooching around wondering whether to have the petrified dim sim, the frozen burger, or hang out 'til you reach the bright lights, one of the band exclaims excitedly, 'Look here! *Gary Puckett and The Union Gap's Greatest Hits*! Only $7.99!' Money is exchanged and soon after, you're pulling out onto the highway as the CD is slipped into the stereo.

'Okay, do you know about the Gary Puckett song cycle?' says the bass player.

'The Gary Puckett song cycle?' you ask, puzzled.

'Yeah. Now, there are only seven songs you need to worry about. But you need to play them in order. Forget Schumann or Schubert. Gazzer says it all in less than twenty minutes. Start with "Young Girl", then "This Girl Is A Woman Now". It's a bit creepy at first, but just go with it.'

It's creepy all right, as a wound-up Gaz tells his budding Lolita to leave *now*, before his urge to have underage sex overpowers him. He wrestles manfully, operatically with himself through a couple of songs, including 'Lady Willpower', until finally, needs must, he gives in on 'The Pleasure Of You'. Everyone breathes a sigh of relief, as his paramour now seems to be of legal age. Gary has waited and sweated and bided his time and at last his dream's come true. This is the high point of the cycle, the resting place, the happy summit before the inevitable descent.

'Woman Woman' introduces the worm in the apple of bliss as the Big G begs to know 'Woman, have you got cheating on your mind?' No sooner thought than done. Everybody can see what's coming big time – just as everybody but Oedipus knows what's going to happen when he meets the old stranger at the crossroads – but we're still on the edge of our seats because it's not the what, it's the how. 'Don't Give Into Him' tells the story we're all expecting. Don't give into him – as if. Amazingly, you're still picking hamburger beetroot from your teeth as Gary performs the mournful last rites. 'Over You' closes the *Liederkreis* with a sad note of resignation: 'Though it hurts, I'll get by.'

Such concision. Such conception and execution. Love's dark flowering, love's bright fulfilment, love's dimming fade. You never knew Gary Puckett was a genius. Does Greil Marcus know about this? Michael Gray? Christopher Ricks?

Rockhampton, 300 kilometres.

YOUNG LOVERS

Young lovers, young lovers, young lovers
I see them everywhere I go
Holding hands in the park
As the sky grows dark
Young lovers don't want to go home

Young lovers, young lovers, young lovers
They drive me right out of my mind
Lying down by the river
Whispering 'forever'
Young lovers, they don't have very long

(Everybody was a young lover once
See that old man coming down the road, shuffling on a stick
Once he pressed a girl against a fence and drank her kiss
And never knew such tenderness
And holds still in his head that bliss
Now he has to sit down to take a piss)

Young lovers, young lovers, young lovers
They seem to get younger every year
Find a job, get a loan
Raise some kids 'til they're grown
Young lovers, they don't have very long
Young lovers don't know what's coming on

Two Dans

Nephew Dan, Martin's son, moved to Melbourne from southern Queensland in 2001, not long after Kaarin and I broke up, and he stayed with me on and off for a year or two.

Growing up, he'd imbibed a lot of music from his parents. His mother Rosie sang and played guitar and there were many records in the house, as well as miles of music on Martin's reel-to-reel tape recorder – Beatles, Rolling Stones, Dylan, Van Morrison, Richie Havens, Pentangle, Steeleye Span, Fairport Convention, Cream, Blind Faith, Led Zeppelin, King Crimson, Yes, Supertramp and so on.

Rosie was born and grew up in England, so that may explain the strong British bias in the above list. Maybe it was just the times. Or Adelaide. This was all music that had seeped into me as well, via my older brothers when I was a teenager. The first rock concert I ever went to was Yes, at the Apollo Stadium in Adelaide, just after *Close to the Edge* had been released. I went with Martin and John and their friends. The concert – and the record – totally rocked my head.

Dan started playing guitar at thirteen and some of the first things he learnt were Steve Connolly's parts on my early records. He had a terrific ear and soaked everything up. He loved U2 and Dire Straits. 'There's other stuff too,' I said, and sent him mix tapes from time to time as part of his education. Occasionally I sent dubs of whole albums. He told me years later that Nick Cave's *Your Funeral . . . My Trial*, backed with Son House, Blind Lemon Jefferson and Robert Johnson, which I'd sent him when he was fifteen, totally freaked him out as he lay on his bed, one thin wall away from the brooding, back-block cane fields looming behind the house. He put it away and didn't discover its dark joys 'til years later.

When he came south in his twenties and we started to see more of each other, the musical influences began to go both ways. Like Declan, who over the years has slipped me lashings of electronica, hip-hop, Ethiopian R&B and cut-up avant-gardists on burnt CDs, Dan has turned me on to lots of new music, including the sardonic, noodling Steve Malkmus and his band Pavement; later on, The Shins, Animal Collective, Beta Band and many others.

Dan was working in a restaurant and writing songs, layering parts upon parts on the DA88 tape recorder in my shed. We jammed a lot at home and started doing a few little gigs together. I love playing and singing with him. Apart from the genetic similarities embedded deep in our cell structure, we have a lot of the same library in our heads, so we're usually in sync without having to think. There are deep roots in his playing which, combined with his eclecticism and his own bent, give him a kooky soulfulness.

'Young Lovers' came from Dan and me sitting around the house with a couple of guitars, making stuff up. The usual goofing around. I was doing a bad impersonation, I realised afterwards, of Bing Crosby singing 'Sweet Leilani'. I didn't think much of it but Dan made me press *record* on the little beat-box and about a week later brought it up again, saying, 'You should finish that one off.' We had a few other things kicking around at the time and all I had for that one was two words and the start of a tune. To me it was just a little jokey squib, not worth putting time into. But Dan quietly persisted over a couple of months, until I finished off the melody and wrote a few more words.

It was still incomplete when we took it into rehearsals with the band for *Ways and Means*. Dan Luscombe added a couple of fancy chords and Bill and Pete gave it the thumbs up, so now the pressure was really on. I spent an afternoon walking up and down Elwood Canal and didn't come home until I had full set of lyrics, complete with talking bit. It was the talking bit that got it over the line for me – it had a nice rhyme density. 'Pressed' roughly rhymed with 'kiss', 'tenderness', 'bliss' and 'piss', as well as sitting snugly with the internal rhymes 'against' and 'fence' and 'drank', all in the space of four lines. And nobody had ever written 'has to sit down to take a piss' in a song before, had they?

Wrong. Six years later, when I was mixing a live version of

'Young Lovers' for a DVD, the engineer laughed when he heard the line about taking a piss and said, 'Did you get that from Randy Newman?'

'What do you mean?'

'You know, that song of his "Shame", where the old guy is talking to the prostitute and says she doesn't know what it's like to have to sit down to piss.'

'No! *Bugger.*'

Yes, true. What can you do? There's nothing new under the sun.

YOU'RE 39, YOU'RE BEAUTIFUL
AND YOU'RE MINE

I don't talk all that much
About my feelings and such
Though I try to keep in touch with this heart of mine
But now I'm gonna speak out loud
'Cause it makes me feel so proud
That we're standing the test of time
You're 39, you're beautiful and you're mine

I wake up every day
On my tongue a song of praise
You still take my breath away in the morning light
Down all the dogging days
You keep on getting better with age
Like a lovingly made bottle of wine
You're 39, you're beautiful and you're mine

Like a sailing ship at sea
Bearing spice and history
You come swaying to me in your prime
You're 39, you're beautiful and you're mine
I'm gonna say it one more time
You're 39, you're beautiful and you're mine

My Shout

Record companies worth their salt like to throw ideas at you. The
ideas are rarely original but I don't mind. Unoriginal ideas keep coming around, in most cases, because they work. And it's nice to know
that somebody other than yourself is thinking about your stuff.

Michael Gudinski bugged me for years to put out a Greatest Hits. I wasn't particularly opposed to the idea but couldn't muster much enthusiasm for it either. The thought of going back and listening through my old records to make a selection made me groan. It was one of those things, like cleaning out the shed, that you know should be done but never get round to. There are always more interesting things to do – like write new songs and make new records.

Michael plugged away, though, and eventually I went out to the shed. Listening to the old songs was quite a shock, often embarrassing, but once in a while a pleasant surprise. Many music fans may not realise that they know a band's records more intimately than the band does. They've returned to a particular record at different times over the years and know it inside out as a result – the singer's every note and inflection, the drummer's fill into the final chorus, the little bendy bit the guitarist played in the third verse. Whereas those of us who made the record, although we listened a lot to ourselves at the time of recording, left it behind once we were done. Or you may say it left us, sailed away like a paper boat out of a child's hands. The singers and musicians I know don't listen to their own records. Why would they? I can think of nothing worse. We listen to music made by other people.

The years go by and we continue to play our songs, though. A performer's work, like an athlete's, is mainly repetition, with incremental changes. Night by night, little variations creep in. You find a more interesting way to sing the second verse. You get bored with the original melody and start to fuck with it a little. You and the band keep yourself interested by finding new ways to play the old tunes. You change the groove, the tempo, turn a tough 4/4 full-band rock song into a tender waltz perhaps, with only one or two instruments. After a while you've completely forgotten how the original version went.

In the shed, dutifully listening to my voice on the old recordings was like listening to a stranger. In the end this detachment made it easier to choose. I didn't need to dwell on what was bad or good. It was supposed to be a Greatest Hits, after all, even though I wasn't a Greatest Hits kind of artist. So I just chose the songs that were popular. Some had got a lot of radio play over the years, while others had become crowd favourites more mysteriously. Twenty songs was enough.

It being 1996, I sequenced them onto a cassette, took it into the Mushroom offices in Albert Park, and climbed the spiral stairs to Gudinski's office, which sat atop the old warehouse labyrinth like an eagle's eyrie. Michael was happy enough with the selection but looked aghast when I showed him a small blurry black and white snapshot of a boy playing cricket on the beach. Me at age ten.

'You're not thinking of using that as the cover, are you?'

'Er . . . yeah.'

He rolled his eyes and shook his head and told me to go and see Pierre in the art department. Pierre has a fantastic collection of old seven-inch soul records and a way with letters, shapes and colours. The cover came together in no time. The album, entitled *Songs From the South*, was released in 1997 and sold more than all my other records put together. It's been updated once and still sells nice and steady. I call it my 'putting the kids through college' record. With a bit of luck, maybe the grandkids too.

Another unoriginal idea record execs like to come up with is the covers album. Or the duets album. Even better, the covers album with duets. A record of duets is often a ploy to revitalise an artist's flagging career. Or putting it more kindly, to connect an older artist with a new generation. There are shades of this on Frank Sinatra's final albums (though Frank's career hasn't flagged since 1952), where he duets with several younger pop stars, including Bono and Gloria Estefan. Call me old-fashioned, but I just haven't been able to bring myself to listen to those records. Maybe there are some good bits.

I've tinkered around over the years with the idea of a covers record. Every now and then I add songs and names to a lengthening list. To put together a coherent album, it helps to narrow the frame, like

K. D. Lang did with *Hymns of the 49th Parallel*, all songs written by her fellow Canadians. I've thought of doing something similar with the Tropic of Capricorn, covering songs of my countrymen and women. Maybe I could call it *My Shout*.

A couple of songs on my shifting list, 'She Speaks A Different Language' and 'This Is Not The Way Home', were written and co-written by Tex Perkins, who's had a protean career in a swag of genre-bending, boundary-pushing bands – Tex Deadly and The Dum Dums, Thug, Salamander Jim, Beasts of Bourbon, The Cruel Sea, and The Ladyboyz. He's also made solo albums with The Dark Horses. In 1993, with Charlie Owen and Don Walker, Tex made a record called *Sad But True* which spent a long time on my stereo. *This is Not the Way Home*, an album released by The Cruel Sea a couple of years earlier, was never far away from the CD pile either. It's a kind of mutant surf/reggae/dubby/widescreen record haunted by the distant ghost of Lee Hazlewood. My kind of mongrel music. Their guitarist, Dan Rumour, is a true original, sounds like no-one but himself.

I run into Tex from time to time. We were drinking at the Prince Hotel one night in St Kilda and he told me that he, Don and Charlie were about to make a new record.

'Maybe you've got a song that might suit us,' he said, necking a lager.

'Yeah, maybe I do,' said I, sipping my Coopers.

'Well, make sure it's a good one. We don't want any offcuts from the back of the drawer. It has to be top-shelf.'

Nothing but the best for Tex, Don and Charlie, I thought to myself, and as they say in Galway, When the quality meets, the compliments fly.

I wanted to do a good job for these guys. Back home I had a song in the workshop, not yet finished, an update on the vintage 'You're Sixteen (You're Beautiful And You're Mine)', recorded in the fifties by Johnny Burnette and covered in the seventies by Ringo Starr. The song, which I'd started in a flurry a couple of years before, was lying in pieces on the floor, like Martin's old BMW did for years until he finally put it together. I hadn't been able to get all the bits to fit. The woman I'd wanted to write it for had recently turned forty-one, so I'd lost some of my motivation.

They don't need to know this is an offcut, I said to myself as I returned to the scene of the debris. Having Tex's voice in my head was like having the missing piece. I tinkered and tapped and bolted the new model together, sang it into a cassette and then dropped it into Charlie's letterbox around the corner from my place.

Nothing happened for a couple of months. Oh well, I thought. Maybe the rivets were too visible. Then one day, out of the blue, I got a call from Don, who said, 'Your song came up pretty well.' Being Don he didn't say much else.

A few more weeks went by. I didn't hold my breath. A song can come up well but still not fit. It ain't final 'til it's vinyl, as they used to say. A month or so after that, Charlie dropped off an advance copy of *All is Forgiven* at my place. 'You're 39, You're Beautiful And You're Mine' had made the cut. Not only that, Tex had rewritten the second line of the song and made it better. ('I guess it's a kind of crutch' was now 'About my feelings and such.') It was a mite cheeky of him not to have checked, but I wasn't complaining.

Charlie said, 'You know, Cold Chisel had a record out in the seventies called *You're Thirteen, You're Beautiful And You're Mine*.'

'Oh yeah, of course. I'd forgotten about that. That's a nice loop. Now I've tripled the Don.'

A year after *All is Forgiven* came out I decided to do my own version of the song. After all, top-shelf songs don't turn up every day. I was recording with Pete, Bill and the Dans again, putting together the songs for *Stolen Apples*. We'd expected 'You're 39' to be one of the easier ones, but as is so often the case it didn't turn out that way. The problem was that Tex, Don and Charlie's version was so authoritative we sounded like we were imitating them. Badly. Their version had come from my demo, so I needed to find another path. We got stuck for a while trying to slice it all different ways – there's half a cassette of offcuts – as we lurched from one dodgy groove to another. Finally Dank hit upon the idea of doing it in 6/8. Suddenly we had an Elvis/ Lefty Frizzell kinda thing going on with Spanish country piano, and we knew we were in the clear, out of the enormous shadows of Tex, Don and Charlie.

Not exactly original but a good little traveller, this song. The woman it was written for was forty-three when our version came out. She's forty-five now. Older by the time you read this. She's an original and she's travelling pretty well too.

YOUR LOVING IS ON MY MIND

The stars out here are so clear in the sky
Everywhere I look they're filling up my eye
The world is turning on its giant wheel
If you were here I'd show you how I feel
Your loving is on my mind
Your loving is on my mind

The curlew just now made its mournful cry
Somewhere someone's just about to die
Your country mouth takes my breath away
I need more sleep before the break of day
Your loving is on my mind
Your loving is on my mind

I was dreaming last night of a big house by the sea
There were people and things and then just you and me
You led me down a path onto the sand
We walked into the water hand in hand
Your loving is on my mind
Your loving is on my mind

He Reproves The Curlew

O curlew, cry no more in the air,
Or only to the water in the West;
Because your crying brings to my mind
Passion-dimmed eyes and long heavy hair
That was shaken out over my breast:
There is enough evil in the crying of wind.

W. B. Yeats

ZOE

Night is falling from above
I'm waiting for the one I love – Zoe
I sing her name inside my chest
The name that never lets me rest – Zoe
Touched by the evening breeze, the trees nod and sway
One by one the stars come out to play
And it seems that I can hear them say, 'She's on her way!'

We are all just tiny beings
In the greater scheme of things – Zoe
But she makes me feel I'm worth
More than the greatest thing on earth – Zoe
Every night I die under her loving touch
Every day we drink the loving cup.
She makes all the lovely stuff come rising up – Zoe

And all I have is all I want when I'm with Zoe

Little Bombs

Six weeks before my first season of A–Z shows, I had no song in the
swag starting with Z. I'd said in my press release that I would write
one by the final night, operating under the risky principle *Say it and
it will come*. Nor did I have a song starting with X or V, but that didn't
concern me. There were ways around that. And I didn't consider skipping those letters a problem. But the season wouldn't be complete
without the final song starting with the last letter of the alphabet.

I played around with a couple of songs in case the muse didn't
come through. (There. I've said it. Hundreds of pages of writing
about music and I haven't used the word 'muse' until now.)

'Zip-A-Dee-Doo-Dah' from Disney's *Song of the South*, and Mel Tormé's collaboration with Was Not Was, 'Zaz Turned Blue', are two songs about as far apart in mood as you can get – a mini A–Z, night-and-day brace in their own right. I had them warming the bench.

Around that time I was jamming once a week with Pete and Bill and the two Dans. We'd toured that year after the release of *Ways and Means*, a record that included a few group-written songs and instrumentals, and were keen to write some more together. I'd been asked to provide songs and background music for a new TV series, *Fireflies*, a drama based on the lives of volunteer country fire-fighters, and coming up with material for that was also on our minds. We were finding a good groove after a couple of years of regular playing. It seemed that every time we assembled in the poky little rehearsal room at Bakehouse we walked out of there with something new.

One day we were noodling around as usual. Nothing much was happening except a few laughs. Dank was playing guitar parts from Supertramp songs, Danel was doing impersonations of Dennis Cometti, the doyen of Australian Rules football broadcasters, and the rest of us were trying not to fall off our chairs. We had a break for lunch and walked up to a Vietnamese bakery on Victoria Parade for the usual pork, salad and chilli rolls. It was a warm, late-October day. You could smell summer coming. We picked up a dozen Tsingtao beers to wash down the rolls and keep ourselves cool and cheerful.

Back in the fetid room with the immovable double-glazed windows looking onto Hoddle Street, Pete and Danel started riffing lines from *Yacht Rock*, the online video series spoofing seventies and eighties soft rock acts – Toto, The Doobie Brothers, Steely Dan, Hall & Oates, and others. They knew all the songs and could do all the voices. This led into our old argument about Steely Dan, a friendly one, the kind of running-gag argument bands carry around for years. I can't remember who said what but I'm sure we would have divided along the usual lines, into those who thought Steely Dan were geniuses and those who thought the world could do just fine without them.

Dank started playing the first couple of bass notes to 'Rikki Don't

Lose That Number', Bill picked up on it, Pete took up the brushes, Danel floated in with some tremolo, and for reasons unknown I was visited by the ghost of Dean Martin singing 'Sway'. A chord here, a chord there, a little wrangle over the bridge, and in less than an hour we had a map of a song, complete in outline, with a woman named Zoe (Greek for 'life') hovering on the edges. All that remained for me to do was pound the pavements of Elwood down by the canal again.

Hemingway once defined beauty as 'grace under pressure'. A fine definition. But what's grace? Is it what happens when a group of people get together and make or do something they can't on their own? When something or someone enters the room but not through the window or the door? When it seems like nothing's happening and then suddenly it does? I've only ever wanted to be taken by surprise, to get to where I don't know myself. To become me no more. Whenever I'm onstage, alone or with the band, I'm always being carried by a cavalry.

I'm yet to write a song starting with X or V. George Strait's 'All My Ex's Live In Texas', and 'Excitable Boy' by Warren Zevon stand by during the A–Z shows. Or my friends The Ukeladies sing 'Xanadu' while I take a break. X, letter of mystery, gives you licence to do anything. I can cover V with 'Viva Las Vegas', which people never seem to get sick of, though I'm starting to.

I still don't have an exact rhyme for orange – 'mélange' is not even close – and I haven't found a good rough rhyme yet either. I haven't been to Brazil. Or Iceland. Nor have I become fluent in another language. I'll never play football for Norwood or test cricket for Australia. Never hear Ruby Hunter's cackling laugh nor argue with Steve Connolly again.

When you're young you think everything's possible. All of a sudden you're past the middle of your life, you've only done a fraction of the things you could have, and the field of possibility grows smaller each year.

As a young man I used to get pulled over by the police quite often while driving. This was before I could afford a boring car. I still remember my shock the first time I realised that the police officer questioning me was younger than I was.

Other little shocks and jolts followed – a thousand cuts. In my line of work, you constantly get those reminders. I noticed in my late thirties, for example, that the record company no longer objected if I didn't put a photo of myself on the front cover of a new album. And of course, those things that happen to everyone eventually happen to you as well. You find yourself lost in some outer suburb one night. You know the name of the street you're looking for and you have a street directory, but your eyes can't read the map. And they haven't invented mobile phones yet. (Well, they have but you're a bit leery of them.) The clincher is when you notice that most politicians and the Prime Minister are younger than you. Even the President of the United States. There's no escaping the fact then that others are coming to take your place.

All these revelations are clichés. Universal experience. This is good, you presume, because there's always someone you can talk to about it. Alas, the attitude of those who've already been through it is generally, Tell me something new. And those yet to get there have no idea what you're talking about.

But there are good things about growing older. For a start you spend a lot less time in bars between midnight and five a.m. thinking that something interesting might happen soon. And the closer death gets, the more intense life tastes. Some days, just the very act of breathing is a song of praise.

More and more, my old friends and loved ones seem like heroes to me. Some have risen, some have moved on, some have broken down. We've lost a lot of things along the way. But through it all we've helped each other out – dealing with the illness and death of parents and friends, raising children, looking for love, trying to find good work.

I play school shows sometimes for students who are studying my lyrics. I walk into the auditorium where they're assembled, all seated in rows with their teachers, and think of W. B. Yeats' description of himself in his sixties, visiting schools in Dublin as 'a public smiling man'. After playing for forty-five minutes or so I answer questions. I get every kind, good and bad. When I respond I try to point the questioners through my songs to other stuff – to other writers, other songs, other people, other stories. I know some of them want little packaged answers they can serve up in exams – the themes of the work, the meaning of the songs, all that guff. I ramble, I digress. I loop around, offering expansion, not reduction. I want to set off little bombs in their brains.

New life begins when strange things connect – a chromosome gets copied a little differently from one generation to the next and joins up with another chromosome in a mutation that takes the population by (slow) storm. Two New York Jewish kids, Jerry Leiber and Mike Stoller, write a song for Big Mama Thornton that gets heard a couple of years later by a shy truck-driving teenager in Memphis, who sings it differently and creates his own storm. Five decades on, Dean Martin and Steely Dan meet in a rehearsal room in Melbourne, long after Dino's dead.

Connect. That's what I want to say to the mixed rows of young faces in front of me, some earnest, some giggling, some bored. Connect. Some distracted, some looking down, some asleep. Connect. That's all I want to say to them – connect, connect, only connect.

Answers & Extras

Page 58

Some may say that life is a piece of cake but I'm here to tell you that's not true. Indeed, it's not all cakes and ale. Ever since she left me I've been burning the candle at both ends. I can't get her out of my mind. I'm gutted, she's seeing a songwriter. Sure, his records sell like hot cakes, but really, could you call what he does art? He's not fit to hold a candle to her. Days, I feel as flat as a cake out in the rain. Nights, I try to write, back on the novel, but my thoughts are all scrambled and my cake is dough. I'm like a candle in the wind. I remember the funny way she used to say 'Hey, sweet baby-cakes.' This love caper's just not worth the candle. I could be philosophical about it, wish her all the best and such, but it'd be like holding a candle to the devil. Revenge is a better option, revenge by art. I'm going to finish this book and then let the world judge its solid worth against his airy confections. The proof will be in the pudding.

Page 112

The drums rolled off in my forehead, the guns went off in my chest 'Wide Open Road' – The Triffids

Well, they blew up the chicken man in Philly last night 'Atlantic City' – Bruce Springsteen

My story is much too sad to be told 'I Get A Kick Out Of You' – Cole Porter

Watching as some old friends do a line, holding back the want to in my own addicted mind 'Wishing All These Old Things Were New' – Merle Haggard

Goddamn you half Japanese girls do it to me every time 'El Scorcho' – Weezer

You've painted up your lips and rolled and curled your tinted hair 'Ruby, Don't Take Your Love To Town' – Kenny Rogers

Jesus died for somebody's sins but not mine 'Gloria' – Patti Smith

Just a little lovin' early in the morning beats a cup of coffee for starting up the day 'Just A Little Lovin'' – Dusty Springfield

I saw a werewolf with a Chinese menu in his hand, walking through the streets of Soho in the rain 'Werewolves Of London' – Warren Zevon

I fell asleep on a tram, Harry Potter in hand, woke up drooling in the south of

Vietnam 'Dan Kelly's Dream' – Dan Kelly

God said to Abraham, 'Kill me a son 'Highway 61' – Bob Dylan

The Mississippi Delta was shining like a National guitar 'Graceland' – Paul Simon

Please allow me to introduce myself, I'm a man of wealth and taste 'Sympathy For The Devil' – The Rolling Stones

It was said of the sheriff to Calhoun Parish not to ever touch his daughter Emily 'High Sheriff Of Calhoun Parish' – Tony Joe White

Hey, Charlie, I'm pregnant and living on 9ᵗʰ Street 'Christmas Card From A Hooker In Minneapolis' – Tom Waits

When I first came to town they called me The Roving Jewel 'Katie Cruel' – Karen Dalton

Early this morning – hooo – when you knocked upon my door, I said: Hello Satan, I believe it's time to go 'Me And The Devil Blues' – Robert Johnson

I found her on a night of fire and noise 'Do You Love Me?' – Nick Cave

Just before our love got lost, you said I am as constant as a northern star 'A Case of You' – Joni Mitchell

Well my friends have gone and my hair is grey, I ache in the places I used to play 'Tower of Song' – Leonard Cohen

You walked into the party like you were walking onto a yacht 'You're So Vain' – Carly Simon

I've been in and out of trouble, mainly in 'Redheads, Gold Cards And Long Black Limousines' – Tex, Don and Charlie

Well, I dreamed I saw the knights in armour coming, saying something about a queen 'After The Goldrush' – Neil Young

I walk 47 miles of barbed wire, I use a cobra-snake for a necktie 'Who Do You Love' – Bo Diddley

A-wop-bop-a-lu-bop-a-lop-bam-boom 'Tutti Frutti' – Little Richard

Page 273
None.

Page 329
The Mystical Art of Track Listing
(Dan Kelly ponders sequencing his 2010 album two days before mastering)
Getting the running order of your songs right on an album is an arcane process. There's so much to think about:
Is the balance of ballads to upbeat numbers right?
Do you start with a party and mellow it out as you go along? Or vice versa?

What about the keys of the songs? Can you have more than three songs in a
    row in the key of E if it's not a Chicago blues record?
What about the general theme – does it tell a story or is it just a collection of
    tunes?
How long is too long, and how short is too short?
Do people even care any more, with iPods and iPhones and shuffling and
    single downloads from iTunes?
Should the falsetto song be straight out there or hidden on the back stretch?
Is it true what Robert Forster says? That the second-last song on an album is
    always the worst?
If so, am I jinxing whatever song I put there?
Should I put a Go-Betweens cover there?
Does the record company/agent/manager have better instincts for a single
    than the man on the street? Or worse?
Or exactly the same?
Will the record reviewers say you're treading water if the opening songs are
    most like the old ones? Or will they be reassured?
Should you put the ones Mum likes all together, or force her to work through
    the record like she's trapped in IKEA for forty-eight minutes when she's
    just trying to buy a lightbulb?
Should I have segues? Or skits?
Should the skits mention the year and trap the record forever in the tweens?
Should I fade the songs?
Or perhaps a cunning fade-in, or try the old fade-out, fade-in again?
How long should the silence be between tracks?
Is it the right kind of silence?
(The story goes that Johnny Marr once took so much coke that he went
    around sampling different silences until he found the perfect one to put
    between songs.)
I have forty-eight hours to find these answers...

Page 341
An onion.

Page 525
It could be one of several. 'Bootylicious' is the only song not about shoes.
'Purple Sneakers' is the only song not to mention shoes or boots. 'Good Old
Shoe', unlike the others, is a parody.

Discography

Post (1985)
From St Kilda To Kings Cross
Incident On South Dowling
Look So Fine, Feel So Low
White Train
Luck
Blues For Skip
Adelaide
Satisfy Your Woman
(You Can Put Your) Shoes Under My Bed
Standing On The Street Of Early Sorrows
Little Decisions

Gossip (1986)
Last Train To Heaven
Leaps And Bounds
Before The Old Man Died
Down On My Speedway
White Train
Randwick Bells
Before Too Long
Adelaide
I Won't Be Torn Apart
Going About My Father's Business
Somebody's Forgetting Somebody
   (Somebody's Letting Somebody Down)
The Ballroom
Tighten Up
I've Come For Your Daughter
So Blue
The Execution
Incident On South Dowling
Maralinga (Rainy Land)
Darling It Hurts
Look So Fine, Feel So Low
Stories Of Me
Don't Harm The Messenger
Gossip
After The Show

Under the Sun (1987)
Dumb Things
Same Old Walk
Big Heart
Don't Stand So Close To The Window
Forty Miles To Saturday Night
I Don't Remember A Thing
Know Your Friends
To Her Door
Under The Sun
Untouchable
Desdemona
Happy Slave
Crosstown
Bicentennial
Bradman
Pastures Of Plenty

So Much Water so Close to Home (1989)
You Can't Take It With You
Sweet Guy
Most Wanted Man In The World
I Had Forgotten You
She's A Melody (Stupid Song)
South Of Germany
Careless
Moon In The Bed
No You
Everything's Turning To White
Pigeon/Jandamurra
Cities Of Texas

Comedy (1991)
Don't Start Me Talking
Stories Of Me
Winter Coat
It's All Downhill From Here
Leaving Her For The Last Time
Brighter
Your Little Sister (Is A Big Girl Now)

I Won't Be Your Dog Anymore
Take Your Time
Sydney From A 727
Buffalo Ballet
I Can't Believe We Were Married
From Little Things Big Things Grow
Blue Stranger
Keep It To Yourself
(You Can Put Your) Shoes Under My Bed
Invisible Me
Little Boy, Don't Lose Your Balls

Hidden Things (1992)
Reckless
When I First Met Your Ma
Sweet Guy Waltz
Hard Times
Other People's Houses
Special Treatment
Little Decisions
Rally Round The Drum
Pastures Of Plenty
Beggar On The Street Of Love
Pouring Petrol On A Burning Man
From St Kilda To Kings Cross
Brand New Ways
Rock 'n' Soul
Yil Lull
Bradman
Ghost Town
Elly

Live, May 1992 (1992)
Foggy Highway
To Her Door
Winter Coat
Taught By Experts
From Little Things Big Things Grow
I Can't Believe We Were Married
Until Death Do Them Part
Same Old Walk
Don't Explain
Stupid Song
Brand New Ways
Stories Of Me
Everything's Turning To White
Dumb Things
Just Like Animals
Keep It To Yourself
I Won't Be Your Dog Anymore
I Was Hoping You'd Say That

Careless
Invisible Me
When I First Met Your Ma
Most Wanted Man

Wanted Man (1994)
Summer Rain
God's Hotel
She's Rare
Just Like Animals
Love Never Runs On Time
Song From The Sixteenth Floor
Maybe This Time For Sure
Ball and Chain
You're Still Picking The Same Sore
Everybody Wants To Touch Me
We've Started A Fire
Lately
Nukkanya

Deeper Water (1995)
Blush
Extra Mile
I'll Forgive But I Won't Forget
Queen Stone
Deeper Water
Madeleine's Song
Difficult Woman
Give In To My Love
I've Been A Fool
Anastasia Changes Her Mind
California
Gathering Storm

*Live at The Continental
and The Esplanade* (1996)
When I First Met Your Ma
Maralinga
God's Hotel
Everybody Wants To Touch Me
Somebody's Forgetting Somebody
   (Somebody's Letting Somebody Down)
Just Like Animals
To Her Door
Pouring Petrol On A Burning Man
Dumb Things
Cities Of Texas
She's Rare
Darling It Hurts
Careless
Summer Rain

Words and Music (1998)
Little Kings
I'll Be Your Lover
Nothing On My Mind
Words And Music
Gutless Wonder
Tease Me
I'd Rather Go Blind
She Answers The Sun (Lazybones)
Beat Of Your Heart
It Started With A Kiss
Glory Be To God
Saturday Night And Sunday Morning
Charlie Owen's Slide Guitar
Melting

Smoke (1999)
Our Sunshine
You Can't Take It With You
Until Death Do Them Part
I Can't Believe We Were Married
I Don't Remember A Thing
Teach Me Tonight
Sydney From A 747
Night After Night
Whistling Bird
Stories Of Me
Taught By Experts
Gathering Storm
Shy Before You Lord

Professor Ratbaggy (1999)
Please Myself
White Trash
Can't Fake It
Moni, Make It Good
Coma
Love Letter
Blowfly
See The Birdie Fly Out
Mannish Woman
Rise And Shine
Oh, Death

Nothing but a Dream (2001)
If I Could Start Today Again
Change Your Mind
Midnight Rain
I Close My Eyes And Think Of You
Somewhere In The City
Just About To Break

Love Is The Law
The Pretty Place
I Wasted Time
Would You Be My Friend
Smoke Under The Bridge

One Night the Moon
(soundtrack, 2001)
I Don't Know Anything Anymore
Flinders Theme
One Night The Moon
Moon Child
The Gathering
Now Listen Here
This Land Is Mine
The March Goes On - The Gathering 2
Spirit Of The Ancients
What Do You Know
Carcass - The Gathering 3
Night Shadows
Black And White
Moment Of Death
Hunger
Unfinished Business
Spirit Of The Ancients
Moody Broody
Little Bones
Oh Breathe On Me
Moonstruck

Silent Partner
(soundtrack, 2001)
Be Careful What You Pray For
Silver's Theme
Is It A He Or A She?
You Can't Take It With You (instrumental)
Silent Partner
Teach Me Tonight
Now's Not The Time For A Hot Sea Bath
Silver's On The Line
Ain't Got The Constitution
Better Prospects
The Gatekeeper
Forest Funeral/Silver Turns To Lead
Little Boy, Don't Lose Your Balls
Silent Partner (reprise)
Royal Road
Ain't Got The Constitution (reprise)
Would You Be My Friend?

Lantana (soundtrack, 2001)
Lantana Part 1
Lantana Part 2
For Eleanor
What's Happening To Us
Through The Window
Numb
Shortcut
Let's Tangle

Ways and Means (2004)
Gunnamatta
The Oldest Story In The Book
Heavy Thing
Won't You Come Around?
These Are The Days
Beautiful Feeling
Crying Shame
Sure Got Me
To Be Good Takes A Long Time
Can't Help You Now
Nothing But A Dream
Little Bit O' Sugar
Forty-Eight Angels
Your Lovin' Is On My Mind
You Broke A Beautiful Thing
My Way Is To You
Curly Red
King Of Fools
Young Lovers
Big Fine Girl
Let's Fall Again

Fireflies (soundtrack, 2004)
Beautiful Feeling
Love Letter
Taught By Experts
Gutless Wonder
Everybody Wants To Touch Me
I Smell Trouble
Boon Companion
Melting
Foggy Highway
Emotional
Gathering Storm
Last Train To Heaven
Los Cucumbros
If I Could Start Today Again
Beautiful Promise

Foggy Highway (2005)
Stumbling Block
Rally Round The Drum
Ghost Town
Song Of The Old Rake
Don't Stand So Close To The Window
Passed Over
They Thought I Was Asleep
You're Learning (with Kasey Chambers)
Foggy Highway
Down To My Soul
Cities Of Texas
Meet Me In The Middle Of The Air

Jindabyne
(soundtrack, 2005)
The Rocks
Jindabyne Fair
Body Drop
Claire On The Road
Mirror
Morning Fishing
Stewart And Claire
Power Lines
Nukkanya
Night River
So Soft
Going To Susan's
Welcome Dance
The Way That I Love You
The Humming Way
Troitsa Bratya
Everything's Turning To White

Stardust Five (2006)
Last Orders
Nightwatchman
Things We Said In The Dark
Pussy Got Your Tongue
Mi Camion Mi Casa
Everybody Loves You Baby
Zoe
Road To The North
Lady With Dog
Lovers' Field
Los Cucumbros

Stolen Apples (2007)
Feelings Of Grief
God Told Me To
Stolen Apples Taste The Sweetest
Sweetest Thing
You're 39, You're Beautiful And
    You're Mine
The Lion And The Lamb
Right Outta My Head
Keep On Driving
The Ballad Of Queenie And Rover
The Foggy Fields Of France
Please Leave Your Light On

Songs From the South
Volumes 1 & 2 (2008)
Vol. 1
From St Kilda To Kings Cross
Leaps And Bounds
Before Too Long
Darling It Hurts
Look So Fine, Feel So Low
Dumb Things
To Her Door
Bradman
Everything's Turning To White
Sweet Guy
Careless
Winter Coat
From Little Things Big Things Grow

When I First Met Your Ma
Pouring Petrol On A Burning Man
Love Never Runs On Time
Song From The Sixteenth Floor
Deeper Water
Give In To My Love
How To Make Gravy

Vol. 2
Nothing On My Mind
I'll Be Your Lover
Love Letter
Our Sunshine
Gathering Storm
Every Fucking City
Be Careful What You Pray For
Love Is The Law
If I Could Start Today Again
The Oldest Story In The Book
Won't You Come Around
Gunnamatta
Your Lovin' Is On My Mind
Song Of The Old Rake
They Thought I Was Asleep
Everybody Loves You Baby
God Told Me To
You're 39, You're Beautiful And You're
    Mine
Thoughts In The Middle Of The Night
Shane Warne

Recordings by other artists mentioned in the text

Be Careful What You Pray For (Vika
    and Linda Bull, *Two Wings*, 1999)
Best Of Your Heart (Christine Anu,
    Women at the Well, 2002)
Before Too Long (Chrissie Amphlett,
    Women at the Well, 2002)
Beggar On The Street Of Love (Jenny
    Morris, *Women at the Well*, 2002)
The Cake And The Candle (Kate
    Ceberano, *Women at the Well*,
    2002)
Difficult Woman (Renée Geyer,
    The Great Renée Geyer, 2001)
Everybody Wants To Touch Me
    (Deborah Conway, *Women at the Well*,
    2002; Paul Capsis, *Everybody Wants to
    Touch Me*, 2007)

Everything's Turning To White (Kasey
    Chambers, *Women at the Well*, 2002)
Foggy Highway (Renée Geyer, *Fireflies*,
    2004)
God's Hotel (Nick Cave, *B-Sides &
    Rarities*, 2005)
Jump To Love (Christine Anu, *Come My
    Way*, 2000)
Special Treatment (Jimmie Dale Gilmore,
    Two Roads, 1992)
The Gift That Keeps On Giving (Bic
    Runga, *Women at the Well*, 2002)
Treaty (Yothu Yindi, *Tribal Voice*, 1991)
You Broke A Beautiful Thing (Renée
    Geyer, *Women at the Well*, 2002)
You're 39 (Tex, Don and Charlie, *All is
    Forgiven*, 2005)

Acknowledgements

Thanks to my early encouragers, Matthew Kelly, Nikki Christer, Mandy Brett, Jane Palfreyman, Richard Flanagan, John Kingsmill, Sophie Cunningham, John O'Donnell, Bill Cullen and Edrei Cullen. Thanks especially to Richard for *The Periodic Table* and perceptive comments on the early chapters. And to Sophie for helpful criticism and support all the way through.

Thanks to all those who exchanged ideas, honed memories, corrected facts and contributed to lists – Dan Kelly, Peter Luscombe, Dan Luscombe, Bill McDonald, Cameron Bruce, Shane O'Mara, Bill Miller, James Black, Brian Nankervis, Angus Grant, Renée Geyer, Chris Langman, Gideon Haigh, Andrew McMillan, Bart Bull, Bleddyn Butcher, Bain Attwood, Howard Pedersen, Steve Hawke, Tom Gutteridge, Bernard Rechter, Joy Kirkpatrick, Kaarin Fairfax, Rosie Jones, Bob Weis, Demos Krouskos, Neil Murray, Don Walker, Alan James, Simon Moor, Damian Trotter, Martin Flanagan and Rachel Perkins. Big thanks to Casey Bennetto for many fruitful discussions on key changes, opening lines and other musical minutiae.

For hunting song lyric permissions through impossible thickets, thanks to Cath Wells and Wendy Richardson. And to Shane and Adam Simpson for invaluable legal advice.

To the onelouder management team, Bill, Edrei and Cath – already mentioned – Nick Walsh and Briese Abbott for a multitude of tasks, thank you. Thanks also to Ann Gibson for close reading and discography research.

Thanks to Sally Warhaft and Ben Naparstek for editing and adapting chapters for earlier publication.

Thanks to my brothers and sisters, Anne, Sheila, Martin, John, Mary-Jo, David, Tony; my cousins Sue, Geraldine and John Hannon, and Alex and Fiona McGregor for much useful criticism and family history.

To my book editors, Ben Ball, Meredith Rose and Michael Nolan, my challengers, confessors and constant supporters, a huge thanks for doing a job way above and beyond my imagining. God and the devil dwell in details. Thanks, John Canty, for the beautiful design. I felt safe as you all tugged me into harbour.

To Sian Prior for your love and support and for living with someone often somewhere else. To my children, Declan, Madeleine and Memphis. Thank you. This book's for you and yours.

The following sections have been previously published in an earlier form: 'My Left Foot' in *The Footy Almanac* 2007, ed John Harms and Paul Daffey, Malarkey Publications, 2007; 'Cities of Texas', 'The Bell and the Ball' and 'Immortal Ones' in *Rolling Stone*; 'Swing Low Sweet Chariot' in *Meanjin* 2009; 'C90', 'The Pretendies' and 'Stories of Me' in *The Monthly*. 'Stale, Mate' borrows heavily from Sian Prior's 'Conversations Behind the Barbed Wire', published in *The Age*, 14 October 2002.

Extracts from the following have been reproduced with permission (unauthorised reproduction is illegal):

Lyrics

Alfred Publishing (Australia): 'I'm In Love With A Big Blue Frog' (words and music by Lester Braunstein, Peter Yarrow and Noel Stookey), 'I Get A Kick Out Of You' (words and music by Cole Porter), 'On Your Way Down' (words and music by Allen Toussaint); Control: 'We Never Cross The Line' from *Shane Warne The Musical* (music and lyrics by Eddie Perfect); 'Prince Alone In The Studio' (by Bill Callahan); EMI Music Publishing Australia: 'Just A Little Lovin' (Early In The Morning)' (B.Mann/C.Weil) © 1968 Screen Gems-EMI Music Inc, 'Look Of Love' (B.Bacharach/H.David) © 1967 Colgems EMI Music Inc, 'High Sheriff Of Calhoun Parish' (T.White) © 1970 Combine Music Corp, 'Our Don Bradman' (J.O'Hagan) © 1930 EMI Allans Music Australia Pty Limited, 'Roll Truck Roll' (T.Collins) © 1966 Central Songs Inc, 'I Found A Reason' (Lou Reed) © 1970 Oakfield Avenue Music Ltd, 'On Your Way Down' (A.Toussaint) (75%) © 1972 Marsaint Music Inc, 'Cradle Of Love' (B.Idol/D. Werner) (66.25%) © 1990 David Werner Music Inc; Hal Leonard Publishing: 'Roadhouse Blues' (words and music by The Doors) Copyright © 1970 Doors Music Co, 'Cradle Of Love' (words and music by David Werner and Billy Idol) © 1990 EMI April Music Inc, David Werner Music, Chrysalis Music, Boneidol Music and TCF Music Publishing Inc; Hello Mr Wilson, Bug Music: 'She Never Spoke Spanish To Me' (Butch Hancock); Mushroom Music Publishing: 'Man Overboard' (written by Bray/Carter/Conway/Philip), 'Took The Children Away' (written by Archie Roach), 'Say Goodbye' (written by Seymour/Archer/Falconer/ Smith/Waters/Howard/Miles), 'I Love My Leather Jacket' (written by Martin Phillips); Mushroom Music Publishing, Sony/ATV Music Publishing Australia: 'Treaty' (written by Kellaway/Mununggurr/Williams/Yunupingu/Yunupingu/Marika/Kelly), 'Leaps and Bounds' (written by Kelly/Langman), 'Rally Round The Drum' (written by Roach/Kelly), 'Our Sunshine' (written by Thomas/Kelly); Mute Song/Mushroom Music Publishing: 'God's Hotel' (written by Nick Cave); Song Cycles Pty Ltd: 'Eulogy For A Black Man', 'From Little Things Big Things Grow', 'Thou Shalt Not Steal', 'This Land Is Mine' (by Kev Carmody);

Sony/ATV Music Publishing: 'A Tiny Broken Heart' (Ira Louvin, Charlie Louvin, Eddie Hill) © 1956, 'Don't Stand So Close To The Window' (Paul Kelly and Alexander McGregor) © Orient Pacific Music Pty Ltd & Sony/ATV Music Publishing; Universal Publishing: 'I Am Woman' (words and music by Helen Reddy and Ray Burton) © Irving Music, Inc/Buggerlugs Music Co, 'Breakfast At Sweethearts' (words and music by Don Walker) © Rondor Music Australia; *and the author also gratefully acknowledges* Campbell Connelly, Music Sales for 'Back In The USA' (Chuck Berry), 'Je T'Aime' (Serge Gainsbourg), 'Who's Been Talking' (Chester Burnett); EMI Music Publishing for 'White Christmas' (Irving Berlin); Prize Music, Urn Music for 'Dallas' (Jimmie Dale Gilmore); Sony/ATV Music Publishing for 'Harry Was A Bad Bugger' (Don Walker), 'Alfie' (Hal David, Burt Bacharach), 'Not Dark Yet, Highlands' and 'Highway 61 Revisited' (Bob Dylan), 'Over You, Woman' (Jimmy Payne, Jim Glaser) and 'Kansas City' (Jerry Leiber/Mike Stoller); Universal Music Publishing for 'Cattle And Cane' (Grant McLennan, Robert Forster), 'Don't Explain' (Billie Holiday), 'Candle In The Wind' (Elton John, Bernie Taupin), 'MacArthur Park' (Jimmy Webb), 'Streets Of Philadelphia' (Bruce Springsteen), and 'Say A Little Prayer For You', 'Trains And Boats And Planes' and 'Don't Know What To Do With Myself' (Hal David, Burt Bacharach); Warner Chappell for 'I Wish I Were In Love Again' (Lorenz Hart, Richard Rodgers).

Texts

Czesław Miłosz, 'I Sleep a Lot' and 'Youth', *New and Collected Poems 1931–2001* (Allen Lane, The Penguin Press, UK, 2001, reproduced by permission of Penguin Books Ltd); Peter McCarthy, *McCarthy's Bar*, (Hodder & Stoughton, 2001); Seamus Heaney, 'Act Of Union', *Opened Ground: Selected Poems 1966–1996* (Faber & Faber, 2002); Cleo Davis, liner notes to *The Essential Bill Monroe and His Bluegrass Boys 1945–49*, Columbia, 1992; Philip Roth, *Sabbath's Theater*, published by Jonathan Cape, used by permission of The Random House Group Ltd; Judith Wright, 'The Moving Image', *A Human Pattern: Selected Poems* (ETT Imprint, Sydney 2009); John Berryman, 'The Ball Poem', *Selected Poems 1938-1968* (Faber & Faber, 2002); Yami Lester, *The Autobiography of Yami Lester*, (Iad Press, 2000); Martin Flanagan, 'Walking the Dog' (*Age* blog, 11 February 2008); Henry Miller, *Nexus*, (HarperCollins, 1971); Jeffrey Eugenides, *Middlesex* (Bloomsbury, 2002); Wisława Szymborska, 'Theatre Impressions', *Poems News and Collected* (Faber & Faber, 1999); C. P. Cavafy, 'Days of 1903', *Collected Poems* (Oxford University Press, 2008).

Photographs

Ten Miles to Saturday Night, Robert Lougheed, Claggett/Rey Gallery; Gough Whitlam and Vincent Lingiari, Mervyn Bishop/Licensed by Viscopy, 2010; SANFL Grand Final 1961, supplied by Norwood Football Club; Johnny Cash and June Carter, GAB Archive/Getty Images; The Beach Boys, Michael Ochs Archives/Getty Images; the graves of Queenie McKenzie and Rover Thomas, Bill Cullen; Frank Sinatra, young and middle-aged, Snap Photo/Austral Press.

While every effort has been made to contact copyright holders, the publisher welcomes hearing from anyone in this regard.

Index Of People & Bands